"BY THE BANKS OF THE THAMES". RUSSIANS IN EIGHTEENTH CENTURY BRITAIN

A. G. CROSS

"BY THE BANKS OF THE THAMES" RUSSIANS IN EIGHTEENTH CENTURY BRITAIN

Oriental Research Partners
Newtonville, Mass.
1980

©**1980**, Oriental Research Partners

(ISBN 0-89250-085-9)

For a detailed brochure of other books
dealing with Russia and East Europe, write
to the Editor, ORP, Box 158, Newtonville,
Mass. 02160.

FOR MY RUSSIAN FRIENDS,
for those who have seen England,
for those who might still, and
for those who never will

CONTENTS

LIST OF ILLUSTRATIONS
(between pages 208 and 209)

PREFACE

For some years I had been gathering materials and writing a number of pre-liminary articles for what is still an unfinished book about the British colony in St. Petersburg in the eighteenth century when I paid a further research visit to Leningrad in October, 1974. It was then that I had the opportunity to work in the Institute of Russian Literature on the archive of A. A. Samborskii, who had been chaplain to the Russian Embassy church in London for a long period during the reign of Catherine II. This archive, hitherto virtually untapped, proved a rich source not only for tracing Samborskii's own very varied activi-ties but for establishing the identities and movements of numerous other Rus-sians visiting England. My interest in this aspect of Anglo-Russian relations, complementing that of the British in Russia, was not new; indeed, my first article, dating from 1964 and re-worked as the concluding chapter to the pre-sent work, was devoted to an individual case-study. The overall jig-saw, how-ever, now began to take on definite shape and many hitherto random pieces fell into place. Subsequent research in British archives and the use of countless printed sources, both primary and secondary, have enabled me to present the sort of wide-ranging and hopefully comprehensive study which has hitherto never been attempted with regard to Russians abroad in any country and in any period, various articles and indeed monographs on Russians in France, Germany, or Italy notwithstanding. Although conceived and written as an independent study, the work, at the suggestion of my publishers, is offered as the first of two volumes on Anglo-Russian interchange in the eighteenth century; the study of the British in Russia, which is to follow, will offer in-evitable close parallels but also revealing differences and divergences which will make it other than a mirror-image.

During the time I have been preparing this work I have benefitted from the support of several institutions and the guidance and encouragement of many individuals. I wish to express my gratitude to the Leverhulme Foundation which funded my visit to the Soviet Union in 1974, which was arranged by the Bri-tish Council and the Soviet Academy of Sciences; to the Warden and Fellows of All Souls College, Oxford for the award of a Visiting Fellowship in the Hilary and Trinity terms of 1978, which allowed me to complete the writing of the remaining chapters in the most civilized and congenial of settings; to the Uni-versity of East Anglia for granting me sabbatical leave and leave of absence at regular intervals. My thanks are due to members of the Study Group on Eight-eenth-Century Russia who suffered offerings at their meetings and particularly to Dr. Roger Bartlett and Professor Rod Home for reading and commenting on individual chapters. Numerous librarians and archivists in Moscow, Leningrad, Birmingham, Edinburgh, London, and Oxford have provided generous assistance. For permission to incorporate in my work materials which appeared in the pages of their respective journals I wish to thank the editors of the *Journal of European Studies, Oxford Slavonic Papers, Slavonic and East European Review* and *XVIII vek*. I am greatly indebted to Mrs. Beryl Ranwell for preparing the typescript with her customary expertise. Finally, in the peace which comes with the end of writing I can only say thank-you to my family for their indulgence and understanding during the fever.

Norwich, November 1978

INTRODUCTION

Much is made, and not without reason, of Britain's "discovery" of Russia in 1553 and of the substantial commercial benefits in particular which ensued, but the Russians, not to be outdone when discoveries and inventions are at stake, have provided 1524 as the year of their own "first-footing" in England. In that year Vasilii III, in response to overtures from Carlos V of Spain to establish diplomatic relations between his country and Muscovy, sent an embassy headed by Prince Ivan Zasekin-Iaroslavskii to Spain. It appears that Zasekin-Iaroslavskii and his secretary or d'iak Semen Trofimov, obliged to skirt France, travelled to Spain via Flanders and England. Further details are not available, but it would seem mere wishful thinking to suggest that the arrival of the Russians caused a particular impact in London and that Willoughby and Cabot were spurred on to their voyages by knowledge of this visit and the lure of Russian furs.[1]

If 1524 or indeed 1553 mark the beginning of contacts between Muscovy and England, there is evidence of much earlier ties from before the period of the Tartar "yoke." M. P. Alekseev looked to links between Kievan Rus' and Anglo-Saxon England in the eleventh century and concluded that the court of Iaroslav Mudryi was visited by the princes Edwin and Edward, sons of Edmund Ironsides, fleeing from England after the death of their father in 1016 and the invasion by the Danes. Better documented is the arrival in Kiev later in the same century of Gita, daughter of King Harold, to marry Vladimir Monomakh.[2] But the generally overlooked candidate for the honour of being "the first Russian in England" was one Rabbi Iza or Isaac from Chernigov who, according to the Jewish historian Joseph Jacobs, arrived in England in 1181.[3]

Such early contacts, however curious, have an accidental character which is totally absent from the links forged between Muscovy and England in the reigns of Ivan the Terrible and Elizabeth I. The extent to which Muscovy impressed itself on the imagination of Elizabethan England and of its poets and dramatists in particular has been exhaustively documented by M. P. Alekseev,[4] and it is pertinent here merely to mention as additional to the influence of "travellers' tales," exerted most notably through the great collection of Richard Hakluyt, the presence of Russian ambassadors and their exotically attired retinues. Diplomats continued to be the most common of still uncommon Russian visitors throughout the seventeenth century, although England also welcomed the occasional escaped Russian slave,[5] and, more significantly, the first Russian students.

In 1602 that enlightened and much maligned tsar Boris Godunov decided to send some eighteen young Russians in groups of six to France, England and Germany to study languages and prepare for a career in the diplomatic service (*Posol'skii prikaz*). In the event, five went to Lübeck and four to England but none apparently to France. In the late summer of 1602 Mikifor Olfer'evich Grigor'ev, Sofon Mikhailovich Kozhiukhov, Fedor Semenovich Kostomarov, and Kazarin Davydov arrived in London, where it was said of them: "We have here foure youthes come from Muscovie to learn our language and Latin, and are to be dispersed to divers scholes, as Winchester, Eaton, Cambridge, and Oxford."[6] Unfortunately it is impossible to say whether they ever enjoyed the fruits of an English public school or university education: certainly the available records of these institutions reveal no trace of them, although there is reference in another source to two unnamed young Russians dying in Oxford of smallpox.[7] Such information, however, conflicts with the details supplied to the Russian authorities when at last, in 1613, enquiries were made about the students: two were then said to be in the East Indies and two in London. Further efforts to get the students back to Russia were made by subsequent embassies in 1617 and in 1622, by which time the two in the East Indies (although possibly in Oxford) were said to have died. Throughout this period only one student, Mikifor Grigor'ev, was actually produced and he steadfastly refused to return to Russia because he had renounced the orthodox faith and had entered the English church. By a sad twist of fate this same Grigor'ev was last heard of in 1643 when he was removed from his office by the Puritans.[8] Despite the melancholy outcome from the Russian point of view of Boris's experiment, Tsar Mikhail Fedorovich consented to send one further student to England in 1617. Ivan Ivanovich Almanzenov, son of a translator in the *Posol'skii prikaz*, went to Cambridge, where he studied English, Latin, and Greek. By 1629, he was continuing his education abroad, in France and Italy, and the tsar was assured that on his return he would then study medicine both in London and at Cambridge. Two years later, similar promises were made in a letter from James I, but whether Almanzenov, or John Elmson, as he was known in England, ever returned to Russia to care for the health of the tsar is unknown.[9]

Against a background of rare and abortive educational initiatives and diplomatic missions, blinkered in attitudes and cautious in objectives, the Great Embassy of Peter I stands out in all its significance. The visit which he and his entourage paid to London at the beginning of 1698 was the key event, both as fact and symbol, for that distinctive period in Anglo-Russian relations that is the eighteenth century. Peter's visit has been and continues to be the subject of much detailed research by both Russian and British historians and it seems unnecessary to give it particular attention here, although inevitably certain aspects—Peter's interests in the navy and in scientific matters, his trip to Oxford —provide appropriate starting points for chapters which follow.[10] British fascination with the character and exploits of Peter was to continue unabated throughout the eighteenth century and was sustained not only by his personal contacts with this country but by a spate of biographies, collections of anecdotes, panegyrical poems, and dramatic works which appeared with great regularity.[11] Only with Catherine II did Russia produce another colourful personality who would compete with Peter for the attention of the British. It was during the reigns of these two monarchs that movement between the two countries reached its heights and although the flow of the British to Russia was impressive, that of Russians to Britain was not inconsiderable. It is to this latter aspect of Anglo-Russian interchange that this study is devoted, to an aspect that has been but barely recognized and scantily documented.

It would, however, be incorrect, not to say immodest, to suggest that nothing relevant to the subject has been written, but with the exception of a single monograph, Professor V. N. Aleksandrenko's *Russkie diplomaticheskie agenty v Londone v XVIII v.* (2 vols. [Warsaw, 1897]), and a very limited number of articles, attention has been focused on an individual or on a particular incident or episode. It would equally be presumptuous to pretend that the visits to Great Britain for various purposes of such figures as Prince Antiokh Kantemir, Count Semen Vorontsov, Princess Ekaterina Dashkova, Semen Desnitskii, Vasilii Petrov and Lev Sabakin were not widely known, but even specialists in eighteenth-century Russian history might have difficulty in producing a further twenty names. The checklist which completes this study certainly contains hundreds of the obscurest Russians ever to be named in a twentieth-century book, but also and more significantly, it includes dozens of Russians who achieved eminence in a wide variety of careers and for whose biographies the connection with Britain provides a frequently unsuspected page. Filling that particular page in the biographies of a host of well-known and lesser-known figures was not, however, the main purpose of this study; nor, for that matter, was the compiling of a longer list of names than had ever been compiled before, although both exercises are not without their interest and value. The book was conceived as an investigation into the activities of Russians in Great Britain over a whole century and an examination of the ways in which Peter the Great's important initiatives were developed, broadened, or neglected.

Establishing the nature of these activities led in its turn to the arranging of the chapters thematically rather than chronologically. Nevertheless, within each chapter the theme is treated chronologically, although the starting point may obviously differ: the reign of Catherine II brought a series of interests and concerns unknown or barely perceptible in the earlier period. Throughout the century at the hub of affairs in the English capital was the Russian ambassador (or minister or resident, as he was variously termed at different times) and it was logical that the opening chapter should be devoted to the embassy and that this should be followed by a study of the Russian church which was soon attached to the embassy and became an equally important and constant factor in the life of Russians in England. Subsequent chapters are concerned with a single wide category, with "students," for it was the urge to learn and to gain practical experience which dictated the sending of the majority of Russians to Britain. There were students in the usual sense of young men taking courses at the universities of Cambridge, Oxford, Glasgow, and Edinburgh (chapters 4-5) and studying painting and engraving at the Royal Academy (chapter 8), but also students of English farming techniques (chapter 3) and apprentices to masters in a large number of trades and skills (chapter 7). The longest-standing of all Russian initiatives to learn from the British was in the area of navigation and shipbuilding (chapter 6). Even the tourists (chapter 9) included in their number men not merely bent on fashionable pleasures but also eager to see and record and add to their knowledge of the world. One of the most eminent of these was the writer N. M. Karamzin, whose writings undoubtedly exerted considerable influence on his contemporaries' views of England (chapter 10).

This study, finally, might be seen as part of a much wider concern with Anglo-Russian cultural relations extending beyond the eighteenth century. Whereas the second volume of this work will explore the activities of the British in Russia over the same period, articles already published, other work in progress, and still further research as yet merely envisaged look to questions of British awareness of Russian culture and of the image of Russia and the Russians as fostered by personal contacts, travel literature, imaginative literature, and translations of Russian works, and to some extent to the formation of similar Russian attitudes towards Britain.

CHAPTER 1
THE RUSSIAN EMBASSY IN LONDON

The arrival in London at the beginning of May, 1707, of Andrei Artamonovich Matveev was an event of no little significance in the general context of Anglo-Russian relations in the eighteenth century. Matveev was the first permanent Russian diplomatic representative appointed to the Court of St James's. Not that Russian ambassadors and envoys had been unknown before that time in Britain, although they were indeed in every sense a rare sight. A hundred and fifty years before Matveev, the first Muscovite ambassador, Osip Grigor'evich Nepeia, had survived a shipwreck off the Scottish coast before eventually arriving in London with due pomp and "barbaric" splendour. In the intervening period, such ambassadors as Grigorii Mikulin in 1600, Gerasim Dokhturov in 1645, Prince Petr Prozorovskii in 1662, and Petr Potemkin in 1681 had visited London, but in every case they had a specific mission to fulfil, on the completion of which they returned to report to their master, recording what they saw and did in the chronologically organized, official embassy reports known as *stateinye spiski.*[1] In the event, Matveev stayed in England only a little longer than some of his predecessors and he came with detailed instructions as to what he should accomplish, but his appointment was also an acknowledgement of Queen Anne's moves to put Anglo-Russian diplomatic relations on a firmer footing and of her initiative two years earlier in sending Charles Whitworth to Moscow as British envoy extraordinary.

Matveev (1666-1728), son of a boiar, was an experienced and shrewd diplomat who had served in The Hague since 1699, but he could hardly have foreseen the trials and tribulations which awaited him during the fifteen months he was to spend in England. His task was basically to propose an Anglo-Russian treaty which would go far beyond the commercial interests that had been virtually the sole topic of his counterpart's negotiations in Moscow and that were to remain throughout the century the dominant factor in British diplomacy with Russia. Peter the Great was anxious to gain British support in his struggle against Sweden and as a gesture of mutual aid was prepared to become a member of the Grand Alliance, formed by England, Holland, and Austria since 1701. He also wished to ensure that England would not protest, if and when he secured the Baltic littoral which was vital to his design of a strong Russia, by holding out the promise of increased trading advantages through such ports as Riga. England, however, was little inclined to commit itself; indeed, the all-powerful Duke of Mal-borough had resolved even before Matveev set foot in London that "it is certain you will not be able to gratify him in any part of his negotiation."[2] And so it proved: Matveev found himself enmeshed in a net of vague promises and distracting civilities. He had already announced his intention to return to The Hague when there occurred an event which, although distressing to him personally, led to the one positive gain of his embassy.

On the evening of 21 July 1708 Matveev, travelling in his carriage to meet some fellow foreign ministers, was attacked and beaten by three men, recruited by creditors to whom he owed some £50. Although he was rescued, temporarily, by people answering his cries for help, his assailants produced documents and were allowed to take him to a debtors' prison on Wych Street off the Strand. He managed to inform his friends about his predicament, but it was only early the next morning that he was released. The outcome of the ensuing protests from Matveev, staunchly supported by all the foreign ministers (the Swedish excepted), whose debts were far in excess of the Russian's, and of the obvious embarrassment of the English government was the Act of Parliament of 21 April 1709 "for preserving the Privileges of Ambassadors and other publick Ministers of Foreign Princes and States."[3] Both Russia and the other European states obviously benefitted from England's recognition of diplomatic immunity—no Russian ambassador after Matveev suffered such indignities, although on at least two other occasions members of the Embassy staff, to whom similar privileges were also extended, found themselves in His Majesty's prisons.[4] Russian ambassadors were now free to put their minds to other sensitive diplomatic issues, such as their rank and standing in the eyes of the English government and their precedence vis-à-vis the representatives of other foreign states, as well as the due recognition of the "imperial" status of their ruler.

Matveev's successor, Prince Boris Ivanovich Kurakin (1676-1727), appointed at the end of 1709 when Peter considered his honour over the Matveev affair satisfied, encountered a cool reception in England, but his tact, his penetrating and educated mind, and his aristocratic bearing made his recall in June, 1711, a matter of regret for the English ministers. He was, however, to be employed by Peter on special missions to England in 1714, 1715, and again in 1716, when Russian affairs in London were successively in the hands of the Prussian Albrecht von der Lith (1711-13) and the Dane Bertram, Baron Schack (1713-16), competent diplomats, but non-Russian and therefore suspect, in the eyes of Peter and certainly of Kurakin, when questions of alliances and treaties were at stake.

Kurakin was undoubtedly one of the outstanding political figures of Peter's reign, masterminding from The Hague, both before and after his appointment to England, the actions of Russian diplomats abroad and aspects of Russian foreign policy. His own initiation into the life of Western Europe had begun early, in 1696, when he was sent to Italy to study navigation, mathematics, and other practical subjects and to acquire a knowledge of Italian brought to perfection by the time of a second visit to Rome in 1707, as Russian ambassador. In the interim he had travelled widely, leaving Russia in 1705 to take the waters at Carlsbad and then residing for some time in Holland. His diaries and notebooks from the period 1705-08 reveal what a perceptive observer he was of the social and cultural life of the countries he visited and make the absence of any such coverage for England highly regrettable.[5] His interest in England, however, was predictable, and even before he was dispatched to London, he had set about compiling a dossier on aspects of its religious and political life. From London he was subsequently to write a series of informative reports on the workings of Parliament, the differences between the parties and questions of legal procedures.[6] In 1711 his continual ill-health led him to journey to Bath and he was able to see a little of the country outside the capital: like his predecessor Matveev, he was entertained by the Duke of Ormond at his estate at Richmond, then he went to Windsor, visiting Eton College, where, he noted, "the children of such honourable people as lords and dukes study Latin, Greek and French, as well as all subjects in the humanities, but not military science."[7] On his return journey, he saw Oxford and was one of the first Russians to visit the Bodleian Library. Generally impressed by what he saw in England, he in turn impressed many who met him. An inconclusive but likely illustration is afforded by a short-lived journal entitled *The Muscovite*, the five issues of which appeared during the time of Kurakin's second visit to England in 1714: the editor passes on his alleged discussions with a Muscovite by the name of Plescou, for whom the prototype may indeed have been Kurakin: "A Muscovite, who having enjoyed a noble Encouragement from his Prince for several Years, has employed it in travelling through the most civilized Countries, where he has filled his Mind with the most valuable Parts of knowledge, but especially with that of Mankind."[8]

As a diplomat in London Kurakin achieved no triumphs, negotiating in difficult times, when allegiances were changed virtually overnight in frantic moves to preserve or restore the balance of power, and yesterday's heroes became today's villains. Peter, after the triumph at Poltava in 1709, could no longer be ignored, but he posed as many threats—a growing fleet, a vast and vastly improved army, territorial gains, export monopolies—as he held out promises—a permanent trade agreement, a strong alliance. Peter's aims and policies were clear and simple; it was the English interpretation or reaction that was changing and complex.[9] The net result was a general worsening of Anglo-Russian relations, accelerating after the Northern Crisis of 1716-17, and leading to a complete breakdown of formal diplomatic links in November, 1720, when the then Resident, Count Mikhail Bestuzhev-Riumin (1688-1760), was ordered to leave. It was the treaty of alliance signed between Great Britain and Sweden in January of that year that had finally brought matters to a head: Bestuzhev expressed the tsar's indignation in a strongly worded "Memorial," which earned him a snub from the Secretary of State Craggs.

Bestuzhev's "Memorial," presented on 17 October 1720, was published early the following year,[10] illustrating a tactic already used by his predecessor, Fedor Pavlovich Veselovskii, Resident between 1717 and 1720. During Veselovskii's time in London, anti-Russian feeling found expression in a stream of pamphlets and newspaper articles, highlighting the expansionist designs of Peter, his conspiring with the Jacobites through the agency of his Scots physician Robert Erskine. In an attempt to counteract the attacks and insinuations contained in such publications as *The Northern Crisis, or Reflections on the Policies of the Tsar* (1716), *Letter from a Gentleman at Hamburgh* (1717) and *Truth is but Truth as it is Timed!* (1719) by making the Russian case known to the general public, Veselovskii published two memorials which he had presented to the British government in 1717 and 1719. The first was an attempt to convince not only George I but "also the whole World . . . of the Uprightness of his Intentions and unblemish'd Conduct, and that all the artful Insinuations that have been spread against his Czarish Majesty, will be dissipated and confounded" with regard to his Swedish designs and Jacobite connections;[11] the second was a far less conciliatory, sharply worded rebuke to the British government for its recent defensive alliance with Austria and Poland.[12] Both *Memorials* were ineffective in influencing either the government or public opinion, but are interesting as the first Russian attempt to meet the challenge of the comparatively free English press other than by libel actions, bribery or physical assault.

Despite Veselovskii's honest endeavours, the tsar was dissatisfied with his lack of success and sent Bestuzhev to relieve him. In the meantime the tsar learned that Veselovskii's brother, Abram, who had been Resident in Vienna, had fled to Geneva on hearing of the execution in Russia of people involved in aiding Peter's son Aleksei to escape abroad. The tsar's anger reached out for both Veselovskiis and Bestuzhev was ordered to arrest Fedor in London on charges of malconverting embassy funds. Fedor fled also, to Marburg, from where he wrote to Bestuzhev that he would never return to Russia from fear of being tortured and interrogated. In 1723 Peter demanded the extradition of the brothers and was infuriated at the British government's unwillingness to refuse them asylum; the following year, however, Russian intervention was instrumental in thwarting Abram's attempt, via a sympathetic Member of Parliament, to become a naturalized Englishman. Of Fedor nothing was heard for many years until the appointment of a new Russian Resident to London in 1731. The Resident's attempts to secure Veselovskii a pardon were for a long time unsuccessful; it was only in 1743, after Veselovskii had followed the Resident to a new appointment in Paris, that the Empress Elizabeth finally allowed him to return to Russia.[13] Veselovskii was the most notable of a number of Russian runaways or, in some cases, castaways in London during the eleven years that official diplomatic relations were broken, who surfaced when the Empress Anna's general amnesty of February, 1732, was made known. Producing an English version of the manifesto and publishing it in the English papers was one of the first tasks of the new Russian representative, Prince Antiokh Kantemir (1708-44).

II

"The prince of Valachia, who arrived here 2 days ago, set out from hence yesterday to go to London as Her Czarish Majesty's resident. I am in hopes his person will be acceptable to your lordship, though he is very young and never was employed in business." Thus did Claudius Rondeau, the British Resident in St Petersburg, introduce his Russian counterpart to Lord Harrington in a letter of 14 January 1732.[14] Despite Rondeau's reservations, Kantemir proved an exceptional ambassador. Son of the Hospodar of Moldavia, Demetrius Cantemir, who sought refuge with his family in Moscow in 1711, fervent supporter of his adopted country, but especially of Peter, the tsar-reformer, widely educated, poet, philosopher, Antiokh Kantemir owed his appointment to London at the early age of twenty three to his steadfast support of the new Empress Anna Ivanovna during the succession crisis of 1730 and his powerful protectors in the "German party," Counts Osterman and Biron. Long desirous of travelling and studying in Europe, Kantemir came to London not with suspicion but with enthusiasm, eager to see, to learn and to mix with scholars and scientists. By nature and inclination preferring the world of books and the company of an intimate circle of friends, Kantemir came to terms with the conflicting demands of the public and the private man and proved a conscientious and respected diplomat, employing his powers of analysis and literary talents to produce a stream of reports which were thereafter regarded as models among the more discerning members of the Russian *corps diplomatique*.[15]

Since the deaths of both George I and Catherine I in 1727 Britain and Russia had been moving towards reconciliation and Kantemir's arrival heralded an era of closer co-operation and less suspicion which was to survive until the last decade of the century. The concept of "the natural allies" was born, although at times its implications seemed strictly negative. At least, Britain and Russia did not go to war against each other, although the diplomatic chessboard occasionally revealed them in unpromising, indeed compromising situations; neither, on the other hand, did they actually make war together, although there were times when Russian forces moved slowly, and ultimately too slowly, to help. But generally there were enough powerful enemies seeming to threaten or indeed threatening both Britain and Russia for the two countries to experience a vague sense of fellow feeling. If this feeling had a hard core, it was distinctly commercial rather than political and the great event that occurred during Kantemir's ambassadorship was the signing in 1734 of the first Commercial Agreement between the two countries, which was to last for fifteen years. Kantemir was not, however, directly involved in its negotiation, for the British insisted, as they were to do throughout the century, that all agreements be reached in St. Petersburg. Nonetheless, the event could not but add to his standing in London, which had already been advanced by his promotion from Resident to Minister.

Kantemir was in London for a little over six years in all, until his appointment as Ambassador to France in April, 1738. It was in Paris that he was to die in 1744, revealing to the end his attachment to England and its culture and eliciting from a French diplomat the "epitaph": "Il est plus à regretter pour la douceur de son caractère et les qualités de l'esprit que par rapport à son amitié pour nous, car il étoit plus Anglois que s'il fut né à Londres."[16] Kantemir indeed was the first of a notable line of distinctly Anglophile Russian ambassadors, whose warm response to many aspects of English life undoubtedly helped to keep diplomatic relations on a generally smooth course. He was also typical in that, although he read English, he spoke it with difficulty and continued to express his admiration in French.

Lack of a proficiency in English proved a stumbling block if not generally at ambassadorial level, then certainly among the lower echelons of the embassy staff. Kantemir had brought with him to London as his secretary and translator a young man by the name of Onufrii Speshnev, who knew German but neither French nor English. He was thus quite unable to cope with the College of Foreign Affairs's demand to translate the "manifesto about Runaways" into English, a task which Kantemir asked in future to be done in Russia.[17] Kantemir was nevertheless obliged to take on an Englishman by the name of William Brown as interpreter and translator, but the latter's addiction to drink made him an unreliable assistant. More reliable as an English interpreter and a valued and cultured friend was Varfolomei Kassano (Cassano), of French and Greek parentage and priest to the Orthodox community in London. A final member of a haphazardly collected embassy staff was Andrei Tret'iakov, a man literally abandoned by the Russian government during the years of broken diplomatic relations and utterly destitute before Kantemir adopted him in 1733.[18] If Kantemir had had his way, the embassy would have acquired another valuable member in Giovanni Zamboni, a Florentine diplomat who was the Minister in London of the Duke of Hesse-Darmstadt. Kantemir's proposal that he should be elected to the new post of Russian Consul was rejected by the College of Commerce,[19] and ambassadors were obliged to take care of commercial affairs and visiting Russian merchants (two of whom, incidentally arrived a year after the signing of the Commercial Agreement) until as late as 1773.

Zamboni was one of Kantemir's closest friends, one of the select group of foreign diplomats in London who formed themselves into a convivial dining, quasi-masonic group, known among themselves as "the Ministerial Club."[20] In addition to Zamboni and Kantemir, other members included at various times Count Giuseppe Ossorio, the Sardinian ambassador, Baron Johann von Loss and Baron von Wasner, the Saxon and Austrian Residents, Giambatista Gastaldi, Secretary to the Genoan Mission, Vincenzo Pucci and Marco Antonio Azevedo, representatives of Tuscany and Portugal respectively. In the summer of 1738, Kantemir wrote to a friend, the abbé Paretti: "Nous avons bu votre santé à la table de notre club, qui va le mieux du monde. Je crois sans vanité que c'est la seule coterie à Londres, où en mangeant bien, on est gai, on se traite en vrais amis."[21] Kantemir's friendship with Italians in particular was stressed by his first biographer, the abbé Octavien de Guasco, himself an Italian, who attributed to them his fascination with the Italian language and love of painting and music. Outside his diplomatic circle, Kantemir was especially close to Paoli Rolli, poet, teacher of Italian to the royal family and director of the Italian opera, which was then enjoying a tremendous vogue in London, supported by the Prince of Wales and his friends in defiance of the king's encouragement of Handel.[22] Kantemir was an enthusiastic supporter of the famous castrato singer Farinelli and more than a little involved with one of the female singers, Francesca Bertolli. But his circle of friends was far from exclusively Italian or indeed foreign; Guasco suggested that: "Dans les intervalles, que les occupations de son minstère lui laissoient, il ne négligeoit rien pour profiter des lumières d'un pays, devenu la patrie des sciences & des arts. Sa maison étoit le rendez-vous des savans, attirés par sa réputation & par l'accueil gracieux qu'il leur faisoit. La façon de penser de cette nation convenoit à la solidité de son esprit; aussi se forma-t'il une idée si avantageuse de Londres, qu'il disoit souvent, que l'Angleterre étoit son centre."[23]

Kantemir found time in London to devote to literature, revising the early Satires which he had written in Russia and writing new ones, which clearly revealed the influence of such as Pope and Locke on his ideas on education and morality.[24] Works by English writers and philosophers, in English or French translations, formed a significant part of the extensive personal library which he accumulated in England and France. He had close connections with the Royal Society and its president, Sir Hans Sloane, and was strongly influenced by the ideas of Newton. Prominent among the translations which he also managed to complete in London (Anacreon's Odes, Justin's History) was his version of Francesco Algarotti's *Newtonianismo per le dame*, the manuscript of which was sent to Russia for publication but was suppressed on the intervention of the Holy Synod.[25] Algarotti, whom Kantemir met in London and whose visit to Petersburg in 1738 he helped to arrange, was to express the hope which was thus not fulfilled that "may he shortly become the propagator of Newton's philosophy in the vast em-

pire of the Russias, and may the new faith soon be spread in new worlds."[26]
Kantemir also became well known to the English Royal family, particularly
to Queen Caroline, with whose encouragement he arranged for the translation and first publication of his father's history of the Ottoman Empire.[27]
The overwhelmingly favourable impression which Kantemir made in London
is evident from a letter which George II sent to the Russian empress on
hearing of his appointment to Paris: "We could not in justice to his merit
dismiss him from Our Presence without acquainting Your Imperial Majesty
how worthy he has constantly shewed himself of the Trust You reposed in
him, and how much to Our satisfaction he behaved himself during the whole
course of his Ministry here, in endeavouring upon all occasions to promote
and increase the happy Union which subsists between Us."[28]

His successor, Prince Ivan Andreevich Shcherbatov (1696-1761), was
also so successful in fostering this "happy union" during the remaining
years of Anna's reign that the king saw fit to make it known that his recall
in 1742 was likewise a matter of regret. Like Kantemir, Shcherbatov was a
protégé of the "German party" in St. Petersburg and his recall was dictated
by the circumstances surrounding the accession of the new empress, Elizabeth, and the inevitable ousting of all who had been connected with Biron
and Osterman. Nevertheless, Shcherbatov's undoubted success as ambassador
and the confidence he inspired in the English ministers with whom he had
dealings led to his re-appointment within two years. Despite certain changes
in the internal situation in Russia, Shcherbatov's years of service pointed to
the essential continuity in foreign policy and the nearness of Russian and
British interests.

Following the successful conclusion of the Commercial Agreement, the
English government made the first moves towards a defensive alliance; Shcherbatov was instructed to make reassuring gestures in that direction but also
to press for British support in their policies towards Sweden. In April, 1741,
an alliance was signed in Petersburg but it was not ratified on account of the
coup in Russia a few months later. An alliance was, however, signed at the
end of 1742, when Russia was again at war with Sweden and eager to involve
England. In the event it achieved little for either side, other than bringing
at long last British acknowledgement of the "imperial" eminence of Russia's
rulers. Throughout the twenty years of Elizabeth's reign Anglo-Russian
diplomatic exchanges are marked by their inconclusive nature, although
for much of the time Russian foreign policy was in the hands of the strongly
pro-English anti-French Chancellor A. P. Bestuzhev-Riumin. He succeeded
in negotiating treaties with Great Britain in 1747 and again in 1755, after
years of protracted wrangling, only to find that by the time the latter convention was ratified in February, 1756, Britain had already signed a treaty of
alliance with Prussia which made it virtually worthless. In August, 1756,
the Seven Years' War began and Great Britain sat on the sidelines, turning

its attention to India and Canada while attempting through its Ambassador Sir Charles Hanbury-Williams and his good standing with the "Young Court" of Grand Duke Paul and Grand Duchess Catherine to counteract the growing French influence in Petersburg.

During Elizabeth's reign Russian affairs in England were in the hands of just four ambassadors, Semen Kirilovich Naryshkin (1710-75), Shcherbatov, Count Petr Grigor'evich Chernyshev (1712-73), and Prince Aleksandr Mikhailovich Golitsyn (1723-1807). Although all with the exception of Naryshkin served long years in London, almost nothing is known of their activities, even as diplomats—which affords a striking contrast not only with their predecessors during the first third of the century but more particularly with the ambassadors of Catherine II. To some extent one might find in this a fitting reflection of the highs and lows of British public interest in Russia and things Russian, a trough of indifference towards a country lacking the interest aroused by Peter I and later by Catherine II. But Elizabeth's ambassadors were not only experienced diplomats but in some cases scholars and men of letters.

Shcherbatov had already studied some three years in England between 1719 and 1721 and on being refused permission to sail with the British Navy, spent his time learning English and producing a translation (1720) of John Law's *Considérations sur le numéraire et la commerce*. When he next came twenty years later, he had behind him years of diplomatic service in Spain and Constantinople and had risen to the presidency of the College of Justice. He was an outstanding linguist, knowing English, French, Latin, Italian, and Spanish and had compiled a number of essays on economic and scientific subjects, all unpublished, including a "Treatise on Russian trade" (1724).[29] His first replacement as ambassador, Naryshkin, was a man of letters of a different species. He was a confirmed Francophile who had spent most of Anna's reign in Paris, where his opposition to the "German party" did not prevent close friendship and probable literary collaboration with Kantemir. Via Kantemir Shcherbatov and Naryshkin in turn "inherited" Zamboni, whose papers contain a number of notes and letters from both ambassadors, increasingly enthusiastic from Naryshkin, who declared that Zamboni possessed "le secret de tout de belles choses."[30] Naryshkin spent nineteen months in London before returning to Petersburg where he produced a number of literary works and translations from French, notably of Strube de Piermont's *Discours sur l'origine et les changements des lois russiens* (1756). Shcherbatov's second replacement, Chernyshev, received within eighteen months of his arrival in 1746 the sort of scholarly recognition which Shcherbatov would more obviously have merited, if the former's election to the Royal Society on 10 March 1748 had been other than a diplomatic gesture.[31] Certainly he seems to have had few intellectual or stylistic pretensions to judge by a complaint from St. Petersburg in July, 1747, about his reports which lacked "clear sense, exposition and style, and the most important passages of which were simply incomprehensible."[32] Such a verdict is hardly contradicted by his one published report, written in response to a demand of December, 1747, to provide a detailed account of the reception and privileges accorded to "ambassadors and ministers of the second rank."[33] Chernyshev nonetheless served nine years in London, enjoyed the favour of George II and was well received in fashionable society. He had brought with him his wife and two young daughters, Dar'ia (b. 1738) who was to marry Fieldmarshall I. P. Saltykov, and Natal'ia (b. 1741), later a Princess Golitsyna who lived to the age of ninety-six and achieved immortality as the prototype of the Countess in Pushkin's *Pikovaia dama* ("Queen of Spades"). It was from another branch of the Golitsyn family that Chernyshev's successor came: Aleksandr Mikhailovich Golitsyn was to return to Russia to become Catherine II's vice-chancellor and be characterized by a British ambassador as "extremely polite and well-bred, but has neither inherited great talents from Nature, nor taken much pains to cultivate those few she gave him. He was several years Envoy in England, but I do not look upon him as very hearty in his good wishes towards it."[34] If the last comment was accurate, Golitsyn at least was exceptional in a court which the new empress had virtually ordered to look favourably towards England.

III

It was said of the Empress Elizabeth that she lived out her life "unaware that Great Britain was an island";[35] Catherine II not only knew its precise geographical location but realized all that this implied and explained, particularly with regard to trade, naval power and attitudes towards the Continent. While still grand duchess, she told her friend, the then British ambassador, Sir Charles Hanbury-Williams, that she considered an alliance with England as both the most useful and natural for Russia.[36] As empress, she appeared to a later ambassador, Lord Cathcart, to be putting such ideas into action: "Russia, to my predecessors, as their correspondence shows, appeared under French influence, from inclination, custom and education. Russia is now, by the Empress's firm determined and declared opinions, and will be so by all her institutions, *decidedly* English."[37] Her Minister Nikita Panin was also to profess his belief in the idea of "natural allies," but both he and the empress repeatedly emphasized that for the British "the natural" was synonymous with "the commercial." For the Empress the British "toujours sont marchands," while Panin noted the government's propensity to treat people purely as merchandise.[38] These particular expressions of irritation were occasioned by the British reluctance to respond to Russian overtures for a renewal of the lapsed defensive and offensive alliance with the same enthusiasm that they had shown in negotiating a

second Commercial Agreement in 1766, but Catherine's recognition thereafter of what was nearest and dearest to British interests made her an astute
and formidable adversary rather than a submissive ally.

That the period of the greatest cultural, technological and commercial
intercourse in the eighteenth century should also be the period of the greatest political and diplomatic tension and confrontation is a paradox already
anticipated in the reign of Peter the Great. Catherine inherited Peter's desire
to make Russia a great power, to improve and increase the army and the
navy and to seek further territorial expansion; she also followed him in
looking to the West, and particularly to Britain, for the expertise and inspiration which would help to make such designs possible. Sandwiched between
the reigns of Peter and Catherine had been some three decades of comparatively easy diplomatic relations and limited Russian political and territorial
ambition but of colourless, at least to British eyes, rulers and virtually non-
existent cultural contacts. In contrast both Peter and Catherine were dynamic, larger-than-life figures who caught the imagination of the British,
and not only the British, public, and whose activities as "enlighteners" of
a backward people seemed to overshadow any threat they posed militarily
or politically. It is interesting that Peter's virtual apotheosis came in biographies published in Britain in the 1740s and 50s, at the time of the emergence of the idea of "natural allies," and these combined to give Catherine
and Russia the benefit of any doubts way into the 1780s. M. S. Anderson
had clearly shown how British public opinion and indeed British politicians
were slow to react to the implications of such events as the Russian naval
victories over the Turks in the Mediterranean in 1769-70, the partition of
Poland in 1772, the formation of the Armed Neutrality in 1780, although
the last action could not but cause deep and lasting scars. However if Pitt
the Elder was able in 1773 to welcome Russian·victories over the Turks
with the words "I am quite a Russ. I trust the Ottoman will pull down the
House of Bourbon in his fall,"[39] Pitt the Younger viewed the renewal of
hostilities in 1787 in a different light precisely because the French now stood
to gain an advantage from Russian success. The previous year had seen the
signing of a France-Russian commercial agreement in Petersburg and the
failure of the British to re-negotiate their own agreement. British suspicions
came to a head in 1791 with the so-called "Ochakov crisis," when Pitt issued
an ultimatum to Catherine to return the captured fortress of Ochakov to the
Turks and to begin peace negotiations. He had, however, seriously under-
estimated the strength of the opposition in Parliament, in the City, and in
many parts of the country and he was forced initially to seek a compromise
and ultimately to withdraw all his demands. For Catherine the hero of the
hour was Charles Fox, whose bust (by Nollekens) she was to place in the
colonnade of the Cameron gallery at Tsarskoe Selo between those of Demos-
thenes and Cicero.[40] But it was Edmund Burke who in a speech at the end

of March, 1791, pointed to the real weakness in Pitt's action: "the considering the Turkish Empire as any part of the balance of power in Europe was
new. The principles of alliance and the doctrines drawn from thence were
entirely new. Russia was our natural ally and the most useful ally we had
in a commercial sense."[41] Catherine's star was again in the ascendant:
her expectedly staunch opposition to the French Revolution and the re-
signing of the Commercial Agreement in 1793 could not but herald a new
rapprochement which continued to her death in 1796, although her role
in the third partition of Poland in 1793-95 lost her many friends, including
Fox.

During the eventful thirty-four years of Catherine's reign Russian interests
at the Court of St. James's were represented by six ministers or ambassadors,
who provide fascinating contrasts in age, experience, provenance, personality
and abilities. At either end of the period were the two brothers Aleksandr
and Semen Romanovich Vorontsov. Aleksandr served for less than two
years, until December, 1763, as did his successor Heinrich Gross, who died
in office in November, 1765. Gross was followed by the first of the long-
serving ambassadors, Aleksei Semenovich Musin-Pushkin, whose twelve-
year period in London was interrupted by the ambassadorship extraordinary
(1768-69) of Ivan Grigor'evich Chernyshev. Ivan Matveevich Simolin served
between 1779 and 1785, when Semen Vorontsov arrived to begin an ambassadorship which was to extend until 1806 and a period of residence in
England which was to end only with his death in 1832. Four of the men were
counts, members of influential and powerful aristocratic families in eighteenth-century Russia, while Gross and Simolin were of non-Russian origin
and had worked their way up the Table of Ranks by dint of long years in
the diplomatic service. Aleksandr Vorontsov, appointed at the age of twenty-
one, was much younger than all his successors, four of whom were over
forty at the time of appointment, and his lack of experience in state service
was equalled only by his brother's.

Aleksandr Vorontsov (1741-1805) was appointed to the London post
not by Catherine but by her husband Peter III. Early in 1758 Vorontsov
had been sent to France by the Empress Elizabeth in accord with the wishes
of the young man's uncle, her new grand chancellor, M. I. Vorontsov, who
was a confirmed Francophile. He remained in France for some two years,
serving in the cavalry at Versailles, before being sent by Elizabeth on diplomatic missions to Spain and Italy. Shortly before her death the empress
appointed him *chargé d'affaires* at Vienna and in February, 1762, Peter III
sent him to London as minister plenipotentiary. It is to Catherine's credit
that she did not recall him immediately after the coup which brought her to
the throne following the murder of her husband, for the Vorontsovs, with
the exception of Princess Dashkova, Aleksandr and Semen's sister, supported
her late husband and their eldest sister was indeed Peter's mistress. Catherine

continued to regard the Vorontsovs with some suspicion for many years but retained Aleksandr in London until the end of 1763 before transferring him as ambassador to The Hague.[42]

The task facing Vorontsov—negotiating a new defensive allinace which would guarantee Russia British support in Poland, Sweden and Turkey— would have taxed and defeated far more experienced diplomats, and he was to plead British unwillingness to be involved in Europe generally as the reason for his lack of success. However, Catherine seemed generally pleased with his efforts, commenting that "je lis avec plaisir vos relations et j'espère que vous continuerez la conduite louable que vous avez eue jusqu'ici," although the following year she was to find certain arguments in his reports "pitiful."[43] Vorontsov's successes were social rather than diplomatic, and he made many lasting friends, as his brother Semen discovered over twenty years later: "J'ai trouvé beaucoup de personnes que me parlent de vous. M-r Pitt m'a dit qu'il sait que vous étiez très-lié avec son père et qu'il se souvient qu'il parlait de vous toujours avec une très-grande estime. Le lord Sydney, qui de votre temps s'appelait Townson et que était parent de Charles Townson, m'a dit vous avoir aussi beaucoup connu, il est actuellement secrétaire d'état pour les affaires intérieures. Le marquis Landsdowne, autrefois Shelburne, a passé chez moi et ne m'ayant pas trouvé, m'a fait dire qu'il désire faire ma connaissance, ayant eu l'avantage d'être de vos amis."[44] If the young and personable Vorontsov earned the esteem of the elder Pitt, he seems to have won distinctly more in the case of the ageing widow, Maria Lady Blandford, about whom a contemporary forecast, if wrongly, "That she will marry Count Woronzow, I no more doubt than that in consequence she will change her religion, and attend him some years hence to his mother country."[45] Despite the strong French influences on his early education and the relatively short period he spent in London, Vorontsov conceived a genuine admiration for many aspects of English life and culture. Shortly after his transfer to the Hague, which was both unexpected and unwished, he wrote: "Je me regarde en quelque façon, comme citoyen de ce pays-là par les communs intérêts, qu'il a avec le nôtre, ainsi que par les bontés, que j'ai éprouvé de tous ceux qui ont été assez justes et éclairés pour reconoître les bonnes dispositions, que j'aurai toujours pour une nation aussi respectable que l'est celle, que j'ai quitté."[46] He was true to his word and his appointment as president of the Commerce College in 1773 brought him inevitably in close touch with British affairs, as did the appointment of his brother to London in 1784. In the way that he had received detailed instructions from his uncle as to his conduct, so he, with the added advantage of his own knowledge of England, advised Semen on its attractions and dangers.[47] During his own period in London he had begun to collect books for what was to become by the end of his life one of the most famous and extensive private libraries in Russia, and Semen readily supplied him with further works which he considered of importance, notably Adam Smith's *Wealth of Nations* in 1786.[48]

An illustration of the curious and arbitrary merry-go-round of diplomatic representation is provided by Vorontsov's successor, Heinrich Gross, who would have been his predecessor, had George III not objected to his nomination in December, 1761, by Peter III, a nomination obviously considered disrespectfully low. Gross was nonetheless "un homme consommé dans les affaires, ayant cependant une figure ignoble et les manières d'un homme d'assez basse extraction";[49] he was already familiar with England, having served in the embassy under Kantemir, who had been taught by Gross's elder brother, a Petersburg Academician, and had then served in Paris and The Hague. As a foreigner in Russian service and at a time of rapidly changing rulers, he was very vulnerable, but he served Russian interests well if unspectacularly during a residence of some twenty-one months, cut short by his sudden death in November, 1765.

Although chronologically, Gross was followed by Musin-Pushkin, the latter was soon transferred temporarily to The Hague to replace Aleksandr Vorontsov and allow Count Ivan Chernyshev to come to London as Ambassador Extraordinary to make what was virtually a last attempt to bring Britain into Catherine and Panin's cherished Northern System. Chernyshev received detailed instructions, in which the Northern System was defined as "the greatest and closest possible union of the northern powers on matters of immediate and common interest with the aim of creating a firm counterbalance to the houses of Bourbon and Austria at the courts of Europe and of preserving peace in the North and banishing completely their influence which had hitherto brought such dire consequences."[50] Having signed alliances with Prussia in April, 1764, and with Denmark in February, 1765, Pussia wanted direct British financial support for the anti-French faction in Sweden and acceptance of Russia's role in Poland as part of a general defensive and offensive agreement. Chernyshev was no more successful than his predecessors had been and he was recalled in November, 1769, after exactly a year in London. It was for things other than high diplomacy that Chernyshev's embassy was remembered.

Perhaps no Russian ambassador before or after was preceded to London by a more devastating characterization than the one Chernyshev received from the British ambassador in Petersburg, George Macartney, in February, 1767, by which time, it appears, Chernyshev had already persuaded the empress to appoint him, although nearly another year was to pass before the official announcement. It is indeed a "portrait at full length," developed with all the considerable, if self-indulgent powers of Macartney's rhetoric, of "our new Ambassador," who is now about forty years old; but retains all the vivacity and petulance of youth; fed by the consciousness of superior talents, and entire security of the favour and friendship of Mr. Panin; his natural parts, though not solid, are lively, and in Russia may well pass to be of the first rate; his reading, such as it is, is extensive, but certainly in the French way, consisting of memoirs, letters, anecdotes, almanacks, and dictionaries. As to the learned languages, he is totally ignorant; as to the modern ones, he possesses many of them; particularly the French and German, both of which he speaks with uncommon fluency and precision. His conversation abounds with wit and entertainment; though often tiresome and disgusting by the exuberance of his expressions; for with him eloquence and talkativeness are the same thing. He seems, in common with all the Russians I have ever seen, to want the discriminating faculty. He is a pretender to all sorts of knowledge, an enthusiast of his own opinion; little scrupulous in point of profession, and seldom very attentive to the obligation of veracity; ambitious even beyond presumption, regarding no elevation too high for his merit and expectations; suspicious of his friends implacably vindictive to his enemies; an imperious Master; false to his patrons, regardless of his dependents, cruel to his slaves, haughty in his disposition, and violent, nay furious, in his temper, filled with extravagant ideas of the greatness and power of his own Nation, and comparatively not entertaining the most advantageous thoughts of others; and as for as I can judge, more likely to blow up or ruffle a negotiation, than to conduct or advance one.[51]

Macartney's successor, Lord Cathcart was much more charitable and in mentioning "the civilities his family show to all the King's subjects (they call themselves la famille anglaise),"[52] was pointing to the boundless, extravagant love of England and the English that could not but strike other observers. It may well be that prior to his own visit Ivan was well disposed to England by what would have been the undoubtedly reasoned enthusiasm of his eldest brother Petr, ambassador in London in the late 1740s; certainly, "their sense of the civilities they received in England" did nothing to dispel it and they were therafter "to show their regard for the nation on every occasion where a British subject of whatever rank comes· in their way," whether it be the notorious Duchess of Kingston, who sailed up the Neva in her yacht escorted by a squadron commanded by Chernyshev, or the much more worthwhile Samuel Bentham. A French diplomat was to comment sourly on "le Comte Ivan, Anglois à l'enthousiaste sans savoir pourquoi,"[53] and indeed the French had particular cause to remember his public dispute with their representative in London.

Catherine in her instructions to Chernyshev had emphasized that he was not to cede precedence on either official or private occasions to diplomatic representatives from other countries, and certainly not from France. At a ball held to celebrate the king's birthday on 5 June 1769 at St. James's Chernyshev was sitting next to the Austrian Ambassador Count Seilern, a position which immediately displeased the arriving French ambassador, the Marquis du Châtelet. What ensued was picturesquely relayed by Horace Walpole to his friend Sir Horace Mann: "Chatelet sidled up to the two former, spoke to them and passed behind them, but in a sudden lifted up his leg and thrust himself between the two imperials. The Russian astonished and provoked, endeavoured to push him away and a jostle began that discomposed the faces and curls of both; and the Russian even dropped the word *impertinent.*"[54] After a seeming reconciliation, the affair flared up again the next day and the king himself felt obliged to intervene. "The public papers, which seldom spare the French," commented Walpole with disapproval, "are warm for the Russian."[55] As for Chernyshev, even after his return to Russia, the mere mention of the incident was enough "to throw him into an apoplexy."[56]

Macartney was correct in suggesting that Chernyshev had "very extravagant notions of the dignity of an Ambassador, and particularly of a Russian Ambassador to England," and no less in forecasting that: "his appearance will be uncommonly splendid and magnificent; for he is a man of great expense and profusion, as you will easily suppose when I inform you, that the state liveries of his servants cost upwards of a hundred pounds apiece. His Lady's diamonds are worth, as he told me, near forty thousand pounds sterling. She is a woman of uncommon beauty, of a sweet temper, and most amiable character, and though I believe by no means happy with him, yet is so dazzled by the idea of his Embassy, that she is determined to accompany him to England."[57] Accompany him she did, and so did such an amount of silver and other effects that he was allowed no fewer than forty three horses for the journey from Petersburg to Riga and special dispensation at the customs. Soon all London was buzzing with stories of their magnificence, "beyond any Publick Minister that has ever been here" and of diamonds, already escalating in value to "fifty thousand pounds worth."[58] No doubt the Chernyshevs returned with yet more effects from London, for one very obvious manifestation of his Anglomania was his respect for items of English manufacture—from saddles and riding whips to shoes, from engravings to objets d'art. He was also interested in the institutions which fostered an interest in both the aesthetic and the practical: he was a member of both the Society of Dilletanti and of the Society for the Encouragement of Arts, Manufactures and Commerce. Himself a founder member of the Russian Economic Society since 1765, he subsequently kept up his interest in English agricultural methods and, as will be seen in a later chapter, even sent one of his serfs to England to gain practical expertise.

For Musin-Pushkin, Chernyshev's predecessor and successor, there was indeed "no happiness like that of returning to England as a private man, and purchasing a farm."[59] At least so he informed Lady Craven in 1786, when he was retired from his labours as a diplomat and, according to another English observer, was indulging himself at the Petersburg gambling tables, dressed in a very striking pink coat[60]—perhaps another vestige of his sentimental attachment to England. Musin-Pushkin, however, had come to know England very well over a fourteen-year period, had a keen appreciation of many aspects of its history and institutions, and spoke the language fluently. One of his most interesting reports clearly reveals his understanding of the importance of agriculture to the British economy, the advances that were being made and the particular role played by the country gentry: "Agriculture, its [the country's wealth] main source, has already been brought to such a flourishing state here that was only to be expected from laws which promise every individual full enjoyment of the fruits of his labours and encourage more and more effort. Significant help comes from the custom of the gentry to live in the country; at their expense experiments are ceaselessly carried out to improve all aspects of rural economy."[61] Other reports described the foundation and workings of the Bank of England, parliamentary elections, the functions of the two Houses, the election of the Lord Mayor of London, the East India Company, etc., Catherine was said to have kept for many months his description of parliamentary elections which arrived during the sittings of her Legislative Commission in 1768, although later both she and Panin expressed displeasure at the lack of political analysis and information in other reports.[62]

It was during Musin-Pushkin's long residence in the 1770s that Anglo-Russian intercourse increased immeasurably in all fields, bringing ever growing numbers of Russians to London. Many of the activities of such as students at British universities, officers in the British navy, craftsmen, mechanics, painters, writers, tourists provide the substance of later chapters, but Musin-Pushkin and the ambassadors who followed him found more and more of their time taken up with duties more readily associated with academic tutors, banking houses, naval commanders, wet-nurses, shopkeepers, and merchants. At least in 1773 one of the heaviest burdens—that of looking after Russian commercial interests—was removed with the appointment of a consul, a post so earnestly advocated by Kantemir nearly forty years previously and now promoted by Aleksandr Vorontsov as Head of the College of Commerce. The man chosen was Alexander Baxter, a member of the Russia Company of twenty years' standing, who was to use his wide contacts in the City and throughout industrial Britain to serve Russians and Russia well over a long period. His appointment was followed by others, to Hull in 1785 and the Isle of Wight in 1788, but the ambassador was still obliged, and certainly in the case of the last appointee with good reason, to oversee their activities.[63]

In the last years of Musin-Pushkin's ambassadorship, as Russia's confidence and prestige mounted and England's fell, particularly following the outbreak

of the American War of Independence and the growing threat of France
through alliances with the colonists and with Spain, Anglo-Russian diplomatic relations entered a difficult period. Turning to Russia for help, through
the agency of its new ambassador James Harris, Britain found only a wish
not to be involved. It seems likely that in pursuing and elaborating policies
as uncongenial to the British as the Armed Neutrality was to prove Catherine
deemed it appropriate to replace the Anglophile Musin-Pushkin by a new
man, unknown to the British but skilled and experienced in diplomacy.
Ivan Simolin (1720-99), son of a Swedish pastor from Reval and with over
thirty-five years of service, almost all in Scandinavian embassies, was such a
man, as Catherine's detailed instructions to him make patently clear:

> From your long experience in a political career you are aware both of
> the nature and state of our present affairs with other European states
> and of England's particular anxious condition arising from its onerous
> war with its American colonies and France as well as the additional
> recent Spanish war. For these reasons we also do not consider it neces-
> sary to expatiate on either subject, for until time and circumstances
> produce new events and with them perhaps new ideas which might
> demand the elaboration of new and immediate plans of action, you
> should keep in the meantime to vague generalities, and we are satis-
> fied that for your course of action we need only point on the one
> hand to your own perspicacity which has ever been guided by your
> patriotic endeavours in our service, and on the other, to the instructions
> given to your predecessors insofar as they are pertinent to the present
> state of affairs, but particularly to the instructions given to the present
> Vice-President of the College of Commerce Count Chernyshev during
> his embassy to London.[64]

"Vague generalities," designed neither to antagonize nor to compromise,
were thus the order of the day, except in one particular area, where Simolin
was requested to make common cause with the Danish envoy in London in
seeking reparation for losses sustained by Danish subjects from the attacks
of British privateers. Solidarity with the interests of Denmark and Sweden,
their mutual right to trade and sail without interference from the warring
powers, England, France, and Spain, was the basis of Catherine's famous
Declaration of Armed Neutrality of 27 February (O.S.) 1780. Simolin was
instructed to re-assure the British government as to Russia's continuing
friendship but to watch with particular care what counter-measures might
be undertaken by the Admiralty, if only in response to British regrets that
"Great Britain, from being the first maritime power in the world, should be
so humbled, in the course of a few years only, as to receive laws from an
empire to which, within the memory of many now living, she taught the art
of shipbuilding and navigating ships of war."[65] No decisive action was,

however, taken, and one of the opposition papers contented itself with insinuations about Simolin's spying activities on behalf of France, which led to a successful libel suit against the editor of the *London Courant*.[66]

As Catherine had hoped, Simolin performed his duties more than efficiently and virtually anonymously. He seems to have made little impact on English society or indeed, it on him, and the few comments on him during his London period all come from Russian sources and all are negative. A young Russian visitor in 1783 considered him "le seul ministre de Russie, que j'ai connu dans mes voyages, qui traite les jeunes russes, à lui recommandés, avec si peu de politesse"; if he appealed to one of his travelling companions, it was simply because "ils courroient ensemble les filles. Ils firent regulièrement la chasse de St James parc pour faire la curée du gibier." A fortnight later, he noted that "Mr. de S. Ministre de Russie s'est brouillé avec son maître d'hotel, son valet de chambre et sa maitresse. Les deux premiers sont congediés et la dernière est à negocier son congé, soutenant qu'il est bon qu'à p. . .er qu'à tousser."[67] Semen Vorontsov also commented on Simolin's unsavoury reputation, as well as suggesting that his reports were merely edited versions of English newspaper reports.[68]

Simolin moved in early 1785 to Paris where he was to remain as Russian ambassador through the French Revolution. Before he left London, he sold his house, 36 Harley Street, to the empress, with the result that for the first time the Russian Embassy in London had a permanent home. Previously, the Russian ambassadors had been provided with accommodation by the British government or, after about 1756, with funds from Russia to hire their own house or rooms. It was thus into Simolin's old house that the new Russian minister Semen Vorontsov moved in early June, 1785.[69]

Catherine's most famous ambassador at the Court of St. James's, this same Vorontsov had been described by the empress as "a dangerous character,"[70] even before the revolution of 1762, which over thirty years later he still looked back upon as "ce jour horrible . . . l'abominable jour."[71] After long years in the wilderness, during which he travelled extensively abroad and later served in the army, fighting with distinction against the Turks and feeling deeply the unjust preferment of others, he was suddenly offered a diplomatic post in Venice. Reluctantly, Vorontsov accepted Catherine's peace offering and in 1782 departed for Italy with his wife, whom he was soon tragically to lose. With his two young children, Mikhail (1782-1856), who was to become a field-marshall and a prince, and Ekaterina (1784-1856), who was to marry into the English aristocracy, he came to England to spend the second half of his long life. He pictured himself somewhat bleakly at this period as "un soldat réformé, un homme jeté, malgré lui et fort tard, sur le declin de ses jours et sans aucune préparation préalable, dans une carrière tout-à-fait étrangère à ses goûts et à ses habitudes, enfin une recrue politique qui faisait son apprentissage entre 43 et 44 ans et qui tâchait de suppléer, par son application pour ses devoirs et par son zèle pour servir sa Patrie, tout ce qui lui manquait de talents acquis et naturels."[72] In addition, he had long suffered ill health and his wife's death affected him so much that "ma vivacité s'anéantit, et mon corps ne put plus supporter ni la fatique, ni le froid."[73] Nevertheless, this "elderly mild tall yellow looking Man," as an Irish girl described him some years later,[74] revealed unflagging energy, firmness of character, and great diplomatic acumen through some of the most difficult years in Anglo-Russian relations.

Vorontsov came to England well primed by his brother as to its dominant characteristics and its beguiling attractions and well disposed by his own experience of life and of the vagaries of autocracy in Russia to respond enthusiastically to "le pays le plus libre qui existe au monde."[75] He was not, however, an Anglomaniac in the mould of Ivan Chernyshev; he was rather a passionate believer in the need for a strong Anglo-Russian alliance, in the concept of the "natural allies," in the fundamental nearness of English and Russian interests. Throughout his letters at different periods of his life in England and in slightly differing formulations occurs the conviction that "tout bon Anglais doit être bon Russe et tout bon Russe doit être un bon Anglais,"[76] and in its defence he was ready to attack anyone, English or Russian, statesman, politician, or journalist, whom he considered was working against the mutual interests of the two countries. His brother had warned him that "c'est un pays pour lequel vous avez toujours eu du faible et auquel il est impossible de ne pas s'attacher à mesure qu'on le connaît."[77] Previous Russian ministers, Aleksandr Vorontsov included, had been unable to preserve the necessary detachment, and Lord Granville, who succeeded the Duke of Leeds as Secretary for Foreign Affairs in 1792, suggested indeed to Vorontsov that he had become "un ami de l'opposition." His reply was revealing: "je ne suis d'aucun parti que celui de ma Patrie, (que) je suis Russe et rien que Russe, (qu')il m'est très indifférent, si c'est son cousin et ami William Pitt, ou Charles Fox, qui gouverne ce pays, pourvu que ce pays fut gouverné par un homme qui désire d'entretenir la bonne harmonie entre la Russie et l'Angleterre, et (que) celui qui aura ce désir, si sensé et fondé sur les vrais intérêts et avantages des deux pays, trouvera toujours en moi un cooperateur très zélé pour la réussite de cette bonne oeuvre."[78] Thus over the years he had made common cause with Fox and opposed Pitt, as later during the Napoleonic wars he was to side with Pitt against Fox. The cause was greater than the man and Vorontsov never betrayed it.

Within days of arriving in England, Vorontsov wrote that "il m'est très avantageux à Londres d'être ministre de la puissance qu'on estime le plus et qu'on recherche preférablement à toute autre,"[79] an impression suggested not least by a conversation he had had recently with Pitt, the minister whose policies during the first six years of Vorontsov's residence were to put the two countries on an inevitable collision course. The principal threat to continuing Anglo-Russian understanding was the willingness of George III, "ce cher roi, le plus fatale pour Angleterre de tous ceux qui y ont régné, . . . de se lier, dans sa capacité électorale, sans rime ni raison, avec le roi de Prusse."[80] In August, 1787, war broke out between Turkey and Russia, and, within a year, between Sweden and Russia: Russian suspicions of Prussian involvement, with British connivance or more, were increased with the signing of an Anglo-Prussian defensive allinace in August, 1788, and confirmed by the Prusso-Turkish alliance of January, 1790. British assurances that the great fleet which was being prepared later that year was destined for North America rather than the Baltic did not satisfy Vorontsov who saw the move as tantamount to a declaration of war against Russia and delivered his own ultimatum in terms which, he assures us in his autobiography, subsequently earned him esteem and renown:

Puisque je vois que le ministère est assez aveugle que de s'obstiner (sous prétexte de conserver Otchakow aux Turcs, ce qui doit être indifférent à l'Angleterre) dans une guerre injuste et dommageable aux deux pays, mon devoir est d'empêcher le mal. Vous aurez sans doute une majorité dans les deux chambres, mais je connais déjà assez ce pays pour savoir que le ministère et le Parlement même n'ont de force que quand ils sont soutenus par le voeu des comtés et des personnes possessionnées et indépendantes, qui en dernière analyse governent le pays. Je vous déclare donc, monsieur le duc [of Leeds], que je me donnerai toutes les peines possibles que la nation soit informé de vos projets si contraires aux intérêts du pays, et j'ai trop bonne opinion du bon sens anglais pour ne pas espérer que le cri général du pays ne vous force à abandonner cette entreprise injuste.[81]

It is a remarkable statement: it reveals not only now quickly Vorontsov had conquered his own initial "ignorance de ce gouvernment si compliqué"[82] but to what extent Russian diplomacy in England came of age with him, for implicit in what he was saying was the recognition of his ability to sway public opinion, to manipulate the press and publishing outlets, to forsake the crude forms of physical assault on opposing voices, advocated as late as 1762 by Catherine to his brother;[83] it testifies no less eloquently to Vorontsov's own admiration for what could be done within the English system and explains perhaps his horror on hearing in the same year of 1790 of "la condamnation du pauvre Radistchef" in distant Petersburg.[84]

1791 was Vorontsov's finest hour as a diplomat, according to his own estimate and that of the considerable number of historians who have studied in detail the "Ochakov crisis." If in the final analysis M. S. Anderson is correct in stressing that "the ambassador and the opposition won a victory, and a striking one, because they had behind them almost the whole of the informed and politically conscious opinion of the country,"[85] Vorontsov's contribution to the defeat of Pitt's policies against Russia was nonetheless considerable. Inevitably, in his campaign he turned to members of the opposition and principally to Fox, whose own degree of involvement was such that he sent one of his own supporters, Robert Adair, to Petersburg as a sort of "oppositional ambassador" during the same period that Pitt's special envoy, William Fawkener, was negotiating with Catherine—a move which was seen, not without some justification, as near to treason. The eloquence of the opposition orators was undoubtedly crucial in Parliament, as Catherine herself recognized, but Vorontsov was also successful in capitalizing on the indecision among the Pittites themselves: Nathanial Dimsdale, M.P. for Hertford, who had assisted his father in the inoculation of Catherine II, and had been generously rewarded by the empress, used his influence to promote the Russian cause. Outside the House, Vorontsov recognized that there was much support in the City, particularly among members of the Russia Company, and throughout early 1791 he used to great effect arguments about the crucial importance of the Russia trade. Russia Company members in a number of manufacturing and industrial towns were prominent at meetings to express disapproval of Pitt's policies. For example, on 28 April 1791, "a numerous and respectable meeting of the Merchants, Manufacturers, and other Inhabitants of the city of Norwich" passed several resolutions condemning any war with Russia and stressing the importance of the city's commercial ties.[86] Both the *Norfolk Chronicle* and the *Norwich Mercury* carried reports throughout April about developments in London and other cities such as Manchester as well as within Norwich itself. Vorontsov mentioned as further examples of popular support country voters who "écriverent à leurs représentants au Parlement, pour qu'ils aient à se séparer de m-r Pitt et voter contre lui" and the London populace which "sur toutes les murailles des maisons . . . écrivait avec la craie: Point de guerre avec la Russie."[87] One cannot but wonder whether the writing was not done by members of the Russian embassy, the deployment of whose literary and distributory talents was an essential element in Vorontsov's campaign:

> Dans 29 et plus de gazettes, qui paraissent ici journellement, il y avait toujours des articles qui sortaient (sans qu'on le sache) de moi et qui éclairaient la nation, qui devenait de jour en jour plus furieuse contre le ministère, et tout cela n'a pas coûté 250 livres sterling à mon cour; mais cela m'a coûté à moi et à tous ceux de ma chancellerie beaucoup de peine. Car depuis le mois de Mars, jusqu'au mois de Juillet que ce combat a duré, ni moi, ni eux nous n'avons pas eu de repos et nous passions les nuits à griffonner et les jours à courir de tous côtés, et quand je prenais quelques moments de repos, eux n'en avaient pas: car c'est pendant les nuits qu'ils allaient porter aux différents bureaux des rédacteurs des gazettes les articles qui devaient paraître le lendemain.[88]

Among his most assiduous helpers were Vasilii Grigor'evich Lizakevich, who had served in the London embassy since 1765, the embassy chaplain Iakov Ivanovich Smirnov, a remarkable figure whose career will be traced in a later chapter, a young Ukrainian translator named Andrei Vasil'evich Nazarevskii, and two men who were not Russian subjects but whose devotion to the Russian cause was invaluable, Vorontsov's private secretary and his son's tutor, a Swiss by the name of Joly, and John Paradise, a Fellow of the Royal Society, Oxford D.C.L., linguist and littérateur. It was Joly and Paradise who were directly concerned with Vorontsov's most effective contribution to the pamphlet war, *Serious Enquiries into the Motives and Consequences of Our Present Armament against Russia* (London, 1791): Paradise rendered into English the French text prepared by Joly on the basis of information and instructions from Vorontsov.[89]

Elated by the turn of events in Russia's favour in the early summer of 1791, and bitterly opposed to revolutionary France, Vorontsov was now to argue for more formal ties between Britain and Russia. In March, 1793, contrary to earlier English practice, two conventions were signed in London: the Commercial Agreement extended the provisions of 1766 for a further six years and the second convention was one of mutual opposition to France and included a naval blockade. This second convention was a source of particular pleasure for George III, for it "so completely destroys the whole Russian system of an armed neutrality, which was in the late war the most inimical measure adopted by any nation."[90] A more comprehensive defensive alliance followed in February, 1795. Thus, despite the mounting disquiet in certain English circles which followed the cynical dismemberment of Poland in 1793-95, Vorontsov by the end of Catherine's reign could feel that the hopes which he had cherished twelve years earlier were at last realized.

The first years of Paul's reign did nothing to disabuse him and his own standing with the emperor was so high that early in 1799 he was offered the Russian chancellorship in succession to the late Count Bezborodko. But by the end of that same year Anglo-Russian relations had rapidly deteriorated after a brief honeymoon which had seen a further renewal of the commercial agreement and Russia's joining a new coalition against France. After initial victories under Suvorov in Italy, Russian forces suffered humiliating defeats in Switzerland and the Netherlands, much of the blame for which Paul attributed firstly to the Austrians and then to the British. Napoleon took his opportunity to woo Paul with such success that the infamous Armed Neutrality was renewed against Britain. Official diplomatic relations between Britain and Russia were broken and Vorontsov, whose distaste for Paul's actions was all too obvious, was dismissed from his post but with permission to remain in England. Early in 1801, Paul's suspicions of Vorontsov were such that "il y avait à Londres un certain gueux nommé Crempin, envoyé par la police de Petersbourg pour nous espionner"[91] and his estates in Russia were confiscated. The winter of Vorontsov's discontent was, however, to be relatively short. In March Paul was murdered and the new tsar was quick to restore Vorontsov to his former post. Immediately he wrote to Lord Whitworth, his former counterpart in Petersburg: "Je m'adresse à Vous Mylord comme à un bon russe pour m'aider à réunir de nouveau nos deux Patries,"[92] and for a few more years he was to work unceasingly for Anglo-Russian harmony. The Anglo-Russian alliance of 1805 allowed him to retire the following year with albeit short-lived equanimity, but July, 1807, brought Tilsit, and the fall of the Russian star in Britain was as dramatic as in 1800. In retirement in Southampton, Vorontsov consoled himself with the thought that he had seen it all before, and that "the Russian God is great and certainly will not desert altogether our poor country which is perishing from stupidity, corruption and treachery."[93] Indeed in 1812 he was witness to "l'enthousiasme qu'on a ici pour les Russes; généraux, officiers, soldats, nobles, bourgeois et peuple, tous sont estimés, admirés, et loués"[94] and, two years later, to the rapturous welcome for Alexander I, the first tsar to visit England since Peter I.

In all Vorontsov spent some forty-eight years in England, broken only by one short visit to Russia in 1802. He was highly respected in London society and had many friends and acquaintances in diplomatic, commercial, scholarly, and scientific circles. Indications of the regard in which he was held were Southampton's conferring on him the freedom of the city and the change after his death of the name of the street in London where he lived for many years, Mansfield Street, to Woronzow Road. He was buried in Marylebone, an area in which he was known for his "good works": he left, for example, £500 in his will to the local poorhouse. By the end of his life he was truly a good English aristocrat in every respect except his continued inability to speak or to write English, and it was in French that he spoke with his grandchildren from the marriage of his daughter with the 11th Earl of Pembroke, who included Sidney Herbert, Britain's future minister of war at the outbreak of hostilities in the Crimea.[95]

IV

With Semen Vorontsov Russian diplomacy in England found its most notable representative and visiting Russian students, as long as they displayed the right degree of patriotic purpose and endeavour, their most steadfast supporter. Although his own dedication was never in question, he would have been, and indeed was, the first to recognize the contribution made by members of the embassy, or "mission" as it was frequently called. To an incomparably greater degree than its counterpart in Petersburg, where the English community took its character principally from the merchant houses, the Russian embassy in London was at the hub of Russian activities in Britain and the demands made upon it were as varied as they were exacting.

Until 1779, when the staff of the embassy was fixed at six—one embassy counsellor (*sovetnik posol'stva*), two titular counsellors (*tituliarnye sovetniki*), one translator and two students or *aktuariusy*—there seems to have been no consistent number. Kurakin in 1711 had merely a secretary and a copyist, while Kantemir's staff fluctuated between four and seven, including at one stage two designated "embassy gentlemen" (*dvoriane posol'stva* or *dvoriane kantseliarii*). In this latter category were to be found young members of the gentry sent to gain practical experience of diplomatic service but also to study. Elizabeth's ambassador Naryshkin was instructed in 1742 to supervise closely their studies in languages and other useful subjects, to ensure that they did not waste their time and to use them for routine embassy chores, should the need arise. If they worked hard, he could seek promotion for them, but if they were lazy, he had the right to withold part of their salary. Although Semen Vorontsov in particular was scathing about the aptitude and qualities of some of the "gentlemen" sent to the London embassy, they remained very much an important part of the staff, even after the edict of January, 1800, which reduced the permanent staff to three—a secretary and two officials—but made provision for "attachés," young men destined for high diplomatic posts.[96]

Vorontsov from the beginning of his residence in London had been in favour of a small permanent staff of three, not merely because he believed that (in normal times) such a number was adequate for the work, but also because he realised that embassy officials were grossly underpaid: a reduction would leave more money for the salaries of the remaining staff without increased costs to the College of Foreign Affairs. Throughout the century embassy officials, to say nothing of ministers, found themselves ever in debt; complaints were legion about the high cost of living in London as well as about totally inadequate salaries, made even more so by the steadily falling value of the ruble against the pound. During Peter's reign, embassy secretaries in London received 300 r.; under Elizabeth, the figure was 400-600 r.; in the early years of Catherine's reign, virtually the same, while for other officials, somewhat less. In 1773, for instance, when the exchange rate was about 4.5 rubles to the pound, the minister Musin-Pushkin, received 8000 r., as well as 200 r. for postage and 2000 r. for accommodation, while his counsellor, Mikhail Pleshcheev, received 1200 r., Lizakevich, 600 r., and others, 400-450 r. In the 1790s, Vorontsov by constant petitioning was able to gain increases for all the members of his staff, but it was only with the decree of 1800 that new significantly higher salaries were fixed: 2500 r. for the secretary and 1000 r. for each of the two other officials.[97]

It is not possible, for reasons of space or lack of sufficient evidence, to trace the careers of many of the countless men who were attached to the

London embassy in the eighteenth century, but one or two examples may
be cited here.

Musin-Pushkin's staff in the 1770s offers interesting contrasts in personalities and abilities. His senior counsellor, Pleshcheev, and one of his
talented *aktuariusy*, Ivan Koshelev, will be mentioned elsewhere in connection with their studies at the University of Oxford, whilst Lizakevich has
already been noted as one of the key figures in Vorontsov's anti-Pitt campaign. He was to be the longest serving embassy official in London in the
eighteenth century, finally heading the embassy briefly in 1800, following
Vorontsov's fall from favour and prior to his own reluctant transfer to
Copenhagen as Russian envoy. "Ce digne homme" was, in Vorontsov s words,
"si pressé par la nécessité que je crains toujours qu'il ne soit réduit ou à se
brûler la cervelle, ou à vendre nos chiffres, ou à communiquer à qui le payera
ce qu'il sait des affaires. J'ai lieu de croire, d'après ce que je vois de son
caractère, qu'il préferera plutôt la première voie."[98] Utterly dedicated and
trustworthy, Lizakevich stood in complete contrast to the type of useless
"embassy gentleman," such as Prince Makulov, denounced by Vorontsov in
1787, or Prince Petr Gagarin, attached to Musin-Pushkin's staff in 1773 and
recalled to Russia in 1784 after unsatisfactory reports. A Russian visitor
in London in 1783 characterized the latter as "un misanthrope à plaindre
dont le seul plaisir est de s'enfermer entre quatre murailles dans la plus
grande ville d'Angleterre."[99] Much more gregarious and industrious were the
Tatishchev brothers, Mikhail and Ivan, sons of a Ukrainian priest who offici-
ated at Elizabeth's court. Mikhail had come to the London embassy in 1766
as a translator and was joined three years later by his younger brother, who
had previously been attached to the Russian mission in Danzig.

The year before Ivan arrived, Mikhail had been arrested on a London
street by a police-officer who mistook him for a wanted criminal.[100] A
victim of mistaken identity in 1768, Tatishchev has been denied any existence at all by a contemporary English scholar, who re-published in 1931
a translation which he had made also in 1768 and which is his only claim to
modest immortality! The work in question is the English translation of
Catherine's *Nakaz* or Instructions to her famous if ultimately abortive Legislative Commission which convened in Moscow in July, 1767. Although the
name of "Michael Tatischeff" appears prominently on the title page and he
proudly states in his preface that "a Work in the Russian language, translated
into English by a Native of Russia, is a Novelty, I believe, never offered before to the English Nation," W. R. Reddaway surmised that "In the age of
Ossian and a thousand lesser impostures, a Russian gentleman translating
from the Russian might well turn out to be an English or Irish gentleman
translating from the French."[101] Reddaway's notes on the inadequacies of
the English translation as well as its frequently "high and sustained level of
nervous eighteenth-century prose" provide nonetheless an accurate assess-

ment of Tatishchev's abilities. Given his relatively short time in England, his achievement was considerable and it is a pity that no later examples of translations into English are known. Undoubtedly, he sought and received help with his translation or rather his English. Perhaps some assistance came from no less a source than the young Jeremy Bentham and his even younger precocious brother Samuel. Certainly the Benthams were already acquainted with Mikhail Tatishchev early in 1768 (Tatishchev's preface to his translation was dated 8 October); in a letter of 12 July, Jeremy speaks of visiting Tatishchev and of his intention to send him a copy of a pamphlet which would be of interest to him, namely John Burton's *Account of the Designs of the late Dr. Bray with an account of their proceedings* (1764).[102] Years later, looking back to this period, he elsewhere recalled how he had begun to read Helvétius's works which together with the translations of Beccaria's *Dei delitti e delle pene* and Catherine's *Instructions* "gave me fresh incentives and afforded me further lights."[103] It should be recalled that at the end of 1767 Tatishchev had in fact published a short *Description of the Manner in which the Commission for Establishing a New Code of Laws, Was Opened at Moscow, on Friday the Third Day of August, 1767* (subsequently reprinted with the *Instructions*) and that this possibly led to the two men becoming acquainted. Bentham was very interested in Catherine's projects and questioned Mikhail and his brother, who arrived in 1769, about many aspects of Russia. He has left a further fascinating glimpse of the two brothers, "whose fondness for each other was perfectly infantine, and whose disputes about the merits of Montesquieu were very amusing. The discussion turned upon fundamental principles, which were fundamental nonsense: it was a perpetual trifling about words to which they could give no definite, and each attached a different, meaning; such as 'honour,' 'virtue,' 'fear': 'honour' being a love of reputation, of as much power as a man could get; and 'virtue' being admiration of a republican government."[104] The only other reference to Mikhail Tatishchev in the Bentham correspondence dates from May 1778 when he was said to be "in a very indifferent state of health."[105] It is possible that he died soon afterwards, for nothing more is known about him from either English or Russian sources. His brother Ivan (1743-1802), on the other hand, returned to Russia in 1775 to pursue a long and successful career. He served in the College of Foreign Affairs until 1799, when he became the Director of the Post Office in Moscow, retiring in 1891 with the rank of Actual State Counsellor (which gave his family hereditary nobility) and several orders. He was particularly active as a translator from several languages, including English. In 1790 he published, at the direct command of the empress, his translation of Sir Joshua Reynolds's presidential discourses at the Royal Academy and later completed an apparently unpublished version of William Robertson's *History of Scotland*.

Far more distinguished, if ultimately very different careers were enjoyed by two other Ukrainians, who were attached at approximately the same period to the London embassy under Count Semen Vorontsov. Both were born in the early years of Catherine's reign and achieved eminence in the reign of her grandson, Alexander I. The elder and less well-known of the two was Vasilii Fedorovich Malinovskii (1765-1814), a younger brother of the writer, dramatist and translator Aleksei Malinovskii.[106] Shortly after graduating from Moscow University, Malinovskii joined the College of Foreign Affairs and, in his words, "in 1789 requested a post in London, wishing to get to know a state famed for the wisdom and happiness of its government and people, and not caring about the effect on my career."[107] He returned to Russia two years later with letters of warm recommendation from Vorontsov. About his stay in England one fact alone, but an intriguing one, is known. In 1803 he published a book entitled *Rassuzhdenie o mire i voine* ("Deliberations on Peace and War"), the writing of the first part of which was completed in 1790 at Richmond, where Vorontsov had his country house. The work is a passionate denunciation of the horrors and senselessness of war and a critique of the usual concept of "the hero": for Malinovskii, the true hero was first and foremost the wise legislator, who brought peace and contentment to a people. The little that is said specifically about England is complimentary: "Englishmen enjoy general respect in Europe, for which they are indebted to men great by their virtues, to the sound organisation of their government and to their personal qualities."[108] Although the ideas in Malinovskii's work belong to a general tradition of enlightened European thought rather than derive from any particular English source, the possibility that he, like several of his predecessors in the embassy, knew Jeremy Bentham personally and discussed with him issues of mutual concern (such as reflected in Bentham's own "Plan for the Establishment of Universal and Eternal Peace") should not be discounted.[109] The second part was completed in 1798, when Malinovskii was living near Pavlovsk with his young family: his wife was the daughter of A. A. Samborskii, a remarkable and long-serving priest at the Russian church in London, and his English wife, and had spent the first twelve years of her life in England. In a story entitled *Pustynnik* ("The Recluse"), written there the following year, Malinovskii put into the mouth of his hero a paean to the joys of family life which he found celebrated in England and which he himself was experiencing.[110] This story, which was not published, was destined for a weekly journal entitled *Osennie vechera* ("Autumnal Evenings"), which he managed to begin only in 1803 after his return from two years in Moldavia as Russian consul-general. The journal continued his ardent pacifist propaganda in a series of searching articles on the contemporary state of Europe and particularly the conflict between France and England. In one long and interesting passage he exploited the contrasts and contradictions of England and the English, emphasizing as the positive aspects of English commitment to enlightenment,

Christian philanthropy, country and family life.[111] In 1811 Malinovskii's career reached its climax with his appointment as the first director of the Tsarskoe Selo Lyceum but within two years he died, depriving Russia and a generation of talented young students, including Aleksandr Pushkin and several future Decembrists, of his guidance, learning and humanity.[112]

If Vorontsov thought well of Malinovskii, he could not praise highly enough Viktor Pavlovich Kochubei (1768-1834), the other young man who came under his supervision in 1789. Scion of a famous line, Kochubei owed his education and early rapid advancement to his uncle, the highly influential Count Bezborodko, who brought him to Petersburg in 1775 and arranged for him to be attached to the Russian Embassy in Stockholm at the age of sixteen in 1784. Before leaving for London, he had gained the favour of the empress, accompanying her on her visit to the Crimea in 1786 and receiving the rank of *kamer-iunker*. He was to remain in London for a little under two years, from the early spring of 1789 to the beginning of January, 1791, before leaving for further study and travel in France and Switzerland;[113] returning to London a year later, he departed finally for Petersburg in July, 1792, destined, at the age of twenty-four, for the important post of Russian ambassador to Constantinople. He was thus absent from London during the height of the Ochakov crisis, but on his return was used on important and confidential work in the embassy. Vorontsov asked him also, for example, to produce for Fox a version in French of the Russian peace treaty with Turkey, signed in 1792 at Jassy, where, incidentally, Malinovskii had gone as secretary to the Russian delegation after his departure from London. He returned to Russia with letters from the ambassador to Count Markov, his former chief in Stockholm, and to Platon Zubov, Catherine's current favourite, in which he was described as "cherchant à s'instruire et s'instruisant beaucoup, modeste, ayant beaucoup de jugement et d'élévation d'âme, parlant et écrivant parfaitement bien en russe et en français, et désirant de servir son pays avec tout le zèle et le désintéressement d'un homme d'honneur."[114] Vorontsov put him among only five young men whom he had met during his diplomatic service who "ont profité des pays étrangers pour être utiles à la Russie."[115] As biased and unfair as Vorontsov's verdict was with regard to numerous other Russians visiting England in the eighteenth century, it revealed once again his strong prejudices that only Russians (and he made no distinction between Russians and Ukrainians), and then only Russian aristocrats and gentry, should occupy the highest diplomatic posts. Kochubei did not disappoint him: managing to retain, most of the time, the favour of both Catherine and of Paul, as grand duke and emperor, and the devotion of the young Grand Duke Alexander, he came to a position of great power and influence when the latter became tsar. The senior of the "young friends," the members of the *Neglasnyi komitet* ("Unofficial Committee"), he shared with them an enthusiasm for reform in Russia and a profound respect for the institutions of England, which he, Adam Czartoryski, Pavel Stroganov and Nikolai Novosil'tsev all knew from first-hand experience. It was their "Anglomania" that F. F. Vigel', the author of the most scathing of all the characterizations of the "young friends," indentified as their common bond, noting of Kochubei that "he better than the others knew the composition of Parliament, the rights of its members, had read all the English publicists and like the young lion in Krylov's fable, was ready to teach the other beasts how to build nests."[116]

CHAPTER 2
THE RUSSIAN CHURCH IN LONDON AND ITS CLERGY

Early in 1741 a translator in the College of Foreign Affairs in St. Petersburg, Iakov Seniavich presented his "Brief Account of the Establishment of the Greek Church in London" to the Russian Vice-Chancellor M. G. Golovkin.[1] A leading role in its establishment had been played by Seniavich himself, when as a member of the Russian Mission in London in 1716, he had addressed a letter to Arsenii, Bishop of Thebes, asking him to send Archimandrite Gennadii to officiate in England, At the end of November Gennadii arrived, together with his nephew Varfolomei Kassano, and regular Orthodox services began that same month in rooms hired by Seniavich in York Buildings in the Strand. Seniavich's appeal had been prompted by fears of the "misfortunes and satanic intrigues" to which the Orthodox brethren in London were likely to be exposed with the archbishop's own departure from England earlier in the year. Arsenii and Gennadii had been in London since 1712, attempting to gain English aid for the Greek Church suffering under Turkish rule, and during their stay had held services, which were attended not only by resident Russians and visiting Greeks but also by Englishmen sympathetic to the possible union of the Western and Eastern churches.[2] Despite some opposition, Seniavich gained the permission of the Bishop of London, Robinson, to establish a church under the protection of the Russian mission, arguing that Peter the Great had granted the English in Moscow similar privileges. Robinson, who was alert to any attempts at proselytizing, nevertheless demanded that the Russians "should conduct their services in private and not permit any Englishmen to attend and should also sing quietly so as not to give offence to the common people."[3]

Despite the rupture in Anglo-Russian diplomatic relations in 1720, the church prospered, in a spiritual if not material sense, throughout the reign of Peter the Great under the care of Gennadii. In 1726 the ageing priest asked permission to send his nephew to Petersburg to be ordained with a view to succeeding him. The request was granted; Kassano was admitted to the priesthood by Archbishop Feofan Prokopovich and returned to London at the end of the year. The first priest to be appointed by the Russian government and clergy specifically for service at the London church and the first of a line of remarkable and talented men to hold that office up to the October Revolution, Kassano continued to serve under his uncle for another ten years. Gennadii, however, felt it necessary to return himself to Russia in 1729 to plead for funds for the church and receive icons and vestments which he brought back in the summer of 1731. In March, 1732, Prince Kantemir arrived as the Russian resident in London and church and embassy entered into a close and productive relationship which was to remain unbroken for the rest of the century.

The church during the first decades of its existence was very much a Greek church: its first priests, Gennadii and Kassano, were Greek, the majority of the congregation were Greeks, services were conducted in Greek and Greek books (and a few in English) were used. It was only after the death of Kassano in June, 1746, that the church came under its first truly Russian priests and carried a new name which emphasized its Russian character: "The Orthodox Graeco-Russian Church of the Dormition of the Blessed Mother of God." In 1737 the Synod had, however, sent from Russia a priest Ioann Iastrembskii and two clerks (*d'iachki*), Aleksei Kamenskii and Stepan Ivanovskii, to help Kassano, who took charge of the church after the death of his uncle earlier that year. Kassano (1697-1746), whose mother was Greek and father French, soon added a mastery of English to his two other languages. Kantemir said of his English that "he spoke and wrote in that language like a native English-man,"[4] and this is confirmed not only by his extant letters in English to Kantemir but also by his translations of a number of church books from Greek into English (which is possibly to be explained by an increasing number of Englishmen in the congregation). At the same time the first books in Church-Slavonic were requested by Iastrembskii from the Synod, to be sent for use in the church.

The church was never rich; it had often to rely on donations from a congregation of whom a Russian ambassador wrote in 1749: "apart from three or four people who have reasonable clothes on their backs and a few Greek merchants who come briefly to trade, all are from the lowest strata: sailors, beggars and similar rabble" and suggested that if anything were to be done about purchasing a permanent home for the church, it would have to be with money from the Russian government.[5] Peter the Great had apparently indicated the need to build a church or buy suitable premises but the matter was not pursued because of the prohibitive costs. The same obstacle remained when Prince Shcherbatov in 1740 and again in 1746 was asked to make enquiries about a house. Something, however, had to be done: in May, 1753, the Russian priest, who was by that time Stepan Ivanovskii, described to the ambassador, Count Petr Chernyshev, the state of the church in York Buildings: "the house in which the church is established, is already so old that every day I expect it to fall down, and is anyway in an indecent and shameful place [the Strand was a notorious haunt of prostitutes]; inside everything is shoddy, the cloths around the holy altar are torn, the curtains, which are used for doors in the screen and at the side have completely fallen apart; the damask covers on the throne and altar are in poor condition; plaster everywhere has begun to fall, all the paint has come off the iconostasis, which has turned quite black. . . ."[6]

Ivanovskii asked the ambassador to seek permission for the church to be moved, although he pointed out that more money would be needed. The plea was heeded and in 1755 the Senate increased the allowance for the rent and upkeep of the church from 200 rubles to 600 (around £120). Suitable accommodation was found at Burlington Gardens on Clifford Street at a rent of £80 per annum compared with the £4 for the former house and the move was effected early in 1757.[7] The money received from Russia was soon to prove inadequate in the face of London's high cost of living and was at all events received only irregularly. The church began its inevitable physical deterioration and by the 1780s complaints similar to those of Ivanovskii's were again being made. Father Iakov Smirnov wrote to his predecessor Andrei Samborskii at the end of 1784, asking for assistance in yet another move, "for I am afraid, if it is long delayed, one day or other we shall be buried in the ruins of this nasty old house, that cracks and shakes whenever the least wind happens, or when the Coaches pass by it. And when ever rainy weather, it runns through everywhere."[8] 1786 saw the next move of the church to Great Portland Street in Marylebone.[9] Catherine on 13/24 November 1786, issued two decrees: the first authorizing annual payment of a rent of £15 and rates of 16 guineas, and the second granting a single payment of £300 for the construction of an iconostasis and for structural alterations to the new building.[10] The London church became at last a respectable place of worship for the significantly increasing numbers of Russians in the English capital in the last decades of the century, although in 1813 a fourth and final home was found for it in Welbeck Street.[11]

Not only the fabric of the church had been in need of attention for so long: the icons, paintings, and church ornaments had not been distinguished by their richness, neither had the vestments of the clergy. Indeed, in 1763 we read that chasubles and a surplice had been made out of "an old padded housecoat of an orange colour," kindly donated by the ambassador, Count A. R. Vorontsov.[12] The clergy itself could ill afford to replace its vestments and the salary, when it came, was soon spent. Gennadii had received 300 rubles a year, whereas Kassano continued to receive a mere 150 as his assistant, although by a decree of 1725 the salary of a priest (*sviashchennik*) was set at 300. In 1754 the Senate kept the salary at 300 rubles for priests and 150 for unordained helpers in the church (*tserkovniki*). With such a salary, Ivanovskii told Chernyshev in 1753, "it is impossible for a poor man like me, with a family, to live in the face of the known high cost of living here and not fall into debt."[13] His predecessor, Antipa Martinianov, who served from 1746 to 1749, had returned to Russia, leaving behind him debts of £182. Chernyshev himself reported that the Russian clergy were paid less than a lackey. Even an increase to 600 rubles in 1764 for priests and to 200 for others was a drop in the ocean. A comparison with salaries received by members of the embassy at this period shows the official equivalent in rank on the civil list to a priest, a titular counsellor (*tituliarnyi sovetnik*) also received 600 rubles, but two other officials received 1200 and 800 rubles and only a translator at 450 and two junior clerks (*aktuariusy*) at 400 received less. Even these received twice as much as the poor *tserkovniki*.

Gennadii ˋhad been an archimandrite, a rank corresponding to the sixth grade on the army, navy and civil lists, but after his death, it was decided that this was too high a status for the head of a small church with an equally small congregation, such as London. All subsequent appointments were subsequently made at the rank of *sviashchennik*, although *d'iakon* (deacon) at the tenth grade, addressed as *podobie* (Reverence) as opposed to *prepodobie* (Very Reverence) of the *arkhimandrit* was also envisaged. There are instances in the eighteenth century of a *tserkovnik* at the London church succeeding the former priest, whereupon he would be recalled to Petersburg to be ordained. Ivanovskii, Samborskii and Smirnov all served as *tserkovniki*, Ivanovskii over twenty years, before proceeding to the priesthood. Smirnov is the only example of a London priest rising in rank while still in office: in 1817, after thirty seven years as priest, he was finally raised to *protoierei* (Dean), equivalent to the rank of the very first priest Gennadii.

After the resumption of diplomatic relations with the arrival of Prince Kantemir in 1732, the Russian ministers in London became increasingly responsible for supervising the good running of the church, for liaising in church matters with the College of Foreign Affairs and through it with the Synod in Russia, for influencing appointments of the priests by conveying the wishes of the congregation or by his own views on certain pre-conditions for the post. Although some of the early appointments were men from monastic orders, it became clear to the ambassadors that such men could only antagonize the English populace by their dress and appearance. 'Ieromonakh' Efrem D'iakovskii (1727?-95), a teacher from the Kiev Academy who was appointed to succeed Ivanovskii (d. 1765), had to be recalled because of the baiting he received. Count Musin-Pushkin reported some months before his recall: "His health has deteriorated and he has been unable to leave his house because he has frequently been subject to insults and injuries from the insolent and rowdy people here on the streets who are not accustomed to his dress, and it is impossible to gain any satisfaction, still less punishment against those who are to blame."[14] His successors, Samborskii and Smirnov, went to the opposite extreme. They shaved their beards and wore, Smirnov especially, English-style clothes. Although Samborskii and Smirnov fulfilled to the letter their obligation "to maintain their rank and calling with dignity sobriety and honour,"[15] they neglected the instruction not to involve themselves in any secular matters, but the ways they found to extend the implications of their office brought only respect and admiration from their English contemporaries and acquaintances. It is the careers of these two remarkable men, representatives of the "new Russia" of Catherine the Great, which are to be examined in detail.

II

Andrei Afanas'evich Samborskii was born on 1 August 1732, the son of a priest and small landowner in the village of Syrovotka near Khar'kov in the Ukraine. He was initially educated at the Khar'kov Collegium (former Belgorod Seminary) and then moved to the Kiev Academy, where he was recruited in 1765 to serve as a *tserkovnik* in London under the newly appointed priest D'iakovskii. With the deterioration in D'iakovskii's health towards the end of 1766 Samborskii assumed more and more responsibility for the good order of the embassy church and showed himself eminently suitable to succeed D'iakovskii. The exact date of D'iakovskii's recall is not known, although it was probably early in 1768. During the rest of that year Samborskii was in charge and only on 9 January 1769 did he receive the order from the Holy Synod recalling him to Petersburg to be ordained. He left for Russia at the end of May, but before he went he married a young English girl, an orphan by the name of Elizabeth Fielding, whom he had met at the church and whom he introduced to the Orthodox faith. It is interesting to note that Elizabeth's godfather on that occasion was Peter Paradise, a former British consul in Salonika and prosperous merchant, who had returned to England some years earlier. Samborskii's last surviving granddaughter who published his short biography in 1888 writes that Samborskii himself translated the orthodox cathecism into English for his fiancée and also acquired for her "a remarkable book on the services of the Graeco-Russian church in English," which became a family heirloom.[16] It is possible that the work in question was the translation of Peter Mohila's *Confessio Orthodoxa*, which had been made by Philip Lodvill, an English clergyman and father of Peter Paradise's wife, and published in London in 1762. Samborskii's friendship with the influential Paradise family is one example of the circle of acquaintances he was beginning to make in London society initially through members of the congregation of the Russian church. Peter Paradise's son, John, who was to become a Fellow of the Royal Society, a close friend of Samuel Johnson and of almost everyone of note in London society during the following decades, proved a good friend to Samborskii and to his successor Smirnov. John Paradise himself was married in the embassy church in 1769 to Lucy Ludwell, the youngest daughter of another well-connected family who were also regular members of the congregation.[17] Another example, more relevant for Smirnov perhaps than for Samborskii, of such important contacts with English members of the Orthodox church is Frederick North, Lord Guilford (1766-1827), the famed Philhellenist and author of a Greek ode to Catherine (1791).[18]

After a short visit to the Ukraine with his brother Vladimir to see his mother, Samborskii returned to St. Petersburg where on 6/17 September he was made a *d'iakon* and on 8/19 a *sviashchennik*. On 22 September/3 October he was presented to Catherine and the following day officially appointed chaplain of the Russian church. Before his departure for London on 29 September/10 October, he met many influential people at Catherine's court, including Grigorii Orlov, Count Zakhar Chernyshev, whose brother Ivan had briefly been Russian minister in London during Samborskii's absence, Nikita Panin, and Archbishop Platon.[19] By the end of 1769 Samborskii was back in London, resuming his duties in the church and renewing close co-operation with Musin-Pushkin, who had just returned to begin his second term as ambassador. Samborskii and Pushkin were to serve another decade before both returned to Russia at the end of 1779.

As chaplain Samborskii was instructed to ensure that all Russians residing in London were attentive to their religion and took communion and confession and to offer all assistance to people of the same faith, particularly Greeks visiting London. He was required to watch in particular over the activities of the increasing numbers of Russian students at British universities or apprenticed to English craftsmen. He later recalled how "when I was not performing my religious duties in the church, I employed all my remaining time not for my own profit but for the general good, using every opportunity and means for the advancement of Russian artists, shipbuilders, sailors and agriculturists."[20] Evidence of his care and attention is found in numerous letters which have survived in his archive from young Russians who continued to correspond with him after their return to Russia. Letters of a different kind came in profusion from almost all the prominent aristocrats of the day, who, competing with the empress in fashionable Anglomania, plagued Samborskii with commissions of every conceivable nature. He seems to have spent half his days, scurrying across London in pursuit of ribbons, watches, buttons, shoes, cloth, saddles, carriages (new and secondhand), telescopes, mathematical instruuments, engravings, books, and maps. The search for carriages in particular gave him endless trouble. In 1773 Prince Nikolai Vasil'evich Repnin, who had been to London on a short visit, left Samborskii with an order for a secondhand, four-seater carriage for a friend in Petersburg; Samborskii visited all the carriagemakers in London without success but eventually found one offered for sale by the Corsican General Paoli at 80 guineas. This was too expensive and only four months later did he manage to get a suitable one. At the same time as he had been attempting to fulfil Repnin's order, he had been trying to get a phaeton for 50 guineas for another correspondent, who had specified the colour he wanted for the paintwork and upholstery.[21] A few years later, Catherine's librarian, the poet Vasilii Petrov, was much taken with the two-seater carriage in which the Duchess of Kingston was driving around the Russian capital and asked Samborskii, "when you have the leisure," to order him a similar one from the London carriage maker Thomas Wright.[22] Fortunately, by the time Catherine got round to ordering "a very commodious travelling-coach, of an uncommon size, and containing a variety of conveniences,"[23] Samborski had left England.

Samborskii's role as errand-boy obviously brought him in contact with a broad cross-section of London craftsmen and merchants; at the same time his own real interests took him into the company of men prominent in the cultural life of the capital. He was very friendly with a number of naturalized Englishmen, such as Matthew Maty (1718-78), his son Paul (1745-87) and Joseph Planta (1744-1827), all of them librarians at the British Museum and also executive officers of the Royal Society as well as Jean Magalhaens (1722-90), who proposed Samborskii for membership of the Society of Arts in 1774. Samborskii's membership of this Society have him the opportunity to meet in particular some of the outstanding agriculturists of the day. Among other notable people whom Samborskii came to know well was Jeremy Bentham, who had become very interested in Russia and the opportunities that Catherine the Great might possibly allow him for carrying out some of his schemes and projects. Jeremy Bentham first mentions Samborskii in a letter to his brother, Samuel, of 23 December 1778 and seems to have met him early the next year, when he notes that "we are as great as Inkleweavers."[24] They met frequently throughout 1779 until Samborskii's return to Russia, where he met up with Samuel Bentham who had preceded him by a few months. Samuel Bentham came to rely on Samborskii's advice and contacts a great deal in the ensuing years and in December, 1782, wrote that "there are few men who I esteem more than this same Sambouski, and the degree of respect he meets with here is exceedingly great."[25]

Apart from his visits to Russia in 1769 and 1779, Samborskii returned on one further occasion in the intervening period. In the summer of 1775 he obtained permission from the empress to recruit a number of students to study agriculture in England and returned with them in June, 1776. The story of Samborskii's involvement in agriculture both in England and later in Russia is more properly the concern of the following chapter: suffice it to say at this point that during his remaining years in England much of his time was devoted to the care of his group of young Russian agriculturists and to dreams of the agricultural school which he returned to Russia in the hope of establishing at the end of 1779. He left England at that time, leaving behind his wife and daughters and convinced that he would soon be returning. Despite the empress's acceptance of his scheme, his life was, however, to take a different turn. There are numerous indications that he was preparing to return to England in late 1780-early 1781, but on 12/23 August 1781, Catherine's state secretary, Count Aleksandr Andreevich Bezborodko (1747-99), informed Samborskii that the empress wished him to accompany the Grand Duke Paul on their European travels.[26] For a year Samborskii acted as domestic chaplain to the "Comte du Nord" as they travelled to Vienna, Venice, Rome, Naples, Florence, Milan, Turin, through France to Paris, then to Brussels, Leyden, Spa, Frankfurt, and Switzerland. Samborskii not only earned the respect of Paul and his wife, which was to stand him in good stead later, but also of influential members of their retinue, such as Prince A. B. Kurakin and S. I. Pleshcheev, who were both convinced Anglophiles. In March, 1783, Samborskii received from Catherine a diamond-studded cross on a blue ribbon for his services and was soon writing to his wife of his intention to return to England. It was, however, only in July, 1784, that he saw England again, for the last time and only briefly. Four months previously he had been given another appointment, this time as spiritual adviser and teacher of English to the Grand Dukes Alexander and Constantine, Paul's sons.

Samborskii had four children during his years in England, two daughters, Anna (1770-1844) and Sofiia (1772-1812), who were always called Nancy and Sophie, and two sons, Aleksandr (b. 1776) and Isaiia (b. 1779). The elder daughter remained a spinster and after the death of her mother in 1794, looked after her father through the serious illnesses of his last years. Her sister, Sofiia, married V. F. Malinovskii (who has already been mentioned as a member of the Russian embassy in London in 1790s) and bore him six children, one of whom was to marry the future Decembrist Baron A. E. Rozen and another to write the biography of her grandfather.[27] The younger son, Isaiia, died in 1783 at the age of four, during Samborskii's absence in Russia; the other son, Aleksandr, who as a child of three had gone to Russia in 1779 with his father, returned with him in 1784 and remained in England to pursue his education. Aleksandr was entrusted to the care of Stepan Semenovich Dzhunkovskii (1762-1839), who accompanied him to Hertford, where he and another young Russian, Petr Ivanovich Balabin studied at the academy of a Dr. Carr. Dzhunkovskii kept Samborskii regularly informed of his son's progress, mentioning that he had done well in English and French, but not too well in Latin, for he was influenced by his English schoolfriends' prejudice against that language.[28] At the end of 1791, alarmed by his son's disinclination to join the church, Samborskii requested the Russian ambassador to send Aleksandr and Dzhunkovskii back to Russia.[29] It seems probable that Samborskii's son died on the return journey in 1792, although Samborskii's niece wrote that he died at the age of twenty-two (i.e., 1794) at Elsinore on a journey from St. Petersburg to London.[30] At all events, Samborskii became subsequently closely attached to Dzhunkovskii, described in one source as his protégé and in another as his adopted son, whom he hoped would succeed to his position.

Since his own return to Russia in the autumn of 1784 Samborskii had assiduously combined his duties as tutor to the young Grand Dukes with those of priest at the church of St. Sophia at Tsarskoe Selo. He had received the latter appointment early in 1780 when Catherine decreed that a new town called Sophia be built. The Scottish architect Charles Cameron began work on the church in 1782, but it was only consecrated in 1788. An incident connected with the ceremony of consecration is revealing for the suspicion with which Samborskii was viewed by many members of the Russian clergy. Despite the favour of the imperial family, Samborskii was considered tainted by western heretical thought and ways, obvious evidence of which seemed his refusal to grow a beard and abandon his English-style clerical dress. The Metropolitan of Novgorod denounced him in the following words: "Do you know what they write from Kiev? There has been a poor harvest because you have shaven off your beard; you have brought in a new heresy! Shaving the beard gives an excuse to schisms and to popular unrest! What are you plotting? Grow a beard or I shall deliver you up to the judgement of God."[31] The chaplain to the English congregation in St. Petersburg at this period, the Reverend William Tooke, noted that "it was as much as she [the empress] could do to screen the rev. Mr Samborsky from the fury of the monks."[32]

Samborskii was, however, kindly regarded by many as the devoted, deeply Orthodox priest he was and his knowledge of England and its ways was much admired. His house in Petersburg became a meeting-place for increasing numbers of Anglophile Russians and for Englishmen both resident in and visiting the Russian capital. It was, for instance, there that the future powerful minister of Alexander I, M. M. Speranskii, met his wife, Elizabeth Stephens, whose mother, a sister of Joseph Planta, had sought Samborskii's help when she came to Petersburg to seek a position as a governess in 1790.[33] Samborskii was frequently visited by Potemkin's gardner, William Gould, and by the empress's watchmaker, Robert Hynam, whom he had helped to gain his position, and Englishmen had good cause to echo Samuel Bentham's characterization of him. Samborskii's home at the end of Dvortsovaia Embankment near the Liteinyi Bridge on a street which was subsequently named after him (*Samburgskii pereulok*) was famous not only for its English atmosphere but also for its adjoining garden, where he grew soft fruit from bushes and plants he had brought from England.[34]

Samborskii's agricultural pursuits during the rest of Catherine's reign were of necessity in a minor key, but he took the opportunity to instruct his imperial charges in the delights and comforts of a farmer's life after the English manner on his estate at Belozerka between Tsarskoe Selo and Pavlovsk; he also assisted Grand Duke Alexander in the laying out of a garden at nearby Aleksandrova. This garden was planned as a representation of Catherine's allegorical *Skazka o tsareviche Khlore* ("The Tale of Prince Chlorus," 1781), complete with grotto and temples to Ceres, Felitsa and "The Rose without Thorns" (i.e., Virtue), set among the hills, woods and lake of an English landscape garden. When Dzhunkovskii returned from England, the first task he was given by Samborskii was to write a descriptive poem about the garden which Samborskii presented to the empress in 1794.[35] The most interesting features of this long and indifferent poem are the opening lines in praise of England and a later stanza extolling agriculture as

> The bliss of society, the glory of the monarch,
> Rural toil, the gift of Ceres!
> The support of health, the delight of the soul[36]

The accession of Paul brought Samborskii some of the financial rewards and honours to which he felt entitled. In a petition to the tsar at the beginning of 1797 he expressed the hope that a new lease would be given to a life "which hitherto has been burdened with extreme poverty and various insults."[37] He was given the estate of Stratilatovka in the southern Ukraine with 500 peasants and made a member of the Bureau of National Economy with the particular responsibility for setting up a practical school of agriculture. After two years in this position he was appointed domestic chaplain to the tsar's daughter, the Grand Duchess Aleksandra, on her marriage to Joseph, Prince Palatine of Hungary, and left Russia with his daughter Anna at the end of 1799. He returned to Russia only in 1804. In the remaining years of his long life he received many favours from his former pupil, the new Tsar Alexander I and divided his time between his estate, where he carried out numerous measures to improve the life of his serfs, and St. Petersburg. He died in 1815 in the Mikhailovskii Castle, where Alexander had provided him with rooms.

Because of his close links with members of the imperial family after his return from England to Russia Samborskii has received some attention from historians, particularly at the end of the nineteenth century; the discussions, however, have been mainly confined to assessing the influence which his religious teaching had on the young Alexander. Almost nothing has been written about his importance for Anglo-Russian cultural relations and of the years which he spent in England, crucial for his own world-view, it has been enough to say "there is as yet no information."[38] The preceding pages, which illuminate at least some of the activities of his "lost years" in England contain, nevertheless, no detailed discussion of his agricultural interests which fused with his religious creed to become the dominating passion of his life, but these are the concern of the following chapter.

III

Samborskii left behind him in England "a worthy successor,"[39] who became one of the most remarkable but least sung figures in Anglo-Russian relations at the turn of the nineteenth century. Iakov Ivanovich Smirnov (1754-1840) now appears as a shadowy and minor figure in narrations of other people's lives and deeds, relegated to a brief and generally uninformative footnote, although he was respected and lauded by the many Englishmen and Russians who met him in London. Smirnov became over the years a sort of repository of Russian knowledge about England. Serving four Russian rulers, from Catherine II to Nicholas I, outlasting a succession of Russian ambassadors, with the career of the most eminent of whom, Count Semen Vorontsov, his own was so closely connected, Smirnov was the person consulted by an endless stream of correspondents, travellers, and students. He was stability in an era of great change, and to a greater degree even than Samborskii he was always at hand and ready to help Russians and Englishmen alike, the supplier of countless letters of recommendation and introduction, dependable for all manner of commissions and errands. No Russian chaplain in England, or his English equivalent in Russia, chaplain to the British community in St. Petersburg, rivalled Smirnov in his length of service or in his range of activities, although several (John Glen King and William Tooke among Englishmen and Samborskii among Russians) achieved greater reputations, but only after their return to their homeland. The announcement of Smirnov's death appeared not in a Russian journal, but an English one: in 1840 *Gentleman's Magazine* briefly recorded: "April 28. In Welbeck-street, in his 85th year, the Rev. James Smirnove, during sixty years Chaplain to the Russian Embassy."[40]

Little is known about Smirnov's early years. The son of a village priest from the Ukraine, he had three brothers: Ioann, a priest, who was granted patents of nobility in Khar'kov in 1794 and died some time before 1800, Stepan, who received his patents at Voronezh in 1788 and was attached to the Caucasian Fiscal Board, and Ivan, who became a translator in the London embassy and died about 1810. The family name was Linitskii, and Smirnov accounts for his change of name in a deposition he sent to the College of Foreign Affairs in 1800 which also contains details about his education. He was at the Collegium in Khar'kov in 1776 when Samborskii recruited him and other students to serve in the embassy as *tserkovniki* and to study English agricultural methods: on the journey to Petersburg they had been advised to modify, or change completely their own surnames, because of alleged prejudice among certain officials against Ukrainians. Thus Linitskii became Smirnov, believing that his original surname "had been derived from the Latin word *lenis*, which means quiet or meek."[41] As Smirnov he arrived in England, and his youngest brother Ivan, who joined him in 1788, also adopted the Russian surname to avoid confusion.

Smirnov remained in England initially for three years until he returned with Samborskii to Russia in the autumn of 1779. A year later, on 9/20 October 1780, Catherine appointed him chaplain and he was ordained by Innokentii, Bishop of Pskov, the following week. After an absence of nearly sixteen months, Smirnov returned to London, where he began his duties in the church; he was to officiate until the middle of 1837, when *ieromonakh* Nifont arrived from Paris to help in the services. Revealing glimpses of Smirnov at various stages of his long career as chaplain are found in a number of contemporary memoirs and travel accounts and they combine to afford some insight into his character, way of life and activities. The first dates from 1787 when Count Evgraf Fedotovich Komarovskii (1769-1843), who was then acting as a diplomatic courier, asserted that "out of all the officials attached to our mission in London there was only one remarkable man: he was the priest of our church, Iakov Ivanovich Smirnov, who was also used in the diplomatic sector."[42]

Some years later, in 1795, the journalist and author Petr Ivanovich Makarov (1765-1804), true to his golden rule of visiting on his travels Russian priests, for "they are generally intelligent people and can be useful because they are well acquainted with the country in which they have long been resident," called on Smirnov. "I was led into a room which was very well furnished and some minutes later there appeared a man who was fairly young, fairly handsome, tall, well-built, erect, impressive in bearing and dressed with the greatest care but without the least hint of unbecoming foppishness: in a word, a young, well educated Lord—and this Lord was Mr S-v, the Russian priest at the Embassy." Makarov was not disappointed, for Smirnov proved "very intelligent; he knows Latin very well, speaks French, German, English and (if I am not mistaken) Italian. He has read a great deal and himself translates and writes. He has an extreme love of Englishmen, for which the English in turn love him. I do not think he would wish to live in any place other than London."[43] A native source provides an amusing footnote to Smirnov's command of spoken English: Martha Wilmot (1775-1873), on her way from Ireland to stay with Princess Dashkova in Russia, met Smirnov in May, 1803, and in a letter to her father wrote: "The Russian Chaplain Mr Smirnove has Call'd upon us here; and seems to take an interest for me I cou'd not have expected. The Elderly lady who is going to see her daughter at Petersburgh he told us is a Mrs Delamain under whose care I cou'd go in the most agreeable manner, dat he was very sure Madlle wou'd much like his contree, and she wou'd be relish'd there."[44] Smirnov's kindness and willingness to help were emphasized by Pavel Ivanovich Sumarokov (d. 1846) in his account of a visit to London in 1819. He carried letters of introduction to Smirnov, who "was very polite, promised to travel around with me and show me everything, and justified reports about his rare qualities."[45] Aleksandr Ivanovich Turgenev (1784-1845), the second of the famous quartet of brothers, received similar consideration and was escorted on his visit to Parliament early in 1826 by "the respected Smirnov, whose appearance was in accord with his calling and good reputation."[46] "Tall, with the accent of a Ukrainian from the Khar'kov region, dressed in a black coat of an old-fashioned, Quaker-like cut," was how Fedor Ivanovich Iordan (1800-83), a student, later Rector of the Academy of Arts, found Smirnov in 1830, but his description of Smirnov at their second meeting recalls strongly Makarov's thirty five years previously: "Ia. I. pleased me greatly, dressed like a lord of an earlier age: in a long frock coat with tails which reached down almost to his heels, with buckles on his shoes, in gaiters [*shtiblety*], with a low, wide-brimmed hat and carrying a large sturdy stick with a silver knob. His whole appearance inspired sincere respect. He walked along quietly, describing circles with his stick, and with his respectable appearance, and his hair in a plait, heavily powdered and brushed back at the temples, he seemed to me a living portrait of the seventeenth-century Dutch school.[47]

It may be assumed that Smirnov remained sartorially elegant until his death, but Nikolai Ivanovich Grech (1787-1867), who provides our last glimpse of him, in 1839, was concerned to emphasize only "Russianness." He found him still "lively in spirit and body" and rhapsodized in terms of the Uvarov-Nicholas formula: "It seemed to me that I had visited a pious hermit living on a lonely island amidst the stormy waves of a foreign ocean. Russian icons, the portraits of Russian tsars, Russian books and a Russian heart—that is all he had saved from the shipwreck. Sufficient for this world—and the next."[48]

In all these recollections and descriptions Smirnov emerges as a sympathetic and attractive man, but it would be a pity to leave him in the hands of the hagiographer Grech and to paint out any "warts." Smirnov, however, seems to have possessed remarkably few. The principal one was perhaps a sense of his own importance and authority which went beyond his calling as a priest but which, as will be seen, was not altogether unjustified by the responsibilities he came to assume particularly in the reign of Paul I. In 1804, Paul Nicolay (Pavel Andreevich Nikolai, 1777-1866), who was a counsellor in the London embassy, wrote to Vorontsov to explain a contretemps with Smirnov over the issuing of passports. He suggested that Smirnov was involving him in unnecessary paperwork out of a desire to sustain "une opinion assez generale parmi les negocians de la Compagnie de Russie dans la Cité et parmi nombre de personnes dans cette partie-ci de la ville, que dans l'absence de votre excellence l'influence du réverend est très-importante ici dans les affaires de l'ambassade."[49] Although in this specific instance a mountain seems to have been made out of a molehill, Nicolay was revealing a facet of Smirnov's character—the desire to cut a figure among Englishmen (seen also in the most obvious sense in his dress)—which was highlighted a few years earlier in a clash with the celebrated Russian Indologist, Gerasim Stepanovich Lebedev (1749-1817). Lebedev returned to England from India in 1799, distraught at the illtreatment he had received from Englishmen both in Calcutta and aboard ship on the return journey, and turned to Vorontsov and Smirnov in the hope of obtaining redress. According to Lebedev's more than somewhat garbled and excited account Smirnov proved hypocritical in words and actions, professing to help him but in fact anxious not to create a fuss with the English authorities. Smirnov also was sceptical about the worth of Lebedev's writings, particularly his Hindustani grammar. In Smirnov's eyes Lebedev was an eccentric and an adventurer, whereas Smirnov appeared to Lebedev "cowardly," "envious," "base," and "tyrannical."[50]

There is no doubt, however, that Lebedev's reaction, although understandable, was exaggerated. Smirnov was animated by a genuine concern to preserve the friendliest relations between Britain and Russia at all levels and was distressed by political and other events which jeopardized them. Devoted to the country of his birth, he was deeply attached to his country of domicile. In this respect he may be compared with Count Vorontsov, to whom their mutual friend Dr. John Rogerson, Catherine's physician, wrote: "et vous connaissant d'être comme moi et bon Russe et bon Anglais (car ils doivent aller toujours ensemble)."[51] Vorontsov was quick to appreciate Smirnov's quality after his arrival as ambassador in June, 1785, and they were to remain firm friends and companions for almost fifty years.

A year after his arrival Vorontsov wrote to Count Bezborodko on Smirnov's behalf, providing a detailed account of his varied activities:

> By his knowledge, the respect which he has earned here in society and his devotion to his country he is very necessary for all our compatriots who are sent here to study by the Admiralty College and other places; to secure teachers for them and all conceivable things for the success of their studies, he is obliged to travel ceaselessly about the city as well as to other places where they are studying. In addition he attends to all commissions for the various instruments which are requested by various institutions. He is so well known and loved here by scholars and craftsmen that out of friendship for him they accept our students to learn crafts to which foreigners have for some time been barred and he succeeded in placing only recently two men from Tula who had been sent by Prince Grigorii Aleksandrovich [Potemkin] to study weapon and steel production. In brief, he has more work and worries than I and Baxter [Alexander Baxter, the Russian consul] put together. In addition, when Mr Lizakevich is ill and I have something for coding, I am forced to use him for it, since there is no one else who is capable of doing it.[52]

Smirnov's services in the diplomatic work of the embassy, which Vorontsov mentions here and which Komarovskii had noted, became an increasingly important, if unofficial part of his activities. As was seen in the preceding chapter the members of the Russian embassy under Vorontsov formed a closely knit group and the ambassador had good cause to esteem the services of Smirnov and Lizakevich in particular in what might be termed "the intelligence sector," the procuring of information useful for the Russian College of Foreign Affairs through their large network of acquaintances and the attempt to influence English public opinion. These activities were outstandingly successful both during the "Ochakov crisis" of 1791 and the events in the years 1793-95, following the second partition of Poland.[53]

Smirnov's competence and success in a field not always immediately associated with the priesthood received further and certainly unsought acknowledgement a few years later in a totally unexpected and surprising way. After Vorontsov's dismissal from his office as ambassador in 1800, Lizakevich was appointed Russian chargé d'affaires in London, but was soon to his despair transferred to a new post in Copenhagen, whereupon an ukaz of 29 September/11 October 1800 named Smirnov as his successor: "In the absence of all accredited personages at the London court you are instructed to inform the Emperor of all you can find out about the projects, armaments, movements, transfers of funds and trading transactions of the English during this autumn and winter. In this important commission you will perceive the Emperor's trust and its justification will depend on your efforts."[54] Smirnov himself never received nor presented letters of accreditation, which was not surprising for in June Paul had ordered the English chargé d'affaires, Justinian Casamajor, to leave Petersburg along with the Ambassador Whitworth, whom he had been sent to replace, and in September had refused entry to the returning English Consul-General, Stephen Shairp.[55] The British for their part had retaliated by informing the Russian consul Baxter that "the exercise of your functions as the Consul General of the Emperor of Russia in this kingdom is to be considered for the present as suspended"[56] and detailed Shairp to watch over Smirnov's activities. On 1 December 1800 Shairp informed Lord Grenville that "I have the strongest reason to believe that Mr Smirnoy [sic] the Russian Chaplain in London continued to carry on correspondence with his country," which indeed he did, sending back reports on political developments and on proceedings in Parliament.[57] At the end of January, 1801, as a result of the British embargo on Russian ships and goods, the Russians decided to recall all the members of the embassy as well as their officers attached to the British fleet. The order came as a predictable shock to Smirnov, but it was never implemented because of Paul's murder in March. "Calm your spirit, your excellency, after its temporary upsets," Smirnov wrote to Vorontsov on 11 March 1801, "Paul I has gone to his eternal rest."[58]

The situation after Tilsit again brought Smirnov unsought responsibilities and in October, 1808, he was once more instructed "to sell the Embassy house for the best price possible, and taking the archive with me, to leave England."[59] Despite the failure of initial attempts to obtain from the Russian government permission for Smirnov to remain in London, he was eventually allowed to stay, perhaps out of consideration for arguments similar to those advanced by Vorontsov early in 1800 when Smirnov had also been threatened with recall— the need to maintain at all times an Orthodox church "so as not to give up the longstanding and useful object of furthering contacts with people of the same faith."[60] The embassy house at 36 Harley Street, into which Smirnov had moved, was not sold, but it waited another four years for the arrival of the next Russian ambassador, Count Khristofor Andreevich Liven (1774-1838), with whom Smirnov was to be associated for twenty-two years.

Smirnov's long years of devoted service in England earned him a good reputation but certainly no fortune. Iordan recalls that Smirnov began immediately to talk about the high cost of living in London and to promise to petition for an increase in his allowance from the Academy. Smirnov knew only too well and hardships which a lack of money brought and he lived in constant fear of the debtors' prison. Smirnov's own situation was especially desperate because of his large family of six children, "for the education and care of whom he is obliged to maintain in his home more people than the high cost of living, which is increasing from year to year, allows him."[61] Over the years Smirnov did receive small financial acknowledgements of his services: £200 in 1791, for instance, for the anti-Pitt campaign and £150 as well as an annual increase of £50 in 1795 for his part in uncovering the Polish plans to resist Russia. However, Vorontsov's request on his behalf after his services as unofficial chargé d'affaires in 1801 was rejected by Alexander after receiving an account "de tout ce qu'il reçoit de différents départements. Il a trouvé une très-forte somme et, je crois, plus de 600 liv. sterling independamment de 1200 roubles d'appointemens avec la bonification du change, et tout en montrant la meilleure volonté du monde de reconnaitre par la suite les services de m-r Sm., il a cru ne pas devoir rien assigner de fine."[62] Financial rewards apart, Smirnov had made some slow progress up the table of ranks. He received the order of St. Anne, 2nd class, and under Paul was made a Knight of the Order of St. John. It was at this time that he petitioned for patents of nobility and sent off to the College of Foreign Affairs in St. Petersburg the depositions regarding the standing of his three brothers and his change of name, which were referred to earlier. This seemingly straightforward matter was not, however, resolved until Vorontsov, during his short visit to Russia at the end of 1802, took up the matter with Count Kochubei. Finally in 1817 the Holy Synod raised him to *protoierei*.[63]

Smirnov's political and diplomatic activities occupied a great deal of his time and energies, but they were only one part, albeit an unusual and important one, of his total contribution. Recruited by Samborskii not only to serve in the church but also to study agriculture, Smirnov proved an outstanding pupil and Samborskii's worthy successor in this sphere as well. His prowess in agriculture, which will be discussed later, was recognized by outstanding English experts such as Arthur Young, who became his life-long friend and who noted that Smirnov "was much employed by the nobility of that Empire [Russia] in agricultural commissions."[64] These commissions were much nearer to his heart than many others he was asked to carry out. He was aware to a greater degree than the naive Samborskii that he was exploited and acknowledged to Vorontsov that "many who have been here remember me after they have gone only when they want me to carry out some commission for them."[65] Both he and the ambassador himself were not infrequently asked to secure the latest fashionable knick-knacks and gewgaws. They also, to be sure, procured many more valuable things. To enumerate these and other commissions would be, however, merely what has been said with respect to Samborskii, but two of the more interesting commissions which Smirnov received might be instanced, although both date from the nineteenth century.

In 1818 the president of the Academy of Arts, Aleksei Nikolaevich Olenin, wrote to Smirnov (and the painter Benjamin Robert Haydon) of his wish to acquire plaster casts of the Elgin marbles. Informed by Smirnov that the cost of the operation would be at least 15,000 rubles, the Academy compromised and ordered copies of "the best pieces" at a cost of 6,000 rubles, to be raised by selling off "various old, useless or broken iron and lead objects which have piled up over many years from building and repair projects."[66] Many years were to pass, however, before the order was eventually fulfilled. In August, 1823, Smirnov informed Olenin that the unfortunate Haydon had been imprisoned for debt and only recently released. He also added that the sculptor Richard Westmacott alone had the right to take plaster casts from the marbles and hinted that were Westmacott to be elected an honorary member of the Petersburg Academy (as Haydon had been), the commission might be more speedily expedited.[67] In the midst of Smirnov's efforts on behalf of the Academy of Arts, his help was sought by the president of another august body. Admiral Aleksandr Semenovich Shishkov, President of the Russian Academy, sent sets of the Academy's official publications to the Royal Society and to Edinburgh University and asked Smirnov to supply translations and explanations of any article in them which might be found of interest. He also expressed the wish that Smirnov "should become a sort of intermediary between our Academy and English learned societies": "in addition you can in many ways put our Academy in your debt and be useful to us."[68] Shishkov in particular wanted Smirnov's help with the Academy's plan to re-issue the multilingual dictionary produced by Professor Pallas by scouring English travel accounts for lists of words from little-known languages.

Smirnov's activities as a translator and writer were alluded to by Makarov and were in evidence in the newspaper and pamphlet "war" waged by Vorontsov in 1791. His own contributions both on this occasion and subsequently are almost beyond establishing: his pen was only one of a number serving the Russian cause. Smirnov is known as a translator principally for his version of Sergei Ivanovich Pleshcheev's *Obozrenie Rossiiskiia imperii v nyneshnem eia novoustroennom sostoianii* (1786), under the title of *Survey of the Russian Empire, according to its newly regulated State* (1792), which supplied the English public with useful and detailed information about the resources and geography of Russia. Smirnov also produced a translation of the new Russian tariff in 1798, which he presented to the Russia Company.[69] In general, however, Smirnov seems to have helped and encouraged others with their translations and works on Russia. He contributed corrections to the Reverend William Tooke's *View of the Russian Empire* (2nd edition, 1800) when it was translated into French in 1801,[70] and his "powerful assistance" was acknowledged by the noted antiquary, Stephen Weston (1747-1830) in his 1815 translation of an undistinguished ode to Catherine written by Ivan Ivanovich Vinogradov in 1785.[71]

Smirnov's last years were plagued by ill health and failing eye-sight. He had an operation for the removal of a cataract in 1836 and came to rely more and more on the attentions of his two spinster daughters. Smirnov had married the daughter of Simeon Koronatskii, a priest, in 1779 and she bore him six children. She died about 1790 and one of her children did not survive infancy. His eldest son, Konstantin, went to Russia at the beginning of the nineteenth century and settled there. His second son, Ivan, (d. 1844?), felt himself very much an Englishman, although his father was determined that he should go to Russia to learn the language and ways of the country. Ivan joined the Ministry of Foreign Affairs and was soon posted to the London embassy, where he made a name for himself in English cultural circles. He became a Fellow of the Royal Society, of the Royal Society of Literature, and of the Medico-Botanical Society. He remained in England until the spring of 1836, when he was appointed Russian Consul-General in Genoa.

An unduly harsh critic once wrote of Samborskii: "By his education Samborskii was not a great theologian, by his character, opinions and sympathies he was more an agronomist than a theologian, more an Englishman than an Orthodox priest, broader in outlook than the rest of his fellow priests but further than they from the purity and spirit of the Orthodox faith."[72] Much of this might be applied to Smirnov, but in praise and not in censure. Like his predecessor, he had no aspirations to being a theologian but there is no reason to doubt the depth and purity of his faith and his willing service to his church. He was in many ways, a parish priest, if an extraordinary one, extending his pastoral care and concern over all the wide-ranging activities of Russians in England. Like Samborskii, he had a veritable passion for agriculture, which he saw as the key to man's "Comfort and real Happiness" on earth. Only his "political" activity might be seen as conflicting with his calling as a priest, although that would be to introduce too fine a distinction in the general patriotic sentiments which moved him. He was to the end a loyal and devoted servant of Russia and a good friend of England, although his patience was tried and his intelligence pained by the antics of first one, then the other.

IV

It is tempting to leave the story of the Russian church at the high point provided by Smirnov's career, but to do so would be unjust to the humble category of *tserkovniki*, from whose ranks no less than three of the four chaplains at the London church during Catherine's reign, Ivanovskii, Samborskii and Smirnov, were promoted. *Tserkovnik* was the general designation of those members of the church who were not ordained and included *d'iachki* (secretaries) and *ponomari* (sextons) who occupied the bottom rungs of the Table of Ranks, together with *pevchie* (choristers). At the time of their appointment they were generally young men who were taken from seminaries in mid-course; they arrived in London, in no way prepared for life in the English capital. Immature, without any knowledge of English or French, hopelessly underpaid, they faced a life of hardship and poverty. Some failed to meet the challenge, but what is remarkable is that so many of them survived so well and put their experience to account, within and outside the church, in England and back in their homeland. The church obviously gained three impressive servants in the *tserkovniki* who became chaplains and there were others who loyally stayed in London for long years until their deaths, retaining their original positions and, unfortunately, their original salaries. Two instances are Nikolai Nekrasov, who was already in London in 1746, when the ambassador reported to Petersburg that he was making deductions from his salary to meet some of his debts,[73] and who died in November 1783, when he was in his seventies. Smirnov reported to Samborskii that Nekrasov had died in delirium, and there survives a letter from Nekrasov, dated two years earlier, which reveals the same condition. It is a pathetic document, written now in English, now in Russian, in which he pleads for help in his poverty and distress.[74] Also in his seventies when he died was Leontii Litkevich, who was recruited by Samborskii at the Khar'kov Collegium in 1780 and remained with Smirnov for almost sixty years.[75]

Other *tserkovniki* were desperately unhappy with their lot and either failed to carry out their duties, which caused them to be sent back to Russia, or sought to transfer into different and better-paid positions. The 1750s and 1760s in particular provide several graphic examples of such cases. In 1758 two young students from the Troitsa seminary, Mikhail Permskii (1741-70) and Klim Tomarinskii, arrived to help Ivanovskii, but two years later were back in Petersburg: the ambassador, Prince Aleksandr Golitsyn had censured them for their conduct but "was quite unable to bring them to their senses and simply did not know what to do with them."[76] One of their replacements, Sila Barkhartov, soon left the rails and at the end of 1762 was imprisoned in the Gate House prison in Westminster for fighting with soldiers: he was to die there at the end of January, 1763.[77] In 1766 Prokhor Ivanovich Zhdanov (d. 1802) informed the ambassador, Count Musin-Pushkin, that "he had no inclination to devote himself to the church" and asked to be transferred to the College of Foreign Affairs as a student. The comment made by Count Nikita Panin in Petersburg on the ambassador's letter on Zhdanov's behalf is very revealing: "all the deacons want to become students; they receive a 100 or 150 rubles, but students receive 300. The ambassador should petition only for those who possess outstanding qualities and talents."[78] Nevertheless, Zhdanov's request seems to have been accepted and he soon returned to Russia. Both he and Permskii, despite their short residence in England, were to put to good account the knowledge they had acquired of the English language and both occupy a modest niche in the history of Russian awareness of English language and literature.

Soon after his return Permskii entered Moscow University and remained there until 1765, when he was appointed a teacher of English in the Naval Cadet Corps. While still at university, Permskii showed his interest in English literature, and contributed to the journal *Svobodnye chasy* ("Leisure Hours") in 1763 and in the following year, produced for another journal his version of Samuel Johnson's *Rasselas*. His duties as a teacher soon brought home to him the need for an English grammar and in 1766 he published his *Anglinskaia grammatika*. Its historical significance as the first English grammar in Russia apart, Permskii's book was of very limited value or interest. It was in no way adapted to the needs of a Russian audience and was simply a direct translation from an English original. Much space is given to the intricacies of punctuation and the work finishes with a long chapter (Chapter IV) on abbreviations, which include: "Anab. = Anabaptist" and "Ast. P. G. C. = Astronomy Professor of Gresham College." Indeed a whole string of abbreviations of the titles of Gresham professors suggest that the work was produced by one of them! The particular irrelevance of some twelve pages on abbreviations is underlined by the closing advice that they should not be generally used.[79]

The Naval Cadet Corps where Permskii worked until shortly before his death in 1770 also became the scene for the activities of Zhdanov, and in 1772 he too brought out his *Angliska grammatika*. Although it is a much more extensive and competent piece of work than Permskii's, the grammar section (which occupies the first 104 pages) finishes with the same extensive list of abbreviations and advice about their usage. The second section (numbered separately, pp. 1-111) is a concise "Vocabulary English-Russian," arranged according to 79 subjects or themes. One such subject is "Excrements of the body," i.e. "The Hair of the Head, the Beard, the Whiskers, a Tear, the Snot, the Spittle, the Dandriff, the Urine." This is followed by a section entitled "Familiar Phrases" (pp. 112-62), including essentials such as "I'll beat your back and belly" and "Take up this Boy, & whip him soundly," and a final section of "Familiar Dialogues" (pp. 163-304). These dialogues cover a wide range of subjects, but among the more interesting are nos. X "To speak Russ" (pp. 203-10) and XI "To speak English" (pp. 211-12), in which Zhdanov gives his views on the relative qualities and strengths of the two languages. The most amusing is devoted to "before going to Bed and after one is in Bed" and includes the following exchange:

> Go with me.
> Why will you have him go with you?
> He is my Bedfellow, or he lies with me.
> Do you fear Spirits?
> No, 'tis because the Bed is cold.
> Get it warmed.
> Where is the Warming-pan?   [p. 169]

If Permskii's work may be considered the first English grammar, the second section of Zhdanov's with its listing of approximately 3000 words is the first English-Russian dictionary. The work as a whole was popular and was revised and reissued in 1801, but the dictionary as such had been superseded by a further work by Zhdanov which he published in 1784. In his eleventh dialogue he had regretted the lack of a dictionary and he immediately set to work to compile one. *A New Dictionary English and Russian: Novyi slovar' angliiskoi i rossiiskoi* was a huge work of some 750 pages and containing in the region of 30,000 words, arranged in alphabetical order. It was dedicated to his pupils at the Naval Cadet Corps, which was always one of the leading institutions in encouraging the study of the English language and where Permskii and Zhdanov were neither the first nor the last teachers to study and live in England. Zhdanov also called in his dedication on his pupils to use their knowledge of English to translate into Russian "all the best works in which England more than any other country abounds."[80] He himself was a member of the Society for the Translation of Foreign Books, set up by Catherine in 1768, and is known to have translated in 1779 two English plays.[81]

The number of *tserkovniki* serving in London fluctuated between one and three and the names of seventeen men who served in that capacity between 1737 and the end of the century are known to me. Nine have already been mentioned. Of the remainder, two came with Smirnov to study agriculture but one of them was more interested in literature than agriculture and may therefore more appropriately be mentioned here. Also two more, the only ones to be appointed during Paul's reign, cannot be overlooked. Aleksei Vasil'evich Kolmakov (d. 1804) returned to Russia in 1784 after eight years in England. He subsequently used his expertise in English both in his work at the Admiralty College in St. Petersburg and as a translator of English works. In 1792 he produced a translation of *The Koran* (from George Sale's version) and followed this with Sterne's *Sentimental Journey* and *The Letters of Yorick and Eliza* in 1793 and Addison's *Cato* in 1804. He also published a number of occasional odes and produced a collection of his original poetry in 1791.[82] Aleksei Grigor'evich Evstaf'ev (1779-1857) and Nikolai Mikhailovich Longinov (1779-1853) also both came from the Khar'kov Collegium and arrived in England at the very end of 1798. They are referred to in documents as *pevchie* (choristers), although all the *tserkovniki* obviously sang in services to the best of their abilities. Their arrival coincided with the rapid deterioration in Anglo-Russian relations in the last years of Paul's reign and changes in the embassy staff. Longinov soon took the opportunity to transfer to the embassy staff as an *aktuarius*, as Evstaf'ev mentioned in a letter to Samborskii, adding "his place remaining vacant and hearing from Iakov Ivanovich [Smirnov] that he is going to write for a replacement, I thought that my brother could take the place for he has all the necessary qualities and although he is not an experienced singer, his voice, if it has not become spoilt, is very good. As long as one has a voice it can quickly be trained here, as was the case with us."[83]

His brother did not come and Evstaf'ev himself continued to sing and serve in the church until he left England in 1808. However, like Longinov, he quickly revealed other and greater talents. Both Longinov and Evstaf'ev were to have long and successful careers in state and diplomatic service: Longinov in St. Petersburg, where he eventually became state secretary in the Office of Petitions from 1826 until 1840,[84] and Evstaf'ev in America, where he was Russian consul in Boston from 1809 until 1827 and subsequently in New York from 1834 until 1847.

Evstaf'ev has, however, another claim to fame as a writer. In London he quickly acquired a profound knowledge of English and he published in 1806 his translation of Aleksandr Sumarokov's tragedy *Dmitrii Samozvanets* ("Dmitrii the Pretender"). The introduction or "Advertisement" finished with the following lines: "To a generous People, celebrated for their benignity to Foreigners occasionally residing amongst them, and for their liberal indulgence to their own Dramatic Authors, the Translator submits the following scenes; in humble expectation of public encouragement (even should they appear to have no higher merit), in consideration of its being the first attempt to present to British readers, a literary novelty—a Russian Tragedy, in a British dress."[85] He was given the "public encouragement" for which he hoped in notices in *Gentleman's Magazine* and in the *Annual Review* and during the remaining two years of his stay in England produced a number of translated and original works which helped to foster British awareness of Russian culture and affairs. In 1807 he contributed to *The Literary Panorama* a translation of an essay by Karamzin on the Russian book-trade and tastes in reading and of a life of Lomonosov. At the same time he revealed his flair as a publicist serving the Russian cause with his pamphlets, *Advantages of Russia in the Present Contest with France* (1807) and *A Key to the Recent Conduct of the Emperor of Russia* (1808). It was this latter work which brought him to the attention of the Russian Foreign Ministry and brought the change in his career. All the works which he published in England appeared without his name and it was only in America that he signed a further series of influential political pamphlets as well as his first original literary works. His tragedy, entitled *Alexis Czarewitz*, appeared in Boston in 1812 and was followed by his long epic poem *Demetrius, the Hero of the Don*. Instances of "Russo-French" authors are not uncommon in the eighteenth and early nineteenth centuries, but Evstaf'ev is probably the first example of a "Russo-English" author.[86]

CHAPTER 3

"TO SPEED THE PLOUGH"

In the second volume of his *Travels in Poland, Russia, Sweden, and Denmark*, published in 1784, the Reverend William Coxe describes the alleged origins of the Russian *Vol'noe ekonomicheskoe obshchestvo* ("Free Economic Society") in 1765:

> The empress one day at table expressing herself with warmth upon the advantages that would result from such a society, first suggested the idea to Prince Orlof, who happened to be present. In conformity to the wishes of his imperial mistress, he and fourteen other persons, partly men of rank, and partly men of learning, assembled in June, 1765, drew up rules, and formed themselves into a regular society. Having laid the plan before the empress, her majesty returned the following answer, written with her own hand:—"The design which you have just formed for the improvement of agriculture and husbandry is highly agreeable to us; and your labours will be regarded as effectual proofs of a true zeal and love for your country. We consider the plan and the regulations by which you have bound yourselves, as deserving our approbation; and we graciously allow you to be called, The Free Economical Society. You may rest assured, that we take your Society under our protection: We not only consent that you use our seal and imperial coat of arms; but, as a particular mark of our good-will towards you, we permit you to bear our device in the center of our imperial arms, namely, a hive to which bees are bringing honey, with the motto 'Profitably'."[1]

It was inevitable that Catherine, the enlightened autocrat, should gain all the glory for the Society's foundation; certainly, it was only in her reign that improvements and reforms in Russian agriculture became a major concern and she gave her blessing to a number of institutions and developments which seemed likely to increase the prosperity of her vast empire. Nevertheless, there were stirrings towards the end of the reign of Elizabeth, principally in the person of the many-talented Mikhail Vasil'evich Lomonosov; as early as 1747 he had produced a translation under the title of *Lifliandskaia ekonomiia* ("Lifland Economy") of Hubertus' *Stratagema Oeconomicum, oder Akker-Student*, a seventeenth-century treatise on agricultural management. Although long since superseded, it apparently enjoyed fairly wide circulation in manuscript (and in other translations besides Lomonosov's) among Russian noblemen, who, following the decree of Peter III which freed them from obligatory state service, had more time to concern themselves with the running of their estates. In September, 1763, Lomonosov acting on an initiative from Catherine formed a commission to consider the possibility of creating "an agricultural class" within the Academy of Sciences, but he himself was to argue in a special memorandum entitled "Mnenie o uchrezhdenii gosudarstvennoi kollegii zemskogo domoustroistva" ("Thoughts on the Establishment of a State College of Rural Economy") for an institution independent of the Academy, which would be devoted to research and experiment not only in agriculture but also in forestry, exploitation of mineral deposits, drainage etc. It is likely that Catherine received a copy of this document and it certainly anticipates some of the concerns of the Free Economical Society. Lomonosov's death early in April, 1765, precluded him, however, from contributing in a more direct way to the formulation of the Society's objectives.[2]

Of much greater impact was the contribution made to the preliminary discussion by Count Jakob Johann Sievers (1732-1808), governor of the Province of Novgorod, who as a young man had served at the Russian embassy in London from 1749 to 1755.[3] In a memorandum prepared for Catherine he wrote:

> May I refer again, Most Gracious Majesty, to the society for agriculture or husbandry. I am bold enough to maintain that the prosperity accruing to the nobility from it would be all the greater, when one considers their present ignorance in the matter of the improvements of fields and meadows, the draining of swamps, the management of households and buildings, the care of forests, etc. Not only would the production of the land be increased considerably, but many products, hitherto unknown, from neighbouring countries would gradually become familiar and would be cultivated. Above all, the southern provinces of your Majesty's boundless dominions would derive benefits from the production of wine and silk and other products which the favourable character of those localities would make possible.

After suggesting the possible composition of the Society's membership and the contents of transactions of the Soceity which should be made available in published form, Sievers adds:

> May I presume to relate that during my stay in England I witnessed the formation of the famous Society for the Encouragement of the Arts, the Sciences and Agriculture. At the beginning the Society distributed prizes of a dollar for sketches, pieces of embroidery, or other small items from English schoolchildren. Its total capital did not amount to fifty guineas. I heard people ridicule the undertaking. Now it distributes several thousand pounds sterling and equips ships in order to send seeds

and produce from Europe to America. Any moderately affluent English-man wants to be a supporter and feels flattered to see his name printed in the list of supporters and encouragers of the Arts, the Sciences and Agriculture. The original founders of this useful society would be more deserving of memorials than the admiral who conquered Havana and the Spanish galleons.[4]

Sievers' last years in London coincided with the efforts of William Shipley (1715-1803) to found the premium society which became known as the Society for the Encouragement of Arts, Manufactures and Commerce. While still living in Northampton Shipley published in June, 1753, his "Proposals for Raising by Subscription a Fund to be Distributed in Premiums for the Promoting of Improvements in the Liberal Arts and Sciences, Manufactures, &c"; at the end of the year he moved to London and published "A Scheme for Putting the Proposals in Execution." After a few months of energetic canvassing for subscribers, Shipley was able to organize the first meeting of his Society which was held on 22 March 1754, and three days later an account of that meeting was published in the newspapers.[5] It was probably from that publication that Sievers gained his initial knowledge of the proposed activities of the Society, particularly of the premiums offered for the best drawings by young boys and girls. The awarding of premiums became from the beginning an essential part of the new Russian Society's activities and the idea was also incorporated into clauses 299-300 of Catherine's famous *Nakaz* ("Instruction") of 1767 to her Legislative Commission. Lomonosov too had recommended the organization of competitions with rewards, and the idea was by no means new (the Dublin Society for Promoting Husbandry and Other Useful Arts had awarded premiums since 1740), although Lomonosov may have heard of the English initiatives through acquaintance with a Scots doctor in Russian service, James Mounsey (1700? -73), head of the Russian medical chancery and the first corresponding member (elected April 1755) of the Society of Arts in Russia.

It was only much later, in 1798, that Sievers was himself elected to corresponding membership of the Society of Arts, on the strength of a paper entitled "On the Manner of Rearing and Treating Silkworms in the Northern Parts of Europe," in which he again alludes to the foundation of the Russian Society and to Catherine's awareness of the Society of Arts' premium system.[6] However, in Sievers' lifetime, both before and after his own election, other Russians as well as Britons residing in St. Petersburg became corresponding members. In 1792, for example, Count Friedrich Anhalt, who was at that time President of the Free Economic Society, was elected, together with Dr. Matthew Guthrie (1743-1807), also a member of the Russian society and of numerous other Russian and British institutions and an important link-man in Anglo-Russian cultural relations at the end of the eighteenth century.[7]

These elections testify to the contacts which were established between the London and Petersburg societies, at an official level, but there were also three Russians who became subscribing members of the English Society during their residence in London. The first was Count Ivan Chernyshev who was one of the founder members of the Free Economic Society and who was elected to the English Society on 31 May 1769, towards the end of his short stay in London as Russian Ambassador Extraordinary. The other two, of much greater significance, were the chaplains Samborskii and Smirnov, and it is through their efforts and contacts that Russian interest in and knowledge of developments in English agriculture were stimulated and deepened. Samborskii was elected on 21 March 1774 and paid his annual dues up to 26 May 1779; Smirnov became a member on 27 March 1782, in 1811 served as a steward of the Society, and remained on the membership lists until his death. Both Samborskii and Smirnov had many friends and acquaintances among the members of the Society, but the men whose friendship they prized the most were Arthur Young (1741-1820), the greatest of all English agricultural publicists, and John Arbuthnot (d. 1801), a gentleman farmer at Mitcham in Surrey.

II

William Coxe in his notes on the Free Economic Society (to which he himself was elected in 1785) added that "the empress, in the true spirit of this institution, sends several young men into England in order to study practical agriculture. They are chiefly recommended to Arthur Younge, Esq. who has distinguished himself by many excellent works on various branches of husbandry; and who was elected in the most honourable manner a member of this Society." He later refers to Samborskii as having "carried from Mr Younge's house, in Suffolk, ploughs, harrows, and other implements of agriculture."[8] Young printed Coxe's remarks in his own *Annals of Agriculture* in 1784 and followed them with "Observations on the Means of Promoting Russian Husbandry," in which he paid his own tribute to Samborskii's "knowledge, industry, and indefatigable perseverance."[9] The beginnings of Young's career as a farmer and writer virtually coincided with Samborskii's arrival in England in 1765 and by the time Samborskii was elected to the Society of Arts in 1774, of which Young had been a member since 1769, Young had established an international reputation. The recipient of several premiums and gold medals from the Society, he was better known for his prolific writings. By 1774 he had published the following works on agriculture: *The Farmer's Letters to the People of England* (1767), *The Farmer's Guide in Hiring and Stocking Farms* (1770), *A Course of Experimental Agriculture* (1770), *Rural Economy* (1770), *The Farmer's Calendar* (1771), as well as the first three of his famous "tours," through the southern (1768), northern (1770) and eastern (1771) parts of England.[10] Arbuthnot is in comparison with Young a virtually unknown figure, respected for his practical activity rather than for any published work. He was the brother of the Right Honourable Robert Arbuthnot and an outstanding example of that peculiar breed of English gentlemen-farmers whom European noblemen, and Russians among them, sought to emulate with a conspicuous lack of success. Apart from two short essays published in 1800 and 1802, his only published work was *An Inquiry into the Connection between the Present Prices of Provisions and the Size of Farms*, which appeared anonymously in London in 1773, but his agricultural experiments were made known to the world at large through Young's description of them in his *Farmer's Tour through the East of England* (1771). Young valued highly his friendship and in his memoirs described him as "upon the whole the most agreeable, pleasant and interesting connection which I ever made in agricultural pursuits."[11] In 1811 Young lectured to the Board of Agriculture on the achievements of "this real genius in Husbandry," who enjoyed "so happy a success, that no person who knew the Man and his Farm, could fail of the most extra confidence in his opinions."[12] Samborskii's acquaintance with the two Englishmen could not but inspire him with ideals of effecting a great agricultural revolution in Russia, one which would ensure the prosperity of peasant and landowner alike and bring people nearer to God by the contentment gained from life in tune with nature. As he was later to write to Alexander I in 1804, his system had always been one of "the religion of the Gospels and the religion of the countryside, from which come good morals and industriousness."[13]

Samborskii had been presented to the empress in 1769 and his name had been mentioned with love and respect many times since then by people close to Catherine, whose interests he had served. It was to Catherine that he turned in 1775 with his grandiose dreams; the time was propitious, for not only did the empress look kindly on the activities of the Free Economic Society but she faced at home the menace of the Pugachev rebellion and a largely disaffected peasantry. A peaceful rather than a bloody revolution was only to be encouraged. In June, 1775, Samborskii obtained the permission of the ambassador, Musin-Pushkin, to return to Russia to present his petition to the empress, a draft of which survives in his archive. Praising Catherine for her wise legislation and her particular attention to agriculture, he continues:

It is undeniable that it [agriculture] has been brought to the greatest perfection in England. Finding myself there under your powerful protection and considering it my esteemed duty to serve the general good, I have for some time now been occupied with its theory and practice. The great and universal fame of Your Majesty is so powerful a guide for me that several eminent Englishmen aid me in my intentions. But since my strength is not sufficient for the study of so vast a science I prostrate myself at your august feet and most humbly beg you to send back with me four able young men who have already acquired some knowledge in science and foreign languages. Success would be ensured for when they have a knowledge of English, they would quickly be initiated into all aspects of agriculture, including that part of chemistry which is concerned with assessing the quality of soil and the use of manure, mechanics for the invention and building of necessary implements and machines, physics for knowledge of plants, livestock-breeding and husbandry in general. Once they had undergone this course of study in the most assiduous fashion, my colleagues could be admitted, following my example, as members of the Economic Society [the Society of Arts], which includes the most learned people, and become acquainted with their inventions.[14]

He concludes by suggesting that when he returned with the students, they could be sent to such places in Russia as the empress would decide and stimulate other Russians with their enthusiasm and knowledge. At the end of the petition, Samborskii provided a tentative list of three students whom he considered suitable. The first, Luka Sichkarev, a translator in the Holy Synod with a command of several languages including English, did not go, but the other two, Mikhail Egorovich Livanov (1751-1800) and Aleksei Vasil'evich Flavitskii were selected. After noting that a fourth candidate would soon be found, Samborskii added later the name of Danilo Samoilovich Samoilovich, already established as a medical authority for his work on the Moscow plague of 1771. Samoilovich was sent instead to Leyden to continue his medical studies and only briefly appeared in England at a much later date.

The empress gave her blessing to the project and Samborskii soon found two more candidates to add to Livanov and Flavitskii: Ivan Mikhailovich Komov (1750? -92) and Evstafii Fedorovich Zveraka (1751-1829). On 10/21 June 1776 Catherine sent an order to her Secretary of State in charge of finance, Adam Vasil'evich Olsuf'ev, to the effect that the four students "volunteering to go to England to study agriculture" should be given an annual salary of £100.[15] Samborskii had brought together a talented group, of whom only Zveraka was not to justify his expectations in the sphere of agriculture. All four were almost of the same age, in their mid-twenties, and with good academic backgrounds and some experience of life, which is more than may be said of many students treated in these pages. Livanov was a graduate of Moscow University, which he had entered in 1767 and where he had been awarded a silver medal in 1770 and a gold medal in 1772. He knew Latin and some French and had studied philosophy, law and medicine. Among his teachers were Professors Desnitskii and Tret'iakov, who had studied at Glasgow University, and M. I. Afonin, "Extraordinary Professor of Natural History and Agriculture."[16] Zveraka and Flavitskii were Ukrainians, both priests' sons, who had studied at spiritual academies, the first in Kiev and the second at the

Krutitskii seminary. Zveraka had then gone on to the main military hospital in Petersburg and from there to the 2nd army field command as a *lekar'* (surgeon).[17] Komov (who is also known under the name Ivan Mikhailov) had the most varied background of the four. The son of a poor village deacon, he had studied initially at the Moscow Slavono-Greco-Latin Academy, where his teacher of rhetoric and poetics had been the poet Vasilii Petrov, who became the great friend of Samborskii during his stay in England between 1772 and 1774; he was then transferred to the Academy of Sciences in Petersburg in 1768 and had taken part in the expedition of Academician S. G. Gmelin which went as far as the frontiers of Persia. The year before he volunteered to go to England, he had joined the Engineer Cadet Corps with the rank of *perevodchik* (translator), and taught classes in history, geography and rhetoric.[18]

Catherine termed the four students who were financed from her office *akademiki*, but there were to be three other students in the party Samborskii took back with him to England in the summer of 1776: they were funded by the College of Foreign Affairs, for their official status was that of *tserkovniki*, and as such two of them have already been named and certain of their functions discussed in the preceding chapter. After a short time in St. Petersburg, Samborskii had travelled to Khar'kov to recruit a number of seminarists who could combine service in the embassy church with the study of agriculture and hopefully on their return to Russia would take orders and so fulfil Samborskii's ideal of the farmer-clergyman. He received the blessing of Aggei, the bishop of Belgorod, and by February the students were selected. The bishop wrote to Samborskii on 28 February/11 March 1776: "Show the students a degree of care in keeping with their hopes, willingness and enthusiam. They came to me today and received their passports and an order for providing them with testimonials. May God speed you in your useful designs."[19] As a later letter indicates,[20] the bishop knew not only the *tserkovniki* Smirnov, Kolmakov and Vasilii Prokof'evich Prokopovich (d. 1792), but also Zveraka and Flavitskii and he remained in touch with the group throughout their years in England. Smirnov, as we have seen, changed his name from Linitskii, on the advice of Samborskii, who for some reason feared opposition to the number of Ukrainians in his party; Prokopovich, Flavitskii and Zveraka likewise changed their names to Prokof'ev, Flavianov and Zverev, but unlike Smirnov, they reverted to their real surnames on their return. Samborskii and his students left Petersburg at the end of June and by August were established in London: the grand project could now be put into operation.

Although a few members of the group had a smattering of English, in common with almost all students sent to England they were obliged to spend some time in London improving or acquiring a knowledge of English and the *tserkovniki* carried out their duties in the church. It was not long, however, before Samborskii began their initiation into "practical farming" under the guidance of Arbuthnot at Mitcham.

Under the supervision of the English gentleman, Mr Arbuthnot, who is generally recognized as the leading and most accomplished agriculturist, and practising in the fields, we have made significant progress in practical operations. I must not fail to mention that the assiduousness of this Englishman is so great that he has allowed us to carry out all our operations on his own fields. In addition he explains to us all the physical and mechanical methods and not infrequently leaves his family and lives from morning to evening with us in the fields. It is true that all Englishmen without exception offer me their services, but he surpasses all of them. And it seems that his chief satisfaction is now to pass on to Russia all the methods of this useful knowledge, i.e., of agriculture.[21]

This letter dates from 2/13 October 1777 and its seems likely that the students began to visit Arbuthnot from the late summer of that year and studied with him for up to two years, according to a remark in a work published many years later by Livanov. Interesting glimpses of them are afforded by letters from Bentham to his brother Samuel at the very beginning of 1779. The Benthams had recently made Samborskii's acquaintance and came to esteem him highly. Jeremy spent the evening of 2 January at Samborskii's house and found "the whole tribe of Russian Farmers there—very good [sort] of folks I liked them mightily."[22] On 26 January he refers to "the 6 Russ: who are studying farming here with Arbuthnot who I think is their instructor."[23]

A few months later Samborskii apparently received instructions from Catherine to return to Russia with a view to organizing a school of practical agriculture. There had been no mention of such an institution in Samborskii's petition of 1775 and the first references to it are found in drafts of two letters to Catherine and to the ambassador, Musin-Pushkin, which are entered in a small notebook and dated 21 August and 22 August 1779 respectively.[24] It is unlikely that the letter to Catherine was sent, for much of it is repeated in the petition dated St. Petersburg, 9/20 December which he presented to the empress on his return. Whether Catherine was responding to an initiative which came originally from Samborskii himself or from some other source, possibly the Free Economic Society, is not clear, but her decision to entrust Samborskii with the setting-up of an agricultural school induced him to give free reign to his ideas. "The more I contemplate the trust which Your Majesty has placed in me with respect ot the establishment of a school of practical agriculture, the more I intent to use my time to advantage. Consequently I fall before your imperial feet and slavishly implore Your Majesty to grant me some infertile land near St. Petersburg which could be drained and manured. This preparatory work is very necessary if we are to begin without delay our agricultural work immediately after our return from England on the completion of our general course of husbandry there."[25] He then asks that a successor to him as chaplain to the London church be appointed so that he [Samborskii] could employ his remaining time in England, inspecting agricultural methods and produce in various parts of the country. Looking ahead to the time when the school would be flourishing under his direction and that of his assistants, he suggests that its graduates could be sent far and wide through Russia to popularize their newly acquired skills. The students would be of two kinds: firstly, "the landowners could send their peasants to the practical school and these would return to their estates after a period to pass on their knowledge to their fellows. And since during the winter a systematic course of lectures will be given, even the landowners themselves would have the opportunity to acquire the rules of agriculture"; secondly, "each seminary could send two of its ablest students who on completion of both the theoretical and practical courses could teach a regular class in the seminaries to priests' sons, who would eventually replace their fathers. A priest who has church lands and some influence among the people can make a great impact by his own example, showing by word and deed the general advantages to be gained. Thus it would be possible at one and the same time to sow both in the earth and in men the good seeds of that science from which by the natural course of things and the general acknowledgement of politicians the prosperity of societies and nations is born."[26]

At the beginning of 1780 Samborskii must have felt that all his cherished dreams were about to be realized but although certain moves were made towards the establishment of his school almost immediately, his career was soon to take a quite different direction. In the preceding chapter an attempt was made to trace precisely his subsequent career in Russia without dwelling on those aspects which were of more relevance to this discussion of the introduction of "English agriculture" in Russia. Viewed from one angle his career presents an upward curve as he enjoys more and more imperial favours from Catherine, Paul and finally, Alexander and seems to achieve a power and influence of which as the chaplain in London he could scarcely have conceived. Seen from another angle, Samborskii from 1780 until his death endured a series of frustrations and disappointments, heightened by tantalising glimpses of the life and activities to which he would have devoted himself with much energy and love. Coxe in his work of 1784 spoke of the school of agriculture as already existing, or at least stated that "at Sophisk, about three quarters of a mile from Sarsko Selo, a farm of a thousand acres is provided with dwelling-houses, and other necessary buildings."[27] He gave details of the proposed courses and types of students, precisely as set out in Samborskii's memorandum of 1779 to Catherine, and this suggests that he had possibly received his information from Samborskii himself, or, more likely, from Smirnov who returned to England at the end of 1780 after being ordained a chaplain. Jeremy Bentham heard in Februray, 1780, from a visiting Russian that "l'Imperatrice va etablir a Petersburgh un Bureau d'Agriculture d'apres un projet dressé par Sambouski. Il doit meme eu etre le Directeur. Tout est arrangé selon ses souhaits."[28] There is, however, no mention of the proposed farm at Sofiisk in

Russian sources, although Catherine seems to have assigned Samborskii at that time land near the newly planned town of Sofia. Arthur Young also gave the projected school his enthusiastic approval, finding that "every feature of the plan is full of intelligence" and that "no man is better qualified for the task, nor more likely to bring it to entire perfection" than Samborskii.[29] In his autobiography, however, he wrote that "the intended establishment of an Imperial farm never took place, and after at least an expenditure of £10,000, the men on their arrival were turned loose, some to starve, some driven into the army, and others retained by Russian noblemen. In this wretched and ridiculous manner did the whole scheme end, which, under a proper arrangement, might have been attended with very important effects."[30]

The "men" to whom he was referring were Komov and his friends who had spent their last five years in England without Samborskii's presence and counsel. Young says that Samborskii "wrote to me at Bradfield earnestly requesting that I would go to London and examine all the young men, that he might take or send them to St. Petersburg. This I accordingly did, and examined them very closely, except one, who refused to answer any questions from a conviction of his absolute ignorance. I gave a certificate of the others' examination, and I asked Sambosky [sic] what would become of the obstinate fool who would not answer. He replied that without doubt he would be sent to Siberia for life, but I never heard whether this happened."[31] He adds that one of them, "by much the ablest", remained in England as chaplain. The note refers to 1784, although Smirnov by that time had been chaplain for over three years. Like much that Young wrote, his note inspires little confidence with regard to detail or chronology. Certainly, although his remarks about Samborskii's school were correct, his description of the fate of the students was, as will be seen, totally inaccurate. Nevertheless, his remarks about the recalcitrant examinee are interesting, but might easily be discounted, given his unreliability on other matters. There were, however, two obvious candidates among the original group of seven students. In his letter to Musin-Pushkin of August, 1779, Samborskii reported that "Evstafii Zverev stopped studying agriculture some time ago and took up medical practice."[32] Samborskii added that despite Zverev's "unjust denunciations and immoderate abuse," he had paid him his annual salary of £100 for the last three years and had the accounts to prove it, and was now leaving him time "for repentance and correction." Zverev, who had worked as a surgeon in Russia before coming to England, had in fact decided that medicine was his true interest and in 1778 or even earlier had gone to study in Edinburgh. If Young's examination of the students did take place in 1784, then Zverev could not have been the man he had in mind, for he had returned to Russia to begin his career as a fully-fledged doctor by 1782. This would leave Kolmakov, one of the *tserkovniki* as the person in question: Smirnov informed Samborskii on 30 April 1782 that "Mr Kolmakove, as ever, remains at home & under pretence of attending the Church never will think to learn anything of Agriculture."[33] Like Zverev, Kolmakov's major interests were other than agricultural, although apart from the literary works and translation to which he subsequently turned, he did produce in 1791 "as an aid to those concerned with the construction of mills and water pipes" a *Karmannaia knizhka dlia vychisleniia kolichestva vody, vytekaiushchei chrez truby, otverstviia ili no zholobam* ("Pocket Manual for Calculating the Flow of Water through Pipes, Openings or Drains").

What had the other students been doing during Samborskii's absence? In the letter in which he describes Kolmakov's lack of activity, Smirnov mentions that "Mr Prokofieve has been in Kent for some time. Mr Livanove and Mr Flavianove are going now to Suffolk. they take Leonty with them."[34] "Leonty" was Leontii Litkevich, yet another *tserkovnik*, who had arrived in London in 1780. It seems probable that he was accompanying Livanov and Flavitskii to Young's farm at Bradfield or that of the Reverend Mr Lord, which was also in Suffolk. It is difficult to say precisely when any of the students first came under Young's supervision. He gives the impression in his notes for 1784 that he met them for the first time at their examination, for previously "two or three were fixed with my friend Arbuthnot, and others in different parts of the Kingdom,"[35] but Samborskii had told Catherine in 1779 that the students were then "in the care of Mr Young and other skilled agriculturists."[36] Certainly in a communication which he sent to the Bath and West of England Society for publication in 1783, Young mentions a visit he had made in the summer of 1779 accompanied by "a Russian gentleman," to inspect the cultivation of carrots in a part of Suffolk.[37] Smirnov was at Bradfield in November, 1783, when Young asked after Samborskii and told Smirnov of his writing of the *Elements of Husbandry*, which is described at length.[38] The Russian students in fact seem to have been in frequent contact with Young throughout their stay and in the reports which they presented to the Free Economic Society after their return, they specifically alluded to the period between 19 September 1782 and 5 October 1783 as spent in Suffolk and supplied crop rotas as employed on Young's farm.[39]

The reports, or rather their summaries as printed, fall into two sections. The first section has the rubric "in the county of Suffolk" and deals under fifty-two heads with all aspects of the cultivation of wheat, barley, and clover (the first twenty-two items, after which comes the dating of the observations given above), then, beans, oats, peas, and turnips. There follow tables showing the rotation of crops on various farms, three for Young varying according to the type of soil, one for Lord, and a final set of rotas for Robert Bakewell. The second section discusses under similar heads as the first section the cultivation of wheat, barley, and vegetables on Bakewell's farm, but then supplies information about his care and breeding of livestock. The introduction of the name of Bakewell (1725-95) and of his farm at Dishley Grange, near Loughborough in Leicestershire, is of particular interest for showing the acquaintance of at least some of the Russians with yet another of the outstanding figures of the English agricultural revolution. There is no indication of the exact period which they spent at Dishley nor of their identity, but one Russian who certainly was there was Livanov, whose debt to Bakewell and to other English farmers will be discussed later.

Surrey, Kent, Suffolk, Leicestershire are thus four counties where the Russians are known to have learned their trade, but they certainly do not exhaust the places that at least one of the party visited. Komov, whom Smirnov did not mention in his letter to Samborskii, was the most independent and mature of the group. His wide knowledge and experience seems to have earned him the respect of his companions, if his own words are to be believed: "Several of them had such trust and friendship towards me that they sought my advice about what they should study above all else. I advised them to neglect the unnecessary and concern themselves with what was important for agriculture, namely physics and practical mechanics, so that they could observe how various English buildings, machines, carts, mills, etc. were made and then note down what they saw. It was not necessary to encourage them in agriculture, but I reminded them that they should prefer it to all other sciences, for such was our duty."[40] Basing himself on little evidence other than this letter, which was undated, Komov's biographer was eager to stress his role as "the unofficial leader" of the group and to reduce Samborskii to a mere "moral" adviser and generally to minimize his influence and significance. The advice Komov gave his colleagues was no more than a re-statement of Samborskii's intentions as outlined in his original petition to Catherine and Komov's leadership of the group would not have been in opposition to Samborskii's but a filling of the gap left by Samborskii's departure for Russia in 1779. At the same time it is obvious that Smirnov, after his return from Russia, in 1780, became as much the leader of the group as Komov, not only because he was chaplain, but also because his knowledge in agricultural matters was recognized. Samborskii noted in 1779 that Arbuthnot's appreciation of him was such as to allow him to manage his farm and Young found him the ablest of the group when he examined them; important recognition had already come in 1782 with his election to the Society of Arts. Nevertheless, Komov was an outstanding agronomist, who used his eight years in England to great advantage. As early as the summer of 1777 Komov had gone to Oxford, where he heard lectures on physics and mathematics and became acquainted with a number of professors. In 1778, when presumably most of the students were with Arbuthnot, he undertook a fortnight's walking tour through parts of England to see local agricultural conditions—and he generally prided himself on his fitness and constant activity.[41] The itinerary of his tour is not known but it seems likely that it was through the east of England. In a work he published later he mentions his observations of agriculture in Suffolk and Norfolk, as well as in Kent.[42] January, 1780, saw him in Bath, where he met members of the Bath Society for the Encouragement of Agriculture, Arts, Manufactures and Commerce. Its secretary Edmund Rack noted in his "Disultory Journal of Events &c at Bath" for 15 January:

> After Breakfast came T. Curtis Esq with Count Comhoof a Gentleman whom the Empress of Rushia sent to England to study agriculture. They came to examine the Societies new Models & machines, the Russian seems a polite sensible man & speaks English pretty well. After looking over the Machines, they Came into parlour & Chatted about an hour, on the State of Agriculture & Arts in Rushia. from what he says it appears that an excellent Police is established in Rushia—that Civilization, Learning Arts & Sciences are making rapid strides in those frozen Regions of the North. The Empress is the *Elizabeth* of the present age; & being Absolute, has nothing to oppose her plan.[43]

Komov obviously impressed the gentlemen of Bath, for on 8 February, after Komov's departure the committee met and elected him "an Honorary & Correspondent Member." Rack "after dinner prepared the Minutes for the papers & wrote to Monsieur Komhoff to inform him of his being Elected a Member, & to request his procuring us some Russian Publications, & seeds of plants from that Country. I suppose its the first Quakerly Letter he ever had." (Rack is referring to the "Thou" form of address.) In February, 1782, Komov was writing to a friend in St. Petersburg that he was now back in London studying chemistry and that in the spring he had decided to return to Oxford to hear lectures on astronomy. He was certainly in Oxford in February of the following year when his name appeared in the Bodleian admissions register.[44] From that time another eighteen months were to elapse before he set sail for Russia on 13 September 1784, a fortnight after Samborskii had left with Kolmakov, Livanov, Flavitskii, and Prokopovich.

At the beginning of 1782 the students still believed that they would be settling in Tsarskoe Selo at the new agricultural school, but on Samborskii's return in the summer of 1784 they knew that this was not to be, for in March of that year he had been appointed spiritual adviser and teacher of English to the Grand Dukes Alexander and Constantine. They thus returned to Russia probably unaware of what the future was to hold for them. Catherine, however, resolved their fates in September, 1785, when in Komov's words, "she ordered them to be sent as assistants to the Directors of Economy in various regions where they could be consulted by people needing advice."[45] Once more, as had been the case with the group of seminarists who were sent to England in 1765 with a view to providing the nucleus of a theological faculty at Moscow University on their return, a project which originally had the blessing of Catherine came to nothing and the participants were scattered far and wide; in contrast, however, some of the men were able to use their acquired skills to great advantage in their new situations. In a directive of 12/23 September 1785, Catherine mentioned the "six professors who had studied agriculture and other sciences in England,"[46] for Zverev, who had returned in 1782 and had worked for three years in St. Petersburg, was also to be reassigned. But Zverev's future long career in the south of Russia was to be as a doctor and is therefore not of immediate concern; the same may be said of Kolmakov, who spent the remaining few years of his life as a translator attached to the Admiralty College, and whose contribution to Russian knowledge of English literature was discussed in the previous chapter. The other four men all rendered great service in the cause of Russian agriculture. None of the six suffered the fate which Young described in his *Autobiography*.

By an ukaz of 1/12 September 1785 from Catherine to Count Iakov Brius, Komov was assigned to Moscow as assistant to the Director of Economy of Moscow province, with particular responsibilities for agriculture.[47] Over the following seven years until his death in 1792, he applied his energies and skills to experiments and to the practical instruction of peasants. Apart from the evidence provided by his published works, which will be discussed later, his activities are known principally from the reports which were sent to Catherine and the Senate by P. I. Eropkin, the governor of Moscow. Eropkin described the difficulties which Komov faced in passing on information about the latest agricultural methods and techniques to illiterate peasants and how he had decided to arrange practical demonstrations. Catherine's permission was sought for establishing what was essentially a minor version of the practical school of agriculture of which Samborskii had dreamed. A suitable area of land was found near the Novodevichii Monastery for ploughing and sowing and other experiments and Eropkin suggested that not only could peasants from neighbouring estates take part but also landowners could come and observe what was being done. In this way the new methods would spread, encouraged both from above and from below. In addition to his work as as instructor, Komov continued his own experiments, principally on a plot of land given him for this purpose by the Procurator-General A. A. Viazemskii on his estate at Aleksandrovskoe near Moscow.[48] Some of the results he achieved wer incorporated into a paper he communicated in 1786 to the Free Economic Society, of which he had been elected a member on 18 October 1785.[49] Komov's writings made his name known and respected in his homeland, although he died in relative obscurity on 13/24 June 1792 in Moscow, having achieved the rank of *kollezhskii asessor* (collegiate assessor). His sad prediction to Vasilii Petrov "Poor I was born, poor I live and poor I shall die despite all my economies"[50] was fulfilled—and it was equally true of all his companions.

Komov and Kolmakov apart, the other "professors" were sent to the south of Russia where in every case they were to spend the rest of their days. They were all Ukrainians and in a sense were returning home, although with the exception of Flavitskii, who settled in Kiev, they were to work in "New

Russia," in the region along the northern littoral of the Black Sea, which was then under the energetic administration of Potemkin. Perhaps Potemkin himself had been influential in persuading Catherine to abandon the idea of an agricultural school and to use the skills of some of the English-trained agriculturists in places where they would bring immediate and important results. The idea of Catherine's visit to see her new territories in the Crimea (which was to take place in 1787) had already been mooted and Potemkin was anxious to show her a prosperous and blooming paradise. In 1783 Samborskii himself had travelled through the Ukraine down as far as Kherson and described the conditions he saw there in a letter to Prince A. B. Kurakin:

> And since in my travels I encountered agricultural practices which previously I had known only superficially, then I considered it highly necessary to investigate all local practices so that I could afterwards apply with greater accuracy to the local climate the rules which I have learned in England and in other places, and I can now say with confidence that it is possible to introduce into all parts of the Russian empire good husbandry which will be highly profitable to the state. As regards the present state of Russian agriculture I can report that it is very poor. The peasants in general do not understand any sort of system; therefore they waste at least one third of their time, which, given the length of the winter, should be very dear to them. They lose almost half of their corn and at the same time exhaust themselves and their livestock, which causes untold harm to the state. I then travelled to Kherson, in order to find out what kind of husbandry could be introduced there. I must say about that region that it abounds in excellent soil. I undertook all this because I know that there will be no opportunity for me to get away when I return from England and take up my post and practical work.[51]

Having appointed Samborskii to a post which would make the realization of his agricultural school impossible, Catherine gave Potemkin the opportunity to use the skills of Livanov and Prokopovich immediately. On 1/12 September 1784, she addressed a directive to Potemkin, putting the two professors at his disposal "as assistants to the directors of economy in the Ekaterinoslav and Tauric regions."[52] It was an appointment which undoubtedly pleased Livanov, for his director in Ekaterinoslav was none other than his old teacher and friend from Moscow University, M. I. Afonin and they entered into a new and productive partnership.[53] In the next few years Afonin, Livanov, and Prokopovich organized and directed activities in every sphere of farming and husbandry: they advised on the laying out of fields and pastures, the techniques of ploughing, the sowing of seed and the care of livestock, the planting of woods and gardens, the development of silk farming and the setting up of factories. At the beginning of 1787 Potemkin sent Livanov and

Prokopovich on a tour of the Crimea to promote improved agricultural methods. Their instructions required them "to organise the whole economy, after taking into account the quality of the local soil, in accord with the latest English inventions, in matters of ploughing, crop rotation, the introduction of new grasses and the best agricultural implements; also to set up threshing-floors and barns, and where no water mills existed, to build windmills."[54] Their work in the Crimea was interrupted by the outbreak of hostilities between the Russians and the Turks and they returned to Ekaterinoslav. Nothing more is known about Prokopovich's activities apart from the date of his death, 25 September/6 October 1792, in Elizavetgrad. Livanov's talents were, however, soon employed in realizing another of Potemkin's projects—the search for deposits of coal, iron and precious metals—and he was outstandingly successful. In the next two years he discovered not only rich deposits of coal but also quantities of silver, gold, iron and marble in the area around Krivoi Rog and revealed conclusively the enormous natural wealth of "New Russia." In 1789, during one of his prospecting expeditions, Livanov, however, suffered a stroke which paralysed his left side and from which he never completely recovered.

His infirmity did not, however, put an end to his career; it merely limited his work as a prospector. He moved to Bogoiavlensk, near Nikolaev, where his health improved a little. Potemkin was not slow in asking him to carry out further searches for coal in the immediate vicinity, while promising him a pension and permission to "take the waters" for his health. When Potemkin died in 1791 these promises were still unfulfilled and remained so for the rest of Livanov's life, despite persistent petitions on his behalf by Potemkin's successor, Admiral Mordvinov. In Mordvinov Livanov found a solicitous protector and friend and with his encouragement Livanov devoted his last years to promoting the cause of English agriculture. It was, nevertheless, in accordance with the wishes of Potemkin that Livanov set up a school of practical agriculture, the first of its kind in Russia, in Bogoiavlensk in 1790, with a view to providing the settlers with practical instruction in the new methods. It was to be one more failure, one more noble project with bright beginnings and gradual but increasing disillusionment. In its early days it gave Livanov a new lease of life, an ability to cope with his physical infirmities. His letters to Samborskii in 1792 reveal his initial enthusiasm when he shared his time between the school and the laying out of a new farm for Mordvinov: "We are establishing near the town of St Nicholas a fine English farm for that noble and good man Nikolai Semenovich Mordvinov. We hope this summer to dig the boundary and inner ditches and to line at least one side with hedges, for we shall not have time to set more. English ploughs, harrows and rollers are gradually being introduced into this region. We firmly hope that all aspects of practical husbandry will be accepted by the local landowners, who are uncultured and steeped in prejudice."[55] He wishes to order through Samborskii quantities of good quality English winter wheat and mentions that the acorns which he had sown the previous year were doing well. At the end of the same year Mordvinov also wrote to Samborskii inviting him to visit "our *farms*, which are established or are being established according to the best principles." He described his own farm as "complete with ditches, divided into fields and being planted with *whitethorn, & timber trees.*"[56] By 1795 the mood had changed. Livanov complains that : "The local climate is so dry that all our work is in vain. Not a single drop of rain fell on the earth during the whole of last spring, and for such reasons my own enthusiasm for agriculture begins to disappear. A fine beginning for all that was sown and planted, but for what: drought, winds and heat destroy everything. All human knowledge can do nothing to avert such ills."[57] Two years later he sadly informed Samborskii that Mordvinov had "virtually abandoned his farm" because of his naval duties,[58] and in a final letter, undated but probably written shortly before his death, he wrote a sad epitaph on his labours: "I had wished to establish an English farm on the banks of the Bug, but God did not will it. . . . I have set up three fine farms in this region, but all have been abandoned for no good reason. My heart is unbearably pained and there is no cure for this illness."[59] He planned to visit a brother in Kiev, whom he had not seen for more than twenty years, but in 1800 he died in Nikolaev, broken physically and spiritually.

III

The story of agricultural students in England does not end with the return of Samborskii's group in 1784; it was only its beginning. Smirnov in his long years as chaplain in London carried on and developed his predecessor's initiatives, consulting frequently with his friend Young. In his autobiography under the year 1781, Young notes that "Prince Potemkin, the Russian Prime Minister, sent this year to England three young men consigned to the care of M. Smirnove, chaplain to the Russian Embassy, who requested that I would fix them in my immediate vicinity, in order that I might pay some attention to their progress and acquisitions. This I readily did, and took every means to have them well instructed in the English mode of cultivating land."[60] It was an experiment which Young wholeheartedly endorsed and he commended to other European landowners "this very noble example of Prince Potemkin, which is certainly one of the best means of introducing a new husbandry that can be devised." Essentially the experiment was for "a peasant's son that has some tincture of education" who would lodge with an English farmer "in order to reap the advantage of the farmer's conversation; but he should have the strictest orders to do all sorts of work with his own hands, in the same manner as an english labouring boy; and he should be left seven years in England."[61]

Smirnov visited the young men at Bradfield in the autumn of 1783 and reported: "The boys seemed to have made as much progress as one could expect in their first year. They plough very well and show great enthusiasm for agriculture. Mr Young has advised me to send them to different provinces and they will be sent off as soon as possible in accordance with his advice and arrangements."[62] They are mentioned in further letters from Smirnov to Samborskii, almost always in connection with Potemkin's failure to send any money for their upkeep. When money came it was £20 short and Smirnov was obliged to write a formal request for money in June, 1786, invaluable above all as the unique clue to the young men's identities.[63] They are named as Grebnitskii, Sofon'kov and Kozlov, who are to be found later working at Bogoiavlensk with Livanov, but whose sojourn in England has hitherto been an unknown chapter in their generally obscure careers. Smirnov soon sent the young men off to further their experience in different areas of England and in 1784 and 1785 they are found, singly, in Hertfordshire, Leicestershire, and Wiltshire. In 1785 Young paid his first visit to Bakewell since 1771 and described in his "Ten Days Tour to Mr Bakewell's" the improvements that had been made in the intervening fifteen years. He was at Dishley between 16 and 18 March, during which time he witnessed an experiment being carried out under the personal supervision of a young Russian, "John Saphonkove." Ivan Sofon'kov had brought together six rams of different breeds,which were being fed in a sheep-house and their respective weights at the various stages of the experiment recorded. The accompanying table was signed by Sofon'kov and dated 2 April, and was obviously sent to Young at a later date for inclusion in his published report.[64] Stepan Grebnitskii was established during the same period with a tenant-farmer by the name of Unhill near Hatfield. A description of the farm and of the sort of life Grebnitskii was leading there is found in the unpublished diaries of another young Russian, Ivan Sudakov, who met Grebnitskii and stayed on the farm during the first two weeks of February, 1785.[65] Sudakov gives the same detailed and itemised account of all aspects of Unhill's farming, such as all the Russian students were obliged to compose, but as an amusing extra describes Mrs Unhill at work in her kitchen and gives the recipe for her plum pudding and lists other dishes which they ate. Among other activities, he accompanied Grebnitskii to the weekly market at St Albans. Sudakov, in his travels had also met the third of Potemkin's "boys," Gerasim Kozlov, who in August, 1784, was lodging with a tenant farmer called Vines in Wiltshire. Sudakov describes Kozlov as engaged in making cheese and he gives a detailed description of the process and of the various utensils used.[66]

After some five years of wide-ranging practical experience, the three Russians left England on 4 September 1786. It seems likely that they had originally come from Potemkin's estate at Krichev in White Russia and perhaps had been recommended to Samborskii in 1781; it is also possible that it was to Krichev that they now returned, for their names (or at least those of Kozlov and Sofon'kov, who seems to have reverted to his former name of Saponkevich) are next encountered in a document of 1787 where they are described as "Krichev *meshchane*."[67] Their talents would certainly have been welcome there, for in their absence great changes had taken place, particularly since 1784 under the supervision of Samuel Bentham. In 1786 Jeremy Bentham arrived at Krichev to join his brother and thus by a strange coincidence the Benthams probably came in contact with yet more Russians who had been trained in England.

They would find at Zadobrast, some three miles from Krichev, a farm organized by Samuel Bentham on English lines. Jeremy Bentham in the year of their return was ordering from England numerous works on agriculture, with Young's publications prominent among them, and quantities of grain and seed.[68] But if they added their expertise to the farming at Krichev, it would not be for long, since Potemkin sold his estate in 1787, and Kozlov and Sofon'kov would seem to have moved south. Their names are listed in the document which has already been cited as people who had received agricultural training and were therefore free from the payment of taxes. It was at this time that they renewed their acquaintance with Professors Livanov and Prokopovich and five years later in 1792 they and Grebnitskii were assigned as assistants to Livanov at the school of agriculture at Bogoiav-lensk.[69] In May, 1792, Admiral Mordvinov informed Samborskii that "Greb-nitskii is employed at the Bogoiavlensk school of agriculture, where he continues his useful service" and in December mentioned that Grebnitskii and Sofon'kov (here called Stepanisevich!) were working with Livanov "to beautify the outskirts of our city."[70] Nothing further is known after that date about the career of Sofon'kov, but Kozlov and Grebnitskii were to leave Nikolaev in 1798 for Petersburg. Livanov, on hearing of Samborskii's appointment as head of the new practical school of agriculture near Pavlovsk, recommended Kozlov to him as a man whose skills in agriculture he knew well;[71] some months later Mordvinov praised Grebnitskii in similar terms.[72] Kozlov's movements cannot be traced further, but Samborskii is found describing Grebnitskii in 1799 as his most energetic and talented assistant at a school, where nearly twenty years after presenting his project to Catherine, his dreams seemed at last to have come to fruition under her son, but where he suffered only bitter disillusionment and failure.[73]

IV

Even before his return to Russia in 1775 to enlist his agricultural students Samborskii's enthusiasm for English agriculture was well known and communicated itself to a number of people who wished to introduce new ways on their estates in Russia. Mordvinov's attempts in the 1790s to set up

English farms in the south with the help of Livanov have already been mentioned, but they were only a final stage in his desire to be an "English farmer." Mordvinov had come to know Samborskii very well during his own stay in England between 1774 and 1777 and his letters of the late 1770s reveal to what extent he had been affected by Samborskii's dreams. Shortly after his return to Russia he requested the best books on agriculture, including Young's *Farmer's Calendar*, as well as instructions on how to sow seeds by drilling rather than by broadcasting.[74] The following year he exclaimed in English: "I come more nearer to you: I become a Farmer; give me good instructions, & I'll go in your ways of Glories." Returning to Russian, he rhapsodized:

> We will gather together ploughs and harrows, rams and bulls; we will feed the hungry, clothe the naked, and bring joy to the soil; we will cover the steppes and bogs with a rich mantle; there will be no more poverty or lamentation; people will dry their tears, will marry and will raise to you, holy Andrei, their psalms and prayers. I have travelled through the villages; everything grows poorly; the peasant sweats and cries at his work. Ignorance is great; everywhere instruction is needed. The main thing is that there are no fields with which I can begin my husbandry. If it is not too late this year to sow, which you will know better than I, then I beg you to send me seeds of rye grass, of the best kind, together with brief instruction on how to sow and harvest it.[75]

Ignorant himself, but in the beginning boundlessly enthusiastic and willing to learn, Mordvinov read his English manuals and then sent off for rye-grass, oats, carrots, turnips, clover, urging Samborskii to enlist Arbuthnot's aid because it was so easy to make mistakes about the best kind of seed.[76] Agriculture was to be Russia's salvation, "let people look at England and they will be convinced." Mordvinov's devotion to English ways at this period of his life was boundless and throughout the 1780s and 1790s he was intent on re-organizing the estates which he and his brother had inherited in the Ukraine. In 1786 he had sent some of his serfs to Samuel Bentham's farm at Krichev, requesting that "vous les employés plutot a labourer la terre & a jardiner; car vous savez que dans notre pays nous avons plus besoin de des *Farmers* que des menuisiers."[77] A few years later in 1792, he was pestering Samborskii to hire him an English farmer. "For a good farmer I would be prepared to pay 1000 rubles or more a year, if you could find or bring one from England who knew his job and could set up in all its parts *an English Farmarship*."[78] In Nikolaev, Mordvinov found a willing Anglophile collaborator in Livanov throughout the 1790s and although Livanov despaired of success and suggested, as we have seen, that Mordvinov had by 1797 "abandoned" his farm, there is other evidence which shows that Mordvinov's interest in agriculture was as keen as ever at the end of 1798. In an interesting letter to Prince A. I. Viazemskii, who had also travelled in England and was a friend of the Benthams, Mordvinov spoke of his *new* school of agriculture at Nikolaev:

> Cet établissement est fait d'après les principes de Mr. Young le meilleur professeur connu d'Angleterre. J'ai deja pour mon Academie deux professeurs Anglois. Vous m'obligeriés beaucoup de persuader a vos amis d'en faire autant [i.e., following Viazemskii's example of sending young men to be trained], car je voudrois que cette école donne au plus vite et en plus grand sphere des fruits de son etablissement, je m'interesse beaucoup au bien qui en pourrit resulter si nos Seigneurs proprietaires des Terres immenses voudroient profiter des avantages que j'ai intention de leur procurer. Leurs sujets avec le terres pourroient etre des Fermiers aussi parfaits que ceux d'Angleterre, et nous avons tous les moyens de les former.[79]

It is, however, unlikely, that the School ever became truly operative, for early in 1799 Mordvinov was relieved of his post at Nikolaev and recalled to St. Petersburg. In the reign of Alexander, Mordvinov occupied a succession of important governmental posts, but an indication of his continuing interest in agriculture was his acceptance of the presidency of the Free Economic Society in 1823 which he held until 1840.

Mordvinov was not alone among Russian landowners in looking to England. Count Ivan Chernyshev, a founder member of the Free Economic Society who had become a subscribing member of the Society of Arts in 1769 during his brief period as Russian Ambassador in London, also knew Samborskii personally and frequently enlisted his help and advice in the following years. At the same time as Mordvinov was writing to Samborskii, Chernyshev was writing for details of English distilling methods and plans of distilleries, then for seeds, then for dogs. At the end of May 1779 he was informing Samborskii that he was about to buy a new estate where "I shall attempt to introduce English agriculture with the help of your instructions."[80] In the same letter he thanked Samborskii for sending him agricultural implements, various seeds, two horses with their harnesses, a number of cows and pigs and an apparatus for butter-making. Despite all the information Samborskii obtained for him, Chernyshev eventually felt that he needed one of his own men trained in England and possibly mindful of the example of Potemkin's boys, decided to send one of his own serfs with Samborskii when he left for England in 1784. On 9/20 June he wrote: "I entrust to your favour and protection the bearer of this, my valet Ivan Sudakov," and asked Samborskii to read through the detailed instructions Sudakov had been given and add to them, if necessary.[81] A year later, almost to the day, Sudakov arrived back in St. Petersburg and disappeared again into the total obscurity from which he had briefly emerged. Absolutely nothing has been recorded about his subsequent activities and he would be known, if known is the word, only for Chernyshev's letter of 1784 and a mention later in the same year in a letter of Smirnov's, if it were not for the fact that the detailed and absorbing journal of his year in England has survived. Sudakov at least has left his own memorial.

His journals begin with a dedication in which he asks his benefactor to receive his work "as a mark of the assiduousness and eternal devotion to Your Highness of your slave, whose education was not of a slave, but of a true noble."[82] This is followed by the detailed instructions he received (I, 4-7v.), ordering him to observe everything concerning agriculture and domestic economy and to keep a diary. His particular concern was to be distilleries and distilling and the first twenty-one of the twenty-six heads of his instructions touch on all aspects of building and organizing a distillery, the organization of its labour-force, the means of production. He was also asked to visit a malthouse and a specific farm near London. Drawings and plans were to be made, whenever possible, and the diaries indeed reveal Sudakov's considerable skills as a draughtsman, as he provides plans not only of a distillery, but of country estates, farm implements, new buildings in endless and rich profusion.

Sudakov arrived in London on 26 July 1784 and within two days was visiting a farm on the Weybridge road and producing the first of his detailed descriptions and meticulous coloured plans. In the course of the next month he was on farms in Ascot and in Wiltshire, describing the making of cheese and butter, the curing of pork, harvesting methods and the raising of calves. He visited local markets and made a tour of the city of Bath. At the end of August he was back in London, consulting with Samborskii, prior to the latter's return to Russia, and engaging to study chemistry with the "most famous" Dr. Bryan Higgins (I, 53v.) (of whom more in a later chapter) and visiting the merely "famous mechanic" Mr. Sharp (I, 59). His activities were described in constant reports to his master Chernyshev, who, however, took exception to Sudakov's pursuits in chemistry. In December Smirnov informed Samborskii: "Mr Soodakoff has received orders from Count Chernysheff not to learn Chemistry but to apply himself more to rural affairs & distilling."[83] Sudakov thereafter devoted himself exclusively to fulfilling these requirements. At the beginning of January, 1785, he visited the distillery of Cook & Co. near London and produced a long report "On English Distilling," complete with plans and his own reflections on English methods and how they could be adapted for use in Russia (II, 20-71v.). In March he went to the malthouse owned by a Mr. Birch in Chelsea and repeated his detailed investigations (II, 72-91).

Volume II of his diaries is devoted exclusively to questions of distilling spirits and brewing beer and he notes that his agricultural activities between

29 January and 14 February are the subject of a separate volume. Volume III is in fact entitled "A Description of Agriculture in the County of Hertfordshire" and describes initially his stay near Hatfield with the tenant-farmer Unhill, with whom, as we have seen, Stepan Grebnitskii, one of Potemkin's boys, was already living (III, 5-56). Sudakov's agricultural studies were not, however, confined to Hertfordshire and after his return to London in mid-February and his visit to the malthouse, he spent varying lenghts of time on other farms around London. Thus, on 22 March, he stayed with Mr. Cooper, the owner of a large farm at Dulwich, and added more to his earlier notes on cheese and butter making. He also watched a Scottish chain-plough being constructed and commented on the various types of ploughs in use (III, 61v.-75). On 25 March he visited Mr. Thompson, a nurseryman at Mill End (III, 75-75v.) and in April was on the farm of a Mr. Edmonds in Battersea. He paid particular attention to types of soil and sowing techniques and gave various calculations about the size of farms, making reference to the views of Arthur Young (III, 90-IV, 38). Other visits took him into Surrey to the farm of a Mr. Nightingale and the market garden of a Mr. Simpson, and his final days included a thorough inspection of the oast-houses of a Mr. Atkins in Esher and the usual detailed notes about hop-growing (IV, 42-54v.). Among Sudakov's other activities his visit to a meeting of the Society of Arts with Smirnov is of particular interest (IV, 38v.-41v.). Although not extensive, Sudakov's account is valuable and possibly unique as an outsider's description of an actual meeting of the Society and it is enlivened by details which do not find their way into official accounts and minutes.[84]

V

Komov and his companions had left England in 1784. Sudakov and Grigorii Sarvilov (another young Russian mentioned in his diary as studying agriculture) set sail in June, 1785, and in 1786 Grebnitskii, Kozlov, and Sofon'kov followed. Strictly speaking, they were the last Russians who came to England specifically to study agriculture, but one more name might be added. The arrival in England in 1784 of S. S. Dzhunkovskii to act as guardian to Samborskii's son, Aleksandr, has already been mentioned, but not the interest he subsequently took in agricultural matters. He first speaks of his agricultural pursuits at the end of December, 1785, but at that time he was more concerned with other studies, and only in 1788 does he again return to the subject, giving Samborskii his observations on French agriculture during a stay of three months at Lille. He subsequently gave more and more time to agriculture and with Aleksandr Samborskii moved to Pinner in 1790 to live on a farm. They remained there for over a year before deciding to go further afield in the autumn of 1791 to study agricultural methods and livestock breeding in other parts of the country.[85] Perhaps

once more Bakewell played host to Russian visitors, before they returned to
Russia at the request of Samborskii in 1792.

Dzhunkovskii subsequently became a member of the Bureau of State
Economy and on its dissolution in 1803 became Secretary to the Free Economic Society, a post he retained until 1828.[86] In the year after he had left
England, that body became linked with a new institution in England which
was specifically concerned with questions of agriculture. A brainchild of
Sir John Sinclair (1754-1835), the Board of Agriculture was formally con-
stituted in 1793 with Sinclair as President and Young as Secretary. Sinclair,
like Young, had many Russian acquaintances and had been in Russia himself
in 1786; he lost no time in informing the Russian society of the foundation
of the Board, promising to send all its publications and requesting news of
Russian developments. Young had been a member of the Russian Society
since 1779 and Sinclair was immediately elected in 1793. The Board of
Agriculture followed suit by electing to its honorary membership P. B.
Passek, A. A. Nartov and J. A. Euler, President and Permanent Secretaries
of the Free Economic Society, as well as the ubiquitous Dr. Guthrie, who
performed the sort of go-between function in St. Petersburg which was to
be fulfilled in London by the Reverend Mr. Smirnov, also elected in the
same year. Evidence of the contacts which were established between the two
bodies is found in the first volume of *Communications to the Board of
Agriculture*. "A Letter form Dr. Guthrie of St Petersburg, to the President
of the Board of Agriculture," dated November, 1793, is followed by "Tables
containing Names of Plants, and Productions cultivated for domestic Economy, and for the Arts, in the District of St Petersburg," "Answers of the
Imperial Free Economic Society of St. Petersburgh to the Queries of the
Board of Agriculture," and a "Translation of a Letter from Count Alexis
Orlow Chesminskoy, to the Rev. Mr. Smirnove," giving information on
Russian horse and sheep breeding.[87]

Smirnov's expertise in agricultural matters gained wide recognition and
was brought to the notice of Catherine herself in an interesting letter from
Baron Friedrich-Melchior Grimm in 1795, in which he passed on advice from
his "oracle," "milord Finlater," on a number of subjects, principal of which
was agriculture. James, seventh earl of Findlater (1750-1813) and son of a
celebrated agriculturist, suggested that Smirnov could play a key role in
furthering in Russia the progress of agriculture, "la mère de tous les arts,
la source des toutes les prospérités." He could be asked to translate key
English works on agricultural matters, such as the *Transactions* of the Society
for Arts, the publications of the Bath Society and books by Sinclair. Findlater also proposed that if Smirnov were to be recalled to Russia, "il pourrait
être mis à la tête d'une société économique qu'il faudrait établir a Kiev ou
dans quelque autre part méridionale de l'empire."[88] Smirnov was entrusted
with none of these specific projects, for as has been seen, he lived out his

long life in England and his translating activity was from Russian to English rather than vice versa. Nevertheless, Findlater's proposals may be pursued further and placed in the context of 1) the translation of English works on agriculture into Russian in the latter part of the eighteenth century and the dissemination of the ideas of Young and others in Russian works and 2) the eventual establishment of the practical school of agriculture in 1797.

The Reverend Coxe mentions that Young's "Six Weeks Tour was translated by particular order of the Empress, for the purpose of diffusing the knowledge of practical agriculture,"[89] but if this was so, the translation is unknown to bibliographers and bibliophiles. The work is not even noted among works which were taken for translation by members of the Society for the Translation of Foreign Books, set up by Catherine in 1768 and existing until 1783. In fact none of Young's numerous works appeared in Russian translation in the eighteenth century and the same is to be said of publications by Arbuthnot, Francis Home, Lord Kames, Sinclair and by any other of the numerous English agricultural writers or of the societies mentioned by Findlater. Their work remained known only to a group of devotees and were read in English or in German or French translations. Sievers in his memorandum to Catherine in 1765 alludes to a translation (into French or German) of an English work "which contains a complete course of agriculture. It is the most recent work on this subject."[90] The book is not named, but was possibly Francis Home's popular *Principles of Agriculture and Vegetation* (Edinburgh, 1747 and editions in 1759 and 1762) or Thomas Hale's *Compleat Body of Husbandry* (4 vols. [London, 1758]); the Russian translation which Sievers was promised did not appear. Mordvinov, who mentions in his early letters works by Young and Lord Kames, sent Samborskii in 1798 Kames's *Gentleman Farmer* (Edinburgh, 1776) which had been translated into Russian by a young naval officer at Nikolaev, S. A. Iuferov.

> I believe that this book can be very useful for Russia and that there are many such works in the English language. This young man translated it very quickly and could produce three books a year which could be sent to you, if he is encouraged. I have now given him Young's agricultural tours to translate. Please tell me how much money your department [the Bureau of State Economy] has at its disposal for translations and how this sum is apportioned. I have a printing press here and would like to use it more for agricultural works. The translations could be sent to you for approval and censorship.[91]

Mordvinov was soon to leave Nikolaev and although the press continued to produce a variety of works until 1803 under the directorhsip of Prokhor Suvorov, a friend of Samborskii's and an Oxford M.A., no work by Kames or Young was published.

In the eighteenth century in fact only one major work by an English agriculturist was translated and published. In 1780 Semen Efimovich Desnitskii, professor of law at Moscow University, who had been at Glasgow University between 1761 and 1767, brought out his *Nastavnik zemledel'-cheskii*, a version of Thomas Bowden's *The Farmer's Director* (London, 1776) with additions from the work of other English writers. In his long dedication to the Grand Duke Paul, Desnitskii extolls the greatness of the English language and the successes of the arts and sciences and hopes that his translation will stimulate other young Russians to undertake the translation of other English books. His foreword is concerned solely with agriculture: he recalls the scenes he witnessed at Smithfield Market and praises the general advance of English agriculture. He argues that reforms will not be effected overnight in Russia, but that landowners should give the practical course of agriculture described in the book a try by ordering implements from England and possibly enlisting the help of an English farmer who would be given a sufficient area of land on which to introduce the new methods and train young Russians committed to his care for seven or nineteen years, after the English custom. He ends by thanking for their help two members of the famous Demidov family who had been in England and two Britons residing in Moscow, Dr. John Grieve and James Rowand, the merchant banker.[92] The book he offered was an extensive treatise on all aspects of English agriculture and husbandry and was accompanied by diagrams of various ploughs used in different parts of England. The following year, Desnitskii's translation was followed by Samborskii's only published work on agriculture, edited under Desnitskii's supervision. Entitled *Opisanie prakticheskogo anglinskogo zemledeliia* ("A Description of Practical English Agriculture"), it was a brief work of some eighty-eight pages, presenting a resumé of the theories of practice of leading British agriculturists, whose works are indicated in the margins. Noteworthy are the references to "the skilled agriculturist Arbuthnot" and Young "whose works are known to the whole world"[93] (possibly the first time their names had appeared in a Russian publication), but on the whole the work is an unsatisfactory compilation. It nevertheless seems to have attracted some notice: a copy in the Lenin Library had inserted sheets with notes in an eighteenth-century hand on the application of the methods described to Russia[94] and at the beginning of the next century Aleksandr Radishchev makes reference to "an Anglo-Russian writer's" four ways of ascertaining the quality of soil in his "Opisanie moego vladeniia" ("A Description of My Estate," 1801).[95]

If the works of the leading English agriculturists were not translated their ideas were disseminated and incorporated in the books produced by the two outstanding "professors of agriculture" trained in England, Komov and Livanov. It is curious that while Komov has been the subject of a biography and a detailed article on his agricultural works in the Soviet period, the equally deserving Livanov has been neglected, possibly because he declares his debt to England more openly and insistently. Nevertheless, both authors adapted what they had learnt to Russian conditions and as men of many years of training and experience voiced their own opinions. Anything less would indeed have been disappointing, not least to the English farmers from whose teaching and advice they benefitted.

The last third of the eighteenth century witnessed the appearance of a number of journals devoted to problems of agriculture and general husbandry produced both by the Free Economic Society and by individuals, notably A. T. Bolotov. In a long survey article Professor K. V. Sivkov has indicated the problems to which writers addressed themselves, stressing those subjects which attracted great or little attention. He does not look beyond the journals to books on farming which frequently were concerned with precisely the topics ignored or scarcely reflected in the journals; moreover, he emphasizes the influence of practices in the Baltic provinces alongside internal Russian experiments and pays no heed to English or indeed general European advances, and it is in books rather than articles that the English influence is paramount. He writes for instance that "the question of agricultural implements is scarcely reflected in the journals under review, despite the fact that one of the aims of the Free Economic Society was to acquaint landowners with new improved models of agricultural implements."[96] Desnitskii's call for English implements to be imported as well as his chapter on ploughs has been noted as well as Samborskii's return from England with implements from Young's farm and the orders of such as Chernyshev and Mordvinov. Vasilii Petrov, after his retirement from court and return to his estates, also sent to England for ploughs and others implements.[97] Sudakov, constantly sketching farm implements, had been very interested in the Repository of the Society of Arts and made a drawing of a tool for digging up and cutting turnips. It is interesting to note that among the subscribers to William Bailey's *The Advancement of Arts, Manufactures and Commerce; or, descriptions of the useful machines and models contained in the Repository of the Society . . . of Arts* (London, 1772) Russian names figure prominently: they include Samborskii, Chernyshev, Musin-Pushkin (the ambassador), Princess Dashkova, Count Razumovskii (2 copies) and a Captain Nepliuev. Komov's first work on his return from England was in this overall context an important one: *O zemledel'nykh orudiiakh* ("On Agricultural Implements," 1785), which came out in a second corrected and expanded edition in 1791, described all manner of implements which he had seen and tested during his stay in England. Livanov in one of his own works wrote: "English agriculturists instead of pulling hay out of a stack cut it with a knife, an example of which can be seen in Professor Komov's book on agricultural implements. I should like to see our own peasants follow this example."[98]

In 1787 Komov published an article in the *Trudy* of the Free Economic

Society on ways of combatting disease in wheat and rye and this was incorporated the following year in his major work *O zemledelii* ("On Agriculture"), which has been hailed as "a sort of Russian encyclopaedia of eighteenth-century agriculture."[99] He defined his intentions as follows: "I shall speak about the characteristics of plants; then, about air, water and earth and how they aid the growth and feeding of plants; then I shall suggest ways of fertilizing the soil; and finally I shall show how and when it is necessary to sow and on what kind of soil vegetables, grain and grass of all types and how to harvest and keep them."[100] He then proceeded to explore under fifty heads many of the main aspects of agriculture, relying on his own experience (gained during the Gmelin expedition of 1768-75 as well as in England) and that of leading Western writers. His attitude to foreign expertise and achievement was as rational and practical as his general *modus operandi*: "to imitate it is not only not shameful but glorious. . . . As one of those sent [abroad] I consider it my duty to use all my strength to realize Her Majesty's intention; and since among the many ways of improving agriculture the quickest is considered to be the description of it in different lands and its publication, this is what I am doing. Because thereby everything which agriculturists in one country use to enrich themselves but which is unknown in another land will become known to all at once."[101] Among the topics which Komov examines are the life of plants and the quality of soil which reflect his knowledge of chemistry which he acquired in England, his propaganda for the cultivation of potatoes, for clover and lucerne, his advocacy of a six-field rotation. Russians with experience of England where the potato was a vital crop were much concerned to promote it in Russia. Sivkov notes that there were some ten articles devoted to potato growing in eighteenth-century journals, beginning with Sievers' account in 1767 of potato-growing in his Novgorod province.[102] Earlier in 1765, seed potatoes were being ordered from London through the Russian charge d'affaires, H. Gross, and bought by Pavel Demidov during his visit in the same year.[103] Komov considered "the earth apple," as it was frequently called in Russia at this time, "the most useful of all vegetables" and gave detailed hints on its planting, propagation and cultivation.[104] Livanov also was a strong supporter, but regretted that it was insufficiently known and grown.[105]

Livanov's *Nastavlenie k umozritel'nomu i deloproizvodnomu zemledeliiu* ("Guide to Theoretical and Practical Agriculture") had appeared in St. Petersburg the year before Komov's work. Produced at the behest of Potemkin as a guide for the new settlers of the Ekaterinoslav and Tauric provinces, it inevitably anticipates some of the subject-matter of Komov's work but is of a more compilative nature. Of particular interest, however, in present context are Livanov's constant references to English authors and to his own activities in England. Examples are Francis Home, Young, "who deserves immortality for the untiring way in which he carries out experiments and makes notes on different soils," John Mills, "although this clever agriculturist frequently makes mistakes," Arbuthnot "with whom I had the good fortune to study for two years," "the most respected English priest and skilful agriculturist Mr Lord," "the noble and enlightened Englishman, Mr Moore," Baker, "famous for his numerous different experiments to promote husbandry," Ellis, Mortimer, and last but not least "Mr Bakewell, skilled in livestock-breeding."[106] This first book of Livanov's like Komov's was devoted to agriculture, not livestock, but Komov had pointed out the close links between the successful cultivation of fields and meadows and the raising of livestock, "for livestock feed and clothe men and help to fertilize the fields; and without them it is impossible to plough or harrow or bring manure to the fields or carry away the corn."[107] Unlike Komov, however, Livanov lived long enough to produce a second work on livestock-breeding, which was dedicated this time to Mordvinov, his benefactor whom he extolled in verse:

> Mordvinov! Sterility and hunger banished by your hand
> Flee from these fields
> On rich pastures the sturdy ox grazes
> And the peasant laughs among the yellow fields.

In his preface he emphasizes, along similar lines to Komov, the importance of livestock-breeding and declares that in producing his work for the benefit of Russian breeders he was following the rules and practice of Bakewell. "Mr Bakewell, an Englishman, burning with love for his homeland, spared no expense nor effort in order to, firstly, investigate in his country all breeds of every kind of domestic livestock, secondly, ascertain which breed in each species brought the most profit and which the least, and thirdly, indicate the signs by which the most profitable breed of each species could be recognized and differentiated from the least profitable."[108] Attempting to popularize the ideas of Bakewell and others (he names Carrington, George Culley, a favourite pupil of Bakewell's and author of *Observations on Live Stock* (1786), Edward Lisle and Tancred Robinson), Livanov has his eyes clearly set on conditions in the south of Russia. He recommends the English method of dividing fields and pastures by ditches to prevent the spread of foot-and-mouth disease and in giving suggestions on the raising of cattle, sheep and pigs, is well aware of the rich potentialities of the southern provinces.

In May, 1795, Livanov sent Samborskii a corrected copy of his book, regretting that the St. Petersburg printers had made all manner of mistakes and omissions. He was equally aware of the advanced nature of his work, remarking sadly that "the Petersburg experts on husbandry will have little trust in the truth of this composition."[109] Livestock-breeding had indeed been accorded little space in the agricultural journals and was generally regarded as a mere adjunct to agriculture. The position was even worse with poultry-farming, which was totally ignored by the journals. Livavov's little pamphlet on this subject, *O ptitsevodstve*, remarkable for the complete absence of references to English expertise, was ready in 1795 but was published only in 1799 at the Nikolaev press together in one volume with second editions of his previous two works.

Komov and Livanov were the most productive writers among the English-trained agriculturists, but some of their companions also left a few articles of interest and in the case of Kolmakov, a book, which has already been mentioned on hydrology. Most were members of the Free Economic Society and it is in its various publications that their works are found. Prokopovich published an article in 1785 "O rashchenii soloda" ("On the Preparation of Malt"),[110] but it was only much later, in 1812, that Flavitskii committed to print the results of his English expertise married to long years of experience in Russian conditions. His "Kratkoe opisanie udobnykh sposobov, upotrebliaemykh dlia vozdelyvaniia mokrykh zemel' " ("A Concise Description of Methods of Reclaiming Marshland") was followed two years later by "Pokazanie sposobov, upotrebliaemykh v Anglii pri vozdelyvanii mokrykh zemel' " ("An Illustration of English Methods of Reclaiming Marshland") and dealt with the important question of draining and reclaiming low-lying marshes and bogs, about which several articles had appeared in the eighteenth century and which had been discussed by both Komov and Livanov in their books.[111]

All the members of Samborskii's group thus made their contributions to the slow advances in Russia of English methods and expertise in all branches of farming. Their articles apart, there were few contributions to the publications of the Free Economic Society which paraded English achievements, at least in their titles: an exception was Ivan Kel'khen's "Novye izvestiia, sluzhaschchie k poznaniiu anglinskoi sel'skoi ekonomii" ("New Information Regarding English Rural Economy"), which was a series of haphazard notes on the preparation of soil, methods of ploughing, turnip growing, and cheese making.[112] It is perhaps indicative of some opposition to English methods that the article based on the reports of the Samborskii group was not published until 1814. It has been suggested that the many-field system, such as indicated in that article and generally favoured by Samborskii and his friends was regarded with no little suspicion throughout the latter part of the eighteenth century. Sivkov has suggested between the 1770s and 1790s the question of the many-field system was frequently discussed, although he refers only to Bolotov's defence of the seven-field system in an article of 1771, repeated without change some seven years later in his own journal, and a curious advocacy of an eleven crop rotation proposed in 1799.[113] He, however, notes that the majority of landowners were reluctant to abandon the old three-field system for the new-fangled ways, the advantages of which Samborskii's school of agriculture attempted to demonstrate.

On 4/15 March 1797 Paul I issued an *ukaz* setting up the "ekspeditsiia gosudarstvennogo khoziaistva, opekunstva inostrannykh i sel'skogo khoziaistva" ("The Bureau of State Economy, Guardianship of Foreigners and Rural Economy").[114] The Bureau was to be under the general supervision of the procurator-general, Prince Aleksei Borisovich Kurakin, and consist initially of two senators and four other members, one of whom was Samborskii. There has been much speculation as to the initiator of this enterprise, but there seems little doubt that Samborskii's influence was crucial. He had enjoyed the favour of Paul since 1781 and was respected by many people in the tsar's immediate circle, not least Prince Aleksandr Kurakin, the procurator-general's elder brother. Paul, when grand duke, had been called upon by Desnitskii in the dedication to his translation of Bowden to foster agriculture and undoubtedly he was pleased to give his blessing to a project over which his mother had shilly-shallied for so long–Samborskii's school of agriculture, the organization of which was to be one of the first concerns of the new Bureau.

The School was allocated a large stretch of land at Tiarlevo between Pavlovsk and Tsarskoe Selo, bordering Samborskii's own home at Belozerka and stretching as far as the Moscow road, where Samborskii, as Director, was to watch over the instruction of the students in the theory and particularly practice of English agriculture. Provision was made for fifty-three students from a variety of backgrounds and in early 1798 Samborskii was recruiting for example eight students from Moscow University and ten seminarists from Khar'kov: other places were for children of both sexes from the foundling hospitals and for state peasants. The course, which was to be of three years' duration, was specifically to demonstrate the advantages of the many-field system, to introduce new crops and implements, to explain techniques for reclaiming bogs and planting hedges. All that was practised at the School was to become "an example to be imitated, for the correcting and perfecting of [all branches of husbandry] throughout the length and breadth of the Empire."[115] The graduates of the School would proceed to spread what they had learned, as officials in government departments, as bailiffs on estates, as village priests, exerting the influence of which Samborskii had always dreamed.

The land was to be divided into four parts, for experiments in 1) agriculture (the seven-field crop rotation), 2) gardening and forestry, 3) livestock-breeding and 4) building and machines, and each section was to be under a supervisor with one or two assistants. The builder, or architect as he was termed, and the mechanic were to be assisted by a blacksmith, a carpenter and a locksmith. A married man was envisaged as the livestock expert with a wife who would teach domestic economy, including care of poultry. In addition there was to be an apothecary, a clerk and a translator, charged with the translation of useful works from German and English. 88,000 rubles were assigned. for the setting-up of the School, including buildings and salaries, and by the end of 1799 some 64,000 rubles had been spent, but seemingly little had been accomplished. In August, 1799, Samborskii was appointed domestic chaplain to the tsar's daughter Aleksandra Pavlovna, but by that time he had already become involved in disputes with other members of the Bureau and much of what he had dreamed had not materialized. He had been unable to secure the appointment as supervisors of several of the people he had recommended and he alleged that not a single building of any sort had been completed nor was any system of husbandry initiated. He was succeeded on his own recommendation by Modest Petrovich Bakunin, a man also dedicated to English ways and author of *Pravila, rukovodstvuishchie k novomu razdelu i obrabotyvaniiu polei* ("Rules for a New Division and Working of Fields," 1800), which advocated a six-field rotation as opposed to Samborskii's seven. The School, however, was soon removed from the authority of the Bureau and existed only until 1803, accomplishing little of lasting value. No works were translated under its auspices, although one of its first students, Efim Petrovich Liutsenko, from Moscow University, issued in 1806 his *Sobranie kratkikh ekonomicheskikh sochinenii, osnovannykh na praktike i opytakh luchshikh angliiskikh fermerov* ("A Collection of Brief Economic Works, Based on the Practice and Experiments of Leading English Farmers"), dedicated to none other than the Earl of Findlater.

VI

For Samborskii the eighteenth century, the age of rational agriculture, ended on a note of bitterness and disappointment. He was not to be involved again in agricultural progress in Russia in a public capacity. Returning to Russia via Odessa after the death in Hungary of Aleksandra Pavlovna, Samborskii wrote to Alexander I in 1804 of his new hopes of bringing light to the steppes, preaching the gospels and encouraging agriculture,[116] but illness and old age led him to devote his remaining energies to Stratilatovka, the estate in the Ukraine which he had received from Paul in 1797. His activities there aroused the interest of the local police chief who sent a report to Petersburg in 1808 and again in 1811. The second report stated that Samborskii had set up

a home for orphans and widows, also a third house for the very old as well as a hospital . . . ; adjoining the hospital there was a rather impressive separate building for medicines and for smallpox innoculations, and moreover another house for peasants suffering from venereal disease has proved an evident curb on licence. The police inspector had also noted that the peasants who had been victim to such weaknesses had now gradually begun to turn more towards sobriety, hard work and good conduct, where hitherto immoderation had prevailed. In addition to these philanthropic institutions, he [Samborskii] has encouraged a village school, where peasant children under the supervision of a capable priest learn reading, writing and arithmetic and supply harmonious singing in God's house; finally, he, Mr. Samborskii, has introduced Spanish breeds of sheep and set up a silk farm.[117]

The reign of Alexander gave new impetus to agricultural reform and particularly to English methods. In 1802 Smirnov in London was hailing both English master and Russian monarch in a letter to Young:

my very worthy Friend and Master, the true original Source of all the rational agricultural Knowledge, now so happily extending through Europe and to the End of the World; [to] the Man, who more than any other Individual without Exception, had ventured to point out to Mankind the true Foundation of their Comfort and real Happiness. Here my dear Sir Divine Providence is visibly raising, in the Person of His Imperial Majesty a very powerful Instrument to spread about your benevolent Views, *to speed the Plough*. Such example will have unbounded Influence, for in Russia, I believe, more than in any Country—Regis ad exemplum totus componitur Orbis.[118]

He recommended at the same time to Young a Mr. Davidson (or Davison), who was head of the farm established near St. Petersburg by Alexander "in Imitation to that of His majesty the King of England" and who had been sent to "stock it with the various Objects proper to that Purpose, such as Implements, Cattle, seeds, workmen, Dairy-maid, et hoc genus omne."[119] In September Davidson was on his way back to Russia with his errand fulfilled and Smirnov was writing to Young "to let the Bull go" which had been selected for the farm.[120] Young was particularly useful in helping Smirnov set up the English farm of Count Fedor Vasil'evich Rostopchin (1763-1826) at his estate at Voronovo near Moscow. He recruited a Mr. Patterson, steward to Lord Hardwick, to manage the estate and a year later received via Smirnov a snuffbox from a grateful Rostopchin, depicting on the inside a building dedicated to Young in Voronovo and the inscription "A Pupil to his Master."[121] At the end of 1804 Smirnov involved Young with Alexander I's plan "to have reports of their Governments [i.e., *gubernii*] made upon the same system as ours, of counties"[122] and did much to help his son, the Reverend Arthur Young (1769-1827), who went to Russia in 1805 to carry out a survey.[123]

At this same period there was active in Russia a leading exponent of English agricultural methods, who, according to his son, had conceived during his year in Britain in 1783-84 "that love or rather passion for agronomy which remained with him for the rest of his life."[124] Dmitrii Markovich Poltoratskii (1761-1818) began to put that passion into action at the estate of Avchurino in Kaluga province in the 1790s. Following English examples in crop rotation and manuring, he also ordered the latest farming implements and machinery from England. He proved in the main a successful owner, achieving good results on the poor soil of Avchurino even in years of generally poor harvests. His expertise gained wide recognition and he was enlisted by Prince Kurakin in 1798 to work in the Bureau of State Economy, where according to one authority, he clashed with Samborskii. If this was so, there was no hint of it when Samborskii visited Avchurino in 1806 and wrote in enthusiastic praise of all he saw to Poltoratskii, while admitting sadly that he himself had never possessed the funds to carry out similar measures. "The implements which you use are of the very best; your horses are excellent and the whole set-up is worthy of general imitation."[125] Poltoratskii had also apparently established a school of husbandry at his estate to which Samborskii had sent three of his own peasants.

Although Poltoratskii was a respected founder-member of the Moscow Society of Agriculture[126] and in 1813 had been created an honorary member of the Khar'kov Philotechnical Society as "an enlightened landowner, renowned for his attempts to perfect agriculture in Russia,"[127] he was censured and ridiculed as an eccentric and anglomaniac. His son wrote that "they criticized his expenditure, rejected and even ridiculed much that he did, but gradually even among his critics there appeared iron ploughs instead of the incredible wooden ones, Scottish threshing and winnowing machines, etc."[128] The superiority of the iron plough over the traditional Russian wooden implement was a reference to a famous dispute in 1806, when a brochure entitled *Plug i sokha* ("The Iron and Wooden Ploughs") making a veiled attack on Poltoratskii appeared. Written "by a nobleman of the Steppes," it was the work of Rostopchin, who but two years earlier had been an enthusiastic supporter of Poltoratskii and a fervent admirer of Young. Disillusioned in the results of his own experiments and widening his well-known gallophobia into an attack on all things foreign, Rostopchin branded as an ephemeral, harmful, and extravagant fashion the cult of English agricultural methods, and lauded the traditional Russian ways and implements. In his turn Rostopchin was attacked by Princess Dashkova, a fervent Anglophile, in her *Mnenie o pluge i sokhe* ("Opinion on the Iron and Wooden Ploughs," 1807).[129]

Despite the blessing of the tsar and a growing number of adherents,[130] English farming continued to make slow and chequered progress in the new century. What popularity it enjoyed at the end of the eighteenth century was due in large measure to Russians who had studied or lived in England and who were affected by the enthusiasm of Father Samborskii, a figure of considerable importance if of little lasting achievement in the development of Russian agriculture. Men from widely differing social positions from serfs to aristocrats benefitted from their years in England and some came to occupy positions, as professors of agriculture, as office-holders in the Free Economic Society and as authors, which allowed them to air their views. The material assembled in this chapter reveals that much more was known among Russians about English farming than is generally appreciated and allows a number of interesting and talented individuals to be rescued from comparative or total oblivion. They were among those who, to paraphrase the words of Mordvinov, "looked to England and were convinced that agriculture after the English model was Russia's salvation."

CHAPTER 4
RUSSIAN STUDENTS AT OXFORD AND CAMBRIDGE

The *Scots Magazine* with its customary attention to news items concerning Russia noted in November, 1771, that "Such is the increasing taste for politeness in Russia, that their youth are all educated in foreign academies; and there are at this time several Russian young gentlemen in our own universities."[1] Although the story of Russian students at British universities in the eighteenth century has its cautionary preface in the experiment of Boris Godunov from the beginning of the preceding century, it is likely that neither Peter the Great nor Catherine the Great knew of it or its sorry outcome; if they did, it would have counted for nothing in their own ambitious programmes of foreign education for certain categories of their subjects.

Peter had no intention of sending students to Oxford and Cambridge: they were destined in the main for the fleet and the shipyards, but he himself did not miss the opportunity to visit Oxford in 1698. Many legends and, as befits the main actor, "tall stories" surround Peter's visit to England in general, and one indeed is connected with his brief excursion to Oxford on 9-10 April, when among the honours allegedly accorded him by the university authorities was the degree of Doctor of Laws. As Leo Loewenson has shown, however, the truth is somewhat different. Peter arrived, incognito as was his wont, in the city late in the evening of Friday, 9 April. The next morning he paid visits to a bookshop, the Sheldonian Theatre (where the University Press was accommodated) and the Ashmolean, where he was seen and described by the museum's assistant keeper, William Williamson, as "a very uncouth fellow," in a long black wig and with dirty hands.[2] After only a few minutes at the museum he went on to the chapel of Trinity College, but on seeing that he had been recognized and that curious crowds were gathering, he decided to leave immediately and return to London. Peter, then, was not the first Russian to receive an Oxford degree, but he might be seen perhaps as the first Russian student, although, as another contemporary English source put it, he left "without viewing those curiosities he intended."[3] Some seventy-two years later, in October, 1770, Oxford was visited by another notable Russian, not the autocrat, but an aristocrat who was in some measure (large by her own estimate) instrumental in engineering Catherine the Great's accession. Princess Ekaterina Romanovna Dashkova (1743-1810), sister to both Vorontsovs who were Russian ambassadors to England, stayed three days in Oxford and was able to visit and describe many things in the city and university, including some which no doubt would have appealed to Peter. In her description of the Ashmolean she mentions "the collections for the study of natural history, both preserved in spirits and stuffed."[4] In the strict sense of course she was no more of a student than Peter was, but while in Oxford she met on at least three occasions a group of six young men who were the first Russian students admitted to Oxford colleges and included two who indeed received Oxford degrees. Inevitably it is their activities over a nine-year period which are best known, but they were preceded by other Russians, some of whom studied briefly in Oxford.

Among the men who accompanied Peter I to England in 1698 was Petr Vasil'evich Postnikov (1666-1731?), who three years earlier had become the first Russian to receive the degree of Doctor of Medicine from a foreign university (Padua) and had joined the tsar in Holland. Postnikov remained in England for a short time after the tsar had left with instructions to visit schools and academies. His travels took him to Oxford where he visited the Bodleian Library and acquired a catalogue of its books to send to Peter.[5] The library was visited some years later by another close associate of Peter's, his ambassador Boris Kurakin, who found it "not to be compared with the one in Rome."[6] The names of neither Postnikov nor Kurakin appear in the admissions register of the Bodleian, but the names of three other men, all of foreign stock but whose lives and activities were closely bound with Peter's Russia, do. On 27 August 1709, the register was signed by Petrus Müller and Laurentius Blumentrost, each designating himself as "Moscoviensis."[7] Both indeed were born in or around Moscow, Müller (Petr Petrovich Miller, d. 1745) the son of the German owner of an ironworks at Ugodka near Moscow, and Blumentrost (Lavrentii Lavrent'evich), the youngest son (1692-1755) of the head of the Russian medical chancery. After receiving their early education at home, both matriculated at the University of Halle, Müller in 1700 in the theological faculty and Blumentrost presumably in the medical faculty. Müller remained at Halle until 1704, when he began extensive travels through Europe. Although he is known to have been in Paris in 1710, his visit to England and Oxford in the previous year seems to be an episode unknown to scholars who have written about his activities.[8] He was a fervent Pietist who maintained close links with German scholars as well as with prominent Russians such as Archbishop Feofan Prokopovich and was active among other things in the acquisition of Russian books and manuscripts for the Halle Pietist, A. H. Francke. Presumably it was the wish to see the rare manuscripts and printed books held in the Bodleian which brought him to Oxford. Blumentrost's biographer writes that by the age of fifteen he had already attended lectures on medicine at Halle and Oxford, which would suggest that he was in Oxford from about 1707.[9] Possibly Müller accompanied him to Oxford at that time. Blumentrost then went to Leyden, where he defended his doctoral dissertation "De secretione animali" in 1714. In 1715 he was back in Russia, where Müller was to be found, close

to the family of Prince Demetrius Kantemir, whose son, Antiokh, was later
to become Russian ambassador in London. Although relatively little is known
of Müller's later life (he inherited his father's iron-works which was sold
off in the 1730s, when Müller was active in organizing schools in the Urals),
Blumentrost's career flourished. He was soon sent abroad again to consult
with eminent foreign doctors about Peter the Great's illnesses and took the
opportunity to widen his medical skills. He was also instrumental in securing
the purchase of Professor Ruysch's famous anatomical collection which became the basis of Peter's Kunstkamera. On the death of Peter's Scottish
physician, Robert Erskine, in 1718, Blumentrost was appointed to replace
him, with responsibility for the Kunstkamera. For all his eminence as a
doctor, Blumentrost's chief claim to fame is in connection with the establishment of the Academy of Sciences, of which he became the first president
shortly after the death of Peter in 1725.

Directly linked with the projected academy was the visit to England of
Johann Daniel Schumaker (1690-1761). An Alsatian by birth and educated
at the University of Strasbourg, he came to Russia in 1714 as assistant to
Dr. Erskine and retained his position under Blumentrost, who also made him
imperial librarian and custodian of the Kunstkamera. In 1721 Schumaker was
sent to Germany, France, and England to establish contacts with foreign
scholars and societies and to visit libraries and cabinets of natural history.[10]
Although relations between Russia and England were at this period particularly strained, he was well received in London, particularly by members
of the Royal Society. He also visited Oxford and Cambridge, saw the collections at the Ashmolean, and entered his name in the Bodleian register on
1 February 1722.[11]

Neither Müller nor Blumentrost left accounts of their visits to Oxford
and Schumaker's report is informative but not extensive.[12] However, an idea
of what they saw and possibly did in early eighteenth-century Oxford might
be gleaned from the diary of Zacharias von Uffenbach (1683-1734), the
noted German bibliographer and scholar who shared similar interests and
background. Uffenbach provides detailed and frequently negative remarks on
Oxford personalities and customs and one can only hope that the Russians
had less difficulty in finding what they wanted in the Bodleian and were more
impressed with its catalogues and librarians than he. He gives also an amusing
description of the oath "pro admissione ad Bibliothecam" which he in 1710,
and undoubtedly Müller and Blumentrost in the previous year, were obliged
to take:

> We were conducted by the Proctor into a small room where he gave us
> the oath to read over: when this had been done, he took a little Greek
> testament out of a bag, placed it open into my hand and himself read
> the oath aloud, whilst I laid the two fingers of my right hand on the

open book and was not allowed to speak it after him. When the oath had been read to us, I was about to return the book, but he guided my hand with the book to my mouth, so that I should kiss it—which is said to be a custom in England for all oaths. Thereupon he asked my brother whether he would also remember what he had read himself and what had just now been read to him. On his answering in the affirmative, he was also obliged to kiss the book. Thereupon the Proctor presented us with a Latin *Schedula* or *Copia Decreti Senatus Academici*, which stated as follows, that our request to be admitted to the library was granted, and the Librarian was ordered to take us up. After we had each of us paid eight shillings, and the Sub-Librarian Mr. Crab had taken possession of the *Schedula* or *Copia Decreti*, we were given permission to go into the library every day from 8 to 11 in the morning and from 2 to 5 in the afternoon with the exception of Saturday, when the library closes at 4 o'clock.[13]

Eight years after Schumaker's visit to England and five years after the Academy of Sciences had begun its activities, a serving Academician, rather than a prospective or former one, the historian Gerard-Friedrich Müller (Fedor Ivanovich Miller) (1705-83) came to Oxford. He had been preceded the previous year by Christian Martini (1699-after 1739), one of the original members of the Academy, Professor of Physics from 1725, Professor of Logic and Metaphysics from 1726.[14] Martini had resigned in 1729, together with Professor Bernoulli, Herman and others, and Müller was sent abroad with a view to attracting new full and honorary members of the Academy. He arrived in London at the end of August, 1730, and visited Sir Hans Sloane, who introduced him to eminent British scientists and promoted his election to the Royal Society (10 December 1730, shortly after Müller's departure). In all Müller spent two and a half crowded months in England, failing to get to Cambridge through lack of time, but visiting Oxford, where he was much taken with the Bodleian.[15]

Both Schumaker and Müller were established scholars and as such essentially peripheral to the discussion of Russian *students* at Oxford, but their visits are mentioned for the links which were maintained with Oxford rather than with Cambridge throughout the century and for the particular reputation Oxford seems to have held until the 1770s, when Edinburgh became a more fashionable rival. The visit in 1748 of Ivan Ivanovich Taubert (1717-71), sub-librarian of the Academy and son-in-law of Schumaker, may be seen in the same light. Taubert had a similar brief to Schumaker's and Müller's—the fostering of relations with the Royal Society, but his visit is of special interest for the particular contacts he made with two Oxford professors, James Bradley (1692-1762), Savilian Professor of Astronomy at Oxford since 1721 and Astronomer Royal since the death of Halley in 1742, and Humphry Sibthorp (d. 1784), Professor of Botany. Taubert visited Sibthorp in Oxford and received from him a large quantity of rare American and foreign seeds to be dispatched to the Academy. Sibthorp expressed his wish to receive Russian seeds and plants in return and to enter into regular correspondence with the Academy.[16] Bradley, reported Taubert, "offered very willingly his services to the Academy and mentioned the most skilled makers of astronomical instruments, from whom I obtained lists of those instruments which are currently most frequently used."[17]

By the time Bradley was visited by Taubert, he had already come into contact with at least one *bona fide* Russian student. Between 1729 and 1760 Bradley read a regular course of lectures (seventy-nine times in all) on experimental philosophy at Oxford. Charging fees of £3. 3s. a course, he had an average audience over the years of fifty-seven. The names of students attending between 1746 and 1760 are extant in one of his registers and in the lists of foreigners at the end appear Crevoff in 1747, Chelverikoff in 1749 and "three Russians" in 1759.[18] It has not been possible to establish the identities of the last three unnamed students,[19] but the typically distorted surnames conceal two of three students sent to England in 1745 by the Russian Naval Academy. The death at the end of 1739 of Henry Farquharson, its Scottish-born professor of mathematics who had been recruited in 1698 by Peter the Great, led the Naval Academy to attempt to find a British replacement through the offices of the Russian envoy in London, Semen Kirilovich Naryshkin. Eventually, by 1745, four possible candidates had been found, but the salaries and conditions they demanded persuaded the Naval Academy to pursue the alternative course which the Russian authorities were naturally predisposed to adopt in all branches of knowledge whenever it seemed practicable. Given a number of teachers and apprentices already schooled by Farquharson himself, the Naval Academy selected three of them to go to England to acquire further expertise and primarily a good knowledge of the English language which would enable them to translate important English works on navigational subjects. A teacher, Aleksei Iureevich Krivov, and two apprentices, Mikhail Chetverikov and Petr Kostiurin, arrived in London at the end of 1745 with a salary of 400 rubles a year for three years. They were to request an extension of their stay so that they could undertake a voyage to America and were allowed to stay a further year, but clearly told that they could get all the practical sea experience they needed on the journey back to St. Petersburg.[20] The three men obviously spent most of their time learning the English language, probably in London under the supervision of the embassy, but Krivov and Chetverikov in particular made such good progress that by the end of 1748 they had completed translations of a number of English works on navigation which they sent back to St. Petersburg, together with the English originals, for examination. The works were passed on to Professors Müller, Lomonosov, and Trediakovskii of the Academy of Sciences for judgment and on 10/21 March 1749 Trediakovskii reported that the translations were basically satisfactory and recommended publication.[21] Bradley's courses of lectures in Oxford provided first Krivov, then Chetverkiov with an excellent opportunity to pursue their studies with the most noted astronomer of the day, the father of modern observational astronomy. In his lectures, which were never written out in full or published, but delivered from notes, he made use of apparatus, much of which he seems to have constructed himself and which included "a small machine to illustrate the doctrine of abberation," that is, the situation of the fixed stars from the progressive motion of light combined with the earth's annual motion which he had established in 1727.[22] In 1752 George II granted Bradley a pension "in consideration of his great skill and knowledge in the several branches of astronomy, and other parts of the mathematics, which have proved so useful to the trade and navigation of this kingdom"[23] and recognition came from academies throughout Europe.

His election to honorary membership of the Russian Academy of Sciences followed on 18/27 August 1754 (at the same time as Sibthorp's). By that time Krivov and the others were back in Russia. All three presented further translations, Krivov of a work on practical astronomy, Chetverikov of the second part of a series of lectures on natural philosophy delivered in Dublin and Kostiurin, who seems to have studied for a while at Cambridge,[24] of a treatise on the magnet and the variation of the compass. Nothing is known of the further activities of Krivov and Kostiurin, but it is to be supposed that they proceeded to teach at the Naval Academy. Chetverikov was raised to the status of teacher and in 1759 published a work on latitude calculation, *Tablitsa raznosti shiriny i otshestviia ot meridiana*, which was re-issued in a revised form in 1765 by A. Panov and later in the century was incorporated with corrections into a navigational work by Nikolai Kurganov, the author of the famous *Pis'movnik* and a prominent instructor at the Naval Academy.

II

Krivov and Chetverikov are examples of the relatively few Russians known to have studied at British Universities during the period following Peter the Great's death up to the accession of Catherine the Great. In Catherine's reign the trickle became a comparative flood. Many Russians had, of course, studied at continental universities and received degrees before Catherine's accession, and while it is true that the first Russians to receive degrees at a British university did so during her reign, the first of these students were sent abroad in the last year of Elizabeth's. Semen Efimovich Desnitskii (d. 1789) and Ivan Andreevich Tret'iakov (1735-76) were originally destined to study at Oxford, but were finally sent, for financial than academic reasons, to Glasgow, where their careers between 1761 and 1767 will be discussed in the following chapter. The Russian links with Oxford in the reign of Catherine continued with Mikhail Ivanovich Pleshcheev, signing the Bodleian register in

June, 1762, as "Michael Pleshcoff, Russus."[25]

Pleshcheev, who was to be a counsellor in the Russian embassy in London for over a decade, seems to have arrived in England that year with the new Russian Minister Plenipotentiary, Count Aleksandr Romanovich Vorontsov. He was well known to all the members of the Vorontsov family and it was probably Princess Dashkova, who met him in England later in 1770, who encouraged him after his own return to Russia in 1773 to submit the series of articles for which he is principally known for publication in the *Trudy* ("Works") of the Free Russian Society at Moscow University. His first contribution appeared in 1775 in volume two, where Dashkova's diary of her visit to Oxford and other towns was also published. Under the eloquent pseudonym of "Angloman" ("Anglomaniac"), Pleshcheev accompanied his translation of Hamlet's "To be, or not to be" with a letter in which he expressed his appreciation of Shakespeare's genius and his criticism of Voltaire's "version" of the same monologue.[26] Apart from its significance in the context of early Russian knowledge of Shakespeare,[27] Pleshcheev's work is a reflection of a generally profound interest in English culture, which is confirmed in further contributions published the following year. The first, which is a translation from English of a letter proposing ways of perfecting the English language, is supplied with notes by Pleshcheev, highlighting the analogies with the Russian situation and, en passant, voicing his opinion of the lack of a "metaphysical language," which is a striking anticipation of Alexander Pushkin's some fifty years later;[28] the second is a poem entitled "Stikhi pisannye odnim Oksfortskim Studentom smotria na Lokkov portret" ("Lines written by an Oxford Student on looking at a Portrait of Locke"), which may be from an English original but is followed by an editorial note which says that it "was composed by the Anglomaniac."[29] If it is Pleshcheev's composition, it is interesting not only for its eulogy of Locke's teaching but also for its conscious parading of the author as "an Oxford student," some thirteen years after his name was registered at the Bodleian. There is no record of Pleshcheev having registered at an Oxford college, but it is probable that over the years he went to Oxford to hear occasional courses of lectures. Pleshcheev's chief, Count A. R. Vorontsov, was himself at Oxford in 1763, when he became in all probability the first Russian to receive an Oxford degree—an honorary DCL at the "Encaenia in honour of the Peace" on 7 July.[30] Pleshcheev may have accompanied him on that occasion, but at all events he was briefly back in Oxford in April, 1766, escorting the first Russians to become full-time Oxford students.

On 6/17 May 1765 I. I. Melissino (1718-95), Procurator of the Holy Synod, received instructions from Catherine II to select ten outstanding students from religious seminaries who were to be sent to England "to study the higher sciences at the universities of Oxford and Cambridge for the benefit of the state."[31] Catherine at this time was greatly occupied with questions of educational reform in Russia and she had appointed a special commission in 1764 to make recommendations. Among other things, Catherine was determined to raise the intellectual level of the Russian clergy and to effect certain reforms within the Orthodox Church which would bring it in line with western Protestant practices. Such views would find a firm supporter in Melissino himself.[32] Catherine also probably envisaged the eventual establishment of a theological faculty at Moscow University, but although subsequently in 1773 recommendations were made, the project came to nothing.[33] Acting immediately on the empress's instructions, the Synod asked the various seminaries and religious academies to send candidates both as students and for the two projected posts of "inspector." The response was so great that eventually nineteen suitable inspectors and students assembled in Petersburg by the summer of 1765. Catherine granted permission for all to go to England, but for some reason the Synod decided to form three groups from a total reduced to sixteen by illness and withdrawal and to send them to Oxford, Leyden, and Göttingen. Cambridge was no longer mentioned and the notoriously high cost of living in England may have been a factor in selecting alternative European universities, as well as a wish to diversify the students' educational environment.

The groups destined for Leyden and Göttingen remained in Russia until June, 1766, but the first group, six strong rather than the originally proposed ten, left Petersburg for London on 11/22 November 1765. In charge was Vasilii Nikitich Nikitin (1737-1809) and he was accompanied by a clerk from Catherine's private office, Aleksandr Sergeevich Bukhovetskii, and four seminarists: Prokhor Ignat'evich Suvorov (1750-1815), Semen Ivanovich Matveevskii (b. 1748?), Mikhail Fedorovich Bykov and Aleksei Georgievich Levshinov. Nikitin and Levshinov were from the Moscow Slavono-Greek-Latin Academy and both were sons of priests. Nikitin had entered the Academy in 1748 and in 1761 had become a teacher of Greek and Hebrew. Levshinov was a student of philosophy and the youngest of three brothers, the eldest of whom was at that time spiritual tutor to the Grand Duke Paul and was to become the most powerful and famed cleric in Russia, archbishop of Moscow and archimandrite of the Troitsa Monastery, Platon (1737-1812). It was Aleksei Levshinov whom Count Nikita Panin (1718-83), Paul's tutor and effectively in charge of Russian foreign affairs, was to commend to the special care of the Russian embassy in London.[34] Matveevskii was recommended by the archbishop of St. Petersburg and Bykov by the Troitsa Monastery. The last of students, Suvorov, was to more than justify the warm recommendation from the rector of the Tver' seminary, who described him as excelling all his fellow students there in application, conduct and ability.

The students were preceded to London by a letter from Panin which included a copy of the detailed instructions given to the group, together with an order for 5000 rubles, which were to be distributed at set intervals to the students so that "they could maintain themselves without excess but equally without want." As will be seen Russian calculations as to the cost of living in England were as always hopelessly wrong. The instructions cover under twenty-four heads the students' courses of study, their duties and obligations, rules as to conduct and dress and outline the special responsibilities of the inspector. The students were specifically required to study Greek, Hebrew and French—it was suggested that they already had a good grounding in Latin and that English would be learnt as a matter of expediency, while German and other Eastern languages were left to individual students' propensities. Other required subjects were moral philosophy, history, particularly ecclesiastical, geography, and mathematical principles. Particular provisions were made for theology: students were encouraged to hear sermons, paying attention "to the purity of their language and to the style of delivery," but the inspector should be alive to doctrinal differences and possible contamination. The inspector's duties extended to every aspect of the students' life: he had to make sure that they performed Orthodox services together and that they went at least once a year to London to take communion with the embassy chaplain; he had to be attentive to their dress, their good conduct and clean living, the company they kept, where they walked and how they relaxed; he was to chastise them, first privately, then if necessary, before their fellows, and ultimately threaten them with the next boat home. Last but not least, as inspector and leader, he was expected to excel all of them in his studies.[35]

The students arrived in London early in 1766, and were taken to Oxford in April by Pleshcheev, armed with letters of recommendation from Lord Litchfield.[36] There they wer visited during the summer by the new Russian ambassador, Count Musin-Pushkin, who reported back to Petersburg that "he hoped not without reason that they would soon be in a position to hear and understand public lectures and would bring their country the benefits expected of them."[37] During the following two years the students virtually disappear: almost nothing is known about their activities or precise whereabouts. In October, 1768, they became members of Oxford colleges; up to that time they had obviously lived in private lodgings, devoting their energies to acquiring a very necessary grounding in English, of which none had the slightest knowledge before their arrival, and to other studies under private tutors. From a document deposited with the Chancellor's court of the University, we learn for example that Matveevskii "was for some time under the tuition of the late Reverend Mr. Stubbs, and whilst he continued under his tuition, there was . . . paid for such tuition after the rate of twenty pounds a year."[38] Subsequently Matveevskii became a member of Merton, Bykov and Suvorov of Queen's, and Levshinov and Nikitin of St. Mary Hall. There is no precise information about Bukhovetskii, but it seems probable that he entered University College: his tutor in 1770 was William Scott, a Fellow of that college.[39]

What sort of place was Oxford at this period? Almost without exception critics both in the eighteenth century (one thinks of such as Jeremy Bentham, Edward Gibbon, and Adam Smith) and since (Christopher Wordsworth, Godley, Hargreaves-Mawdsley) see it as a place of torpor and stagnation, in a state of "euthanasia," as one puts it, or "at the nadir of somnolence," in the words of another.[40] Even Princess Dashkova notes that the University "has now fallen far from what it was."[41] The satires and poems of the period dwell on the free and easy life of the Fellows, the privileged gentlemen-commoners, the so-called "Smart" or "Lounger," who spends his day in idle pursuits, lolling in the fashionable coffee-houses, paying court to "the Toasts," as the belles of the day were known, partaking of a little sport—billiards or hunting or cricket or boating, drinking too heavily in the ale-houses and avoiding all study.

From the coffee-house then I to Tennis away,
And at five I post back to my college to pray:
I sup before eight, and secure from all duns,
Undauntedly march to the *Mitre* or *Tuns*:
Where in Punch or good claret my sorrows I drown,
And toss off a bowl 'To the best in the town':
At one in the morning, I call what's to pay,
Then home to my College I stagger away.[42]

James Harris, the first Earl of Malmesbury, later British ambassador to the court of Catherine the Great, painted a similar picture of his life at Merton between 1763 and 1765:

In fact, the two years of my life I look back to as most unprofitably spent were those I passed at Merton. The discipline of the University happened at this particular moment to be so lax that a gentleman commoner was under no restraint, and never called on to attend lectures, chapel or hall. My tutor, an excellent and worthy man, according to the practice of all tutors at that moment, gave himself no concern about his pupils, I never saw him but during a fortnight when I took into my head to be taught trigonometry. The set of men with whom I lived were very pleasant, but very idle fellows. Our life was an imitation of High Life in London; luckily drinking was not the fashion, but what we did drink was claret, and we had our regular round of evening card parties, to the great annoyance of our finances. It has often been a matter of surprise to me how so many of us made our way so well in the world, and so creditably.[43]

The professors are portrayed as reluctant to lecture and the Fellows as loathe to tutor. Serious study is said to have engaged but few of the Fellows, who tended to enjoy their dinners too well and drink too deep from the bottles in the college cellars. They engaged in internal politics, bent on preserving their privileged status quo, and took infinite interest in the college accounts and appointments, on the lookout themselves for the better Preferments and college livings, when marriage should decree that they at last abandon their asylum. The Russians would find an Oxford punctilious about class distinctions, attentive to regulations on dress and headgear, an Oxford rigid in its adherence to the Church of England and true blue in its politics, still tainted by its adherence to the Jacobite cause. Of course, they found much to respect and commend; they met students keen to study and professors prepared to teach, and they never had the money to indulge themselves in much social intercourse, although one was to contract for a tutor in a coffee-house and another to run up a fat buttery bill for wines and spirits. They were also in Oxford at a time when it was given a major facelift. In 1771 work began on the construction of a new market, on the demolition and replacement of Magdalen Bridge, the removal of the remaining old gates of the city, a general improvement of the streets by paving and lighting. A year earlier in 1770 the new Radcliffe Infirmary was opened.

In the 1760s and 1770s there was a considerable increase in expenses for Oxford undergraduates, which only added to the generally parlous financial position of the Russians. A writer in the *Gentleman's Magazine* in 1771 suggested that "a complaint is daily made that the admissions into our Colleges are much fewer than they formerly were. This diminution is attributed partly to the perhaps unavoidable increase of the expense of an Academical Education."[44] It is obvious that for the very beginning their allowances were inadequate and they became woefully so when the students moved into colleges and when at the same time at least three of them suffered prolonged and costly illnesses. The reasons for moving into college were obvious: they were able to enjoy the considerable academic and material advantages and privileges available to people on the inside of a system in which the university signified little and the college virtually all. The cost, however, became clear to the Russian ambassador only early in 1771 at the time of the departure for Russia for the first of the students, Levshinov. Levshinov had spent two years at St. Mary Hall, pursuing studies in theology, dialectics, ecclesiastical and general history, and to the obvious consternation of Musin-Pushkin running up debts of £180. In his explanation Levshinov had put the blame on their move into college and on to the delays in receiving money from Russia, which obliged them to negotiate loans at crippling rates. Musin-Pushkin told Nikitin that he had always opposed the move into college, but that living in college did not explain why eight times as much money was owed by Levshinov for gloves and chocolate as for books.[45] In a series of letters throughout 1771 Nikitin mixed abject apologies for possible excesses in their way of life with a detailed and spirited account of what living in Oxford involved. Reiterating Levshinov's reasons for their financial plight, Nikitin sent a list of their debts and expenditure. In February, 1771, the debts of the group stood at £1242. 6s. 9d., with an extra £562. 9s. 11d owing for exceptional expenditure, primarily medicines and treatment. They were beset by creditors, as the following passage well illustrates:

> For cloth part was paid in August 1769, but since that time we have not been in a position to pay. The doctor for Semen Matveevskii has not been paid since May 1769, since when S. Matveevskii has three times been grievously ill with his eyes, and a doctor was necessary on each occasion. I have not paid the doctor for a year, Mikhailo Bykov since last year. None of us has paid for medicines since 1767. Some have been owing for coal for two years, others for less. The tailor has not been paid since August 1767. For stockings, shirts, etc. since last year. Matveevskii has not paid for tea, sugar, etc. since 1768.[46]

He explained that on their move to college they were obliged to pay caution money, which varied according to college, as did the expenditure on rooms and commons. Some of them faced particular problems. Bukhovetskii was given a set of rooms in a poor state of repair. He was obliged to engage bricklayers, carpenters and decorators to make his rooms habitable. The Russians were dogged by ill health, almost always by afflictions to the eyes, an indication, if the ambassador needed one, that the students were working assiduously rather than indulging in "the intemperance and indulgence" with which Panin was later to accuse them.[47] Bykov and especially Matveevski were so seriously and consistently ill that they could not continue their studies and it was decided to send them home in 1771. They were due to leave early in the year, but it was July before they eventually set sail. Matveevskii had fallen so ill again that it was feared he would become totally blind. He recovered his sight in one eye and had a long and inevitably costly period of recuperation before he could leave. By the summer of 1771 only Nikitin, Suvorov, and Bukhovetskii remained but they continued to be harrassed by debts and even threatened with debtors' prison. The Russian authorities simply stopped sending money for their maintenance between 1772 and 1774. In January, 1773, Musin-Pushkin wrote to Petersburg, describing their situation and explaining that "they are mistrusted by everyone to such a degree that no one will feed them on credit or even loan the most essential things."[48] Nikitin described the worsening situation to Father Samborskii, chaplain to the Russian church in London, in a letter of 18 November 1773: "I would be glad to go to prison if that would only satisfy our creditors. But some merchants have thought up yet another way of making me wretched. Mr. Prince and a few others have decided to write to the English Ambassador in Petersburg, requesting he should inform Her Majesty that English merchants are unjustly being refused payments for things which we have taken."[49] He added that he was reluctant to accept charity from English friends when he should be able to rely on his own people, but only in October, 1774, did Panin send the money to pay their debts and to meet the expenses of their return journey. By that time, however, Nikitin was involved in a protracted and unpleasant case before the Chancellor's Court.

In June, 1774, Richard Davies, Sub-Warden of Merton, brought was was called a "libel" action against Nikitin for non-payment of tutorial fees allegedly incurred by Matveevskii.[50] The disputed sum was £60, which was £20 for each of the years 1769, 1770, and 1771 during which Matveevskii had been at Merton. The case was resolved only on 24 February 1775 and was something of a *cause célèbre* in Oxford that year. The well-known diarist, the Reverend James Woodforde, noted: "Very few at the High Table to day on Account of many going to hear a Trial in the Vice-Chancellors Court between Davies of Merton Coll one Niketen a Russian concerning the Tutorage of one Mattafusci. Holmes pleaded & very well indeed for Davis, and one Archibald Mac-Donald a London Counsellor for the Russian & he came on Purpose—It lasted from one o'clock till five, when the Judge, Jumper Cox, gave it entirely against Davis & all Costs and Damages to be paid by Davis. Davis intends appealing to the Court of Delegates of Congregation."[51] Thus was British justice upheld in allegedly xenophobic Tory Oxford.

The depositions of Nikitin to the Court provide some interesting sidelights on Oxford and Matveevskii's life at Merton. One of the points at issue was the status of Matveevskii at the college. Davies was claiming fees on the scales apparently paid by Gentlemen-commoners and bachelors and he called as witnesses the butler, second butler, and sexton of Merton who testified that Matveevskii's name had been entered in the buttery book since 24 October 1768 "among the names of the Batchelors in the said Book, not where the names of Gentlemen Commoners are usually written but immediately under the Batchelors where Post Masters and Commoners are placed on taking their Batchelors Degrees."[52] Nikitin argued that Matveevskii "could not be deemed to have any claim to the rank of a Gentleman Commoner, nor looked upon as such in the said College, as he, the said Simeon Matfievskoi paid his caution or Deposit money and entrance fees as a Commoner," although he conceded that he sat with the bachelors "as a compliment paid him by the Society merely on account of his being a Foreigner, and not as a Gentleman Commoner." This was to establish that Matveevskii was liable only to pay "eight guineas a year for Tuterage or thereabouts." Nikitin was also insistent that Matveevskii was under Davies's care for two years at the most and that although Matveevskii continued to reside at Merton until July, 1771, he had withdrawn from his studies in 1770.[53] Nikitin's case is substantiated by his letter of 6 March 1771 to Musin-Pushkin where he says that "at the end of the year 1770 I took him away from his tutor so that he should not pay him for a year for nothing."[54] Matveevskii originally entered Merton as Davies's pupil after coming to an arrangement with him in one of the coffee houses and without Nikitin's prior knowledge or consent. Nikitin in fact had intended Matveevskii to enter Hertford under the tuition of the Rev. Blany. Nikitin indeed took his duties as inspector very seriously and acquainted the various tutors with the study plans formulated by the Russian authorities.

All the students studied a wide range of subjects, to some degree, if unknowingly, in accord with the B.A. Provisions of the Laudian statutes of 1636 which laid down courses of study for the seven years between matriculations and the M.A. degree but which by the middle of the eighteenth century were largely inoperative.[55] Bykov and Suvorov at Queen's studied law, modern and ancient languages, theology, philosophy, and history, Bukhovetskii, philosophy and other sciences,[56] Matveevskii theology, philosophy, mathematics, civil law, and ancient languages. In accordance with the wishes of the Russian authorities, all the students requested annual testimonials from their tutors. Perhaps the most substantial and amusing was the one given on behalf of Bykov and Suvorov by the Rev. Stubb of Queen's in 1771.

They first studied jurisprudence, then Hebrew and theology. At the same time, occasionally diluting the serious with the gay, they read many volumes in Greek, Latin and English, some of which entertain with things which have happened, other with things, invented by the Muses; some abound in maxims and rules about righteous living and morals, others teach the elements of the highest sciences, useful in times of peace and of war. In particular, from their great love of the Greek language, they read that intricate [uzlovatyi] author, Thucidides. In short, both had come to that age when it is necessary to study not merely the names of things, but the things themselves, their nature, their causes and relationships. I am delighted to find in both of them such sharpness of intellect and power of reason that I believe they will never undertake anything without benefit. . . . From the beginning of the year they have worked at French with unbelievable diligence, but have not neglected either philosophy or history for which they have a particular bent and have continued to study Hebrew. It would take too long to list all the authors they have studied in the past year and with such success that they can interpret French, Greek, Latin and English authors without any difficulty. There was little problem over which preceptor or example they followed, for respecting reasons and the causes of things and not caring *who* said what, but only *what* was said, *why* and *whether it was just*, inspecting carefully, they acquired a truly mature opinion about everything and became completely proficient in philosophy.[57]

If the various testimonials are to be believed, all the Russian students showed a greater degree of application than the majority of Oxford undergraduates and although four of them returned to their native land without degrees they had more than acquired the grounding necessary for a B.A., which was usually taken after three or four years' residence. Indeed it has been said that "Oxford gave her degrees really for residence, on the basis of the plausible and pleasing convention that Universities being places of study are inhabited by students, and that residence implied the habit of serious study."[58] At the same time the actual B.A. examinations were a farce, well illustrated in the famous story of Lord Eldon, who as John Scott took his Bachelor's Degree on 20 February 1770. "I was examined in Hebrew and in History. 'What is Hebrew for the place of a skull?' I replied "Golgotha." 'Who founded University College?' I stated (though by the way, the point is sometimes doubted) "that King Alfred founded it." "Very well, Sir," said the Examiner, "you are competent for your degree.' "[59] Levshinov, Bykov, and Matveevskii left after not much more than two years in college, but Bukhovetskii, who remained until the beginning of 1775, might well have qualified by successful studies and a sufficient period of residence. It was left, however, to Suvorov and Nikitin to achieve the formal honours.

Nikitin, it will be remembered, was expected to excel and although the degree of Master of Arts he received *honoris causa* on 2 May 1770[60] might be seen as the University's recognition of the group sent by the great Catherine in the person of its leader, it was no less a tribute to Nikitin's abilities which he had already been given a notable opportunity to reveal. The previous year there had occured the transit of Venus over the sun, an event for which the scientific communities of Europe had been eagerly preparing for a number of years. It took place eight years after the previous transit in June, 1761, following a similar dual occurence in 1631 and 1639. In the preparations for observing the phenomenon the Russian Academy of Sciences played a key role, organizing a number of expeditions to set up observatories in various parts of the Russian Empire. There were to be no less than 149 observing stations throughout the world and the British, Danes, Swedes, and French sent expeditions to such places as California, the Hudson Bay, Tahiti, and Pekin. Although possibly mindful of the dangers inherent in inviting foreigners (in 1761 the French astronomer Jean Chappe d'Auteroche went to Siberia to observe the transit and afterwards wrote, in addition to his *Mémoire du passage de Vénus sur le soleil* (St. Petersburg, 1762), a *Voyage en Sibérie*, which incurred the wrath of Catherine and her riposte under the title of *L'Antidote*), the Academy president, Count V. G. Orlov allowed Louis Pictet and Henri Mallet from Geneva and Christian Maier from Manheim to come to Russia as observers. From 1767 the Academy was in correspondence with the Royal Society in London, negotiating the purchase of the best astronomical instruments and informing it of Russian preparations. In September, 1769, the Royal Society received a report about the Russian observations and Johann Euler was asked to send two copies of Russian printed reports.[61] By that time there had already arrived in St. Petersburg a letter containing information about the successful observation of the transit by Nikitin in Oxford, probably to the complete surprise of the Academy. The letter was written in Latin by Thomas Hornsby (1733-1810), Savilian Professor of Astronomy and Reader in Experimental Philosophy at Oxford, who declared that he "could not sufficiently praise the untiring application and profound love of philosophy and astronomy" of Nikitin, who "intended to devote himself completely to practical astronomy."[62] In a paper published in the Royal Society's *Philosophical Transactions* Hornsby gave a detailed account of the Oxford observations, which had allowed him to deduce a Solar Parallax of 8.78", virtually identical with the best modern results. Hornsby and seven assistants were involved, stationed at six different places in Oxford. In "an unfurnished room of the Hospital that commanded the north-west part of the horizon," wrote Hornsby, "Mr Nikitin of St Mary Hall, and inspector of the Russian gentlemen sent here for their education by the Empress of Russia, and Mr Williamson, of St Alban Hall, both well versed in the Mathematics, made . . . observations of the transit, with a reflector of 10 inches, and a refractor of 8 feet."[63] The observations were the culmination of a course of lectures which Hornsby had begun on 24 May. The prospectus, published on 9 May, announced "a Course of Lectures on the TRANSIT of VENUS. . . . In which the History of former Transits will be delivered; the Method of computing the Places of the Sun and Planets explained and exemplified in the Case of the ensuing Transit; the Method of computing the Effect of Parallax, and of finding the Places upon the Earth's Surface, where Observations may be made with the greatest Advantage, will be pointed out; and the manner of determining the Quantity of the Sun's Parallax from some of the Principal Observations made in the Year 1761 will be shown and illustrated by Examples."[64] Students were to be charged one guinea and were given a list of books to obtain, which included Sherwin's *Logarithms*, Halley's *Astronomical Tables* and the Abbé de la Caille's *Tables of the Sun*.

Nikitin had thus come under the wing of James Bradley's successor in the Savilian professorship and there is every reason to suppose that during the remaining six years of Nikitin's residence in Oxford they were in close and constant association. It was Hornsby who furnished Nikitin's annual testimonial, praising his outstanding work in astronomy, chemistry, and mathematics and arguing in 1773 for an extension of his stay in Oxford.[65] Although Hornsby was one of those professors specifically attacked in 1776 by Adam Smith for having "for these many years given up altogether, even the pretence of teaching," he was by other accounts a dedicated and energetic scholar and teacher.[66] A contemporary student, Henry Best, has left a warm and amusing description of his lectures, which he delivered in clear and precise language. He is perhaps best known for his efforts in establishing the Radcliffe Observatory. The conditions in which the transit of Venus was observed in 1769 made clear the crying need for adequate provision of a well-equipped observatory and in the previous year he had presented the University with a petition outlining his recommendations for a building and instruments. Work on the Radcliffe Observatory began in 1773, but it was completed only after Nikitin's departure.

Suvorov, whose praises had been so warmly sung by the late Rev. Stubb, continued to astonish his subsequent teachers. George Murthwaite, Fellow of Queen's, wrote in December, 1772, how he had been impressed during the twenty months Suvorov had been under his tutorship by his abilities and the unbelievable application he showed in his private studies and in following the courses of the professors, at least of those who read lectures, Murthwaite added in a pointed aside.[67] In 1773 Nikitin wrote on Suvorov's behalf to Musin-Pushkin, describing his outstanding work in mathematics and astronomy.[68]

The seal on the Oxford careers of Suvorov and Nikitin came on 2 June 1775 when they were both awarded the degree of Master of Arts by diploma. Nikitin and Suvorov and their Russian biographers (Sukhomlinov, Bobynin, and Aleksandrenko) made much of this award, and perhaps rightly so. In his service record (*posluzhnoi spisok*) of 1793 Nikitin describes it as "an unusual honour for foreigners . . . which gave me the right to all the advantages and privileges of that learned society"; in Suvorov's record, this is rendered as "the right to enjoy not only the advantages of that learned society but also all the privileges of a native Englishman."[69] Musin-Pushkin in a letter to Panin dated 2 June 1775 on the eve of their departure from England wrote: "I consider it my duty to do justice before your Excellency to their notable successes in the sciences and their exemplary conduct. These brought them the highest respect and love of all worthy and learned man. The University of Oxford indeed gave them public and highly flattering proof of this by raising them to maître-ès-arts out of respect for their worth and without any outside petitioning, and moreover against a strong oppositional party."[70] This last enigmatic phrase had hitherto elicited no comment, but it is substantiated by yet another entry in the Woodforde diaries. "At 12, went to the Convocation House, where it was proposed to confer the Degree of Master of Arts by diploma on Mr. Nikitin and Mr. Sufferof two Russians that have been in the University for 9 years—There were many non Placets from many Parts of the House, therefore the Proctors took each Members Voice by which the Placets had the Majority—I was a Placet. The Convocation House very full on the Occasion."[71] Such divisions over the award of the M.A. degree were not uncommon in eighteenth-century Oxford and candidates were constantly rejected. The rejections were motivated more often than not by political and moral rather than intellectual considerations. One can only conjecture why there were so many non placets. Possibly in some cases the reasons were political and xenophobic, but it seems more likely that many remembered the recent case of Davis against Nikitin and took an opportunity of showing their displeasure at the verdict. But Nikitin and Suvorov had obviously made many friends.

Apart from their tutors and professors it is difficult nevertheless to list with any certainty who their particular friends might have been. There was, however, one closed society of which both Suvorov and Nikitin were members, and to which once again Woodforde is the key. His diary entry for 21 April 1774 includes the following: "I went with Holmes today to the Free-Masons Lodge held this day at the New Inn, was there admitted a Member of the same and dined & spent the afternoon with them. . . . Paid on Admission for Fees &c. 3:5:0). It is a very honourable as well as charitable Institution & much more than I could conceive it was. Am very glad in being a Member of it."[72] Throughout the following weeks until his eventual departure from Oxford in May, 1776, Woodforde diligently attended meetings of the Lodge and entered details of the brothers present and the bestowal of the various masonic degrees. On·23 February 1775 among the list of those present is "Suzzerof the Russian," which is followed by the information that "Kempson & Suzzerof made Apprentices & Fellow Crafts."[73] Suvurov is mentioned as attending on 9 March, and on 16 March he was raised to Master Mason. Suvorov's name appears for the last time on 1 June when he became Junior Warden of the Lodge.[74] Suvorov thus achieved a position of some standing in the Lodge, although Woodforde himself seems not to have mixed socially with him. Woodforde makes no mention of Nikitin in connection with masonry, but fortunately the Lodge's records survive and have been the subject of a detailed paper published in 1909 under the title "Two Old Oxford Lodges" by E. L. Hawkins. Nikitin in fact was admitted to the Lodge and raised to Fellow Craftsman on 4 May 1775 and the following week made a Master Mason, during a short period of absence from Oxford by Woodforde.[75]

The "Lodge of Alfred," to which Suvorov, Nikitin and Woodforde belonged, was warranted on 2 December 1769 and existed until 10 February 1790. It was one of two lodges in Oxford, catering exclusively for "the gown," whereas "Constitution Lodge" (1770-89) served "the town." A full list of members of the Alfred Lodge has been supplied by Hawkins and it is not appropriate here to dwell on the people with whom Suvorov and Nikitin came into contact, other than to point out that its Master during the time of the Russians' attendance was the Rev. John Napleton (1739-1817), who in 1773 had written a pamphlet entitled *Considerations on the Public Exercises for the First and Second Degrees in·the University of Oxford*, which argued for reforms in the award of degrees and the institution of honours degrees. Undoubtedly Suvorov as Junior Warden would have known Napleton fairly well and have been abreast of the first important stirrings for educational reform. One must, nevertheless, exercise caution in suggesting more than a nodding acquaintance between the Russians and some of the Masons. It has only to be remembered that Richard Davis who brought the court action against Nikitin was also a member of the Alfred Lodge.

But one particular friend Nikitin had, who subsequently came into contact contact with other Russians visiting London and played an important if completely unsung role in part of their education. In the village of Plumtree near Nottingham there is on the wall to the right of the altar in the Church of St. Mary the Virgin a plaque "Sacred to the Memory of the Reverend James Williamson B.D. late of Hertford College, Oxford, and RECTOR of PLUMTREE NOTTINGHAMSHIRE: who spent a long life in the pursuit of literature and science at home and in other parts of Europe; embracing every opportunity to enrich his mind with various knowledge; but deriving his chief eminence from rare attainments in the higher branches of Mathematicks. He was born in the Capital of Murray in Scotland in the Year 1740; and died at the rectory of Plumtree on the third of January 1813." This was the James Williamson in whose company Nikitin had observed the transit of Venus in 1769. After studying at Aberdeen, Williamson went to Oxford in 1768, taking his B.A. in 1772 at St. Alban Hall and his M.A. in 1775, the same year as Nikitin, and eventually proceeding D.D. from Hertford in 1783. He was an outstanding mathematician and in a letter of January, 1770, wrote that "I believe were there a vacancy in the professorship of Geometry, few, if any would oppose me."[76] In 1779, an undergraduate, John James, junior, of Queen's, noted that "Hornsby, Professor of Astronomy, Williamson of Mathematics, and the Vinerian Professor [Richard Wooddeson], all of them clever, are either reading or preparing lectures at present."[77] At Aberdeen Williamson had been the friend and pupil of the noted poet and Professor of Moral Philosophy, James Beattie, and it is through his letters to Beattie over the period from 1768 to 1791 that we learn of his life in Oxford and London. There is no mention of Nikitin, but testimony to the friendship between the two is found in the diary of James Beattie himself, who came to Oxford in July, 1773, to receive the honorary degree of Doctor of Civil Laws. The entry for 8 July reads: "went wt Williamson to the Angel-Inn where I had left my baggage and from thence to St Mary Hall, where a Russian gentleman one Mr Niliken (a great friend of Williamson's) had a bed provided for me. Mr. N. was exceedingly kind and during my stay in Oxford did everything in his power to oblige me."[78] Beattie spent two nights at St. Mary Hall, dining there on the second with Williamson and Nikitin. Undoubtedly among the things they discussed were Beattie's "Essay on the Nature and Immutability of Truth" and particularly his poem "The Minstrel," which Williamson constantly mentioned in his letters and a copy of the first part of which he had presented to Thomas Gray in Cambridge on his *walk* from Aberdeen to Oxford in 1767. The ceremony at which Beattie received his degree was one of a number following the installation of Lord North as Chancellor of the University, and among the other recipients of degrees whom Nikitin may well have seen was Sir Joshua Reynolds. Nikitin's friendship with Williamson was founded on their mutual love of astronomy and mathematics and Nikitin's respect for his friend's abilities led him to introduce him to at least one other Russian who came to Oxford to study in 1775. The minutes of the Alfred Lodge held on 4 May, at which Nikitin was admitted, also record the presence as a visitor of "Bro. Karsakoff, of the Lodge of the Muses at Petersburgh in Russia."[79] This was Nikolai Ivanovich Korsakov (1749-88), an engineer officer who had been sent to Britain primarily to study canal construction. Both before and after his tour through England and Scotland to inspect factories and canals (May-December, 1776), Korsakov attended lectures at Oxford on higher mathematics and experimental physics and in an entry in his diary for January, 1773, he records his respect for both Williamson and Hornsby: "depuis quelque tems il y a à Oxford des professeurs fort habiles, dans ces sciences, et sur tout dans les matematiques, comme Mr Williamson, qui est un des plus subtils Mathematiciens, qu'il y ait en Angleterre; Mr Hornsby, professeur de physique experimentale; et à Astronomie, est aussi un homme fort renommé dans son genre."[80]

A decade after Korsakov wrote these lines, Nikitin and Suvorov, who had returned to Russia in the summer of 1775, renewed, as it were, their own links with Oxford and with Williamson in a work published by them in English and in London. *Elements of Plane and Spherical Trigonometry, Written Originally in Russian, and Translated into English by the Authors* appeared in 1787, at approximately the same time as the Russian version in St. Petersburg, with the dedication "To the University of Oxford, in testimonly of gratitude for the academical advantages, of which they were admitted to partake, during a residence of ten years; and for the honours conferred upon them" and with a long list of subscribers, prominent among whom was James Williamson. In a long preface, dated Cronstadt, 1 October 1786, the authors presented their work "as the fruit of that learning, which was so cordially and so liberally communicated to them in England."[81] They praised the British as great mathematicians and appended a list of authors consulted. In their conclusion they spoke of their intention to move next to Euclid and in their work to use the pioneer studies of Simpson and Williamson.[82] In fact, already in 1784 they had published their *Evklidovykh stikhii os'm' knig*, translated allegedly from the original Greek with corrections, corrections, which, in the view of a later Russian translator, "left scarcely a shadow of the original."[83]

At the end of his 1893 article Aleksandrenko writes that almost nothing is known about the fate of the various Russian students after their return from Oxford and refers merely to the fact that Suvorov was professor of mathematics at Moscow University at the beginning of the nineteenth century. Aleksandrenko's assertion is true only with respect to some and not all of the students; about the subsequent careers of Nikitin and Suvorov in particular a great deal is to be found. On 20/31 December 1771 the Holy Synod received official notification from the College of Foreign Affairs that Levshinov and Bykov had returned and undertook the business of finding them posts.[84] Levshinov, who had received special commendation for his diligent studies, became initially sacrist at the Moscow Uspenskii Cathedral, where his elder brother, Aleksandr, was dean. His duties included "the composition and delivery of sermons," but how much he was influenced by the Oxford ecclesiastical manner, which he and his fellows had been instructed to observe, is impossible to say. In January, 1776, he petitioned the Holy Synod for a new post, asserting that his worsening state of health made it difficult for him to take proper care of the vestments and other objects with which he was entrusted. The Synod agreed to his request and he became dean at the Spasskii Cathedral in the Kremlin.[85] He was still living in 1805, when his eldest brother, Archbishop Platon, told Reginald Heber that "his brother was, with many other young men intended for orders, sent over to England and was educated at Oxford; an experiment which, has not, apparently answered; he is only a secular priest, so that he has no opportunity of rising."[86] Bykov became a teacher of the upper classes at the seminary of the Troitsa Monastery in February, 1772, but was dismissed in 1773 on the orders of Platon for refusing to teach the catechism to the congregation.[87]

Having settled Levshinov and Bykov, the Synod apparently forgot about its remaining charges in Oxford until the Senate inquired after their whereabouts in 1780. The Synod in its turn addressed a note to the College of Foreign Affairs, which, one can only suppose in the absence of the requisite documents, informed it that all had long since returned.[88] Nothing is known about Bukhovetskii's fate, although it is probable that he again took up his post in the empress's secretariat. Of Matveevskii we have a mere glimpse: apparently restored to health relatively quickly, he was assigned in September, 1771, as interpreter to the British iron-masters Joseph Powell and Adam Ramage on their journey to the foundries at Lipetsk, near Voronezh.[89]

Within weeks of their return to St. Petersburg, Nikitin and Suvorov were assigned to the Naval Cadet Corps at Cronstadt on the specific orders of Catherine. The Corps' director, Admiral Ivan Logonovich Golenishchev-Kutuzov, entrusted to them the teaching of mathematics; Nikitin was asked to read a course of Wolffian mathematics and experimental physics, Suvorov to teach mathematics "by the reading of lectures after the university manner."[90] Nikitin also taught classes in Latin and Russian language and Suvorov, in mythology, ancient geography, English and literature. For almost twenty years Nikitin and Suvorov were to devote all their time and energy to the pedagogic needs of the Naval Cadet Corps, teaching the widest range of subjects, preparing study programmes and composing and translating textbooks. They were to move more or less in step up the table of ranks, receive the same honours and awards and retire within two years of each other. Their service records survive and show that on 1/12 November 1783 both were promoted to majors of the first rank (*premier-maior*) and Nikitin made Inspector of Classes in the Corps and Suvorov Assistant Inspector. On 17/28 November in the same year they were made members of the newly formed Russian Academy, at the same time, incidentally, as Catherine's librarian and court poet, Vasilii Petrov, who had also studied in England in the early 1770s. Undoubtedly, the Academy's president, Princess Dashkova, remembered them kindly from their Oxford days. On 22 September/3 October 1785 they were made knights of the order of St. Vladimir in the fourth class (a military order established by Catherine in 1782) and on 22 June/3 July 1791 they were raised to lieutenant-colonel, with the civil equivalent of which in the sixth rank, Collegiate Counsellor (*kollezhskii sovetnik*), they eventually retired. Nikitin retired in March, 1794, and was succeeded as Inspector by Suvorov, who remained in the post, however, only until 24 March/4 April 1795.[91] It was as if Suvorov felt lost without his constant companion and friend, for he was still only forty-five years of age. Indeed Nikitin and Suvorov were a sort of eighteenth-century Bobchinskii and Dobchinskii, or more kindly, in view of their constant authorial collaboration, the I'lf and Petrov of Russian mathematics. Sukhomlinov in his history of the Academy wrote: "Both participated in the composing of books in which it is impossible to say what is attributable to the one and what to the other. Even their affairs they conducted together, sending the Russian Academy letters under their joint signatures. To judge by their extant correspondence it would seem that not only did they live and work together, teach and study together, but even fell ill together, informing the Academy's secretary on one occasion, under their joint signature, that illness prevented them both from attending a meeting."[92]

As Academicians Nikitin and Suvorov proved conspicuously ineffectual. They were overwhelmed by the honour which had come to them "exceeding our every hope and expectation" and willingly involved themselves in the work of the Academy in the preparation of its dictionary. At least they undertook to gather all words beginning with the letter 'R', but a year later they were writing to the Academy's secretary regretting that their teaching in the Cadet Corps had prevented them from doing the work. They finished with assurances that they would speedily accomplish anything the Academy might entrust them with in the future, but the Academy seems not to have made any further demands. Nevertheless, in September, 1793, at a formal

gathering of the Cadet Corps, Suvorov in the course of a long and involved
oration on the occasion of the peace between the Russians and Turks combined fulsome eulogy of Catherine with praise of the Academy. He saw
monarch and Academy united in their love of all things Slav, particularly
the Slavonic language. Suvorov's own concern with the language, its character and enrichment, was passionate and deep-seated. Among the subjects
he eventually taught in the Cadet Corps were Russian grammar and style
and his views on the language were clearly revealed in his and Nikitin's
Euclid of 1784. There they stated that the Russian language "is extremely
abundant and rich in every way, excelling all modern European languages
and even Latin," a sentiment not unfamiliar to readers of Lomonosov and
Sumarokov. Suvorov and Nikitin systematically replaced foreign words by
Russo-Slavonic ones, declaring "Foreign words were introduced in Russia
by foreign scholars, i.e., by people who did not know Russian, and at a time
when we were not concerned with words: we needed then subjects, things,
not words. Many nations observe the rule of not using foreign words: the
Greeks, the Romans, the Arabs avoided foreign words in their philosophical
and mathematical works. The Germans are now doing the same. If borrow-
ings from Latin are found in Romance languages, it is only because these
languages derive from Latin." Examples of their substitutions are *cherta* for
liniia, ostie for *tsentr, polurazmer* for *radius, myslie* for *teorema, kupa* for
summa.[93]

By the time of his 1793 speech Suvorov's views had received in his own
eyes at least further confirmation by events in Europe. He moves from
questions of language to an attack on the false philosophers Voltaire and
Rousseau who sow anarchy and disorder and he opposes them to Montesquieu whose views "permeate the writings and institutions of Catherine."
The identification of Gallicism with revolt became particularly evident
among members of the Academy and provided the stimulus to Admiral
Aleksandr Semenovich Shishkov's *Rassuzhdenie o starom i novom sloge
rossiiskogo iazyka* (1803), a violent attack on the linguistic reforms associated
with the name of N. M. Karamzin.

Although the bare facts of Suvorov's and Nikitin's careers with the Naval
Cadet Corps suggest steady promotion and recognition, their letters reveal
some of the setbacks and tribulations they endured. In 1778 they threatened
to resign, not merely because they disliked living in Cronstadt and were
unhappy at their low salaries, but because their projected reforms in the
teaching programme of the Corps met with strong opposition from the other
professors. The director of the Corps, however, had assured them that their
new plan would be introduced and the text-books which they recommended
would be published. It is obvious that Nikitin and Suvorov had returned
from Oxford with high hopes and ideals which were beginning to founder.
Deprived of understanding, they proposed to send their new project to

Hornsby for sympathy and approval. Nikitin felt strongly that Suvorov's rare abilities were disregarded and unappreciated.[94] Further evidence of the Russian authorities' blindness to their own resources and exaggerated respect for foreign competence is provided by an incident in 1786. In that year Count I. A. Osterman wrote to the Russian ambassador in London, S. R. Vorontsov, requesting him to find an able English mathematician who would be willing to join the Russian service in what one would have thought was a particularly sensitive area, the cypher department of the College of Foreign Affairs. Vorontsov certainly thought so, and although he went through the motions of finding an Englishman, he reported back to Osterman on 6/17 November 1786 that he had met with no success, and that anyway the salary which would be demanded would be to high. He further wrote that "at Oxford they answered that they were astonished that since we have in Russia Fuss [Nicholas Fuss, 1755-1829], Suvorov and Nikitin, we should still be seeking a fourth Algebraist, and praising very highly the first of these, they also praise highly Nikitin and Suvorov, who were respected in Oxford among skilled algebraists and mathematicians." He suggests trying Suvorov, who was considered more able than Nikitin, and adds that "it would be strange if they could not do what Aepinus did."[95] There is no indication, however, that the College of Foreign Affairs acted on Vorontsov's proposals.

The career of Nikitin ends with the Naval Cadet Corps and nothing is known of his remaining years in retirement. Suvorov, on the other hand, after a short retirement of three years, again entered service in October, 1798, as professor of English in the School of Navigation at Nikolaev in the southern Ukraine.[96] There he continued to show all his old energies and dedication as a teacher and from 1800 held the office of supervisor (*smotritel'*), but without its salary. In the same year he became a State Counsellor, the fifth point in the table of ranks and the highest he was to achieve. For more than four years he was also director of the printing press at the school, supervising the printing of a number of works which included his own textbook for use in his English classes as well as a further oration on the coronation of Alexander I.[97] Retiring in 1804 as a result of ill health and with the warmest regard of the school's director, Count Voinovich, Suvorov and his family (he had married in 1794 and had two sons and two daughters) returned to Moscow. A further career still awaited Suvorov, for in 1810, at the age of sixty, he was appointed Professor of Higher Mathematics at Moscow University, acclaimed by its curator P. I. Golenishchev-Kutuzov, son of his old chief at the Naval Cadet Corps, as "an exceptional man, without peer among Russians or foreigners at the University for erudition or moral character."[98] Napoleon's advance on Moscow which led to the University removing to Nizhnii Novgorod was soon to sever Suvorov's connections. At the end of 1812 he wrote to Count N. S. Mordvinov (who had been head of the Black Sea Naval Administration at Nikolaev until 1800) of his family's tribulations as they sought sanctuary away from the invaders. He had not received official permission to retire, but could no longer serve the university "for reasons of illness and distance," yet he still hoped that his abilities could be of use to his country in some capacity. He sent Mordvinov a copy of what was probably his last work, "Glas Rossiianina k sootechestvennikam" ("The Appeal of a Russian to his Fellow-Countrymen").[99]

Suvorov died in 1815, forty years after his return from Oxford. Petitioning for a pension for his widow, Golenishchev-Kutuzov described Suvorov as "known in our country for many useful works which do him honour and worthy to stand alongside the most distinguished and learned men."[100] Literally hundreds of naval cadets and students benefitted over the years from Suvorov's and Nikitin's abilities and devotion as teachers and it is in this sphere of activity that their greatest claim to gratitude and respect is located. Oxford, even in an alleged period of stagnation, was largely responsible for providing the generally beneficial milieu for the development of their talents, and gave them a period in their lives to which they looked back with warmth and gratitude. To some extent their activity and achievements vindicated Catherine's decision to send them abroad to study, although not in any way she had envisaged. The creation of a theological faculty at Moscow University was not realized and no significant improvement occurred in the general intellectual level of the Russian clergy. Very few of the students who returned from Oxford, Leyden, or Göttingen took orders or achieved eminence as clerics; the others were scattered throughout Russia and with few exceptions lived and died in obscurity.

As is evident from the references to Korsakov, Russian links with Oxford in the eighteenth century did not cease with the departure of Suvorov and Nikitin. In February, 1773, a young secretary from the embassy, Ivan Rodionovich Koshelev (d. 1818), who the previous year was, according to the ambassador, "si enfoncé dans son anglais que je ne le vois qu'au hazard," went to Oxford for six months to hear lectures in experimental philosophy, probably from Hornsby.[101] Korsakov heard Hornsby and Williamson in 1775 and again in 1777, with his companion Neverov. Korsakov's descriptions of the university, its institutions, its professors and tutors, its social and academic life are detailed and overwhelmingly appreciative. Not all Russian visitors, however, shared his enthusiasm. Princess Dashkova's opinion has already been noted and Prince Aleksandr Borisovich Kurakin (1752-1818), who passed through Oxford a year later, in December, 1771, also commented that "Oxford a beaucoup perdu de son ancienne célebrité."[102] Another aristocratic traveller spent two days there in September, 1783, and after giving a series of objective and accurate notes on university institutions and expressing his amusement at the current academic dress, allowed himself a few observations on the academic consequences of contemporary freedom: "La jeune noblesse fait aujourd'hui ce qu'elle veut; et quand suivant les lois de l'université un jeune homme est condamné de traduire quelques chants de Virgile ou d'Homère, ou un autre morceau de quelque auteur ancien, il trouve pour son argent tout plein de servants aux colleges qui font la besogne pour lui. Les tuteurs ferment les yeux à cette fraude, parceque ces servants sont leurs creatures, à qui ils aiment faire gagner quelque chose."[103] He mentions no professors by name but records the disparaging observation of a Frenchman whom he met that the then Professor of Astronomy was "trop riche pour être poli."[104] This was none other than Hornsby, about whom other Russian students felt so differently, and the last reference to a Russian at Oxford in the eighteenth century dates from that year when Ivan Ivanovich Komov, who had been in Oxford in 1777, returned to hear Hornsby's lectures on astronomy, and sign the Bodleian register.[105]

III

In June, 1793, an Oxford don, the Rev. John Parkinson met in the town of Sarepta on the Volga "an old painter who had passed three or four years in England and spoke English perfectly well. One of these years he resided in Oxford, where he did not learn much; though he preferred it to Cambridge, which appeared he said to be a dirty place."[106] Compared with the wealth of information available about Russian visitors and students in Oxford, knowledge about the activities of Russians in Cambridge is meagre and seems to support the preference of Russians for Oxford.

After the period spent at Cambridge by Ivan Almanzenov in the reign of Mikhail Fedorovich more than a hundred years were to pass before another Russian is found studying at the university although Schumaker, unlike many of the other travellers who visited Oxford, also managed to get to Cambridge in 1721. In 1742 Baron Aleksandr Ivanovich Cherkasov (1728-88) and his younger brother Ivan (1732-1811), sons of the Empress Elizabeth's Privy Secretary (*kabinet-sekretar'*), arrived in England and apparently soon proceeded to Cambridge. Unfortunately, there is no trace of them in contemporary Cambridge records and what precisely they did and how long they remained can only be surmised on the basis of vague and frequently contradictory references in Russian biographical sources. Aleksandr Cherkasov is said to have studied with distinction the humanities and to have returned to Russia in 1747 or even later with a fluency in five languages: Greek, Latin, English, French, and Italian. He left behind his brother but returned to England again in June, 1752. The brothers eventually left England in 1756.[107] It may well be that during his second visit Cherkasov turned his attention to medicine and indeed went to Edinburgh to study it. Oliver Goldsmith, who was himself studying medicine at Edinburgh, wrote in a letter of 8 May 1742: "Tis he [the Professor of Medicine, Alexander Munro], I may venture to say, that draws hither such a large number of students from most parts of the world, even from Russia."[108] The Edinburgh University records provide no evidence to corroborate this statement, but Aleksandr Cherkasov seems a likely candidate. Given the number of years he spent in Britain, it is not surprising that he "achieved such a proficiency in the English language as to enable him to read any author and carry on a conversation with ease," and the English Ambassador, John, 2nd Earl of Buckinghamshire, whose estimate this was, suggested that his success at Cambridge had been achieved "by dint of his great application," since "his parts are rather slow than brilliant."[109] Under Catherine, who shared his Anglophilia and admired his wide knowledge, Cherkasov reached positions of eminence, which gave him opportunities to exhibit his threefold interest in medicine, agriculture, and legislation. The first of these found expression in his efforts as president of the Medical College to reform the Russian medical services in the 1760s and in his negotiations to bring Dr. Thomas Dimsdale to Russia to inoculate the empress in 1768;[110] the second in his role as a founder member and later president of the Free Economic Society; the third in his advice and help to Catherine in her work in preparing her *Nakaz* for the Legislative Commission in 1767.[111]

Ivan Cherkasov enjoyed an unbroken stay of some fourteen years in England and after completing his course at Cambridge, went on to study navigation. The interesting glimpse of his interests and activities in the 1750s is provided by the Petersburg journal *Ezhemesiachnye sochineniia* ("Monthly Compositions"). In 1755 it carried his review of Robert Wood's *The Ruins of Palmyra* (1753) and later the same year, his translation of an essay from *The Guardian*.[112] On his return to Russia he served with his brother in the Preobrazhenskii Guards and became aide-de-camp to the Emperor Peter III in 1762. After Peter's overthrow, he was arrested, along with S. R. Vorontsov, for his loyalty to the tsar and seemingly remained in disgrace for some years. In 1771, however, his career took a turn for the better. He became Commissioner General of the Navy in 1771, was made a member of the Admiralty College in 1777 and reached the rank of vice-admiral in 1782.

Although Cambridge was designated originally along with Oxford as the destination of Catherine's seminarists, it was eventually replaced by Leyden and Göttingen. Finance has been suggested as one consideration, but there may have been others. Among them were possibly Russia's stronger links with Oxford (the Cherkasovs and Kostiurin apart), the presence at that time in St. Petersburg as a member of Catherine's commission on school reform of Dr. Daniel Dumaresq (1713-1805), a former chaplain to the British Factory in the Russian capital and a graduate of Pembroke College, Oxford, who had returned to his university to take his D.D. in 1752. In terms of their social and academic life there was little to choose between them: Cambridge could provide as many examples of idle students, recalcitrant professors, and gourmandising Fellows, illustrated by a similar wealth of contemporary satires, squibs and memoirs, although it also had a reputation, somewhat exaggerated on the evidence, for Whiggism, latitudarianism and free thought. A decade later it addressed itself to questions of academic reform with more attention than was the case at Oxford. A more vociferous advocate of change than Napleton in Oxford was his contemporary John Jebb of Peterhouse, who campaigned energetically but ultimately unsuccessfully between 1772 and his retirement from Cambridge in 1776 for a unified system of annual examinations. Evidence of Cambridge's more liberal attitude in religious matters were the hesitant moves a few years earlier to oppose the obligation to subscribe to the thirty nine Articles. One aspect of the Cambridge system which may have been influential in bringing to Cambridge one Russian student later in the century was its emphasis on mathematics rather than on the classics and theology which in 1774 had engendered a poem against the excessive study of the subject, "The Academick Dream."

"Hard at Mathematicks" in Cambridge in 1779 was another young Russian, Aleksandr Alekseevich Chesmenskii (1763-1820).[113] Chesmenskii was the illegitimate son of Count Aleksei Grigor'evich Orlov (1737-1808), the third of the famous quintet of Orlov brothers. He had been educated as a boy at a school in Halle and on his return to Russia in 1774 had entered the Guards. In 1778 the empress, in the words of the British ambassador in Petersburg, had "gradually withdrawn her confidence and good-will from Count Alexis Orlov" and had "refused him some trifling favours he asked for his natural son."[114] As a result Orlov decided to send Chesmenskii to England and entrust him to the care of Henry, Lord Pembroke, whose son George, Lord Herbert, together with his companion, the celebrated Rev. William Coxe, had just returned from a visit to Russia. Chesmenskii arrived in London early in 1779, when Lord Pembroke noted that "he is going by way of learning the language to a Parson at Hampstead, & Pouschin [Musin-Pushkin, the ambassador] proposes to send him afterwards to Oxford."[115] He went instead in June to Cambridge, a choice probably influenced by the fact that Coxe was a Fellow at King's. In January, 1780, Coxe informed Lord Herbert that Chesmenskii "is settled for some months at Cambridge, he is not in any College, but is in a private house. He is very much liked and everywhere well received. He applies himself very much and talks English surprisingly well."[116] He remained in Cambridge until the summer and soon returned to Russia to resume a long and active career in the army, fighting successively against the Swedes, Turks, and Poles between 1788 and 1793. Retiring as a brigadier in 1795, he spent the rest of his days near to his father in Moscow. He shared his father's enthusiasm for things English, particularly horses and horse-racing, and on his estate at Sadki, near Moscow, he set up in 1804 a factory, run on English lines and with many English craftsmen, to produce a wide range of agricultural machines. A contemporary remarked that "Visits to the factory have become very fashionable, and if the road were better, the whole of Moscow would go there to admire the enterprise."[117] On the death of his father in 1808, Chesmenskii took over management of his estate at the request of Orlov's legitimate daughter.

The last known Russian student to study at a Cambridge or Oxford college in the eighteenth century was Ivan Ivanovich Grebenshchikov (b. 1760?), a teacher of mathematics and colleague of Suvorov and Nikitin at the Naval Cadet College. In June, 1785, he was sent to England "to complete his studies, particularly in the theory of shipbuilding."[118] Admitted fellow-commoner to Christ's College on 28 June 1786, he matriculated in December of that year and resided until the early summer of 1789. He then spent a few months in London before leaving for Russia in August of that year.[119] In the eighteenth century Cambridge colleges admitted undergraduates as noblemen, fellow-commoners, pensioners or sizars. The fellow-commoner, although paying less in fees than the nobleman (but more than the other two categories), enjoyed many special privileges, including exemption from attendance at lectures and from performing most of the exercises demanded of other undergraduates: many of them carried on an easy, idle life and were content to leave the university without proceeding to a degree. It is evident in Grebenshchikov's case, however, that he was granted the status on account of his comparative maturity and considerable competence in mathematics. Grebenshchikov came to Cambridge to "learn more fully the Newtonian philosophy," but if he expected to hear words of wisdom from one of Newton's successors in the Lucasian Chair of Mathematics, he would have been very disappointed. Edward Waring had been elected to the chair as a bright young Fellow of twenty-five in 1760 and although he remained professor for thirty-eight years, there is no evidence that he ever lectured. After his death, a contemporary suggested that "the profound researches of Dr Waring, I suppose, were not adapted to any form of communication by lectures."[120] Indeed, it is probable that Grebenshchikov never even saw him, for in 1776 he went to live in Shrewsbury and then retired to his Shropshire estate. Mathematics was, however, the dominant subject in Cambridge and instruction in the colleges by tutors was reputed to be of a high standard and it is likely that Grebenshchikov had ample opportunity to acquire the knowledge for which he had come.

Grebenshchikov was a contemporary at Christ's of Henry Gunning (1768-1854) and although Gunning makes no mention of him in his *Reminiscences of Cambridge*, the memoirs provide a vivid picture of the Cambridge of the day and of numerous characters with whom the Russian may well have had contact. When Gunning went up in October, 1784, he was one of only three undergraduates in his year; seven were admitted in 1786 along with Grebenshchikov and he would have had a nodding acquaintance at least with almost all the members of his college. Two men whom he would have come to know well were the Christ's tutors, Thomas Parkinson and the Rev. John Barlow Seale, under whom both he and Gunning were admitted. Parkinson, was in Gunning's considered estimate, "one of the most kind-hearted and benevolent men breathing; and in spite of his occasional peevishness, I believe him to have been much interested for all his pupils."[121] He lectured on all aspects of mathematics, at such a pace that "it was impossible for any one, not previously acquainted with the subject, to understand or to keep up with him," which extended poor Gunning but should have presented few problems to Grebenshchikov. Gunning also mentions Parkinson as the author of a formidable work on mechanics over which Gunning laboured and "made myself master of that part of it which treated on elastic balls, and was able to investigate the centres of oscillation, gyration, and percussion (as taught in his book), very much to his satisfaction."[122] Gunning studied Euclid and algebra, for which the text-book was Colin Maclaurin's *Algebra* (London, 1748). The Junior Tutor, the Rev. Seale, lectured in classics, moral philosophy and logic. An audience of a dozen or so students from different years would gather for his lectures, which Gunning found very interesting, except for those on "the Metre of the Greek Choruses, of which I knew nothing, but on which he had (unfortunately for me) published a book":[123] Seale's work on *Greek Metres* (Cambridge, 1785) was followed during Grebenshchikov's time by another on the *Analysis of Greek Metres* (1789). Gunning in general highly appreciated Seale and declared that "nothing could be pleasanter than the hour passed at Seale's lectures,"[124] and among other lectures he mentioned were ones on Grotius and Locke. If Gunning is to be believed, both he and Grebenshchikov were fortunate in their tutors at a time when standards were not particularly high.

On his return to Russia in 1789 Grebenshchikov resumed his career in the Naval Cadet College, where he is described as one of its outstanding instructors at the beginning of the nineteenth century.[125]

CHAPTER 5
RUSSIAN STUDENTS AT THE SCOTTISH UNIVERSITIES

On 30 June 1782, Dr John Carr was fulminating from the pulpit of St Mary's against "the scandalous neglect of order and discipline throughout the University" of Cambridge, stressing that

> few gentlemen or noblemen admitted their sons but rather chose to send them to a foreign academy; that the expensiveness of their education here made it almost impossible for common folks to do so without ruining themselves and sons; that the Scotch Universities gained ground upon them every day; that though the world's eyes were upon them, and it was a time of reformation, yet the carelessness of Heads and Tutors was scandalous; that the great endowments were not bestowed for Fellows of colleges to spend their days idly in dissipation, dress and vanity like men of fortune, but to mind their institution.[1]

By the 1780s the Russians had long since taken the hint and although the occasional student was still to be found at Cambridge and Oxford, Edinburgh in particular had emerged as the centre for a sounder and cheaper education. It was to Glasgow, however, that the first Russian students were sent as early as 1761.

I

It seems likely that when Semen Desnitskii and Ivan Tret'iakov left Moscow University for London, they believed their ultimate destination was either Oxford or Cambridge; that it became Glasgow was the result of the ambassador, Prince A. M. Golitsyn's attention to comparative costs.[2] To be fair, the ambassador may also have been swayed by academic considerations, manifest in the choice of Glasgow rather than of Edinburgh, Aberdeen or St. Andrews. For in the 1750s Glasgow boasted a corpus of scholars possibly without rival in Great Britain. Although Dr. Francis Hutcheson, Professor of Moral Philosophy, had died in 1747, his links with Glasgow were perpetuated by the publication there in 1755 of his *System of Moral Philosophy*, by which time the subject was in the hands of the already famous Adam Smith (1723-90), Professor of Moral Philosophy since 1752 and soon to publish his *Theory of the Moral Sentiments* (1759). One of Smith's colleagues was Joseph Black (1728-99), who had succeeded William Cullen as Professor of Medicine in 1756, and among less well known but respected scholars were Robert Simson (d. 1768), Professor of Mathematics, John Anderson, Professor of Natural Philosophy, and during the time the Russians were studying at Glasgow, James Millar, the Professor of Civil Law from 1761, and Thomas Reid, Smith's successor in 1764. Many of these men were members of flourishing and influential societies, pre-eminently the Politicial Economy Club, founded by Provost Andrew Cochrane in 1743, and the Literary Society, which was the sounding-board for some of the most important ideas and theories of such as Smith and Black.[3]

Desnitskii, like so many of the students to come to England, was a Ukrainian, the son of a *meshchanin* from the town of Nezhin, and had been educated at the Troitse-Sergeevskii seminary and the University gymnasium, before entering the University itself in 1760. He remained there only for about a year, but his evident talents led him to be selected for study abroad, along with Tret'iakov, the son of an army officer from Tver' and educated in the local seminary. In 1760 Tret'iakov was twenty-five, Desnitskii possibly a few years younger, although his date of birth is not known, and they would find themselves at Glasgow among youths frequently in their early teens. The education they would have received in Russia, however, would have been rudimentary—a fellow-countryman visiting Scotland in 1776 commented that "l'universite de Moscou ou on n'en donne que les commencements [of literature and the sciences], ne peut etre comparée même avec les Ecoles que se trouvent en Angleterre"[4]—and they would have been hampered initially by their lack of English, even though their knowledge of Latin would have allowed them to converse with the professors, very few of whom, however, continued to use it in their lectures. Nevertheless, the Russians seem to have adapted themselves quickly and to have embarked upon a course of studies which was to take them to their M.A. degrees in 1765. Their fellow students came from every class of society and many countries, particularly Ireland. A Glasgow professor noted in 1760: "Near a third of our students are Irish. . . . We have a good many English and some foreigners; many of the Irish as well as Scotch are poor, and come up late to save money."[5] In this last respect the Russians were in good company, and it is their financial plight which first finds reflection in the records of both Glasgow and Moscow Universities. We have already encountered instances of the Holy Synod, the College of Foreign Affairs and private individuals reluctant to provide for the men they sent abroad; in this case Moscow University failed miserably to meet its responsibilities.

At a meeting of 11 August 1762, the Glasgow University Senate considered the financial difficulties of "the two Russian Gentlemen sent to this University by the recommendation of Lord Mansfield communicated by the Earl of Errol" and decided to advance them £40 until "their remittances shall arrive."[6] Desnitskii and Tret'iakov wrote to the new Russian Ambassador in London, Count A. R. Vorontsov, about their predicament and he took up their case, describing their academic successes and the Scottish university's generosity.[7] His intercession proved successful, for the Glasgow

Senate at its meeting in October, 1762, was able to return the students' "obligation" on their repayment of the loan.[8] This did not, however, signal the end of their financial worries, since the new Curator of Moscow University, V. E. Adodurov, professed to be unaware of both the academic and financial arrangements made for them by his predecessor. In 1765 matters came to a head when the students approached the Moscow authorities for money to pay their debts. Moscow demanded further details of their courses and instructed them "meanwhile to be content with the stipend they were receiving and not to complain."[9] This was in February and Desnitskii and Tret'iakov might well have been content with their 420 rubles a year (which were then worth about £80 and as such much more than many of their fellow students were surviving on), if in fact they had received the money. They were, however, obliged to borrow from moneylenders at crippling rates of interest and also to seek another loan from the university. In October they wrote that they were owing about £160 to teachers, tradesmen and booksellers. Adodurov demanded their return, outraged by the "coarse and threatening expressions" of their letter,[10] but they were to remain for reasons which will become clear almost two more years. When finally the students arrived back in Petersburg in July, 1767, they were penniless and the Senate, which was obliged to meet their bills, soon demanded its rubles from Moscow University "to pay for their passage from Scotland to Petersburg, for their maintenance here and during their journey to Moscow."[11]

Adodurov and his colleagues were inclined to attribute Desnitskii's and Tret'iakov's financial difficulties to the expenses they were incurring in studying an unnecessarily wide range of subjects: ". . . they were attending at the same period lectures on law and medicine and in addition to mathematics, were studying book-keeping from a teacher who had only practical knowledge of the subject, and because of this their whole course of studies has been declared by our professors unsystematic and leading to no obvious end."[12] They were clearly ignorant of the broad studies which were generally pursued at the Scottish universities for the Master's degree, which Tret'iakov received in 1764 and Desnitskii in 1765. Although it is not possible to re-create fully the curriculum which the Russians followed, documents discovered in the Glasgow University archives and published in recent years by Archibald Brown and reports from Moscow University edited by N. A. Penchko reveal both the principal subjects they studied and the names of some of the professors who taught them. In a letter of 31 December 1765 Desnitskii and Tret'iakov spoke of "our attendance on Dr Smith's class of Ethicks and Jurisprudence and our attendance for three years on Mr Millar's classes of civil law,"[13] emphasizing in this instance their particular fittedness to proceed towards a doctorate in law and highlighting the two men whose teaching and ideas were of paramount importance for their present and future careers. Adam Smith resigned from his professorhsip early in 1764, but in the preceding two years the Russians followed not only his lectures on Ethics and Jurisprudence, but also on Rhetoric and Belles-Lettres. Desnitskii and Tret'iakov enjoyed an especially close relationship with James Millar, himself a pupil of Smith's a few years earlier. They continued to follow his course on Roman law in 1766, when they also studied British law.[14] In addition, they had earlier attended classes in mathematics conducted by James Williamson, Robert Simson's successor, but clearly regarded these as something of a chore. On their return to Russia, the authorities at Moscow University insisted on testing their mathematical prowess: Desnitskii refused, but Tret'iakov, who submitted to the demand, failed utterly.[15] Of more significance was their attendance at the lectures given by Joseph Black in the winter of 1764-65. Some years later, in 1780, Black in reply to a query from James Watt about foreigners who had heard him explain his important discoveries on latent heat, specifically recalled the Russians.[16] It was Black who, together with the University Principal, William Leechman, supplied Moscow University with testimonials of the students' progress in 1765.[17]

Having achieved their Master's degrees, the Russians sought "a Liberty of offering ourselves Candidates for a Degree in Law, and of Submitting ourselves to the Trials, which are requisite in order to obtain it."[18] Although by this time they knew of Adodurov's demand that they should return to Russia and their departure date was set for March, 1766, they took advantage of the confusion caused by the death of the Russian envoy in London to extend their stay. Millar, appointed to examine the Russian students privately, reported favourably on their qualifications and they were then examined publicly on 16 January 1766. "The meeting approved of the specimen they had given of their knowledge and Law and calling them in, acquainted them therewith and prescribed to Mr. John Tret'yakov the Title 4 of Book 2nd of the Pandects, 'De in Jus vocando' as the subject of a thesis which he is to read and defend in public, and to Mr. Simeon Desnitskoy, Title 1st of the Pandects, 'De testamentis ordinariis'."[19] Within a month the Russians had produced their theses which were approved in April, 1766, and recommended for publication. Although in their next letter to Moscow they were already calling themselves Doctors of Law,[20] the degree itself was not awarded for another year. In the interim they took courses with Professor Millar as well as "readings in selected English poets."[21] Eventually, after Desnitskii had been involved in a most unpleasant incident with John Anderson, the Professor of Moral Philosophy, which would have ruined his career, had the Rector of the University not given a remarkably humane judgement,[22] the Russians received their degrees. At its meeting of 20 April 1767, the Faculty considered a petition from them and resolved to dispense "with their defending their Theses in public as appointed in a former meeting, and being satisfied with the specimens given of their knowledge in the Civil

Law, appoints the Degree of Doctor of Law to be conferred upon them by
the Vice Chancellor when he shall judge it convenient."[23]

Treated with great consideration by a foreign university, the Russians
returned to their home university to meet suspicion and hostility. Adodurov
and the predominantly German professors of Moscow University were reluctant to recognize not only Desnitskii's and Tret'iakov's qualifications but
also those of other students, such as M. I. Afonin and A. M. Karamyshev,
returning with doctorates from Upsala and both highly praised by Linnaeus.
Desnitskii managed to avoid his oral examination in mathematics, but Professor Rost reported on Tret'iakov that "it became clear that the examinee
does not know even the basic principles of pure mathematical analysis and is
quite incapable of teaching mathematics, which he readily acknowledges
himself."[24] It was, of course, law which they wanted to teach and they
passed convincingly their searching examinations in this discipline. It is
interesting to note that some of the questions put to them had been supplied
by the Procurator-General Prince A. A. Viazemskii and that his secretary,
Samuel Dähn, was present at the examination.[25] Viazemskii had recently
been appointed President of Catherine's Legislative Commission and the
empress was obviously eager to learn of current British thinking on a variety
of issues. It was probably on account of Dähn's report of the performance
of Desnitskii in particular that he was invited or encouraged to write his
*Proposal concerning the Establishment of Legislative, Judicial and Executive
Authorities in the Russian Empire (Predstavlenie o uchrezhdenii zakono-
datel'noi, suditel'noi i nakazatel'noi vlasti v Rossiiskoi imperii)*, which he
dedicated to Catherine in 1768. As Brown has shown, Catherine incorporated
many points, frequently word for word, from Desnitskii's *Proposal* into the
Second Supplement of her famous *Nakaz* which she completed in April,
1768.[26] Although she was probably unaware of Desnitskii's own more
than general debt to the ideas of Adam Smith in his *Proposal*, the Anglo-
Russian link in legislative thinking established between the empress and
Desnitskii was re-established some years later. In 1776 she wrote to Baron
Grimm of her enthusiasm for William Blackstone's *Commentaries on the
Laws of England* (1758-62)[27] and four years later there appeared the first
part of Desnitskii's translation of the first volume of that work, *Istolkovanie
Angliiskikh zakonov* (3 parts, 1780-82), produced "at the command of the
Great Russian Legislatress."

Although Desnitskii and Tret'iakov were obliged to read their first trial
lectures in Latin because of the inadequacy of the examining professors'
Russian, their first public lectures and subsequent courses taught by them
after their appointment as Professors of Law (24 May 1768) were given in
Russian. Once again, it was as a direct result of an initiative from Catherine
who on her arrival in Moscow in 1767 to open the Legislative Commission
informed the Director of the University, M. M. Kheraskov, of her wish for

lectures in all three faculties to be given in Russian "for the better propagation of the sciences in Russia."[28] The first public lectures by Tret'iakov and
Desnitskii were delivered in 1768, but as Brown has demonstrated on the
evidence of a copy annotated by Desnitskii,[29] Tret'iakov's *Discourse on the
Origin and Foundation of State-Supported Universities in Europe (Slovo o
proizshestvii i uchrezhdenii universitetov v Europe na gosudarstvennykh izh-
diveniiakh*) was merely delivered by him but was in fact the work of his
much more talented and prolific friend. Only two other works are credited
to Tret'iakov, dating from 1769 and 1772, and the second of these, *A Discourse on the Causes of Public Opulence and the Slow Enrichment of Ancient
and Modern Nations (Razsuzhdenie o prichinakh izobiliia i meditel'nago
obogashcheniia gosudarstv.* . .), has been shown by Professor Norman Taylor
to be little more than the re-jigging of notes from Adam Smith's lectures.[30]
Nevertheless, although Tret'iakov has little claim to originality, he undoubtedly shared with Desnitskii and the other young Russian professors at Moscow University progressive and radical views which brought him into conflict
with the university authorities and hastened his premature retirement in
1773.

Desnitskii held his chair for twenty years, until 1787, and by his lecturing
and writing fully earned the title of the "father of Russian jurisprudence."
Apart from the *Proposal* for Catherine (first published in 1905) and the
speech delivered by Tret'iakov, eight public lectures by Desnitskii were
published at the Moscow University Press between 1768 and 1781. He was
one of the few practising translators from English and he produced, in addition to his Blackstone, a version of Thomas Bowden's *The Farmer's Director*
in 1780 (which was discussed in Chapter 3). In 1783 he was elected to the
newly established Russian Academy and joined Nikitin, Suvorov and Petrov
as one of a number of strongly Anglophile scholars recruited by the president, Princess Dashkova, who had herself but recently returned from Edinburgh, where her son had gained his M.A. Like Nikitin and Suvorov he was
asked to contribute to the Academy dictionary, but unlike them, he con-
scientiously filfilled his task, contributing many of the legal and political
terms. A further aspect of his activity which aligns him got only with Nikitin
and Suvorov but also with the former *tserkovniki*, Permskii and Zhdanov,
was his teaching of the English language. Unfortunately, the grammar which
he is said to have produced for the use of his pupils at Moscow University has
not survived. It is, however, as the first *gifted* follower of Adam Smith that
he lays most claim on the attention of the student of Anglo-Russian relations.
Before recording the enthusiasm which the publication of *The Wealth of
Nations* (1776) brought from Russians such as Mordvinov and members
of the Vorontsov family (the ambassadors, Aleksandr and Semen, and their
sister, Princess Dashkova), Academician M. P. Alekseev wrote of Desnitskii:
"Desnitsky's works constantly reveal obvious traces of the influence of his

Scotch professor. However, there is no reason to believe that these were merely clever interpretations of the ideas he had heard advanced in the lecture room of Glasgow University, as was the case with his friend and companion, Tretiakov. In Desnitsky we have a mature and original thinker whose literary talent and vast knowledge made him one of the most influential professors of Moscow University in the late eighteenth century. . . ."[31] The researches of Archibald Brown reveal for the first time to what extent Desnitskii's ideas and writings were permeated with the influence of Scottish thinkers, predominantly of Smith but also of Millar. Desnitskii himself made no attempt to conceal his own general indebtedness and Brown is scrupulous in emphasizing the Russian's very real and original contribution to the comparative-historical school of jurisprudence and to economic and socio-political thought in Russia.

II

By the time Desnitskii and Tret'iakov left for home the group of students under their "inspector" Nikitin had settled in Oxford. When in the following decade Russian students are again found in Scotland it is in Edinburgh rather than Glasgow.[32]

At the beginning of the eighteenth century Edinburgh University had some eight professors and 300 students; by 1800 the figures had increased to 21 and 1200 respectively. During the 1760s and 1770s the university had been transformed under the dynamic leadership of William Robertson, who had been appointed Principal in March, 1762. Professors left Glasgow for more promising positions in Edinburgh and the University quickly gained a European reputation. Tieman, a Hungarian literator living in Paris wrote in 1781: "Whenever the English mention Scotchmen to me in that contemptuous tone they sometimes affect, I advise them to go to Edinburgh to learn how to live, and how to be men. Your learned men, Robertson, Black, and Hume are looked upon here as geniuses of the first rank. Only two days ago, I saw Comte de Buffon, who named them all to me at his finger's tip, just as you might name Newton and Locke."[33] Simply to enumerate the names of some of the holders of chairs during the period which particularly concerns us is to help justify the title of the "second Athens" or "the Athens of the North" which Edinburgh soon received: Adam Ferguson, Professor of Natural Philosophy from 1759, of Moral Philosophy from 1764 and of Mathematics from 1785, together with John Playfair, himself later to hold the chair of Natural Philosophy on the death in 1805 of John Robison; Dugald Stewart, Professor of Mathematics from 1775 until he moved to Moral Philosophy in 1785; John Pringle, later President of the Royal Society, Professor of Universal Civil History and Antiquities from 1755; Hugh Blair, Professor of Rhetoric and Belles Lettres from 1762; John Hope, Professor of

Botany from 1761 and founder of the Edinburgh Botanic Gardens in 1776; Alexander Munro, son of the founder of the Edinburgh Medical School and his successor in 1754 to the chair of Anatomy; Joseph Black, Professor of Chemistry from 1766, late of Glasgow, as was William Cullen, Professor of Chemistry before Black, then of Institutes of Medicine and finally, until just before his death in 1790, of the Practice of Physic, in which his predecessor had been John Gregory. It was men of such calibre whom a Russian visitor in 1776 had in mind when he wrote in his journal in his execrable French: "L'université d'Edinbourg est tres fameuse il y a des professeurs forts eminent dans tous les genres et particulièrement dans la medicine c'est ce qui y fait venir les etudiants de tous les pais de l'europe."[34] In 1790, another Russian traveller commented that "to the extent that London is a merchant's city, so Edinburgh is a scholar's. It has world-famous doctors of medicine and of jurisprudence. All who wish to perfect their knowledge of medicine come here to study."[35] And in the years 1774 to 1787 the foreign students included at different times some sixteen Russians, several of whom studied medicine.

By a curious coincidence it was a graduate and former teacher of Glasgow University who was instrumental in establishing the first direct Russian links with Edinburgh University. A close friend of James Watt and of Joseph Black, whom he succeeded as Lecturer in Chemistry in 1766, John Robison (1739-1805) left Glasgow in December, 1770, for St. Petersburg. He went in the capacity of private secretary to Admiral Sir Charles Knowles whom Catherine had invited to re-organize the Russian navy. For almost two years Robison worked with Knowles but his own reputation as a mathematician together with the sound grounding in Russian which he soon acquired led to his appointment as Professor of Mathematics at the Naval Cadet Corps at Cronstadt in the summer of 1772. The following year he became Inspector of Classes and was busy composing a mathematical and navigational primer for the cadets when he learned of his election to the chair of Natural Philosophy at Edinburgh. Before returning to Scotland, he suggested to the Director of the Cadet Corps that he should not only remain in correspondence with him about naval and scientific matters but also "take with him two pupils from the Corps, one to study under his supervision mathematics and ther other, the humanities."[36] In the event he returned with three young cadets in the early summer of 1774 and they became the first Russians to appear on the matriculation rolls of Edinburgh University.

Stepan Ivanovich Rachinskii, a twelve-year old corporal, was selected "for his excellent comprehension and sharpness in the sciences, exhibited during his three years in the Corps,"[37] and he was joined by Nikolai Ivanovich Beliaev and Ivan Nikolaevich Shishukov. Although the Naval Cadet Corps was one of the few Russian institutions at this period to include English in its curriculum, it is probable that the young boys gained their first smattering of the language from Robison during the voyage to Scotland and spent their first months studying it in Edinburgh. Nevertheless, Rachinskii and Beliaev enrolled for Robison's first course at the university in the autumn of 1774. They continued with Robison in 1775, when they were joined by Shishukov, and all three enrolled for the first lectures of Dugald Stewart as Professor of Mathematics. Shishukov's name does not appear again on the rolls, although in the following year Rachinskii and Beliaev continued with Stewart. Only Beliaev's name figures in 1777 as a pupil of the Professor of Moral Philosophy, Adam Ferguson.[38] Nothing further is to be gleaned from the university records, but it seems likely that they all returned to Russia together. Early in 1779 Samborskii, the Russian chaplain in London, spoke of them to Jeremy Bentham: "One of them did extraordinarilly well, and made a great proficiency in the Mathematics—the two others but indifferently. They were allow'd to stay but 3 years (which is another fault with us; we do not allow time enough for education.) At their return, the proficient in Mathematics was sent to sea: the two others were retained as Mathematicians."[39] On the evidence of the courses they took it might have been assumed that it was Beliaev who proved the outstanding student, but subsequent records show that it was Rachinskii who became the sailor and his friends became teachers not of mathematics but of languages.

It is possible that the Russians returned from Leith to Cronstadt on a Russian warship and thereby came to meet another Scotsman in Russian service: on 9 October 1777 Admiral Samuel Greig (1735-88), the commandant of Cronstadt, left Edinburgh after a triumphant first visit to his homeland since he joined the Russian navy as a captain in 1764.[40] Greig was obviously impressed with Rachinskii, who a year or so later was appointed his adjutant with the rank of lieutenant. Beliaev and Shishukov became instructors in French and English respectively at the Cadet Corps, where they were still teaching in the early years of Alexander's reign. At Cronstadt English was already being taught by Zhdanov, once of the Russian church in London, and Suvorov, recently returned with his colleague Nikitin from Oxford. Shishukov was to complement Zhdanov's English-Russian dictionary with his own Russian-English dictionary, *Slovar' rossiisko-angliiskii* (2 parts [St. Petersburg 1808-11]), which unfortunatley he completed only as far as the letter "R." Beliaev too retained his proficiency in English and the one translation he is known to have done was by a strange coincidence of a work by his old teacher, Robison. In 1800 Robison was elected an Honorary Member of the Petersburg Academy of Sciences, succeeding the recently deceased Joseph Black. Three years later he sent the emperor a copy of his edition of Black's lectures (1799) and received from him a diamond ring. Informing Watt of the emperor's regard, he said of his book: "It will be immediately translated by a Mr Belaieff, one of my old pupils from the Marine Academy."[41]

One further aspect of the activities of the Russians shortly after their return to Cronstadt is interesting for its British connections. On 1/12 December 1779 a new Masonic Lodge called "Neptune" was founded at Cronstadt, receiving its warrant from Prince G. P. Gagarin, Grand Master of the recently instituted Grand National Lodge, according to the Swedish ritual. The overwhelming majority of the members of the Lodge were officers in the Baltic Fleet or connected with the Cadet Corps and include many Masons who were either British or Russians with some experience of England and service in the British navy. Admiral Greig, who was Senior Warden of the Lodge in 1780, became Master in 1781, a position he retained until his death. Rachinskii, Beliaev and Shishukov all had attained the degree of Master Mason by 1781 and fulfilled other offices in the Lodge, Rachinskii, that of Orator, and Beliaev and Shishukov, successively that of Secretary.[42]

III

During their second year at Edinburgh the three cadets were joined by an equally young but far more privileged student, Prince Pavel Mikhailovich Dashkov (1763-1807). His mother was Princess Ekaterina Romanovna Dashkova, whose name has appeared more than once in these pages and whose extensive travels through parts of the British Isles will be considered in a later chapter. As "a red hot English woman,"[43] Dashkova had always envisaged a British education for her son and on her first visit in 1770 had considered entering him at Westminster School. In October, 1776, she came again to London, having already begun to make arrangements for him to start his studies at Edinburgh in the New Year.

In three letters to William Robertson, written between late August and early November,[44] she explained her reasons for selecting Edinburgh, tried to persuade the Principal to take personal supervision of her son's studies, and countered the suggestion that she should delay his entry to the university by detailing his accomplishments and potential. In her second letter she outlined the course of studies which her son had previously pursued and would ideally follow at Edinburgh over a period of two years or five terms:

1. Semestre, Langues Rhetorique, et Belles lettres, Histoire et Constitutions des Gouv: Mathe: Logique.
2. Semestre, Langues, Rhet: Hist: et Consti: des Gouv: Mathem: Philos: rationelle, Physique experi:, Fortifications, et Dessein.
3. Semestre, Belles lettres, Hist: et Consti: des Gouv: Fortification, Droit de Nature, et droit public univer: et positif, Mathem: Physique et Histoire Naturelle, Dessein
4. Semestre, Morale Mathem: fortifications, Droit des gens Universel, et Positif, Principes generaux de Jurisprudence, Architecture Civile
5. Semestre Morale Repetition de Physique, premiers principes de Chymie, et ensuite Repetition generale et Logique[45]

Such were the studies, she suggested, which were necessary for the prince's
speedy advancement in his military career. Her letters clearly revealed the
degree to which she combined in her character the traits of a doting, protec-
tive mother and a dominant aggressive father, and the phlegmatic Robertson must have awaited with some trepidation the arrival of the "Scythian
heroine"[46] and her family, whose journey north was scrupulously chron-
icled by the London papers.

The Dashkovs arrived in Edinburgh on 8 December 1776 and took a
house in the New Town, on or near George Street, the elegant centre of
high society life, far removed from the teeming wynds and closes around the
university. The prince was soon embarked upon his studies and during the
next three years he enrolled for courses given by Blair (twice), Robison
(twice), Bruce (twice), Dugald Stewart (twice) and Adam Ferguson. Rhetoric,
Logic, Natural and Moral Philosophy, Mathematics, which these professors
taught, all had found a place in Dashkova's ambitious plan, as did Chemistry,
taught by Black. In a letter to Black after his return to Russia, Dashkov
spoke of "the many kind instructions and all the good offices I received
from you."[47] In reply, Black mentioned "your professor Ferguson" and
mentioned another of his old acquaintants, William Greenfield, an eloquent preacher, who was to succeed Black in 1784 in the chair of Rhetoric
and Belles Lettres.[48] Of Dashkov's particular friends among the student body
nothing is known with the exception of the young Irishman William Drennan,
later to achieve renown as a poet and politician. Drennan noted that "Prince
Dashkov attends his classes with great assiduity and has perfectly melted
away all the Russian Boorishness in French courtesy."[49] Dashkov by all
accounts was a model student, assiduous and polite, but leaving no impression
of a strong personality. He was very much under the watchful eye of his
mother, who carefully supervised *all* moments of his time: "by way of amusement and exercise for my son I gave a dance every week; I also made him go to
a riding school, and an excellent fencing master who happened to be living in
Edinburgh gave him lessons every other day."[50] She kept open house for "the
immortal Robertson, Blair, Smith and Ferguson (who) came twice a week to
spend the day with me," and her admiration for the Edinburgh scholars was
sincere and boundless: "I made the acquaintance of the University professors,
all of whom were generally esteemed for their intelligence, intellectual distinction and moral qualities. Strangers alike to envy and to the pretentiousness
of smaller minds, they lived together in brotherly amity, their mutual love
and respect making of them a group of educated and intelligent people whom
it is always an immense pleasure to see and whose conversation never failed
to be instructive."[51]

By the end of March, 1779, the prince had "undergone before the faculty
of Arts the trials appointed by the Statutes of the University for Candidates
applying for the degree of M[r] of Arts" and he proceeded to his "publick

trials" on 6 April.[52] The princess with the pride of a mother "who has fulfilled the functions and duties of a tutor" described his success: "The audience was prodigiously numerous, and so amazingly successful were his answers to the questions on all his subjects that the audience could not refrain from clapping (even though this is forbidden)."[53] It appears that the prince had to write a thesis in Latin as part of the requirements for his degree. Although the work is not mentioned in the Edinburgh records, a copy found its way to Russia to Samuil, Archbishop of Rostov and Iaroslavl'. Unimpressed, he sent it on to the young Prince I. M. Dolgorukii, who was himself toiling with Latin syntax, with the comment, "Ejus stylus magnopere mihi arrisit. Ex animo vellem, ut ei palmam praeriperes."[54] On 7 May the Lord Provost gave a reception for the prince and made him a Freeman of the city.[55] At the beginning of June the Dashkov family left Edinburgh for the last time, but not before the princess had made one final impressive gesture of esteem towards the university. She presented the university with a magnificent cabinet containing a complete collection of Russian medals from the birth of Peter the Great to the birth of the future Alexander I in 1777. Robison was charged by the Senate with the preparation of a detailed description, but at his death some twenty-five years later only two sheets of paper were found which seemed "to be all that he performed in the way of a Catalogue."[56]

Dashkova'a departure undoubtedly removed a colourful character from the Edinburgh social scene and many of the professors whose acquaintance she cultivated had cause to remember her kindly. Blair, who had given her a copy of his first volume of sermons (Edinburgh, 1777), sent her the second volume (1780) with a letter in which he declared "his high regard for one for whom he entertains sentiments of the greatest and most real esteem, as well as the most profound respect; to have had access to whose society, and to have enjoyed any degree of her friendship, he will always esteem a peculiar honour and felicity in his life."[57] Back in Russia in 1782 and, after a rapprochement with the empress, appointed Director of the Academy of Sciences and then President of the new Russian Academy, Dashkova did not hesitate to use her authority to confer honours on two of the outstanding Scottish scholars. On 28 January/8 February 1783 Robertson and Joseph Black were elected Honorary Foreign Members of the Academy of Sciences,[58] and Black was soon requested to correspond with the Academy on chemical matters. In this respect one of his letters to Dashkova in 1787 is of considerable interest. Mentioning Dr James Hutton (1726-97) as Dashkova's friend who had "assisted in making the catalogue of your beautiful Collection of Derbyshire fossils," he went on to give a detailed exposition of Hutton's revolutionary theory of the origin of the earth's crust, a theory in which he found "grandeur and sublimity."[59]

Although Dashkova's own son was elected FRS in 1781 at the tender

age of seventeen,[60] he never fulfilled his promise or his mother's expectations. What his mother did not at all expect but what was frequently ru-
moured was Paul's candidature for "the highest office in the land"—that of
Catherine's "favourite." Equally devastating for his mother was the manner
in which even such rumours became a thing of the past: Paul contracted an
unfortunate marriage in 1788 with a former shopkeeper's daughter while
serving with his regiment in the Ukraine. A colonel at twenty-one, he became
a general under Paul with supreme command of the army at Kiev. Although
his mother was exiled from Petersburg by Paul, the prince became the close
confidant of the tsar, until he too was dismissed in 1800. In the reign of
Alexander he lived in Moscow with his mistress, becoming a marshal of the
Moscow Nobility, but died suddenly in 1807 at the age of forty-three. Many
Englishmen visiting Russia made his acquaintance and in general found him
"a most accomplished and very honourable young Man," although as Jeremy
Bentham suggested, "too free in his speech, and overrun with Vanity."[61]
His death, according to another observer, came "from disappointed Ambition
& other inward causes of distress."[62]

IV

Apart from cutting a figure in Edinburgh society and caring for her son,
Dashkova was occasionally required to extend her protection and help to
other Russians who came to study in Scotland. Taking three of the same
courses as her son in 1778 was Ivan Stepanovich Sheshkovskii (1763-1818),
whose father was none other than the infamous head of Catherine's Secret
Chancellery. The young Sheshkovskii was followed to London by a letter of
recommendation from Archbishop Platon to Samborskii, in which the esteemed cleric spoke of the father as his great friend and recommended the
son to Samborskii's protection.[63] But even during his brief stay in London
Sheshkovskii revealed his true colours. It seems that he immediately incurred
the Russian ambassador's displeasure by leaving London for a jaunt to the
bright lights of Paris.[64] In Edinburgh he soon neglected his studies (with
Robison, Ferguson and Blair) to idle away his time and to indulge in acts
of tomfoolery which were characteristic of him most of his life. "I don't
know why Sheshovskii has not visited me for the last five weeks" wrote
Princess Dashkova in February, 1778, "but he comes to see my friends and
sits and smokes with them. Certainly he had a reason three weeks ago, when
he was ashamed to see us, for after watching an artist perform on a tight-
rope, he decided to dance himself on the rope, fell and banged and cut his
head, and then stayed away from the university for the next three weeks."[65]
By October she had more or less washed her hands of "that brainless youth":

I recommended him to all the best people here, including the professors, whom I consulted about his expenses and his plan of studies,
which I sent to his father. He lived five weeks in my house before
moving to Dr Blackley's (?) boarding-house, which is considered the
best, about a week before I left for Buxton, and he seemed content.
After my departure, however, he fell ill and gave up the best doctor
there is [Dr. William Cullen], who attends me and to whom I had
recommended him. He changed his rooms, his doctors, bought a huge
library, a horse, etc., etc. He did all this in my absence, taking finally
to live with him my son's former tutor whom I had dismissed for
his madcap nature and unworthy actions, and although the latter
is considered by people here as a madman and a litigant, Mr Sheshkovskii befriends him even as he, Hermann, slanders me. Thus I am repaid,
Father, for my solicitude by Mr Sheshkovskii, but I attribute his
behaviour to his poor intelligence, I forgive him and will not write
either to his father or to Aleksei Semenovich [Musin-Pushkin, the am-
bassador] in the hope that he will come to his senses and mend his
ways, but although his father put him completely under my authority, he not only does not ask permission but also disobeys me.[66]

Sheshkovskii's association with Jean-Frédéric Hermann (1743-1820), who
had been her son's tutor since 1773 and who was then in the process of
bringing a law suit against her for unfair dismissal,[67] was obviously the
last straw. But however prone to exaggeration and dramatization Dashkova
may have been, her stories about Sheshkovskii were well founded. She went
on to mention the enormous debts which he was piling up and in the following year he suffered the ultimate indignity of the debtors' prison. In the
Samborskii archives are four letters written between 9 April and mid-May,
1779, from the notorious Tolbooth Prison in Edinburgh. A frightened,
thoroughly chastened and repentant Sheshkovskii pleaded for help from
Samborskii, describing how he had been imprisoned at the request of one of
his creditors by the name of Angelo, how he was ill and alone and would
be eternally grateful if the ambassador could save him from "a situation
which is like death itself."[68] He seems to have remained there for at least
the month during which debtors could be retained at the expense of their
creditors, in the dark, dank and filthy prison which was later that year to
be visited by the great prison reformer John Howard.[69] It would be unjust
to wish on worthy sons retribution for the misdeeds of unworthy fathers,
but it is not difficult in the case of the miserable Sheshkovskiis to feel that
one more smear on the family honour does not come amiss.

   Sheshkovskii left England in the spring of 1780, studiously avoided by
another young Russian, Aleksei Levashov, who noted "I didn't travel with
Sheshkovskii, firstly because you know what sort of person he is and secondly, because I was afraid of making my relations and protectors ashamed."[70]

Little is known about the remaining forty years of Sheshkovskii's life in Russia. He eventually achieved the modest rank of brigadier and gained something of a reputation as a patron of literature. He was the dedicatee of a mock-epic published in 1791 by N. P. Osipov, a mark of gratitude from a man who had just escaped unscathed from questioning by Sheshkovskii père in connection with the Radishchev affair.[71] A surprisingly positive appraisal of Ivan Sheshkovskii came from a Saxon diplomatist G. A. W. von Helbig, who met him at this time. A scathing characterization of the father is followed by the remark that he had a son "distinguished for his knowledge, good intentions and pleasant manner."[72] But it is a last glimpse of Sheshkovskii from 1813 that is much more in character: Sheshkovskii and a man called D'iakov were involved in a brawl in the Petersburg shopping arcade, chasing each other through the aisles with a riding-whip.[73]

Dashkova found a more deserving and grateful person for her solicitude in Evstafii Zverev. Zverev, it will be recalled, was one of the group of agricultural students whom Samborskii had brought to England in 1776, but he had abandoned his studies in London to follow his real interests in medicine. He had complained in London that Samborskii had not paid him his official allowance and in Edinburgh his situation was desperate. With a compassion that was not without its admixture of self-esteem, Dashkova wrote that

> Pity, which forms a major element in my moral being, did not allow me to leave poor Zverev to starve to death. A fever and the lack of any food but potatoes had broken him. I allowed him to live in my house because he has no money to pay for either rooms or food; I can't give him any money because we don't receive our own income, but as long as I have coal and a crumb of bread I shall always share them with a fellow-countryman, whatever kind of man he is. But humanity will not allow me to abandon him to such an unhappy fate and I am sure you will agree. In addition his decision to go without food, which he has done for the past three-weeks, and not to incur debts deserves in my opinion praise.[74]

Later she was to describe Zverev as "a reliable man, assiduous in his studies."[75]

Zverev followed courses in the Edinburgh medical school, but the degree of M.D. which he received on 24 May 1779 was awarded by the University of St. Andrews. The degree was conferred *gratis* on account of personal merit and circumstances, unspecified but almost certainly financial, on testimonials furnished by Drs. James Hamilton and Andrew Duncan.[76] Although it is well known that "St Andrews and Aberdeen made a regular traffic in degrees, giving them for fees to persons who were never examined, or on the certificate of two obscure physicians"[77] and that even Edinburgh and certainly Glasgow had not been free from such accusations in earlier days, Zverev was a deserving case. The degree he gained was a passport to advancement in his profession on his return to Russia. Before he left Scotland he was elected an honorary member of the Edinburgh Physical Society, an association of doctors and medical students which had been founded in 1771 and was to gain its Royal charter in 1788.[78]

The Russian Medical College granted Zverev the right to practise on 15/ 26 February 1782 and he embarked on long years of devoted service.[79] After three years as Director of the medical office in Petersburg, where, incidentally, he gained a reputation as one of the leading exponents of Rosicrucianism with its devotion to alchemy,[80] he was assigned to New Russia, where he spent the rest of his life. In 1797 he was appointed the head doctor of the Elizavetgrad general hospital and director of the attached school of surgery. He was soon transferred to the naval hospital at Nikolaev where he was to renew acquaintance with his "old protector" Admiral Mordvinov.[81] His final post, which he was still administering at his death at the age of seventy-eight, was Inspector of the Bessarabian Medical Commission at Kishinev.

Despite his abandonment of agricultural studies, Zverev was at one stage appointed a professor of agriculture, but it is as a doctor, trained in Scotland, that he made his real contribution to improving the quality of life in Russia.

IV

The fame of the Edinburgh medical school attracted other Russians besides Zverev—and not only Russians, but students from America and all parts of Europe. Closely modelled on the celebrated medical school of Leiden, Edinburgh had achieved by the 1770s a reputation already surpassing it as a centre of medical scholarship and instruction. Under its founder Alexander Munro it had already achieved excellence but in the days of his son and of Cullen it exercised an enormous and deserved influence. In 1750 there were some sixty students of medicine, in 1766 some 160, but by 1800 the numbers had reached an incredible 600. An incomparable picture of life as an Edinburgh medical student in the 1770s with vivid cameos of the professors, of city notables, and of the activities of the various societies is provided in the diaries, both published and unpublished, of Sylas Neville, M.D. (1741-1840). It was he who wrote: "we have still Dr. Cullen, the greatest medical character that has appeared in the world since the days of Boerhaave. His fame is not confined to the British dominions—it is now extended all over the Continent & his Book is taught in the principal schools of Physic in Holland, France & Germany. Dr. Black is without an equal in Chemistry. Anatomy, Botany & all the other branches of medicine are taught by men, who (to say no more) do honour to them."[82]

Neville had been a member of the Medical Society (founded in 1737) since April, 1773, but it was only at the end of the following year that he was called upon to read a paper, as required of all members by the statutes of the Society. Still at work on it on 7 January 1775, he missed a business meeting of the Society, but noted in his diary: ". . . was prevented going to the private business, which however did not signify much: only I intended speaking a little for Mr. Keir and Dr. Italinski from Russia: the latter proposed as an Honorary member. They were both admitted & therefore no harm was done from my absence."[83] Neville's Russian friend was Andrei Iakovlevich Italinskii (1742-1827), of Cossack nobility stock who after some preliminary medical training in Moscow and Petersburg had left Russia a few years earlier to study at Leiden. He received his M.D. in 1774 and then came to Scotland. His name is inscribed in the medical matriculation rolls for the 1774-75 session and he remained in Edinburgh until mid-June, 1775. Neville elsewhere spoke of him as "a very sensible good kind of man [who] speaks 5 or 6 languages and knows a great deal both in medicine & other sciences"[84] and he was indeed by all accounts a remarkable and talented individual, whose future career and fame was to be as a diplomat. He returned in 1776 to the Ukraine, leaving behind by accident in London what was probably the first Russian translation of Cesare Beccaria's *Dei delitti e delle pene* (1764), a key work of penal reform widely used by Catherine in her *Nakaz*.[85] Back in Paris by 1780, he was presented by Baron Grimm to Grand Duke Paul, an occasion which lead to a marked rise in his fortunes. He was an honorary Counsellor at the Paris embassy but was soon transferred to Naples, where his talents were given opportunity to develop. Shortly after his accession Paul made Italinskii Russian Ambassador in Naples and in 1801 Ambassador in Constantinople. 1812 saw him leading the negotiations with the Turks that led to the Treaty of Bucharest, before he finally returned to his beloved Italy to combine his work as a diplomat with his erudite interest in archaeology and classical art. He was a member of many Russian and European academies and scholarly bodies and his association with England, which he maintained by correspondence with such scholars as the Sanscritologist Johnson, was crowned by his election to the Royal Society in 1814.[86]

Frightened by Italinskii's stories of the high cost of living in England but undoubtedly attracted by his account of British medical achievements was his friend and compatriot Dr. Aleksandr Mikhailovich Shumlianskii (1748-95), known in Soviet medical histories as "the father of Russian histology."[87] In 1782 Shumlianskii had finished five years study at the University of Strasbourg and was hoping to visit London, Paris and Vienna to gain further experience. In the event he was obliged to return to Russia without visiting London, but two years later in connection with the establishment of the Petersburg Medico-Surgical Academy he was sent abroad to study foreign hospitals and teaching establishments. His companion was Dr. Martyn Matveevich Terekhovskii (1740-96), famed for his contribution to Russian biology and an earlier graduate from Strasbourg.[88] They arrived in London in December 1785, but they were by then scarcely on speaking terms and soon incurred the displeasure of the Russian ambassador, who branded them as "deux fols, remplis d'un amour-propre qui les conduira aux petites maisons."[89] Although they were meant to visit Edinburgh together as part of their project, Shumlianskii decided to stay in London, before leaving alone for Russia at the end of June, 1786. Terekhovskii remained some months in Edinburgh, where, according to one report, he did nothing but sit in his lodgings, designing a hospital building which Vorontsov considèred totally unsuitable for Russian conditions. He was, however, accorded a cordial welcome in Edinburgh medical circles, for shortly after his arrival, he was elected an honorary member of both the Medical and Natural History Societies.[90]

The latter society had been founded only in 1782 on the initiative of six medical students and was devoted to the study of chemistry and natural history. Its activities received the active encouragement of Professors Hope and Black, who were honorary members, while another professor, John Walker, joined as an ordinary member. It was one of the best run and disciplined societies, meeting regularly at 7 p.m. on Wednesdays from November to May, and fining one guinea any member who failed to produce a dissertation for discussion on the fixed day.[91] Its membership was truly cosmopolitan and Americans, Swiss, Irish—and Russians took part; indeed, Russians played a more conspicuous role in this society than in any other. Terekhovskii's speedy election is probably explained by the fact that one of the four annual presidents elected on 1 December 1785 was a Russian nobleman, Iurii Alekseevich Bakhmetev.[92]

Bakhmetev was the son of Aleksei Ivanovich Bakhmetev, a recently deceased official in the Salt Office (*Solianaia kontora*) in Moscow and seems to have studied initially at Moscow University before coming to England in 1776 in the care of Samborskii. He spent some four years in London, studying Latin and Greek in addition to English and eventually went to Edinburgh in 1780. He was elected to the Medical Society on 20 December 1783 and to the Natural History Society on 2 December 1784. The first paper which he delivered to the Natural History Society was entitled "On the Use & Action of Quicklime & Other Calcareous Earth as a Manure" (31 March 1785), and this was followed during his term as President by one "On Coal" (15 December 1785). The texts of both these papers are to be found among the records of the Society.[93]

By December Bakhmetev was already working on his doctoral thesis and sought to dedicate his work to Vorontsov. The embassy suggested that he might rather approach the empress, who gave her gracious permission.[94] The subject was one in which Catherine had a keen interest—smallpox inoculation, and Bakhmetev's thesis, *De variolis inserendis*, which he defended on 12 September 1786, contained numerous references to Dr. Thomas Dimsdale's *Tracts on Inoculation, Written and Published at St. Petersburg in the Year 1768* (London, 1781). Bakhmetev was also awarded an M.A. from St. Andrews in 1786 and shortly after his graduation was elected a Fellow of the Royal College of Physicians.[95] He was highly regarded by Black as "a young man of abilities & good sense,"[96] but after his return to Russia in October, 1787, he seems to have made no mark. One of the few medical sources even to mention his name simply notes that "he did not take up practice or serve in the Medical Chancery."[97]

A doctor who did put his considerable knowledge and expertise to practice in his homeland was the third Russian to gain an M.D. from a Scottish university. Daniil Iakovlevich Pischekov (1758-1825) had a similar background to many of the young men treated in these pages. A priest's son, he studied at the Khar'kov seminary, before electing to train in medicine and transferring to the Moscow General hospital in 1775. He was working at the Petersburg naval hospital in 1776 when Samborskii left with the group of young "agriculturists" who included his friend Flavitskii, and he himself was soon to think of studying in London, which was "the first place in Europe particularly with regard to its medical faculty."[98] He spent some ten months in Stockholm, pursuing his medical studies before returning to Petersburg late in 1778. In the next few years he received a number of unsatisfactory and dismally paid jobs in hospitals, as well as acting as tutor to Samborskii's son for a short period and improving his knowledge of English by taking lessons from an Englishman in the Russian capital. He eventually arrived in England in 1782 and enrolled for classes in the Edinburgh school of medicine the following year.[99] Like Zverev before him, Pischekov had neither the time nor the money to qualify for an Edinburgh degree, but was awarded his M.D. from the University of Aberdeen at the end of 1784 through the sponsorship of his friends, Drs. Gardner and Charles Keith, the second of whom was himself an Aberdeen graduate and the author of a number of medical works.[100] His doctoral thesis, *De novo methodo psoram sanandi*, was published in Edinburgh and was to be translated into Russian and published in 1786 as *Novyi legchaishii i bezopasneishii sposob lecheniia chesotki* (2nd edition, with slightly altered title, in 1792).

Pischekov sailed for Russia in the spring of 1785, but early the following year the findings in his thesis were to receive wider dissemination among the British public through the publication of a letter, signed "Medicus," in *Gentleman's Magazine*.[101] Medicus was contributing to discussion on remedies for "the itch" and recommended "vegetable acid," such as used by Pischekov in 1780 in Voronezh province and later described in his thesis. "As the distribution of this pamphlet has been confined to the narrow circle of a few friends," continued Medicus "I should be glad to have an

opportunity . . . of making the author's practice more generally known."
Pischekov employed various vegetable distillations as well as *kvas*, the pro-
perties of which for curing skin diseases, including scurvy, were to be sung
a number of times in British sceintific publications in the late eighteenth
century. Scurvy, in fact, was one of the subjects which Pischekov touched
upon in an article published in 1787 in an organ of the Free Economic
Society (to which he had been elected in 1784). "O novom sposobe pere-
chishcheniia povarennoi soli dlia bezvrednogo onoi upotrebleniia" ("About
a New Method of Purifying Cooking Salt so that It May Be Used with
Safety") described how he had tested a method about which he had read in
Scotland in the Earl of Dundonald's *Thoughts on the Manufacture and Trade
of Salt, on the Herring Fisheries, and on the Coal-Trade of Great Britain*
(Edinburgh, 1784), but only when a solution of his own devising was added,
was pure salt obtained. His prescription for its use—two teaspoons in a glass
of cold water before meals—reads like an early advertisement for Enos
Salts.[102]

Although Pischekov had not stuided agriculture in England, certainly
not of a practical kind, he was appointed a Professor of Agriculture along
with his friends. His first post was as assistant to the Director of Husbandry
for the Petersburg region. In 1790, the year he resigned, he published a
Karmannyi lechebnik, which was basically a translation of Sir John Elliott's
Medical Pocket-Book (1781), but with numerous additions, corrections and
prescriptions of his own. It proved popular and went into a second edition
in 1794, by which time Pischekov was working at Roslavl' in Smolensk
province, short of money but not dissatisfied with his lot. He was soon to
move, however, to the South and it was in connection with an epidemic in
Novorossiisk province that his experience and knowledge of skin diseases
proved invaluable and brought him his mite of official recognition. He wrote
a *Nastavlenie v pol'zu poselian, boleznuiushchikh tsingotnoi bolezniiu* ("Instruction for Peasants Suffering from Scurvy"), for which he was commended
by the Medical College in 1798, and his work in general at this time received
Imperial approval—if belatedly, in 1816. The nineteenth century dawned
for Pischekov with a new post at the Taganrog quarantine office and the
curatorship of the local botanical garden. Here he spent fourteen quiet years
until his retirement in 1814. He retired to his native Ukraine, near Belgorod,
where he continued to offer medical aid until his death in 1825.[103]

It is possible to add one more name to the list of Russian medical students
and doctors in Edinburgh in the 1780s—that of Danilo Samoilovich (1743-
1805), a noted epidemologist and prolific author. Originally selected by
Samborskii as a member of his agricultural group, Samoilovich went instead
to Leiden, where he took his M.D. in 1780. Further studies in Paris and
Strasbourg were followed by a brief trip to London and Edinburgh in late
1783. A member of twelve European academies, which he would carefully

list on the title pages of his later works, Samoilovich seems not to have been so honoured in Britain. The only trace of his visit to Scotland is the recording of his gift of copies of his works on the plague, including *Mémoires sur la peste* (Paris, 1783), to the Royal Society of Edinburgh.[104]

V

Doctors apart, there were other Russian students at Edinburgh in the 1780s, three of whom were noted or notorious for their Anglomania. D. M. Poltoratskii's passion for English agriculture has been described in an earlier chapter, but it is not generally known that during his tour of Britain in 1783 he stayed in Edinburgh long enough to take courses with Ferguson and Adam Fraser, the Professor of Civil History, as a follow-up to his studies at Stuttgart, where he had obtained his degree.[105] Poltoratskii's Anglomania manifested itself in agricultural pursuits, that of Vasilii Zybin in Ivanushka-like posturings of "foreignness." Zybin earned a place in M. I. Pyliaev's work on Russian eccentrics and originals for his affecting to have forgotten the Russian language during his long years abroad and for his contempt for the ignorance of the Russian people.[106] Almost nothing is known about his origins or subsequent life, but in 1780-81 he took courses at Edinburgh with Bruce, Ferguson, Blair and Robison.

Considerably more is known, however, about Pavel Petrovich Bakunin (1762-1805), for he was to succeed Princess Dashkova as Director of the Academy of Sciences in 1794. He was the son of the senator Petr Vasil'evich Bakunin and related both to the Princess who nominated him as her successor, and Count Vorontsov, the Russian ambassador in England, who had hardly a good word to say about him. "Bacounine, qui est mon neveu et qui était près de deux ans avec moi," he wrote to H. L. Nikolai, the new President of the Academy of Sciences, "n'est qu'un étourdi présomptueux et ignorant; c'est l'homme le moins propre à être à la tête d'une Académie et le plus capable à introduire des désordres et des confusions là où il n'y en avait pas même avant."[107] He proved a dictatorial and arbitrary director, an unhappy choice, but not the "person of little education" whom Vucinich describes.[108] He was in Britain for some two years between 1785 and 1787, officially attached to the London embassy, but spending most of his time studying at Edinburgh. He was elected a member of the Natural History Society on 27 April 1786 and in the following year duly read his required paper "On the Means Used by Nature for the Preservation of Vegetables from the Effects of Cold during the Winter in High Latitudes."[109] Later that same year he was elected a corresponding member of the Society of Antiquaries of Scotland, a position held by four notable members of the British community in Russia, Drs Matthew Guthrie and John Grieve, Rev. William Tooke and Samuel Bentham.[110] A Scottish scholar whom Bakunin held in particular respect at this time was Dugald Stewart and it was his subsequent determination to emphasise that respect by engineering the Scotsman's election as an honorary member of the Academy of Sciences in September 1795 that led to one of the many "incidents" during his directorship.[111]

However unfortunate the circumstances regarding Stewart's election, it was yet another link between Scotland and Russia, and given the worthiness of the scholar, essentially no different from the honorary memberships of Robertson and Black, bestowed by Dashkova, and from that of Robison, who succeeded Black, proposed by Nikolai. A recent writer on eighteenth-century Scotland has termed the period between 1770 and 1800 the "age of recognition" and Russia was by no means the last among European nations to honour Scottish scholars. Under Dashkova's predecessor, S. G. Domashnev, the Academy of Sciences had elected on the same day, 29 December 1776 (O. S.), Sir John Pringle, by this time President of the Royal Society, to foreign honorary membership and Dr. John Rogerson (1741-1823), Catherine's physician, to honorary membership.[112] Rogerson, who had received his M.D. at Edinburgh in 1765 and entered Russian service the following year was in every respect a key figure in the very active cultural intercourse between Scotland and Russia during the reign of Catherine.[113] It was he who was responsible for bringing Robertson's *History of the Reign of the Emperor Charles V* (1769) to the empress's attention and for transmitting his request for information about Russian discoveries along the American seaboard in connection with his work on *The History of America* (1777).[114] Catherine's interest in Robertson's works undoubtedly led to their inclusion among books for translation by the Society for the Translation of Foreign Books (1768-83). Volume I of *Charles V* appeared in 1775, translated from the French version of 1771, and Volume II three years later, but although a third volume was translated, it was never published. A similar fate befell *The History of America*, of which only the first part appeared, this time translated directly from the English original, in 1784.[115]

After Robertson, the Scottish scholar best represented in Russian translations by the end of the century was Blair: *Essays on Rhetoric* appeared in 1791, and separate lectures, "The Rise and Progress of Language" and "Eloquence of the Pulpit" in 1799 and 1899 respectively.[116] Blair's eminence as a preacher had indeed been described by a Russian visitor who published his impressions in 1796:

I heard both of the most celebrated local preachers, Doctors Blair and Greenfield. In Moscow there are many connoisseurs of bells and sermons. In the sermons which I heard there was much knowledge, they were of the kind to impress a person and sow in his heart good rules not only for the eternal but also for the present bliss of man. For instance, Greenfield showed that virtue and happiness are indivisible, while Blair warned his listeners of the dangers of hardheartedness and false sentimentality, which manifests itself only in empty expressions of compassion and pity. In short, their sermons demonstrated that they know both the Bible and the human heart. Blair is considered the best of the British preachers. . . .[117]

Two other works by Edinburgh professors found their way into Russian— John Gregory's *A Father's Legacy to his Daughters* (1774) in 1791 and Francis Home's *Principia medicinae* (1762) in 1786, but much of real importance and value was neglected. This is not to say, however, that the major works of Edinburgh professors, and of Scottish literati and philosophers in general, did not find their way to Russia in the original English or in French or German translations. The esteem in which Adam Smith's *Wealth of Nations* was held by the Russian ambassador in London, S. R. Vorontsov, as well as by his brother Alexander, to whom he sent a copy of the book in 1786, and his sister, Princess Dashkova, is well known,[118] but the evidence of Vorontsov's brother-in-law V. N. Zinov'ev has never been quoted. Zinov'ev met Smith in Edinburgh in August, 1786, and described him to Vorontsov as "the author of that book, esteemed by both you and me."[119] Zinov'ev also mentions a meeting with James Burnett, Lord Monboddo, author of *Antient Metaphysics* and *Of the Origin and Progress of Language*, who spoke of sending his works via Vorontsov to Catherine the Great.[120] Robertson, Blair, Smith, Monboddo, as well as Henry Hope, Lord Kames, David Hume, all had their admirers and contacts in Russia[121] and reflect perhaps merely the tip of the iceberg in terms of Russo-Scottish contacts at every level. The traffic was by no means one way: the Edinburgh professoriate had in its number for the last quarter of the century Robison who had personal knowledge of Russia and at Glasgow for a similar period there was William Richardson (1743-1814), Professor of Humanity who had earlier been tutor to the children of Lord Cathcart in St. Petersburg and who produced his *View of the Russian Empire* in 1784. As Franco Venturi has shown in a recent article,[122] Scottish scholars, such as Richardson, Millar, Robertson and Kames, showed much interest in Russian historical development, particularly with regard to their debates on feudalism.

Unlike the Russian students at Glasgow, Desnitskii and Tret'iakov, their counterparts at Edinburgh who pursued courses in the humanities left little evidence of any influence their Scottish teachers may have exerted. They left no original writings or took part in any of the translations which have been mentioned. It was left to the doctors, men committed to, and needing to live by, their profession, rather than the Zybins, Sheshkovskiis and, indeed, Dashkovs, to reveal what they had learned in their dissertations and articles, and, most importantly, in a land desperately short of trained doctors, in their practice. It is indeed appropriate to end this account of Russian students at the Scottish universities by highlighting medicine, for it is in this area that Russo-Scottish ties are at their strongest and most apparent. Scottish doctors made a distinctive contribution to the improvement of medical standards in Russia throughout the eighteenth century and Rogerson was far from unique in achieving imperial recognition. It was on the recommendation of Dr. James Mounsey, the last "archiater" or head of the Russian medical chancery, who returned to Scotland in 1762, that his kinsman Rogerson went to Russia. Although Mounsey was not a graduate of Edinburgh, two graduates of that university, James Grieve (M.D., 1733), Mounsey's father-in-law, and North Vigor (M.D., 1747) were practising successfully in Moscow and Petersburg during his period in Russia. Grieve's son, John (1753-1805), a graduate of Glasgow (M.D., 1777) also worked in Russia and became physician to Paul, a post shared by James Wylie (M.D., Aberdeen, 1794). John Grieve was in Edinburgh in 1784 and was friendly with Pischekov and other Russians there. Graduating in the same year as Bakhmetev was John Rogerson, junior, whose success was witnessed by his father returning for a short period from Russia. Rogerson, jr., did not practise in Russia, but George Cayley (M.D., 1789), son of the British consul in Petersburg and a close friend of both Bakhmetev and Bakunin, did.[123] Examples such as these could be multiplied, but they are more than sufficient to suggest the common bonds of medical knowledge and shared experience which united some Russian and Scottish doctors towards the end of the eighteenth century.

CHAPTER 6
ON BRITISH SHIPS AND IN BRITISH YARDS

If Peter the Great himself were to arrange the sequence of chapters in this book in accordance with his views on the importance of their subject-matter, he would undoubtedly begin with this chapter. Peter's fascination with the sea and with the building, manning and navigating of ships, his liking for the company of foreign skippers and shipwrights, his own prowess as a sailor, his labours in the shipyards of Holland, his visits to Greenwich and Deptford, and his relentless drive to secure outlets to the seas in the west and in the south are legendary and occupy a prominent place in the numerous histories and collections of anecdotes to which his life and reign gave rise. By the time a suitable shrine was built within the grounds of the Peter and Paul Fortress to house "the little boat of Peter the Great" which he had sailed on the lake at Preobrazhenskoe over sixty years before, the Russian navy which the tsar had lived to see gain its first important victories and some measure of international recognition had already suffered a decline and fall; it was only under Catherine the Great that it once more became an effective fighting force and achieved great prestige. At all stages throughout the century, however, England had a significant and telling contribution to make, both by allowing British officers and shipbuilders to serve in Russia and by receiving Russians to train on ships of the British navy and to learn the skills of shipbuilding in British yards. The exploits and achievements of British officers in the Russian service have received detailed attention for a number of reasons; for a number of reasons, the adventures of Russians in England have not.

I

Perhaps Peter himself should be regarded as the first Russian seaman to visit England[1] and the amount of time he devoted to nautical matters during his three months stay is a clear indication of their importance for him. After a few weeks in a house in Norfolk Street, convenient nevertheless for the Thames, he moved to Deptford, to John Evelyn's home, Sayes Court, where when he was not making his own opening in Evelyn's prize yew hedge, he was slipping through a gap specially made in the boundary wall to give him easy access to the royal shipyard. Keenly interested in every aspect of shipbuilding, Peter was also allowed to indulge his passion for sailing. A small yacht, the *Dove*, was put at his disposal and he sailed it frequently and not without incident: on two occasions he seems to have managed spectacular collisions. A special demonstration of firing by a bomb-ship was arranged for him at Woolwich, and he was also taken further afield, to Portsmouth to witness a specially staged mock battle. In constant attendance on the tsar throughout his stay were Vice Admiral David Mitchell, who had escorted him from Holland, and Rear Admiral the Marquis of Carmarthen, who became a bosom friend. According to a reliable Russian source, Peter was subsequently to say that "if I were not the tsar, I would wish to be a British admiral."[2] It was with Carmarthen in particular that Peter discussed ways in which a navy "after the English manner" could most readily be created; Carmarthen advised the recruiting of master builders, "ingenious English sea-officers" and as many "Able English Seamen as His Majesty shall think sufficient to be mingled with his own Subjects on board . . . for the more speedy instruction of them in the practice of the English Navigation and Discipline."[3] Many Britons were to follow the tsar to Russia to begin a century during which a significant number of Russian ships were to be built by British masters and during every year of which at least one British officer was in command of a Russian man-of-war. Only the last of Carmarthen's suggestions was Peter unable to follow and the "more speedy instruction" of Russian seamen was to take place on British ships. Indeed Peter took immediate steps to place some members of his entourage with the British fleet: at the end of March, 1698, the Admiralty agreed to accept nine men for service with the Straits Squadron, and at the beginning of April considered Peter's request that "Alexander Petelin and Gabriel Cabullion" be placed on ships going to the Mediterranean and that the second of the two men be instructed in gunnery.[4]

Among members of the British community in Moscow near to Peter was the merchant Andrew Styles, who had received a monopoly of the export of pitch and tar and, according to the British ambassador, generally had "so great an interest with the first favourite [Menshikov], and even with the Czar himself."[5] Styles had a brother, Thomas, in London, also a member of the Russia Company, and after Peter's return to Russia they carried out various commissions from the tsar, including the recruiting of British specialists and naval officers, and were also instrumental in bringing some of the first Russian seamen and boatbuilders to England. Evidence of this last activity is contained in a petition sent to the tsar from London in July, 1708, by Petr Lunevskii and Ivan Michurin, who "as young men had been entrusted to Mr Stiles for our education." They had been in England seven years and after studying "navigation and engineering" were then engaged with shipbuilding. They were in urgent need of money in order "to live without dishonour to Your Majesty and to find out the secrets of shipbuilding, for we know the language and the ways in which money is used here to obtain knowledge."[6] Lunevskii and Michurin were to stay thirteen years in all in England and by the time they returned to Russia the sending of Russian seamen had long followed a regular pattern.

In June, 1705, after hearing that Queen Anne was reluctant to release more

British officers for service in Russia, Count F. S. Golovin, Peter's minister for foreign affairs in all but name, informed the recently arrived British Ambassador Charles Whitworth that he had proposed to the British merchants "the taking on board their ships at the Czar's charge five or six youths, who are bred up in the mathematical school here, and had learnt part of the theory, but now wanted to see the practical part of navigation, as they would in such a voyage; and if hereafter some of them might be allowed to make a campaign of two on board a man-of-war, he said it would be a greater obligation."[7] Whitworth was much in favour of the idea and thought that if the British did not accept the Russians, other European nations would. Without committing his government, he had suggested that a dozen or so young Russians might be accepted the following year. And a year later the tentative offer was taken up and a list of not twelve but thirty names was submitted to Whitworth. In the interim, however, a few Russians had already been assigned to merchant ships and indeed "were now some of them aboard the fleet."[8] It was, however, with the group of thirty "lusty young men and few or none under twenty years old" that the scheme was first put on a more or less official basis. The British contribution was not only in the willingness to receive the Russian seamen but even more significantly in the initial preparation of suitable candidates: the seamen came from the Moscow School of Mathematics and Navigation, founded in 1701 after the model of the Royal Mathematical School at Christ's Hospital and directed by Henry Farquharson, a former teacher at Marischal College, Aberdeen, who was assisted by two former pupils of Christ's Hospital, Stephen Gwyn and Richard Grice.[9]

1706 thus saw the launching of an operation which was not to be matched in scale throughout the rest of the century; over the following ten years or so groups of young Russians, both commoners and nobles, were to be sent to Europe to gain practical experience on board the ships of the foremost maritime nations of the world. Although the English role was considerable, the European dimension was always present: Russians sailed on Dutch and Danish, and later Venetian and French ships as well as on British, and after 1708 the activities of the various groups were coordinated, or supposed to be coordinated, from Holland. It is virtually impossible to give precise numbers of Russians sent abroad during Peter's reign or even to give in every case the destination of those known to have been sent, but around 150 would seem to have been in England at one time or another, including those who were later sent specifically to study various aspects of the building and arming of ships. Of the Russians who trained in England none is known to have left an extensive account of his experiences, and an impression of what they did has to be gleaned from various letters and official documents. Max Okenfuss has recently and rightly taken issue with the prevailing dismissive attitude towards Peter's "great experiment" and anyone who reads the documents rather than the oft-repeated anecdotal accounts of historians cannot fail to be struck by the serious and clearly defined aims which prompted the exercise as well as to understand the causes of the all too frequent mishaps and the significance of the more rare attainments.[10]

Members of the first two groups from the Moscow School sent in 1706 and 1707 found themselves plunged immediately into the War of the Spanish Succession as hapless "volunteers" in the British navy. Vasilii Shapkin, a seaman in the first group, later reported that "on our arrival in England seventeen of us were allocated on the orders of Her Britannic Majesty to two men-of-war, on which we served only three weeks before we were captured in battle and taken to France where we remained in captivity eighteen months."[11] The second group the following year was intercepted on its voyage from Archangel to London and was imprisoned for a year before eventually reaching England at the beginning of 1709.[12] By the time these seamen were released, a third group, twenty-eight strong, all commoners like their predecessors but including not only immediate graduates from the Moscow school but also *podshturmany* ("sub-navigators") i.e., men with some naval experience, was on its way to Amsterdam to be placed under the supervision of Prince Ivan Borisovich L'vov. In June, 1708, L'vov had been sent to Holland as the "commissar for the supervision of young noblemen" ("kommisar dlia nadziraniia znatnykh osob detei") and he was to carry out his duties until 1716. The first group of young noblemen, destined for command positions in the Russian navy, numbered twenty-three; they were followed in 1709-11 by further groups of eight, thirteen and ten. Over the slightly longer period of 1706-11, 129 commoners were also sent.[13] Thus L'vov had during his first three years alone over 180 men under his supervision, and something of the scale of his responsibilities can be immediately appreciated, before any of the attendant difficulties are even itemised.

L'vov seemed from the beginning overawed by his duties. Before he left Russia, he submitted a list of nine queries, touching on the studies, financing and control of the young noblemen assigned to his care, which Peter answered decisively if not always helpfully.[14] There was no mistaking the basic aim— "the study of navigation in the winter, and in the summer cruises on men-of-war, so that they should subsequently become naval officers," but this, like many of the other instructions, left so much to chance or to a continuously ideal situation in which money flowed without hindrance from Russia, foreign powers strained to cooperate and the young students behaved in exemplary fashion. The 1709 group of commoners was given similar orders, designed to produce complete navigators, but a petition from this group before they departed, drawing attention to their almost complete lack of the necessary navigational instruments, highlighted some of the hidden problems particularly of a financial nature.[15] Lack of regular and adequate funding once again proved to be the inescapable stumbling-block of all young Russians sent abroad at government expense and became the insistent refrain of numerous letters from L'vov, his agents, and the navigators themselves. Whitworth from the very beginning had insisted that all the men sent from Russia for service in the British fleet should come within the category of "volunteers," freeing the British from all financial responsibilities for their maintenance. Frequently cut off for long periods during sea voyages from sources of money, i.e., L'vov and his agents, Van der Berg in Amsterdam and Thomas Styles in London, the Russian sailors were soon heavily in debt. It is small wonder that many were threatened with debtors' prison, were in a state of near starvation and occasionally expressed their despair in wild behavior and heavy drinking. These latter aspects of the Russians' conduct have inevitably attracted most attention and of course there are ample quotations at hand in the reports of such as L'vov and Styles to be paraded, if frequently out of a more meaningful general context. In May 1709 Whitworth mentioned in a letter to London that "Mr. Stile's brother has often complained of the russian voluntiers and desired they might be taken out of his hands, being so very dissolute and unruly, that he could not keep them within their allowance, nor in any tolerable way of living."[16] Between 1711 and 1713 there was a flurry of similar reports between L'vov in Amsterdam, von der Lith, the Russian diplomatic representative in London, Count G. I. Golovkin in St Petersburg and Count Boris Kurakin in The Hague, in which appear such colourful details as "I have tried to appease an Englishman who has had an eye put out by one of the Muscovites, but he is demanding £500," "many have gone astray and spend their nights on the streets to the shame of our nation," or "in England both the old and the new navigators have run up debts and they want to beat to death secretary Siniavich who is hiding from them and has forsaken his responsibilities."[17] But even more in evidence are the genuine difficulties of the Russian navigators. Lith told of one navigator who was shipwrecked off the Danish coast on his way to London from Russia and who arrived eventually without possessions or money but was refused help because "almost all the money here has gone"; L'vov wrote about Grigorii Khlebnikov, a member of the 1710 group who from poverty had decided to change his religion and join the British navy "and others are doing the same."[18] A letter sent by fourteen seamen to Prince Menshikov in February, 1713, puts their case eloquently:

> Having been at sea for six years and more, we have studied naval practices with all our strength and all our power and have learned what we were able. Having been out of England in distant parts for two or three years at a time and not having received the pay granted us by His Majesty, we have contracted debts which are inconsiderable against the money which is our due. Now that we have returned to England from distant parts we wish to be in the service of His Majesty, but we are oppressed by our debts and there is no money to pay us with and we are refused our pay for reasons we truly do not know and this is for us a great mis-

fortune for, with so much money spent on us and our having studied sciences in practice, we are left in foreign parts. Therefore servilely and tearfully we beseech Your Grace to intercede with His Majesty to pay our debts and provide us with books and instruments without which we cannot serve at sea His Tsarist Majesty and to send us to Russian ports so that we shall not be deprived of serving in His Tsarist Majesty's service, for we truly wish to serve and die in His Tsarist Majesty's service.[19]

The plight of the navigators was not shared by most of the nobles who received money from their families, although others, including L'vov himself, were not rich enough to survive without government support and were reduced to poverty. Their problems were somewhat different, arising in some cases from their distaste for a naval career and their apparent lack of preparation (some were apparently illiterate).[20] They included in their number sons of some of the most distinguished families in Russia—Sheremetevs, Dolgorukovs, Golitsyns, Cherkasskiis and last but far from least Naryshkins, cousins of the tsar. Many of the noblemen were very young and Aleksandr and Ivan Naryshkin among the youngest, being fourteen and eight respectively. The Naryshkins travelled separately from Russia in an English man-of-war, preceded by letters of recommendation from Whitworth. They were presented at Court shortly after their arrival in London and received special favours, which displeased Peter, who had wished them to live incognito and soon had them transferred to Amsterdam under the direct supervision of L'vov. L'vov, Whitworth reported, was instructed "to order m-rs Narishkin, prince Dolgoruky and the two counts Golowin, wherever they are, to repair to you immediately, and, if they refuse to come, you are to go yourself and fetch them, and see that they diligently apply themselves to the study of navigation."[21] Most of them were to do precisely that, but there were inevitable exceptions. L'vov reported in 1711 that Prince Sergei Shcherbatov "has gone mad from melancholy and sits naked in his house, and there is no one to pay for him and nothing to pay with. What is to be done with him? The owner of the house wants to put him in a madhouse." On another occasion he wrote that the rich and lazy among the noblemen would become even more idle when they saw the lack of care for those who studied diligently, and they would be content to remain abroad, paying heed merely to their whims.[22]

So much for the difficulties and negative aspects of life abroad for both commoners and nobles; what of the positive attainments? Despite L'vov's long litany of his own ill-health, of an existence that was worse than death itself, of letters and requests for money and instructions unanswered in Russia, his efforts were not all in vain. The impediments were greater than they might have been, for he complained with justice that he had no official standing, that he was "not a public commissar" and that he could not approach directly English and Dutch officials; he also knew no languages but Russian and he

frequently requested money to hire an interpreter.[23] Nevertheless, other reports reveal that, if with difficulty, placements of the young Russians on European warships were being regularly effected, that vital practical experience
was being gained by commoners and nobles alike on frequently long and hazardous voyages to America and in the Mediterranean, as well as between London and Archangel. Batches of seamen were being sent back to Russia from
1711 on after they had been abroad for some four years at least. Of the 129
commoners sent to Europe by 1711, eighty-two had returned by 1713, although others were to stay for ten years or more. In 1714 L'vov sent back a
report which detailed the activities of forty-nine of the young nobles sent to
Amsterdam between 1708 and 1713. The majority had had experience at some
time on British ships and had travelled far and wide. Typical examples are such
as Aleksei Petrovich Sheremetev and his younger brother Ivan:

1) voyage on a Dutch ship and back to Holland.
2) to England on an English ship where they remained.
3) on a British man-of-war in British service.
4) on British ships separately to the Mediterranean, and I have heard that
   they were also in the West Indies.
5) from England to the Mediterranean and I have heard that they went to
   Venice, where they are now.

or Nikolai and Aleksandr Golovin:

1) in the Dutch service on a Dutch man-of-war to the Baltic return.
2) on a British ship to Portugal and back to England.
3) to Portugal and in the Mediterranean to Smirna and then to Cyprus and
   Candia and along the Egyptian coast, without leaving the ship for more
   than a year and a half, and now back in England.[24]

Count Aleksandr Petrovich Apraksin, nephew of Admiral F. M. Apraksin, arrived in Holland in 1709, but soon was attached to the British navy and served
for seven years. He made several long voyages and L'vov reported in 1713 that
he had been in the Mediterranean for some twenty-two months and was soon
to undertake another long voyage. A number of letters to him from his uncle
are of interest for showing not only how the rich families were able to send
considerable sums of money to help sons in debt, whereas the commoners
were generally left in desperate need, but also the family concern tha Apraksin should do well and earn the tsar's favour: "for God's sake show firm application in the work entrusted to your and practise without rest in order to fulfil the will of the Tsar, and if you do not, do not expect to return home until
you know naval matters from keel to pennant, as behoves a skilled seaman. . . ."
Admiral Apraksin also warned his nephew that he would be strictly examined
on his return and "you must acquire especially all the skills of a navigator and
boatswain (*nauku shturmanshuiu i botsmanskuiu*)." He later suggested that before he left, he should attempt to get as many testimonials (*sertifikaty*) as he
could from commanders of ships on which he served. His nephew eventually

reached Russia in 1716 and was deemed satisfactory and confirmed in the rank of ensign. The following year he was again sent to England to buy ships and help recruit skilled tradesmen for service in Russia. He then enjoyed a steady if unspectacular career in the Russian navy until his early death in 1725.[25]

Admiral Apraksin's fears about his nephew proved unnecessary, but the performance of certain noblemen who had returned earlier had prompted them. In April, 1713, he noted that "several of your comrades on their arrival here were quickly reduced from ensigns to ordinary seamen and only Mr. Zotov retained his previous rank."[26] It was such an occurence that led John Deane, who had been the the tsar's service for a number of years and who was later to write a well-known "History of the Russian Fleet during the Reign of Peter the Great," to pronounce negatively on Peter's experiment as a whole:

> For the Russians in general have an aversion to sea, and no manner of inspection was made into the genius and inclination of these youths; many of them sons of such as were suspected to be the least favourable to the Tsar's designs of altering their customs, and new modelling their country; and these retaining a spice of their father's disaffection were the less intent on making a progress; and the rest of the men of fashion, having credit at large, launched out into all manner of effeminate and extravagant living, frequenting the play-houses, gaming tables, &c., according to the prevailing gust of the nation they conversed in, not caring how little they went to sea; and upon their recall, undergoing a strict examination, were found instead of attaining the rudiments of a seaman, to have acquired only the insignificant accomplishments of fine gentlemen. And the Tsar, incensed thereat, gave directions to reduce 'em to common seamen, and employed them constantly in the most servile part of their work. In a word, this great expense was to very little purpose; for out of the many sent abroad, only those of meaner circumstances being obliged to be more at sea, of consequence made a better improvement.[27]

Here the undoubted fact of the incompetence of certain young men has been associated with an anti-Petrine "conspiracy" and much exaggerated by a naval officer's contempt for a nation of "landlubbers", and particularly for its more "effeminate" representatives. Equally hostile was the British minister in Russia in 1715, George Mackenzie, but he on the contrary saw a threat in the expertise gained abroad rather than relief in the incompetence: "it is known that in both our last wars with France, there were still a great number of Muscovite Gentlemen aboard our own Fleet, and but too much encouragement given them, to instruct themselves in not only the Art of Navigation, but also of our different workings in Presence of an enemy; and insomuch, that Apraxin, the Muscovite Admiral, told me one Day at the Czar's Court, that they would even defy any of our Flags to put a Stratagem on them in case of an Engagement."[28] Other British observers saw the experiment as producing positive results and it should not be overlooked that the tsar himself, quick to give vent to his ire against those who failed him, also pronounced himself more than satisfied.[29] An examination of the subsequent careers of many of both the navigators and the nobles in the Russian "Naval List" shows why.

Some of the men died abroad or soon after their return—one indeed was soon run through by the sword of a Dutch officer in Russian service, who was banished to Siberia; others either immediately or later had unhappy chequered careers—Petr Rameikov, a navigator of the 1707 group, was subsequently dismissed for "drunkenness and decrepitude," re-instated only to be again reported for "wild behaviour" and assigned at his own request to the port at Astrakhan "for ever," and Prince Aleksandr Urusov was eventually dismissed for "incomprehension of the sciences and for ignorance and for failing to carry out duties."[30] However, literally dozens of others served through the 1720s and 1730s with distinction, rising steadily and performing notably in the navy and in other branches of government service. Vasilii Shapkin, already mentioned for his period of captivity in France, made several voyages on British ships and during 1714-15 assisted Fedor Saltykov, Peter's special undercover agent, in the buying of ships and the recruiting of personnel for Russian service. He used his time to good effect in other ways and in 1715 wrote to the tsar about a machine which he had invented for propelling barges, which would need only two men to man them and would go "with the wind as well as against it." On his eventual return to Russia in 1719 he was made a Ship's Secretary (*korabel'nyi sekretar'*) and soon promoted to lieutenant. He performed many important commissions until his death in 1732, rising in rank to captain-lieutenant and being assigned as assistant to Admiral Saunders on canal and dock construction at Cronstadt.[31] Shapkin's command of English was not the least of his accomplishments, put to good effect in liaising with the non-Russian speaking British officers, and the navy throughout the century was for obvious reasons the stronghold of the English language. One of Shapklin's comrades, Aleksei Zverev, who shared with him identical promotions on the same days and outlived him by a mere three weeks, was responsible for translating the British Naval Regulations for the Russian Admiralty College in 1723. The following year he acted as translator for William Cooper, a former Portsmouth naval storekeeper appointed as Equipage Master, or Master Attendant of the Cronstadt Dockyard, and in 1726 was sent to Revel by Catherine I to hand a letter for Queen Anne to the admiral of a visiting British Fleet. In the last year of the tsar's life, Zverev had also been commander of the imperial yacht, the *Princess Elizabeth*.[32] At least three future admirals spent some of their time abroad in England and all were noblemen, although Denis Spiridonovich Kalmykov (1687-1746), a son of a boiar, was in the first group of navigators. He rose in the reign of Elizabeth to be a rear-admiral, member of the Admiralty

College and Commander-in-Chief of Cronstadt, and earlier he had used his knowledge of English when enticing English and Dutch junior officers and ratings from merchant ships visiting Riga as well as for translating English naval codes and regulations. Count Nikolai Fedorovich Golovin (d. 1745), who spent nine years in Europe, eight of them with the British fleet, became a full admiral and President of the Admiralty College in the reign of Anna Ivanovna, while Konon Zotov (1690-1742), son of Peter's tutor Nikita Moiseevich Zotov, added to his difficult years as supervisor of Russian naval students in France in 1715-19 and his eventual rank of rear-admiral the authorship of several works on naval strategy and seamanship.[33] The elder of the Naryshkins, Aleksandr, also had a significant contribution to make in a different if related area. He and his brother returned to Russia only in 1721 after thirteen years of the most varied experience including long periods on British and Dutch ships and periods in Italy and France. Ivan Naryshkin was soon to retire from the navy on grounds of ill-health, but Aleksandr became governor of the St Petersburg Naval Academy in 1722 and together with another officer who had served abroad, was "responsible for restructuring the curriculum of the academy to make it a more practical prelude to naval apprenticeship. Together these two men transformed the Naval Academy in the twenties into the kind of school Peter had envisaged."[34]

Such a transformation was indeed timely, for the programme of foreign training for nobles and commoners alike had virtually come to an end. As early as August, 1713, L'vov had reported that the recently concluded peace between England and Holland and France made the placement of Russian seamen on men-of-war very difficult and newly arriving groups from Russia would only add to the problems.[35] But the groups continued to arrive and indeed became more varied. In 1715 and 1717 some sixty-four men, one third of whom were from noble families, were sent to England and Holland specifically to be apprenticed to English and Dutch masters in all aspects of shipbuilding —the making of masts and rigging, the production of cannon, anchors etc., and considerable sums were paid on their behalf.[36] It seems, however, that there was increasing opposition in Britain to the acquisition by foreigners of "trade secrets." In 1719 the Russian Resident in London, Veselovskii, informed Peter that complaints had been made to Parliament about the French in particular, but also about "the Russian apprentices who are studying here, stating that the training of them was highly prejudicial to England, because on their return to their homeland they would carry on the trades they had learned here and thereby affect the sale of British manufactured goods."[37] At the end of 1716 the first Russian "marines" (*gardemariny*), nobles who had studied at the elite Naval Academy set up in St Petersburg in 1715, were sent abroad—some fifty-one to Venice and France and twelve to England, but it is probable that none of the latter received the hoped-for training in London. Peter himself in Amsterdam in 1717 wrote that "they are not accepting our marines for training in England."[38] This was a time of worsening relations between the two countries and although young Russians already placed on British ships continued to serve until the early 1720s, 1719 marked the end of an era. In March of that year Prince Ivan Shcherbatov, who was much later to come to England as Russian ambassador, failed to get himself accepted on a British man-of-war, despite the representations of the Russian minister.[39]

Although acknowledging the significance of the rupture in relations between Russia and Britain, a Soviet scholar has nevertheless asserted that "the Russian educational system which Peter created was by that time completely satisfactory and able to cope with the preparation of Russian specialists without costly foreign training" and even pronounced the Russian fleet by the end of Peter's reign to be "the best in the world."[40] Without following him into a world of make-believe, it should not be denied that Peter's achievements over a quarter of a century were spectacular in the creation of a fleet from virtually nothing, in the transformation into seamen of large numbers of noblemen and serfs who probably previously had not even seen the sea, and in the establishment of schools and academies vital for adequate instruction in naval skills. It is equally obvious that without foreign officers and without the sending abroad of hundreds of young men much less would have been achieved. The tragedy for the Russian navy was that Peter's immediate successors cared little for the continued improvement and expansion of what he had initiated and neglect was the order of the day. Nevertheless, foreign officers, including many British, continued to serve through the reigns of Anna and Elizabeth and indeed there was further recruitment from Britain in 1734-38. An ever decreasing number of Peter's foreign trained Russians were navigators and officers during the same period, but no real attempts to revive the earlier practice were made, and a mere three young men from the Naval Academy, Chetverikov, Krivov and Kostiurin, whose studies at Oxford and elsewhere have been discussed in an earlier chapter, were to be sent to England in 1745. The period of stagnation was ended only with the accession of Catherine the Great.

II

"Il faut avouer," wrote Catherine after a review of the Russian fleet off Cronstadt on 8/19 June 1765, "qu'ils ont l'air de la flotte pour la pêche des harengs, qui part d'Hollande tous les ans, et non en vérité d'une flotte de guerre, pas un vaisseau ne tient son rang."[41] She had already taken steps to effect a remedy and predictably she followed Peter's tactic of inviting experienced officers into Russian service and arranging to send groups of her own young officers abroad. The results were highly successful in both respects and, although a few officers from other countries were recruited and a small number of Russian officers sent to Venice, Britain played a far more dominant role than it had done even in Petrine times. Catherine was largely fortunate in the calibre of the British officers she recruited early in her reign and again in the late 1780s and by selecting for training in England only officers who were genuine volunteers and who also frequently had considerable naval experience, she exacted the maximum benefit. She did not, however, long persist with the regular dispatch of naval officers and only in the last years of her reign was she persuaded by her ambassador in London, Semen Vorontsov, to resume the practice. It was, however, his brother Aleksandr who was responsible for the placement of the first party of Russian officers who arrived in London in January, 1763.

Catherine's approach for British help in the first months of her reign met with a warm welcome from a British government delighted to forge even closer ties with a nation whose opposition to France had been so strongly expressed. The commanders at Cronstadt, Revel and elsewhere were soon instructed to submit names of volunteers to serve with the British fleet and a group of twenty, ranging in rank from a captain of the second rank, through sub-lieutenants and midshipmen, to *konstapeli*, was selected. In the event, a party of fourteen left Cronstadt in October, 1762, and were joined en route by two midshipmen from Revel. The Admiralty College drew up a long and detailed list of instructions and for once made careful financial arrangements, so successfully that there were to be none of the problems which had beset Peter's navigators in England.[42] Only one thing proved disappointing; on their arrival, the officers wanted to be assigned to men-of-war engaged in military operations, "but when they were told that a peace had been concluded between the English, French and Spaniards, and that it was difficult to find opportunities to fight, they became very sad and expressed their regret that the fighting had ceased."[43] Vorontsov nevertheless submitted a list of sixteen officers to Lord Granville, indicating the desired destination for each: eight were to be sent to America, two to the Mediterranean and six to the East Indies. Only the last six could not be placed on men-of-war, but representations were made to the East India Company which agreed to take three pairs of officers on trading vessels.[44] Later in 1763 the remaining four members of the first group arrived, as did at least five members of a second group. Although two more officers came in 1765 and two more the following year, the dispatch of Russians had virtually stopped before there had even been an opportunity to assess the results. The performance of almost all the officers in the Russian service after their return could only suggest that the experience had been eminently successful and relations with England continued to be completely cordial. Perhaps the expense involved was considered excessive, perhaps the positive impact of the British officers in Russia was already felt—the records of the Admiralty College provide no answer.

With the exception of Petr Valles, a lieutenant of possibly Dutch or English descent, who deserted in 1769 after three years in England,[45] and of two officers who died during their service on British ships, the Russians included in their number men who were to give long and meritorious service to the Russian navy. A member of the first group had already had an opportunity to distinguish himself in Catherine's eyes, for Mikhail Kozhukhov was the intrepid midshipman, mentioned but never named in most accounts of the "revolution of 1762," who stood on guard at Cronstadt harbour and refused to let Peter III land: the empress added to the recommended two-rank promotion a bonus of a two years' salary. Daniil Volchkov, who also went to England in 1762, was another rewarded by the empress for his services on that fateful day. Ill-health subsequently forced Volchkov to retire early, but among posts which he filled was that of Russian Resident in Danzig. Kozhukhov served until 1783, retiring with the rank of brigadier.[46] The 1762 group produced no fewer than four admirals: Ivan Antonovich Borisov (1729-90) and Timofei Gavrilovich Kozlianinov (d. 1798) rose to be vice-admirals and Efim Maksimovich Lupandin and Petr Ivanovich Khanykov (1743-1813) became full admirals in the same year, 1799. Kozlianinov took over command of the Russian fleet after the death of Admiral Greig in 1788 during the war against the Swedes and later became Commander-in-Chief of Archangel, where he died; Khanykov was Commander-in-Chief of Cronstadt in 1801 but his career ended in disgrace a few years later, when he was sentenced to be reduced to the ranks for one month for incompetence and cowardice in the face of the enemy, who for the first momentous occasion was the English during the brief period after Tilsit. Khanykov was then an old man of sixty-five, whose earlier bravery in countless campaigns would seem to give the lie to the accusations, but perhaps his close contact with the British on many occasions during his career had inspired more than a healthy respect for their fighting abilities.[47] A fifth admiral with long experience in the British fleet in the 1760s was Sergei Ivanovich Pleshcheev (1752-1802) who arrived in England with his brother Ivan in 1765 and sailed with the British fleet to America. Sergei Pleshcheev's promotion to vice-admiral in 1797 came at a time when he had become an adjutant-general and he was in high standing with Emperor Paul, whose patronage since 1781 had led to a change in his career and personal fortunes. On his return to Russia Pleshcheev had nevertheless embarked on a successful naval career which included periods as commander of the imperial yacht and a position virtually as naval attaché in Prince Repnin's embassy to Constantinople in 1775-76. In 1781, however, he became attached to the "little court" of Grand Duke Paul and accompanied him and his wife on their European tour in that same year. His description of their tour was one of several works he published in the 1770s-80s, mainly of a geographical nature. He translated from English Lord Baltimore's *Travels from Constantinople . . . to London*, but he is best known for *Obozrenie rossiiskoi imperii . . .* ("Survey of the Russian Empire . . . ," 1786), which he had prepared initially for the Grand Duchess Mariia Fedorovna, whose tutor he was.[48] It was this latter work which was recommended for translation into English by a Scottish traveller, Andrew Swinton, who met him in Petersburg in 1791, and a version in fact appeared in London in 1792, prepared by the Russian chaplain in London, Smirnov. It was a fitting compliment to "un excellent homme et demi-Anglais,"[49] to a man who was an ardent Anglophile and always remembered his years in England and in the British navy with great affection. Swinton, for example, recalled how "a picture in this Gentleman's drawing-room attracted my attention: it was the loss of the Centaur, on her passage from the West-Indies to England. Monsieur Pletscheyeff noticed the portraits of several officers in the boat: 'these,' said he, 'I am well acquainted with.' He mentioned all their names, and particularly that of Captain Inglefield."[50] It was also said of Pleshcheev that by the time of his return to Russia from England he had virtually forgotten his native tongue, which he had to re-learn, although all his life he preferred to write in English.

Pleshcheev and his brother were still in England in 1770 when they were ordered to join a squadron of the Russian fleet putting in to Portsmouth on its way to the Mediterranean and to the great victories over the Turks which were to announce to the world the coming of age of the Russian navy. The Mediterranean expedition brought together most of the Russians who had served in England and the recently recruited British officers, of whom Admiral Elphinston and the then Captain Greig are the best remembered. At the beginning of March, 1770, the Admiralty College wisely decided that there should be on each man-of-war leaving for the Mediterranean at least one Russian officer who could speak a foreign language and act as liaison officer between the foreign officers and the Russian crews, but it soon discovered that it was difficult to find enough men with this competence, particularly in English. Kozhukhov, Ivan Samsonov, and Ivan Seniavin, who had all been in England, were then assigned to the fleet and orders were sent to the Pleshcheevs.[51] At least fifteen of the officers who had trained in England took part in the famous battle of Chesme and served throughout the campaign, and one of them, Fedor Dubasov, was to die in the Mediterranean, when his ship, the *Aziia*, sank in 1773.[52]

The visits of the Russian squadrons for repairs and victualling both at the time of the Mediterranean campaign and later gave many other Russian officers brief opportunities to see something of English life in towns such as Hull and Portsmouth. In 1776, for example, the young Aleksandr Semenovich Shishkov (1754-1841), then a lieutenant but eventually to become an admiral, President of the Russian Academy, and prolific author of naval and philological works, visited Portsmouth, touring the town and attending the local theatre.[53] The systematic dispatch of officers for training in England was not however revived in the 1770s, although one or two officers are found with the British fleet during that period. An interesting example is Grigorii Ivanovich Mulovskii, the illegitimate son of Count Ivan Chernyshev and probably accompanying his father to England in 1769 on his appointment as Russian ambassador.

Shortly after his return to Russia in 1771 Mulovskii was appointed adjutant to Admiral Sir Charles Knowles at the latter's request and went with him to Moldavia to supervise the construction of a Black Sea flotilla. After many years of active service, Mulovskii was given command of an expedition which was to explore the North Pacific, but the outbreak of the Russo-Swedish war brought its postponement and Mulovskii was to distinguish himself in a number of battles before meeting his death in action in July, 1789. Described by the English ambassador in Petersburg as "an excellent officer formed in the English navy," Mulovskii enjoyed particularly good relations with British naval officers in Russian service, especially with Captain James Trevenen, who had submitted a scheme to Catherine for an expedition similar to that to which Mulovskii was appointed and indeed would have accompanied Mulovskii, if he too had not met his death in 1790.[54]

By coincidence, Admiral Knowles's senior adjutant at the time of Mulovskii's appointment was Nikolai Semenovich Mordvinov (1754-1845), son of an admiral and himself to become a full admiral during the reign of Paul. It was on the specific recommendation of Paul that Mordvinov was sent to England in 1774: "I know no one of his age more dedicated to knowledge or of better conduct. I know this from personal experience, having seen him daily. His ability, his behaviour and his qualities persuaded me to send him to England to study naval affairs."[55] Mordvinov more than justified Paul's assessment and apart from gaining much experience at sea during his three years abroad, he interested himself in many other aspects of English life, notably agricultural and political, which were to be clearly revealed in his subsequent career. Mordvinov sailed to America, but he also took the opportunity to travel on the continent, visiting Germany and France, and his last summer, when he was much affected by news of his father's death, was spent in Portugal with an English family. It was with another English family living in Livorno that Mordvinov was to be connected a few years in a more significant way. In 1783 he was in command of a ship in a Russian squadron under Admiral Vasilii Chichagov which sailed to the Mediterranean and it was at Livorno that he met Henrietta Cobley, an orphan living with the family of her brother-in-law, a prosperous merchant by the name of Partridge. The meeting is recalled in the memoirs of the painter Benjamin Robert Haydon, son of another Cobley sister: "The Admiral and officers were often entertained at Partridge's table: and one of them, a Captain Mordwinoff, fell in love with the girl. His prospects being very good, consent was given, and Mordwinoff and his young wife started for Russia, taking with them one of her brothers who had expressed a great desire to enter the Russian army."[56] Henrietta's brother, Thomas, made a very successful career in the Russian army, distinguishing himself at the storming of Ochakov in 1788 and eventually becoming a general and Governor of Odessa in the reign of Alexander I. It was to be with southern or "New" Russia, those territories of the Crimea and along the northern shores of the

Black Sea which were wrested from the Turks in the course of the two Russo-Turkish wars of 1768-74 and 1787-92, that Mordvinov's own career was linked in the remaining years of the eighteenth century. In 1785 he was appointed to Black Sea naval administration and on his arrival at Kherson took command of the Black Sea fleet. He was soon involved in actions against the Turks after the outbreak of hostilities in 1787 and was promoted to rear-admiral later the same year. Shortly afterwards Mordvinov came into conflict with Potemkin and left the naval service, and it was only after Potemkin's death that Mordvinov was persuaded by Catherine to re-join the navy and made head of the Black Sea naval administration. In 1792 he settled with his family at Nikolaev, the new town and naval yards established a few years earlier, and it was here that Mordvinov brought to fruition many of the projects initiated by Potemkin and introduced many innovations of his own. Mention has been made in an earlier chapter of his interest in introducing English agricultural methods in the area with the help of one of the English-trained professors of agriculture, Livanov; he also encouraged the setting up of a printing press with which another Russian whom he had known in England, the Oxford graduate Suvorov, now a teacher in the naval academy in Nikolaev, was closely involved. In many respects, indeed, the Mordvinovs created "a nest of English folk" in Nikolaev, consisting of other Russians who had been in England as well as English officers serving with the Black Sea fleet. In 1800, the noted traveller Edward Daniel Clarke observed that "English officers, and English engineers, with other foreigners in the Russian service, residing here, have introduced habits of urbanity and cleanliness; and have served to correct, by force of urbanity, the barbarity of the native inhabitants."[57] Rightly conscious of English influence, Clarke might have attributed it with more justice to Mordvinov, whom he had met and admired, and to his wife.

A man of great integrity, fiercely independent, enthusiastic, markedly liberal in his views on a wide range of social, economic and political matters, Mordvinov finished the reign of Paul in disgrace and out of the navy for the second time in his career. But he was an obvious candidate for high position at the beginning of Alexander's reign, at one in general outlook at least with the Anglophiles of the "Secret Committee" and with the Vorontsovs. He was also therefore an equally obvious candidate for a pen-portrait from Vigel':

Well known for his good intentions, wide knowledge, lively imagination and pretensions to candour, Nikolai Semenovich Mordvinov more than ever before was boiling with projects at this period. He was considered our Socrates, Cicero, Cato and Seneca. This political dreamer, with his lofty ideas, his false concepts about Russia and what was to its advantage, was naturally in accord intellectually with the young legislators. In addition, he was married to the Englishwoman Cobley, spoke English and lived completely in the English way. But he was Minister for the

Navy for only three months. He imagined that we really had a Parliament; his opinions were so bold that two years after the death of Paul
they seemed even rebellious, and he was obliged to cede place to his
friend Chichagov.[58]

Despite the exaggerations and errors, Vigel' managed to convey something of
the essence of the man, whom Pushkin and the Decembrists towards the end
of Alexander's reign were to regard as a martyr to be admired. After a few
years in the wilderness between 1802 and 1810, Mordvinov was reconciled
with the tsar, became a member of the State Council, and occupied other government positions. He was active in other fields, including the founding and
presidency of the Moscow Agricultural Society in 1820. The previous year he
had paid a second visit to England as part of an extensive European tour and
renewed acquaintances with such old friends as Semen Vorontsov and Jeremy
and Samuel Bentham.[59]

The Benthams may well have met Mordvinov during his first stay in England in the 1770s, although his name does not figure in their letters during
this period. One Russian naval officer they did befriend was Iakov Iakovlevich
Lomen (Johann Lohmann), son of a court physician who arrived in England
in 1778 with his brother Fedor. Iakov met Samuel Bentham at the Royal Naval
Academy at Portsmouth where they were both studying and boarding with
one of the masters, the astronomer and mathematician George Witchell (1728-
85). Jeremy Bentham, who met Lomen a little later in London, thought him
"a fine young fellow" with "an amazing deal of vivacity for a Russian."[60] Lomen was offered a commission aboard the *Thunderer* under Commodore Wal-
singham which sailed for the West Indies in 1779 to join Lord Rodney's fleet
in action in the American war and met his death the following year when his
ship sank during a hurricane. His brother (d. 1822), whom apparently the Benthams did not meet, served with the British fleet until 1780 and then returned
to Russia to continue a naval career which saw him rise to the rank of vice-admiral and commander at Revel in the reign of Alexander.[61]

The Benthams were also acquainted with at least two other young Russians
of somewhat different interests and status whose presence in England suggests
that the need to provide a corpus of native shipwrights which was so much a
concern of Peter's was not overlooked by Catherine. Indeed, already in 1765,
an apprentice shipbuilder by the name of Mikhail Portnov had been dispatched
to France and England "for the better observation of ship architecture and related matters." Four years later, having seen "almost all the ports in Europe
and all types of ships," he was sent back to Russia to apply his newly acquired
expertise to the preparation of the Mediterranean expedition. Within months
of his return at the beginning of 1769, the Admiralty College approved of his
design for a machine for transporting heavy cannon and equipment and he
was also assigned to build a 66-gun man-of-war, which was launched in March,

1770. Naval records show him very active in shipbuilding at various Russian yards over the next two decades and his steady rise in rank.[62] It was possibly his success which encouraged the sending of further apprentices in 1776. The Benthams' interest in them was obviously not without ulterior motives: the idea of Samuel seeking his fortunes in Russia was already well advanced. In April, 1778, Jeremy wrote to an English friend in Petersburg:

> There are three young Russians I understand in England to learn Ship-
> building: but there are only in Merchant's Yards. The King's Yards are
> by the rules of the service altogether inaccessible to them as foreigners.
> I question whether the Empress has any persons in her service who have
> been brought up in any of those yards: certainly none of any education.
> I dare affirm that my Brother is the only person in his line at this time
> in England who is of any tolerable family and education, and who has
> any improving views. In the mere routine of practise he had and will
> have had more means of getting information than can ordinarily fall to
> the lot of a working Shipwright.[63]

The Benthams' schemes received encouragement from the Russian chaplain Samborskii, who had particular charge of a man called Afanas'ev: "he is at present with a Mr. Mistiers at Rotherhith. He does not like being there—Mistiers understands buying Timber very well but does not trouble himself about the building part. He is about 22 or 23. He has not had much intellectual education—no languages—Arithmetic and perhaps a little Geometry—a very good moral education—understands something of shipbuilding."[64] Afanas'ev was soon to leave Rotherhithe and with reason—"He could not bear to stay there any longer. They have him for a Bed fellow a Mulatto prentice who used him brutally: amongst other things taking offence at him for disturbing some birds the Mulatto was going to shoot at, he (the Mulatto) fired at him and shot him in the breast."[65] In several letters in early 1779 Afanas'ev's name was linked with a Kudigen or Kutigen, in fact Ivan Kutygin, "the son of a man who is Quartermaster on board the Grand Duke's Yacht . . . who struts about and gives himself the airs of a Macaroni."[66] Kutygin was already placed with Thomas Mitchell, a shipwright who was then First Assistant to the Surveyor of the Navy, but Jeremy was anxious that Samuel should take both the men under his tuition and arrange for them to work in the Admiralty shipyards in Portsmouth. However, Samuel's decision to leave for Russia in August 1779 led to a loss of interest in the apprentices; nothing further is heard of them in the Bentham correspondence—and little elsewhere.[67]

In the 1780s there were, according to Semen Vorontsov, a further eight or nine young men studying "la théorie et la pratique de la construction des vaisseaux," and although "tous ont plus ou moins bien réussi," two in particular, Stepanov and Sarychev, had distinguished themselves.[68] Mikhail Stepanovich

Stepanov, described as a "secretary" from the Admiralty College, was obviously a man of some ability. Although in March, 1785, he was based in Greenwich learning about shipbuilding, he went the following year to study mathematics at Edinburgh University, where he was later elected a member of the Natural History Society. During his time in Scotland he was used as an intermediary in negotiations between Vorontsov and Charles Gascoigne, soon to leave Carron for Russia.[69] Stepanov, Sarychev and three other shipwrights, named Kanaev, Masal'skii and Pospelov, all sent to the Admiralty College drawings of vessels they had seen in English shipyards between 1784 and 1788, clearly showing their attention to "making improvements in the art of Shipbuilding and of building either better ships on the present plans for the present purposes or even upon new plans for the old purposes, or even for new purposes if any such can be pointed out."[70] Pospelov, for instance, who seems to have gained access to the naval yards, sent plans of a 38-gun frigate being built after the design of a captured French frigate. Razumov, a member of a later group of shipwrights, worked in a merchant's yard on the Thames and sent in 1796 a description of a 36-gun frigate and of two 18-gun sloops. "In addition, he mentions that attempting to note at every stage differences between Russian and English shipbuilding, he had observed that the caulking of ships was performed by a method which was not only different from the Russian but also from that previously employed in England."[71] A final example of the range of activities of Russian shipbuilders in England is provided by an apprentice named Kurepanov at the very end of the century, who put his knowledge of English to the translation of *The Ship Builders Repository*, for which he was warmly commended.[72]

If there were few Russian officers with the British fleet in the 1770s there seems to have been only one in the 1780s. Grigorii Alekseevich Seniavin was Vorontsov's brother-in-law and a relation he was more than ready to ackowledge: "je dois rendre cette justice à mon beau-frère qu'il . . . n'a pas perdu son temps à Londres, étudiant tous les matins avec beaucoup d'assiduité. Il s'est conduit ici d'une manière qui m'a fait beaucoup de plaisir. Les marins qui ont servi avec lui dans les Indes occidentales et dans le Nord de l'Amérique m'en ont dit beaucoup de bien. Il est fort doux de caractère et si passionné pour son métier, que je me flatte que ce sera un bon officier pour notre flotte."[73] Seniavin spent over four years in England, making voyages to America and later to the Mediterranean; he studied geometry with Williamson, the former Oxford don who was the close friend of Nikitin and the other Russian Oxonians; he spoke English fluently, and was, in the words of another Russian in London, "in every respect an excellent naval officer and well liked in the English fleet." He recalled how Seniavin had rowed him and another friend down the Thames to inspect the ship on which had had just returned from the West Indies; they were all soaked to the skin and Seniavin took them to a coffeehouse frequented by naval officers and "ordered 'half-and-half punch,' that is, half rum and half French brandy, and he drained a huge tankard as though it was nothing."[74] Seniavin returned to Russia in the spring of 1788 in time to take part in the war against the Swedes, serving with distinction.

His success in that campaign greatly pleased Vorontsov and he went on to remark with no little exaggeration that "par une singularité qui pourtant s' explique, m-r Lizakevich et notre aumonier [Smirnov] ont trouvé que tous les officiers russes qui servent dans la marine et qui se sont distingués dans cette guerre ont appris leur métier dans la marine anglaise."[75] Elated by Russian naval victories both against the Swedes and the Turks, he was ready to affirm that "notre service, depuis le chevalier Knowles et surtout par les soins de l' amiral Greigh, était sur le pied anglais,"[76] but he also felt strongly that the solution to Russia's general difficulties in providing an efficient officer corps lay not in the recruitment of senior English officers but in the experience to be gained by young Russians serving with the British fleet. Therefore, although attempting to carry out the empress's directives both before and after the Swedish war to recruit British officers, he urged her to re-institute the regular dispatch of Russian officers to England. His efforts were thwarted in the 1780s by what he considered was the continuing resentment of the British against Russia for the Armed Neutrality, but by the early 1790s the situation had changed, particularly after the resolution of the Ochakov crisis. Vorontsov's scheme was "to select twelve young and disciplined lieutenants from the fleet and send them . . . to serve four years without a break on English ships at sea; Then to send a similar number of officers for the same period to replace the first group and to repeat this constantly, so that in the space of every twenty years we should have sixty men worthy of commanding ships."[77] In 1793 the empress indicated her willingness to adopt her ambassador's suggestions, and fourteen officers were sent in October of that year. Four years later, Paul I consented to the dispatch of another group of twelve officers.[78] To these two groups may be added the two Chichagov brothers who came by private arrangement in 1792 and the two Baratynskii brothers who were sent by Grand Duke Paul in 1795 to give a total of thirty officers serving with the British fleet in the 1790s. In general all these officers were better prepared and more experienced than their predecessors earlier in the century: many of them had seen action in various engagements during the Swedish war, frequently serving with or under British officers. In terms of their later careers, however, the pattern was very much the same: six became admirals, several served long years in lower ranks, others left the navy soon after their return for careers in different fields, and at least three died during their time on British ships. They were all in Britain during a remarkable decade when relations between the two countries see-sawed in the most confusing and rapid fashion. Although 1800 saw Russia aligned with France against England, the preceding five years had seen close Anglo-Russian co-operation, manifest above all in joint naval and land ventures against revolutionary France. The latter form a background, and in some cases more than a background, to the activities of the Russian officers in the British fleet.

In 1794 a Russian squadron under the English-trained Vice-Admiral Petr Khanykov was sailing in English waters and a Russian diplomat commented that "il en résulterait d'abord quelque bien pour la cause commune, et en-suite un grand bien pour notre marine. Les officiers se formeront; ils profiter-ont des manoeuvres savantes des amiraux anglais."[79] It was, however, only the next year, following the signing of a defensive alliance between Russia and Great Britain in February, 1795, that these hopes had a real chance of be-ing fulfilled. Although the treaty envisaged the use of Russian land rather than naval forces, in the event it was Russian ships which were most needed by a hard-pressed British navy engaged in maintaining the blockade of the Dutch ports where an invasion force was gathered. In June, 1795, a force of twelve battleships and eight frigates, under the overall command of Khanykov, as-sisted by Rear-Admirals Mikhail Makarov and the Scotsman George Tate, sailed to join Vice-Admiral Adam Duncan's North Sea fleet. The Russians were to be subordinate to Duncan's command and their task, according to the letter he sent to Khanykov on 21 August 1795 was to "protect British trade; intercept the enemy's trade; destroy Dutch merchant and men-of-war; strength-en British convoys they may fall in with."[80] Duncan was particularly anxious about problems of different procedures, such as the line of battle—and also of language. He took aboard his own ship, the *Venerable*, one of the 1793 group of Russian officers, Mikhail Ivanovich Baskakov, who had just returned from the West Indies, to act as interpreter and liaison officer, but the real problems which arose came essentially from the distrust of the Russians' competence and motives, the generally poor condition of their ships, misunderstandings between some of Duncan's officers, particularly Sir Richard Onslow and Vice-Admiral McBride, and some of the Russian commanders, particularly Tate. The usefulness of the Russian presence was also soon reduced by the change of rulers back in Russia and Paul's eagerness to undo whatever his mother had instigated; in the early summer of 1797 he ordered Khanykov to withdraw, leaving the British navy at a time when it had barely emerged from the great mutinies at Spithead and then the Nore in the spring of that year. In that con-nection, however, it should not be overlooked that the Russian fleet had con-tinued at sea during April and May when the British fleet was at its most vul-nerable. The following year, the Russians re-appeared and the frequently tense and unhappy alliance continued until Paul's revival of the Armed Neutrality in 1800, an action which brought genuine despair to many of the Russian officers, including Makarov and Chichagov. An Englishman who was in Pe-tersburg when the crews arrived back even doubted whether they would fight against the British and added "So superior do they consider themselves to their brother-sailors at Petersburgh, that they disdained to associate with them and were always seen in knots together. They spoke openly in favour of

England, and refused to throw aside their blue jackets and trousers, notwithstanding the emperor had issued two orders to that effect."[81] It had been an episode which was unique in the eighteenth century for never before had the two navies attempted to work together so closely; whether Russian naval presence was a factor of any importance in averting invasion remains a matter of conjecture, as does the degree to which the Russians may have benefitted from the "manoeuvres savantes des amiraux anglais." There were certainly benefits of a more immediate kind which the Russians reaped: many of their ships received extensive repairs and overhauls in British yards; they were liberally victualled, so much so that in 1796 the crews, with the connivance of their captains, were doing a brisk trade with the Kent merchants and townspeople in superfluous flour, bread and brandy;[82] their numerous sick received prolonged and expert treatment from doctors such as Gilbert Blane and in hospitals in Yarmouth, Deal and Chatham.[83] The Russian admirals found only one matter for real complaint: in 1802 Makarov and Tate put forward a claim to a share in the prize money, an action which incensed Duncan whose earlier somewhat philosophical attitude towards his allies abruptly changed under the threat to his own and his crews' financial rewards. He argued that the Russians had captured but one prize ship and that they had generally defied his orders—but in vain, for judgment was given in favour of the Russians.[84]

The commander of the Russian ship which took the prize in 1796 was Pavel Vasil'evich Chichagov (1767-1849), whose fascinating and involved relationship with England extended far beyond the joint naval operations of 1795-1800.[85] As a young boy of fifteen, Chichagov had had his first glimpse of England during a cruise to the Mediterranean as adjutant to his father, Admiral Vasilii Chichagov; a decade later, when he was already a captain with conspicuous service in the Swedish war behind him, he persuaded his father to arrange for him and his younger brother Vasilii to be sent to London for further "practical naval experience." Accompanied by their tutor in mathematics, Semen Emel'ianovich Gur'ev (1764-1813), the future Academician, they were to stay about a year, initially studying English at "l'académie soi-distante de Tooting," which deflated Pavel's earlier high opinion of English schools, and then at the naval academy at Portsmouth, ending with a voyage on a training ship. It was probably during that voyage that he encountered a Captain Knight, "une bête brute, sans éducation, sans connaissances, grossière et insolente," who soon corrected his ideal of the English naval officer.[86] Nevertheless, he returned to Russia in 1793, full of enthusiasm for many aspects of English life. His next visit in 1795-96 as commander of the 66-gun *Retvizan*, a former Swedish man-of-war which was now part of the Russian squadron acting with the British fleet against the French, only served to strengthen his attachment to England: while his ship was in Chatham dockyards for extensive repairs, he became friendly with the family of Captain Charles Proby, a Commissioner of the dockyards, and particularly with Elizabeth Proby,

whose fiancé he became, despite the opposition of her father. 1796 was also
memorable for Chichagov because of his meeting and ensuing friendship with
the famous inventor and instrument-maker Jesse Ramsden, "ce grand génie"
whose death he was to mourn four years later and who assisted him in making
a navigational aid which was fitted to the *Retvizan*.[87] In contrast 1797 was
the beginning of the most harrowing periods of his life when he came into
conflict with the new emperor Paul. In September Chichagov resigned from
the navy because of preferments given to officers junior to him and retired to
his estates near Mogilev, from where he wrote to Vorontsov of his wish to return to England "pour apprendre l'agriculture . . . la meilleure occupation, je
crois, pour un homme à qui la retraite est l'unique ressource dans son pays."[88]
News of Captain Proby's death and Elizabeth's wish to see him only increased
his resolve but his application for permission to go abroad and to marry brought
the tsar's ruling that "there are enough girls in Russia without having to look
for them in England." At the same time Paul ordered Chichagov back into the
navy, promoted him to rear-admiral and assigned him to the Russian fleet sailing to rejoin the British. However, further misunderstandings arose and Chi-
cagov found himself stripped of his rank and imprisoned in the Peter and Paul
Fortress in June, 1799. But within two weeks Chichagov was released and restored to his rank and given permission to marry, which he did on 5 November
in the Russian chapel in London. It is little wonder that Chichagov and his
new wife left with reluctance and no little trepidation "le pays de la liberté"
in June, 1800, for a Russia which confirmed his worst fears, but the death of
Paul soon afterwards brought to Chichagov, as it did to so many of his kind,
new hope.[89]

Married to an Englishwoman, disgraced by Paul, noted for his strongly Anglophile and liberal views in addition to being the son of an admiral who had
become an admiral in his turn, Chichagov at the beginning of the new reign
seemed to be another Mordvinov and duly received similar treatment both
from Alexander and later, from the pen of Vigel'.[90] One of Alexander's first
acts was to send him to Revel to negotiate with his hero Nelson, who after his
victory at Copenhagen had turned his attention to Russia, the heart of the
Northern Alliance of 1800-01 against England. Chichagov was then made a
member of the committee for the reform of the Russian navy and waited with
genuine enthusiasm for the arrival of the new Minister for the Navy Mordvinov,
who "pourra peut-être soulager le sort des marins."[91] It was unfortunate that
the two men, although devoted to reforms along English lines, were unable to
work together, and Mordvinov's resignation after barely three months in office was due in some measure to his "former friend's" readiness to by-pass
him with recommendations to the tsar. There is no doubting, however, the
energy and originality which Chichagov, first as deputy minister for the navy,
and then from 1807 as minister, brought to the organization of naval affairs,
but he too fell victim to the machinations of others and the tsar's whimsical

changes. In retirement again, he decided in 1809 to go abroad with his family, hoping that should peace come between France and its ally Russia and England, "le seul pays qui honore l'humanité et mérite le nom de patrie pour ceux qui ont la bonheur d'y appartenir, je puisse m'y transporter avec toute ma famille et passer le reste de mes jours dans ce paradis terrestre."[92] It was, however, to be the body of his wife, who died in Paris in 1811, that he transported back to Petersburg, sending only his three daughters to England to the care of Vorontsov and his daughter, Lady Pembroke. In Russia Chichagov found his services once more in demand and he became not only Minister for the Navy but also Governor of Moldavia and Wallachia which brought with it command of the Black Sea fleet—and of the Danube army. It was in this last role that he suffered the worst setback of his career, failing to prevent Napoleon and his army crossing the Berezina on their retreat from Moscow. The reasons were all too clear to his countrymen and to the fabulist Krylov:

> When cobblers take to making pies,
> And cook his hand at cobbling tries,
> You'll look for useful work in vain.[93]

At this low ebb in his life he thought once more of settling in England and this time he succeeded in reaching London and rejoining his "father" and benefactor Vorontsov. It was the summer of 1814, the summer of the triumphant visit to England of Alexander and his suite, but for Chichagov it was the beginning of two years of intense and bitter dissillusionment with his "paradis terrestre." His was an England of the past or rather, of the imagination, and his reaction could be described in the words he had used for his experiences even in 1792: "cette indignation qui vient toujours de la bonne opinion frustrée dans son attente."[94] He was not to be reconciled with "cette île, jadis l'asile de la liberté, aujourd'hui ouverte pour les nègres de l'Afrique, fermée pour les blancs de l'Europe"[95] and he left for the Continent again in 1816 to spend years of wandering before finally settling in Paris, from where he still poured out his bile against nineteenth-century England in his letters to Vorontsov. But the story of his stormy relationship with England was still to have a final chapter: in 1834, having renounced his Russian citizenship in his anger at Nicholas I's decree that all Russians living abroad should return to Russia immediately or suffer confiscation of all their property, he came once more to England to petition for naturalization. Although he returned almost immediately to France to live out the remaining fifteen years of his long life, it was as an English citizen that he died.

The 1793 group contained a number of interesting individuals in whose lives England played perhaps an even more decisive role in purely naval terms than in Chichagov's; they certainly gained much greater experience on board ships of the British fleet in many parts of the world and frequently in com-

bat. Arriving in Hull in early January, 1794, the Russians travelled to London
to spend their first few months acquiring some knowledge of English, but in
April they received their assignments to British ships. Half the party seems to
have sailed to the Mediterranean, where Lt. Iakov Bering, the grandson of the
famous explorer Vitus Bering, was soon to lose his life, and the other half to
the West Indies, where there occurred the sudden and tragic death of Captain-
Lieutenant Semen Velikii (b. 1772), the illegitimate son of Grand Duke Paul
by an attractive young Polish widow.[96] In this second party were two men
who were subsequently to gain fame as Russia's first circumnavigators and
whose connections with the British navy merit special attention.

Ivan Fedorovich Kruzenshtern (Adam Krusenstern) (1770-1846), from an
impoverished gentry family from Revel, and Iurii Fedorovich Lisianskii, the
son of a priest from Nezhin in the Ukraine, met as cadets in the Naval Cadet
Corps at Cronstadt in the 1780s and served with distinction against the Swedes.
Kruzenshtern served under Mulovskii, who was still hoping to command his
expedition on the conclusion of the war, and Lisianskii under Grevens, who
had been chosen to accompany Mulovskii, and it was probably at this period
that they both became interested in voyages of exploration, an interest which
only increased during the six years they sailed on British ships. In May 1794
they sailed for America in the squadron under the command of Rear-Admiral
George Murray, Lisianskii on board the frigate *L'Oiseau*, captain Robert Murray, and Kruzenshtern on the frigate *Thetis*, captain Alexander Cochrane. Of
Lisianskii's adventures at this period we can read in the account of his life
which he published for English readers many years later:

> Near the coast of the United States he was at the taking of a large fleet
> of American ships, which were bound for France with provisions, under
> the convoy of the French frigate La Concorde, and other armed vessels.
> It was then he saw, for the first time, the activity of the British fleet in
> chasing an enemy. By her superior sailing, the L'Oiseau captured, be-
> sides many merchant-vessels, an armed brig, called Chigamoga, on board
> of which was Monsieur Belgard, a black general, well known in the
> French West-India islands.
>
> After this capture, the L'Oiseau repaired to Halifax to refit, and then
> sailed on a winter cruise. During this cruise she was blown off the coast
> of the Chesapeak, sprung a leak, and was carried to the West-Indies.
>
> There the writer of these memoirs was attacked by the yellow-fever,
> which ranged through all the islands; and he has no doubt that he should
> have fallen a victim, but for the kindness of captain Murray, who not
> only have up for his accommodation part of his cabin, but employed
> every means in his power to counteract the violence of the distemper.
>
> In the year 1795 he left the frigate L'Oiseau, and proceeded on a
> course of travels in America. He passed through the United States, from

Boston to the Savanna; and, after spending the winter in Philadelphia, returned in the following year to Halifax; where, finding that his old commander and friend had sailed for England, he entered on board the frigate La Topase, commanded by captain Church. In this frigate he was in a very smart engagement with L'Elizabeth, a French frigate of equal force, which ended in the capture of the enemy.[97]

Kruzenshtern enjoyed a similarly eventful time, using the opportunity when the *Thetis* was undergoing repairs to visit the West Indies and later, according to a less reliable source, also travelling through America, meeting President Washington, as Lisianskii had also done. The two men, however, met up again in 1796, when together with another Russian officer, Baskakov, they returned to England on board the *Cleopatra*, captain Charles Penrose, which barely escaped capture by the French off the coast of Ireland.

In 1797 the three Russians, excited in Lisianskii's case by the desire "to see, if possible, every part of the world," and in Kruzenshtern's, also by his interest in "the English trade with the East Indies and with China," managed to be placed on board the man-of-war, the *Reasonable*, captain Charles Boyle, sailing for the Cape of Good Hope.[98] At the Cape Kruzenshtern and Lisianskii were to part company. Kruzenshtern joined the frigate *L'Oiseau* to India, where he was to remain a year before finally getting to China. Lisianskii fell ill again at the Cape and took extended shore leave, but managed to travel widely in South Africa, visiting Dutch settlements and collecting specimens for a herbarium; he then joined a man-of-war taking troops to India and visited Calcutta and Bombay. The two officers sailed back to England independently on merchantmen in 1799, Kruzenshtern proceeding straight to Russia and Lisianskii following in 1800 after a further winter in London. The Russian navy thus welcomed back two vastly experienced and well-travelled officers, who were to be re-united two years later, when Kruzenshtern's long-cherished project for opening up Russian trade with the East was accepted and he selected Lisianskii to command one of the two ships in the expedition. In 1802 Lisianskii, together with the shipbuilder Razumov who had trained in English yards in the 1790s, was sent again to England to purchase two suitable ships, which he did for the sum of £17,000, although another £5,000 had to be spent on making them truly seaworthy. He also bought a wide range of medicines, clothing, bedding, chronometers by Arnold and Pennington and astronomical instruments by Troughton. The English contribution to the material side of the great expedition was thus considerable, although both crews and the achievement were solely Russian. The two ships, re-named the *Nadezhda* and the *Neva*, set sail from Russia on 7/19 August 1803 on their momentous voyage which was to end for Kruzenshtern three years and twelve days later and for Lisianskii soon afterwards. For just as during their careers in the British navy, they were apart more than they were together: their ships sailed together for only

375 days or just over one third of the time taken on the voyage. Kruzenshtern as the instigator of the voyage and overall commander of the expedition rightly received the major honours, but Lisianskii's role was crucial and he deserved more recognition both from his government and from immediate posterity. Only in the Soviet period has the balance been righted. Kruzenshtern's account of the expedition was the first to appear, in 1809, and German, and English translations were quick to follow. Lisianskii's independent account was held up by the Russian naval authorities and he was obliged to publish it at his own expense in 1812. In retirement since 1809, he came once more to England in 1813 to publish an English version which he had prepared himself and which he justified in his preface as follows: "From the different destination of the two vessels on their arrival in the Pacific Ocean, and from their frequent and unavoidable separation, it fell to the lot of the Author, to visit, without his companion, the Easter and Sandwich Islands, to pass more than one whole year on the island of Cadiack and at Sitca or Norfolk Sound, and to discover an island and a shoal, hitherto unknown, but of no small importance to the navigation of the South Sea."[99] Kruzenshtern's career prospered and he eventually became an excellent admiral and director of the Naval Cadet Corps, where he introduced many reforms in keeping with procedures he had admired in England. He was also the source of inspiration for the spate of Russian circumnavigations which took place in the reigns of Alexander I and Nicholas I. He too paid a further visit to England in 1814 to collect instruments for the voyage of Otto Kotzebue, who had been a cadet on the *Nadezhda*, and also to renew old acquaintances and to re-visit naval establishments at Plymouth, Portsmouth, Chatham and Woolwich. With a justified belief in the abilities of Russian seamen to undertake hazardous voyages, he nevertheless never lost his admiration for, or slackened his personal ties with England.[100]

The 1797 group of Russian officers did not ultimately produce as many distinguished naval commanders as its predecessor but all its members had ample opportunity to see active service at a particularly eventful time in English naval history. Their service was, however, interrupted in 1800 by Paul's renewal of the Armed Neutrality which led the British to retaliate by expelling Russian officers from British warships. When after Paul's death, permission was again given for them to join the fleet, two of the Russians refused, declaring that they had learned all they could and wished only to return to Russia.[101] One of these men was a particularly interesting character, Nikolai Nazar'evich Murav'ev (1775-1845), who is an example of someone who made his considerable reputation outside the navy. Shortly after his return to Russia in 1802 he retired and entered the civil service, becoming eventually governor of his home district of Novgorod, a state secretary and a senator. Like his friend Mordvinov, he also took a keen interest in agriculture, developing a strain of rye which was to bear his name—*murav'evka* and becoming a leading light in the Moscow Agricultural Society. Like Sergei Pleshcheev, he also devoted him-

self to literature and history. An unexpected manifestation of English influence was his translation of excerpts from *The Seasons* of James Thomson, a
poet he admired for his eminence in descriptive poetry, which he published in
1805, the year which also was an "Opyt o Velikobritanii" ("Essay on Great
Britain"). In this essay he argued that Russians would do well to emulate the
English brand of patriotism with its self-centered reverence for its own culture and traditions and contempt for all things foreign.[102]

Peace once more established between the "natural allies", the Russians were
quick to arrange in 1802-03 the dispatch of two further groups, one compris-
ing comparatively experienced officers and the other, raw midshipmen, who
quickly found themselves on active service and some of whom were at Trafal-
gar.[103] In 1804 Chichagov wrote to Vorontsov of his wish for Russian ordinary seamen to serve on English merchant ships, and rumour had it that some
300 midshipmen were also to be sent to England, which brought protests
about the possible threat to British supremacy reminiscent of those voiced by
pamphleteers in the reign of George I.[104] If Chichagov was at one with Vorontsov and indeed with the great Peter over the great benefits to be gained
by sending Russian seamen abroad, he felt that the time had come when Russia could dispense with foreigners in its own service. Arguing against Vorontsov's wish to place a young English midshipman, he declared: "Quant à moi,
je dois vous avouer que vu le très-grand mal et déshonneur qui résulte à notre
pays de l'emploi que l'on fait des étrangers, je suis d'avis qu'on n'en prenne
plus."[105] After Tilsit, however, Britain was inclined to leave Russia to it and
seems not to have received further Russians into the British navy on any regular basis. But over the preceding century it had provided vital and rigorous
training for many Russian officers who had given great service to their own
country on their return: that chapter, like the present one which has attempted to retell it, was now at an end.

CHAPTER 7
"LEARN FROM THE BRITISH"

Exactly a decade after it had published a note about the presence of Russian students at British universities, the *Scots Magazine* informed its readers about the steady stream of young Russians who came to pursue studies "in the useful line".

> The plan the Empress of Russia is upon for introducing useful knowledge into her empire can hardly fail of being successful: There are always forty young men educating in England. They come over eight every year at the age of twenty or twenty one, and eight every year go back, consequently they remain here five years. The objects they are directed to pursue, are all in the useful line: in agriculture, there are ten; in the woollen manufacture, four; in the art of engineering, particularly canalling, four; in physic, two; in surgery, four, in merchandize, six, in engraving, two; in painting, two; in the hardware trade; six. Upon their arrival at Petersburg they are strictly examined, and promoted according to their progress; two or three have been imprisoned for deficiency, one banished to Siberia, and one or two put into the ranks as common soldiers, but if they have made a useful and satisfactory acquisition of knowledge, they are very liberally rewarded.[1]

It is an arresting if somewhat misleading paragraph. It bestows the dignity of a plan, or general design, on what were at best haphazard ventures or initiatives, originating not merely with Catherine but with a number of institutions and individuals; it imposes a timetable and system and suggests a pre-meditated range of activities which are contradicted by available evidence. But for all that, it is near enough the truth as a general indication of Russia's willingness to learn from British expertise and of areas for investigation beyond those examined in earlier chapters. In 1781, there were indeed ten students of agriculture still in Britain, including the three sent by Potemkin to study under Young, but of the alleged thirty in other categories no more than a handful are known; there were certainly two Russians studying engraving and one painting (who will be discussed in the following chapter) and several working with leading London instrument-makers and craftsmen. Some years earlier three young engineers had studied canal construction, and later in the 1780s and 90s other mechanics and technical specialists came in one and twos or in small groups to consult with English masters and to visit the most advanced industrial concerns like the Carron factory near Falkirk and Boulton's enterprises at Soho near Birmingham. There may never have been forty Russian students at any one time in eighteenth-century Britain, and those that came did not arrive and depart with the precision suggested by the *Scots Magazine*, but nevertheless, the story of some of these young Russians is worth the telling.

I

Among the many British specialists whom Peter the Great enlisted for service in Russia during his famous visit to England in 1698 was John Perry (1670-1732), a hydraulic engineer. Perry's generally frustrating experiences in Russia were described in his book, *The State of Russia under the Present Czar*, published in 1716 after his return to England; he also provides important information on the tasks with which he was burdened, particularly the various canal projects to link the Volga and the Don and St. Petersburg and the Volga. A later British engineer, who worked in Russia in 1783-85, referred to Peter's plans in the following lines: "Peter the Great, Czar of Muscovy, amongst his other grand designs, had planned a navigation for conveying all the rich goods of Persia to his new city of Petersburgh, but, alas! the death of this great man prevented the perfect accomplishment of this noble undertaking, which would have made Petersburgh, perhaps, the most populous and profitable place of traffic in the world. What was left undone by Peter the Great, is however now carrying on, with the greatest assiduity, by the immortal Catherine,"[2] but it was as much the departure of such men as Perry and the inability to recruit competent replacements as the death of Peter which delayed Russian canal construction for so long. Catherine certainly revived her predecessor's projects and attempts were made throughout the 1760s and 1770s to find foreign engineers who could direct the work. Foreigners, such as Bayerns and Bilistein, who were given contracts, failed miserably to live up to expectations and it proved impossible to entice leading British specialists.[3] The Russians were obliged to fall back on their own resources and it was in connection with the training of Russia's own canal experts that the head of the Petersburg Engineer Corps, General Mikhail Ivanovich Mordvinov, decided to send three of his young officers on extended tours of Europe in the early 1770s. In view of the virtual absence of information about Russian as opposed to foreign canal engineers, this mission is of great interest and can be described in some detail on the basis of the unpublished journal of the most gifted of the trio, Nikolai Ivanovich Korsakov.

Korsakov arrived in London in April, 1775, and remained until July, 1777. Unfortunately, a complete record of Korsakov's activities has not survived and the notebook, written in uncertain French, which has been preserved in the family archive in Moscow covers only the period from May, 1776, to the summer of 1778, representing about one third of the total period Korsakov was away from Russia, but most of the important months of his travels in Britain.[4] During his first year in England Korsakov studied at Oxford, meeting there his fellow-countrymen, Nikitin and Suvorov, and forming a poor opinion of the young Russian, Prince Dmitrii Grigor'evich Babichev, who had been assigned to accompany him.[5] The extant journal opens with the comment that "Mr Babitcheff, qui devoit être mon Compagnon, n'étoit propre qu'à me causer de nouveaux embarras dans mes voyages" (f. 3) and in the event, Korsakov set out alone from London on 27 May, on a tour which in the following five months would take him to Scotland, where he remained for almost three months, and then back to London, via Yorkshire, Lancashire, Staffordshire, and Warwickshire.

Korsakov was fortunate in securing letters of introduction to the great civil engineer John Smeaton (1724-92) and "autres personnes qui pourroient m'être utiles par leur lumiers" (f. 3) from Alexander Baxter, the Russian Consul-General in London. Baxter, who had a long career as a merchant behind him (he had been a member of the Russia Company since 1752), had been appointed by the Russian government in 1773 and many Russian visitors and correspondents were soon to profit from his advice and wide circle of acquaintances.[6] Early in 1776 Baxter had undertaken to consult Smeaton on the best itinerary for the Russians and on 13 February he wrote to Korsakov in Oxford to pass on the views of "the first Engineer in this Country or perhaps, in Europe—in the planning & execution of Canals." He included the following extract from Smeaton's letter:

> The only Canal works now going on whose Engineers I am acquainted with, are the Forth and Clyde Canal by Mr. Mackell; and the works of the River Air, and the Canals to Selby, by Mr. Jessop, who was brought up with me, and who I believe you have heard of upon another occasion. Those works are in this Country.
>
> In answer to your Query, whether it will be best for the young Gentlemen to begin their Surveys in the North or South, I would advise their beginning with the Forth and Clyde Canal, for though it is a Canal of the largest dimensions, yet as everything is done in the strongest and simplest manner, without any Pedantry or affectation, my belief is that They will get more real knowledge by considering the Construction of this Canal than all the rest put together. After this they can proceed with the rest to what Extent They find their curiosity and appetites to extend, and it might not be amiss to cast their Eye upon Upper Calder Navigation, which is a Specimen of the making a River Navigable according to its own Course, and this upon one of the most rapid Rivers in the Kingdom, of its Size, and quantity of water that comes down its Valley in time of Floods and which having occasioned uncommon difficultys, the Expedients made use of have been in proportion. This was one of my first works in that way.[7]

On his way northwards Korsakov made a first unsuccessful attempt to find Smeaton at his home near Ferrybridge, and then journeyed on to Newcastle, where he was to stay for a few days until he had "examiné tous ce qui est remarquable" (f. 7v.). A great deal of English life and ways fell within Korsakov's interpretation of "remarquable," but first and foremost throughout his journey it was the industrial and technological achievements of Britain—canals, mills, foundries, manufactories, machines of all kinds—which held his attention and brought his most careful and detailed descriptions. Thus in Newcastle, after a few comments on the character of the city, he wrote of smelting techniques, of a "fire-engine" and of the coal-mining and the boats that carry the coal to London. Korsakov was anxious not only to record accurately what he saw but also to assess its importance and relevance for Russian developments and conditions. He was impressed by the number of inventions that had been made but no less by the way these inventions were adapted, developed and perfected by other factory-owners and industrialists: "toute invention utile ne manqueroit pas d'etre imitée dans ce pays-ci, ou il n'y a presque pas un maitre de fabrique qui ne soit Mathematicien et philosophe. Il est bien à souhaiter qu'en Russie cette sorte de gens s'appliquent plus serieusement à ces sciences qui sont si indispensables à leur propre interêt" (ff. 4v.-5). Similarly he praised the wise British government policy in encouraging the coal barges and again conjectured what might be attempted in Russia.

Korsakov was to see Newcastle once more, nearly three months later at the end of July, when he visited a Mr. Hodgson, partner in a factory at Whitehall, and was allowed to make a sketch of a machine for boring gun-barrells. The friendly reception he was accorded was in no small measure the result of the warm recommendation he was given by Robert Mackell, with whom he had spent much time in the intervening period in Scotland.

Mackell is one of the least sung of the eighteenth-century canal-builders but he enjoyed the respect of such as James Watt with whom he collaborated in the early 1760s and of Smeaton, who, as we have seen, commended him and his work on the Forth and Clyde Canal to Baxter. Smeaton's name rather than Mackell's is of course more frequently connected with the planning and construction of that canal, but Mackell was involved with the first survey of 1762, a year before Smeaton was recruited. It was Smeaton, however, who was appointed Head Engineer with Mackell as Sub-Engineer when the canal project was given royal assent in March, 1768. Smeaton and Mackell worked happily together until August, 1774, when Smeaton resigned and Mackell continued as engineer in charge until his death in November, 1779.[8] Korsakov found Mackell a delightful and obliging host, who willingly showed him the plans of the canal and explained to him all the difficulties and technicalities in its construction. Although the canal was not finished until 1790, by 1776 considerable progress had been made and the canal had been filled as far as Stockingfield. Korsakov made copious notes and sketches and was so enthusiastic about what he had seen that he launched into a paean to British canal-building and with Mackell's help drew up an appropriate itinerary for his subsequent surveys. He was so taken with Mackell that he wrote it would be to Russia's advantage to invite him to Russia to advise on engineering matters and instruct pupils, probably unaware that Mackell had been approached and offered a three-year contract in 1774.[9] That was at a time when Mackell was unfairly accused of mismanagement and incompetence by the canal board but defended by Smeaton for "his great merit in conducting the works."[10] Mackell's uncompromising disdain for vested interests frequently brought him into conflict with other bodies, such as the Carron ironworks, intent on altering the course and specifications of the canal. Korsakov, who was anxious to visit "la fameuse fabrique de fer fondu de Carron," also noted that Mackell "n'étoit pas bien avec les proprietaires" (f. 9).

Korsakov did manage to visit the ironworks of which he provides a general description, but he was not allowed to see the secret cannon-boring machine or make drawings during his tour. Korsakov's technique was to look very closely at what he was shown and draw from memory as soon as he could get back to his lodgings. This was a period of widespread industrial espionage and piracy and English firms and inventors were naturally suspicious of foreign, and not only foreign, attempts to steal secrets and bypass the patent system, of which Korsakov on another occasion spoke highly. His own remarks in this general context are interesting:

> Les canons de fer qu'on fait a Carron tant pour l'Angleterre que pour les pais étrangers sont tous fondus en solide; et on y fait percer ensuite les cilindres par le moyen d'une machine de leur invention. Je fis mon possible pour voir cette machine, mais on me dit qu'on en fait un secret pour tout le monde, c'en fut assés pour me faire perdre l'esperance de satisfaire ma curiosité - il faut avouer qu'on est fort jaloux dans toutes les fabriques en general; si vous etes admi a voir leur machinerie et leur ouvrages, c'est qu'il y a de leur interet, mais on ne vous permet pas de lever un plan de la moindre chose. tous ceux que je donne ici ne sont point tirés des machines qu'ils representent; car cela n'est pas permi (f. 11)

His sketches were thus frequently of no use other than to give a general impression of the various machines, but in the case of Carron's specific secrets Russia had not long to wait, for in 1786 Charles Gascoigne (1738?-1806), director of the ironworks, entered Russian service and reorganized their foundries and cannon-production.[11]

Korsakov spent three months in Scotland, deeply impressed by the hospitality of the people and the general level of enlightenment. He spent most of his time in Glasgow, where he was apparently made a honorary freeman of the city, and he visited the university there as well as in Edinburgh, where he spoke with Professor Robison, who had arrived back from Russia two years previously.

Travelling south into England again at the end of August, 1776, Korsakov made another vain attempt to catch Smeaton at home before visiting a number of the famous northern canals. Korsakov had first a chance to see the second canal construction specifically recommended by Smeaton to Baxter and the first on which Smeaton himself had worked at the very beginning of the canal era—the Aire and Calder navigation, which as Smeaton had mentioned, was part canal, part canalized river. It was, however, two of the canals associated with the most famous of all English canal-builders, James Brindley (1716-72), which commanded the Russian's attention. With his customary thoroughness he described first the Leeds and Liverpool canal and then, after stays in Halifax, where he enjoyed the generous hospitality of a local merchant by the name of Hardcastle, and in Manchester, where the local inhabitants, he thought, were less polite, the Bridgewater Canal. Work on the Leeds and Liverpool Canal had begun in 1770 and although it was not until 1816 that the whole of its 127 miles were completed, by 1776 good stretches had been finished from both eastern and western terminals. Brindley had surveyed the route but his own involvement was cut short by his death in September, 1772. It was, however, the Worsley and Manchester Canal, or the Bridgewater, as it was called after Brindley's great sponsor, Francis, 3rd Duke of Bridgewater (1736-1803), which had brought Brindley his initial fame. Compared with other canals already fully or partially built in 1776, the Bridgewater Canal was a modest affair, some 10½ miles in length and following a level course. But this level course was made possible by the construction of high embankments and an aqueduct over the River Irwell at Barton which was acclaimed as "perhaps the greatest artificial curiosity in the world."[12] It was on this aqueduct, on 17 July 1761, some two years after construction work had begun, that the first boatload of coal from the duke's mines at Worsley had sailed on its way to Manchester, almost a symbol of a new era. Korsakov's detailed description reflects his keen interest and his appreciation of the significance of this historic canal. Korsakov had no opportunity to meet the Canal Duke himself and Brindley was dead, but a few days later he travelled down from Manchester to Newcastle-under-Lyme, where he was introduced to Brindley's brother-in-law, Hugh Henshall. Henshall, together with other talented former assistants of Brindley, such as Robert Whitworth and Thomas Dadford, were carrying on and completing the major works which led to the realization of Brindley's vision of the "Grand Trunk," the network of over 260 miles of canals which would link the Mersey, Severn, Thames, and Trent and revolutionize the internal communications system of England. In 1776 Henshall was finishing the Trent

and Mersey Canal (Derwent Mouth to Preston Brook), the vital link in the
overall design; his reception of Korsakov was polite, as was his refusal to
allow the Russian to copy his plans.

Korsakov was introduced to Henshall by a man to whom he had himself
letters of introduction from the Russian Ambassador and from Baxter—
Josiah Wedgwood (1730-95). It was Baxter who had negotiated with Wedgwood about the famous dinner service, known as "The Frog," which had
been dispatched to Russia in 1774 for use in Catherine's new palace of
Kekerekeksinskii (renamed in 1780 the Chesmenskii).[13] Among the 1,224
different views which Wedgwood included on the 952 pieces in the service
was at least one of the Bridgewater Canal at Worsley Bridge, complete with
passenger and goods barges.[14] Wedgwood had been desperately anxious to
provide speedier and cheaper means of obtaining the raw materials for his
great pottery enterprises and had been closely associated with the Duke of
Bridgewater and Brindley since the 1760s, when the Trent and Mersey
Canal was devised and begun. Korsakov, however, communicated little about
the local canals or indeed about Wedgwood's potteries: noting simply that
"il y a plusieurs fabriques de fayence dans ces environs [Newcastle], dont la
plus considerable est celle de Mr *Wedgewood*" (f. 31v.), and he was soon
devoting his attention to the famed Boulton and Fothergill manufactory at
Soho in Handsworth and providing enthusiastic appreciations of its pro-
prietors:

> Mr Bulton qui est un homme de Genie et de connoissance tres super-
> ieures a trouvé le secret de donner a toutes ses ouvrages des beautés
> réelles et immortelles telles que nous admirons dans les productions
> des anciens artistes. Comme je lui avois été recomandé de la part de
> Mr Wedgewood, il me recut tres poliment, et m'expliqua lui même
> tout ce qu'il a curieux dans la Manifacture il me donna même un jeune
> homme pour m'accompagner dans toutes les fabriques de la ville.
> Mr Fothergill ne fut ni moins civil, ni moins obligeant, envers moi;
> ils me firent plusieurs invitations de venir dans leurs maisons (ff. 33v.
> -34).

Matthew Boulton (1728-1809) and John Fothergill, who had been in partnership since 1762, were very used to visits from foreigners, anxious to tour
their factory and glean whatever they thought might be of use to their own
interests and their governments; at the same time they were as eager as
Wedgwood to increase their business with Russia (Fothergill indeed had
already paid a short visit to St. Petersburg in 1776) and were intent on
producing a good impression on their Russian visitors.[15] Boulton was well
known to the current Russian Ambassador in London, Count Musin-Pushkin,
from whom Korsakov carried further letters of recommendation to Boulton's
other partner, James Watt.

Watt had come into contact with Russians over a decade previously when his expertise as an instrument maker at Glasgow University so impressed the young Desnitskii that in one of his first works published after his return to Russia he wrote of the desirability of bringing him into Russian service.[16] The suggestion was not pursued, but in 1771 Watt was urged by his old Glasgow friend, John Robison, at that time in Russia with Admiral Knowles, to take up the post of "Master Founder of Iron Ordnance to Her Imperial Majesty," which Watt declined.[17] At that time Watt was in partnership with John Roebuck of Carron, who was soon to be declared bankrupt. However, when the Russians, through their Ambassador Musin-Pushkin, again attempted in 1775 to enlist Watt's services,[18] he had joined forces with Boulton, who had accepted Roebuck's share in the patent of Watt's steam engine as payment of his debts. Watt fully realized the benefits which his partnership with the resourceful and energetic Boulton would bring and could not be persuaded. Nevertheless, as Korsakov indicated, Watt looked forward to supplying his engines to Russia. The lines which Korsakov devotes to Watt reveal how taken he was with him as a person, but they also show that in common with many other intelligent people Korsakov did not realize the full potential and application of Watt's invention and advised continuing with the old (Newcomen) engine, if Watt's charges seemed high.

la personne dont la connoissance me prometoit le plus de profit, étoit Mr Watt, un compagnon nouvellement reçu dans leur manifacture. Cet homme a inventé une machine à feu, sur un principe tout à fait nouveau; qui avec 120 livres fait monter 20.000 pieds cubes d'eau a la hauteur de 24 pieds selon la mesure angloise. à son grand Genie d'invention il a joint des connoissances profondes de chymie et de Phisique. enfin c'est un homme qui despute en gloire a Mr Smeaton dans son metier. . . .
C'est un homme d'un grande modestie. Il fait volontiers part de son savoir aux autre; excepté qu'il n'a jamais voulu mexplequer la construction de la machine, qu'il a Inventée. Peut etre que c'est son interêt d'en faire un secret jusqu'a un certain tems. Il me fit comprendre qu'il espere avoir des ordres de S.M.I. des Russies, pour un grand nombre de ces machines. Si Mr Watt vouloit les faire pour un prix ordinaire, il seroit fort utile de les introduire dans notre pais, puisque on pourroit épargner une quantité considerable de charbon, ou de bois qui est nécessaire pour les faire jouer, mais s'il prétend en tirer des sommes considerables pour sa nouvelle invention, il est beaucoup mieux à nous en passer, et d'user des machines à feu de la vielle construction. Car tout l'avantage des premières n'est que dans la depense du bois ou du charbon. c'est ce dont nous ne manquons pas jusqu'à present (ff. 34-35v.).

Korsakov was to meet one further outstanding representative of the British industrial revolution before he left the Birmingham area—the iron-master John Wilkinson (1728-1808). Once again the Russian had the necessary letters of introduction (in this instance, from Baxter) which brought him a kind reception from Wilkinson and an invitation to visit his two foundries at Bilston and Broseley. Korsakov provided descriptions of two of the important inventions with which Wilkinson's name is connected, firstly of the "soufflets," the blowing machine for coke-smelting iron ore, and secondly, of a cannon-boring machine which Wilkinson had patented in 1774. He also noted two further machines, for making nails and for producing small pieces of iron, which he considered would be very useful in Russia.

Early in October Korsakov was informed by the Russian Embassy that an engineer officer by the name of Neverov had arrived in London to replace the unsatisfactory Babichev; he was obliged to curtail his tour and return to the capital to arrange affairs for his new colleague, who "ne parlait que sa langue maternelle" (f. 39v.). Korsakov spent the rest of the year in London, apart from a brief excursion to Southampton and Portsmouth and a visit to Leeds on 25 December to meet at last Smeaton. Smeaton entertained him royally, showed him all his plans and even managed to get a model of a steam engine in working order to demonstrate its action. The impressed Korsakov noted that if Watt enjoyed all the glory at the moment for his invention, justice should nevertheless be paid to Smeaton for his role in the development of the steam engine. We learn little of what Korsakov did in London: he stressed that he and Neverov were busy making plans of the various canals Korsakov had seen, which they continued to do during a second stay at Oxford in the first six months of 1777. All the plans were eventually dispatched to General Mordvinov in July, 1777, through another and more famous Mordvinov, Nikolai Semenovich, who was returning to Russia after three years with the English navy.

Korsakov's journal reveals the immense impact which Britain had on him. He constantly relates what he sees and hears back to his experiences of Russia. Appreciating the advantages of certain British institutions or inventions or traditions, he frequently implicitly and explicitly criticizes Russian deficiencies or backwardness; he does not, however, offer his observations in blind deference to all things British; he is on the contrary balanced and objective, conscious that he had been sent abroad to learn and report and to contribute to the bright future which he earnestly believed awaited Russia. Education was a subject which perhaps preoccupied him more than any other. He found that "les sciences sont tres cultivees en Angleterre, comme cela est connu de tout le monde, les anglois ont peut etre plus de Genie, et de vrais savants, qu'aucun nation europenne" (f. 42) and suggested that the working classes, although without formal education, showed great application and specialization which resulted in excellent workmanship and expertise. He was much taken with both English and Scottish universities and almost the last entry in his journal from England sees him returning to the theme of the need to accelerate enlightenment in Russia by the establishment of new institutions of learning:

> Peut etre qu'en Russie il ne manque pas aussi d'hommes de genie pour toutes sortes de sciences; mais il n'y a pas presques aucuns moyens de leur faire acquerir des connoissances. nous navons que des corps de cadets pour les militaires; mais pour la littérature, et d'autres sciences nous n'avons presque aucune institution. l'université de Moscou ou on n'en donne que les commencements ne peut etre comparée même avec les Ecoles qui se trouvent en Angleterre, mais quand elle servit dans un état beaucoup meilleur quelle est a present, elle servit tres peu de chose pour un pais aussi vaste que la Russie, ou il y a pres de trente millions d'habitant, et ou dix universités aussi grandes que celle d'Oxford pouroient a peine fournir suffisament pour les besoins de l'Etat. quel nombre de gens d'education ne nous faut-il pas pour notre ministère, pour nos tribunaux civils, et pour nos ecclesiastiques, en considerant les succes que nos affaires ont eu à présent, nous devons avouer à la verité qu'il falloit que les Russes eussent en general beaucoup de genie naturel, vu que cette nation fut particulierment favorisée de la grace du tout puissant, car autrement jamais nous n'aurions pu parvenir à ce point de grandeur, ou nous sommes à present, ayant tant des nations belliqueuses et civilisées pour rivales à tous nos progres; mais sous le reyne present de notre auguste Imperatrice, il y a tout à esperer. elle a deja fait beaucoup pour planter les sciences dans son empire, et pour eclairir ses peuples, et elle ne manquera pas de venir a bout de son dessein, en fondant quelques universite dans les differentes provinces de ses etats, pour faciliter à ses sujets les moyens d'acquerir autant de gloire par leur erudition, qu'il en ont acqui par leur armes (ff. 48v.-49).

Korsakov left London on 21 July 1777, but over two years were to elapse before he returned to Russia. He was yet to visit France (ff. 50-80 of the extant journal) and Italy, meeting more and more scholars, surveying more and more canals, including the great canal of Languedoc. Korsakov is the first Russian known to have been sent abroad to study canal construction, at a time when Europe's, and particularly Britain's, canal-mania was reaching its height. It is only to be regretted that a man who, in the assessment of an Oxford friend, possessed "great abilities & the finest field in the world for showing them to advantage"[19] was prevented by a tragically early death from achieving the eminence which seemed his almost for the taking.

Korsakov's first assignment on his return to St. Petersburg was to help in the initial construction work on the embankments of the Fontanka (which was only completed in 1789), but he was far from content with his lot during the two years or so he spent in the capital.[20] By the end of 1782, however, Korsakov had received a new appointment in southern Russia. Korsakov seems to have come to the notice of Prince Potemkin, who had him appointed director of building at Kherson, where work had begun in 1778 under Ivan Abramovich Gannibal, Alexander Pushkin's grandfather, to create the major trading centre of southern Russia and shipbuilding yards for the Black Sea fleet. The formal annexation of the Crimea in the summer of 1783 added further territory to that already acquired by Russia in 1774 and Korsakov's skills were soon employed in surveying the site of a new port and shipyard on the Black Sea itself. As a result of his findings, it was decided to transform the little Tartar village of Akhtiya'r into Sevastopol' and work began in 1786.[21] At the end of 1784 Korsakov was ordered to construct bridges to facilitate the farming of salt from the Perekop and Kozlov salt-lakes and to erect buildings suitable for storing the salt, which was a significant source of state income.[22] Kherson remained, however, Korsakov's main concern in these years and Samuel Bentham noted in June, 1784, that "Cherson to be new fortified and other fortresses in abundance all under his direction."[23] At Kherson in 1786 Korsakov was visited by Elizabeth, Lady Craven, who was clearly impressed by him. In a letter to the Margrave of Brandenburg-Anspach, she wrote: "I am going to see the Dock-Yard here and the fortifications, which are to be new done by a Colonel Korsakov, a very civil spirited young man here, who seems to have the welfare of this place and the honour of his nation very much at heart."[24] She later confessed that she was "not soldier enough to know what fault there was" in the existing fortifications, but she had no doubt that Korsakov's "active and studious spirit" would be equal to any challenge.[25] She met with Korsakov his old friend Nikolai Mordvinov, who had come to Kherson at the end of 1785 to head the naval administration, and found them "much more like Englishmen than any foreigners I ever met with."[26]

Korsakov's work at Kherson was interrupted by a new outbreak of hostilities with the Turks in August, 1787. He was soon involved in the fighting, alongside Mordvinov and the ubiquitous Samuel Bentham. In July, 1788, Potemkin wrote commending Korsakov for his part in the destruction of the Turkish fleet in the battle in the Liman and, shortly afterwards, informed him of the award of the order of St. George, 4th class.[27] The Russian mastery of the Liman led to the seige and eventual capture of the fortress of Ochakov on 6/17 December, but Korsakov was not to witness the final victory, for early in October he "was killed by falling down a precipice near Ochakoff as he was working on the batteries."[28] The news was communicated to Jeremy Bentham by Samuel, who had not mentioned Korsakov in his correspondence for some four years. "To me it was no great loss," Bentham continued, "for he was become my enemy; but it was a most unlucky death for a man to meet with in the sight of the enemy. His character was so much changed within these 2 years that I have scarcely found a single person who regretted him." Whatever the reasons for their rupture (and Bentham's general conduct and attitudes hardly suggest that he himself would be totally blameless), it is a pity that Bentham felt the need to bolster his own disillusionment with an unworthy generalization. Russia certainly had lost what it could ill afford—an enlightened and experienced officer and a highly skilled and resourceful engineer.

Despite his training and experience gained in Europe, Korsakov was never employed on the construction of canals, although his general expertise as an engineer was certainly exploited. In the 1780s work was continued on what was to become the Volga-Don canal under the supervision of an English surveyor, John Phillips, who described his melancholy experiences in his *General History of Inland Navigation, Foreign and Domestic* (London, 1792). After some nineteen months "he returned to Petersburg, without doing any thing but cutting down a few thousand timber trees."[29] Although Phillips's books were very popular in England they were probably too general to be thought worth translating into Russian. An indication of continued Russian interest in English canals, however, was the publication in 1800 of *Opisanie sudokhodnykh kanalov, vykopannykh v Anglii s 1759 goda* ("A Description of Navigable Canals, Constructed in England since 1759"), translated from the German work of J. L. Horewe, with numerous plans. By coincidence, the next Russian engineer known to visit England to study the canal system was Korsakov's nephew, Lev Savel'evich Vaksel', who arrived in 1802, bearing a signet ring from the tsar for Thomas Telford.[30]

II

In January, 1701, Peter the Great established in Moscow the School of Mathematics and Navigation. At its head was Henry Farquharson (d. 1739), an Aberdeen scholar recruited personally by Peter in 1698, and he was assisted by two young alumni of the Royal Mathematical School of Christ's Hospital, Stephen Gwyn and Richard Grice. The venture reflected the tsar's concern to create a corps of men essential for the realization of his new Russia, skilled in mathematics, navigation, surveying. Farquharson during his forty-year service in Russia far exceeded possible Russian expectations by his dedication, his versatility and influence on whole generations of young Russian naval officers, engineers and technologists.[31] Russia needed, however, not only trained men but also machines and scientific instruments. Increasingly throughout the century and particularly after the establishment of the Academy of Sciences which brought close contacts with the Royal Society, England became the source of all manner of instruments—telescopes, orreries, sundials, astronomical and navigational aids. Instruments from the great English masters, Culpeper, Rowley, Bird, Dolland, Short, Arnold, made their way to Russia.[32] English instrument-makers were also attracted into Russian service—John Bradlee in the reign of Peter, Benjamin Scott under Elizabeth, Francis Morgan and Robert Hynam under Catherine. Their contracts stressed not only their obligation to produce instruments, but also to train young Russian craftsmen. Bradlee in 1710 "promised to instruct in all kinds of instruments two young men from among the cleverest school pupils who have passed their examination in geometry" and he was to "receive for this instruction 100 rubles for each of them on the condition that he teaches them to work as well as himself."[33] The alternative to bringing foreign masters to Russia was, of course, to send promising young Russians to study abroad, although this could be an expensive and unpredictable undertaking. However, whatever the strategy, the ultimate aim was the same: "se passer des secours étrangers dans la fabrication des instrumens."[34]

If we discount the young sailors and ship-builders sent to England by Peter, the first instrument-maker and mechanic to visit London was the accomplished Andreĭ Konstaninovich Nartov (1680/93-1756), a former student of the Moscow School of Mathematics and Navigation and from 1709 head of its turnery.[35] In 1712 and 1713 he had designed and built lathes of an advanced type and was appointed personal turner to the tsar. Shortly after his visit in 1716-17 to France, where he had shown particular interest in the operations of the Paris mint, Peter decided to send Nartov to Europe. Nartov set out in the summer of 1718, visiting first the King of Prussia, whom he instructed in the art of turning, to which Friedrich-Wilhelm was as much addicted as Peter, and arrived in London on 8 January 1719, accompanied by two apprentices, Zhurakovskii and Bezobrazov. Nartov's mission, according to his own testimony, was "to attempt to obtain information about the new method of preparing and bending oak for the construction of boats, together with plans of the necessary ovens [for steaming the wood]" in London, and in both London and Paris, where he was to go later in 1719, "to collect mechanical and hydraulic models from the best scientific instrument makers to show to his monarch."[36] There is no evidence to suggest that Nartov was successful in discovering the secrets of preparing oak, but he used his nine months in England to great effect. He found no English lathe-masters who were able to construct lathes from plans which he had brought from Russia, but he saw a wide variety of machines unknown in Russia and collected a number of English books on technical subjects. Peter had instructed him to find out about making snuff-boxes from tortoise-shell and he soon found a craftsman willing to reveal his technique for a consideration of two guineas and to undertake to instruct Bezobrazov for twenty pounds more.[37] On 20 March 1719 he sent a long letter to Peter, summing up what he had accomplished and the machinery which he had seen, which included a screw-cutting lathe and the use of hardened dies for the mint, a machine to cut gear teeth on iron wheels and another for boring barrels.[38] From England Nartov moved on to Paris, where he made contact with a number of scholars in the Academy and had an opportunity to show his paces on a lathe which Peter had presented on his visit in 1717.

Nartov returned to Russia to enjoy Peter's favours and a long career which involved him in the construction of more advanced lathes, in the re-organization of the Moscow Mint and the Sestroretsk foundry and in the directing of the machine shop of the Academy of Sciences in the last two decades of his life. He was a turner, a gun-founder, a medallist, Russia's first great mechanic. He had a haughty disdain for foreigners, matched only by the disdain for Russians evinced by some foreigners—and both were excessive, but he was a true "Petrine fledging," who spent the last years of his life writing his "Dostopamiatnye povestvovaniia i rechi Petra Velikogo" ("Memorable Deeds and Words of Peter the Great").

Acquainted with Nartov towards the end of his life was the young Nikolai Galaktionovich Chizhov (1731-67), who had been first a student, then an apprentice in the Instrument Department (*Instrumental'naia palata*) of the Academy of Sciences since 1741, training under F. N. Tiriutin. By 1759 he had shown such skill in the making of various instruments that it was decided to send him for a year to England to widen his experience, but also to fulfil a number of specific commissions from the Academy. He arrived in London towards the end of the year and worked for some eight months until August, 1760, with the famed optical instrument maker George Adams, the elder (1710-73) in Fleet Street. Also with a shop in Fleet Street was John Cuff (1708-72), who described himself as a "Spectacle & Microscope Maker, who makes and sells Wholesale & Retail all manner of curious Optical instruments," and the particular curious instrument which the Academy of Sciences was anxious to obtain was his double microscope (patented in 1744). Chizhov was instructed to buy "two double microscopes with their equipment and most recent additions," having first thoroughly tested them. Cuff, however, had no microscopes in stock but prepared one on Chizhov's order at a cost of six guineas.[39] In July Chizhov was able to report that he had fulfilled all that had been asked of him and asked permission to return to Petersburg, but the Academy sent a detailed second instruction requiring him to visit the Greenwich Observatory, using the good offices of Bradley, an honorary member of the Academy, to look at the new twelve-foot telescope constructed by James Short, and to bring back to Russia as many instruments as possible.[40] After his return to Petersburg, Chizhov soon became head of the Instrument Department at the Academy and worked for Lomonosov on his improved Newtonian telescope.

England again proved popular for young Russian instrument makers in the 1780s, and rightly so, for it was the era of excellence and attainment. In 1780 the Academy of Sciences sent a young man by the name of Vorob'ev to England and France "pour apprendre à faire toutes sortes d'instrumens de mathématiques etc."[41] The little that is known about his activities in England is contained in an interesting letter from Andreas Johann Lexell (1740-84), the Swedish-born astronomer and professor at the Petersburg Academy of Sciences since 1768. Lexell was sent on a fact-finding tour of Europe by the Academy also in 1780 and in April of the following year met in London Vorob'ev, who had been working under Kenneth McCulloch, compass-maker to the Duke of Clarence:

> Après avoir été chez le maitre de Mr. Worobief, je vois bien qu'il ne profitera beaucoup chez lui, puisque ce Mr. Culloch travaille principalement en cuivre, et ne s'occupe point de tout de tout [sic] de l'optique, d'ailleurs chez quelque maitre qu'il soit à Londres, il pourra travailler toute sa vie, sans être mis à portée, de connoitre la composition d'un instrument, puisque pour chaque partie d'un instrument, il y a differens ouvriers. Or comme à Paris tout ces fait chez le même maitre, il sera la plus à portée d'apprendre tout le detail, pour les instrumens d'Optiques.[42]

Vorob'ev in fact left London in the middle of May for Paris, where he made a good impression. By 1784 he was back in Petersburg with the position of Academy mechanic.

During the same period that Vorob'ev was in London, there were two graduates from Petersburg's other academy, the Academy of Arts, apprenticed to leading English instrument makers. Osip Ivanovich Shishorin and Vasilii Konstantinovich Sveshnikov had been students together at the Academy of Arts from 1764 to 1772; they then began to learn their trade as instrument makers under the guidance of the newly arrived Francis Morgan (1742?-1802), who combined appointments with the Admiralty and the Academy of Arts. It seems likely that Morgan himself conducted his apprentices to London in the spring of 1780 and established them with English masters whom he knew and respected. Shishorin was five years with John Stancliffe and Sveshnikov worked for the same period with Simon Spicer.[43] The only glimpse we have of them during this period is a letter which they wrote to the Academy early in 1785, painting a familiar story of funds irregularly, if ever, received from Russia and of insistent English creditors who would not allow them to return to their homeland. One detail is, however, of interest: they were obliged to use "a considerable sum to acquire from knowledgeable workmen the information that the masters usually from malice or envy conceal, particularly from foreigners."[44] Money from the Academy was eventaully forthcoming and the two men set out on 8 August 1785. By December both were made joint heads of the mathematical instrument making class at the Academy, where they remained until the mid-1790s, when for the first time in thirty years their paths diverged. Shishorin set up in private practice in Petersburg, making a variety of instruments including sundials, before becoming director of the navigational instrument workshop at the Admiralty dockyard in 1804; Sveshnikov went to southern Russia in 1794, yet another addition to the group of English-trained sailors and specialists at Kherson and Nikolaev.

III

Machines—"fire-engines," cannon-boring machines, heavy presses, lathes of all kinds—rather than scientific instruments were the major concern of other Russian "mechanics" sent to Britain in the 1770s and 80s. They included in their number men whose exploits have become the stuff of legend and folklore. In the first two decades after the Second World War some writers followed official Soviet policy in combining cheap xenophobia with glorification of Russian pre-eminence in seemingly all fields of human endeavour. The self-seeking and pernicious adventures of foreigners in Russia were portrayed in dark colours and forgotten native Russian heroes were resurrected and their discoveries and achievements triumphantly paraded. Pre-Revolutionary historians and writers were castigated for being duped by the myth of the qualitative and quantitative contributions of foreigners to the industrial and cultural development of Russia from the time of Peter and for their neglect of Russian pioneers, at least of those of lower station. Despite the obvious extremism of this trend, important correctives to the general picture were introduced, and indeed the accounts of some of the Russians in eighteenth-century Britain unfolded in the present work argue in the same direction and highlight the frequent neglect of their talents in their homeland.

In his historical narrative *O masterakh starinnykh* ("Masters of Yesteryear," 1953), Viktor Shklovskii links the stories of some of the outstanding mechanics of the famous Tula factory in the eighteenth century with those of other mechanics whose contacts with Tula were somewhat indirect, namely Nartov and Lev Fedorovich Sabakin (1746-1813), both of whom visited England. Although we shall return to Sabakin, it is the Tula masters, Aleksei Mikhailovich Surnin (1767-1811) and Iakov (Ivanovich?) Leont'ev, who are of immediate concern, for they are connected with an earlier and more famous fiction than Shklovskii's. In 1882 Nikolai Leskov published his *Skaz o tul'skom Levshi i o stal'noi blokhe* ("Tale of the Left-Handed Workman from Tula and the Steel Flea"), in which he related how the skill of Tula workmen allowed Nicholas I a moment of triumph over the English. During a visit to England Alexander I received a present of a minute clockwork flea; sometime after succeeding his brother, Nicholas sent the flea to Tula to see whether his workmen could outdo the English; their response was to shoe the flea and sign their names, while a third workman, the "levsha," produced the nails for the shoes. Levsha was then sent to England with the shoed flea and won the admiration of the English for his skill. Although the action of the story was set well into the nineteenth century, the historian of the Tula factory, S. A. Zybin, suggested in 1905 that Surnin and Leont'ev provided the joint prototype for Leskov's hero. Thus a legend was born, which literary critics and historians have subsequently been at pains to dispel. It is acknowledged, however, that information about Surnin's and Leont'ev's activities in England, known to Leskov through letters of Count Vorontsov which were first published in 1876 and 1879, was used in the description of Levsha's reception in England.[45]

Surnin and Leont'ev arrived in England in November, 1785. They both came from families of experienced Tula craftsmen and had probably worked long enough in the arms factory for their potential to be realized. In 1782 Catherine had issued an ukaz to effect the re-organization and rebuilding of the factory and to raise standards among the workmen. Prince Potemkin, as head of the Military College, had particular interests in Tula and it was on his direction that two apprentices were chosen to train in England and four to work with a master in Petersburg, "in order to see whether the latter achieve better results than those sent to England."[46] In London, the two young men came under the care and supervision of Father Smirnov, who placed them in a local school to learn English, drawing and other subjects which would be of use in their subsequent technical training. In the summer of 1787 Surnin and Leont'ev sent off on a tour of industrial centres, including Birmingham and Sheffield, England's Tula. There was obviously much for them to admire and see, not only the already famous "fire-engines" of Watt at Soho, but all manner of processes in button making, silverplating etc. A Russian who visited Soho the year before Surnin and Leont'ev described his guided tour as follows: "The skill of the works is excellent, the machines are ordinary and I'm sure we have similar ones in Tula; but the great advantage of these factories is that they employ where appropriate women, children and grown-up men and frequently place a child with a man. I don't know whether we polish steel with bare hands, but they do here. Some 300-400 workers are employed at this factory."[47] An English account from the same period speaks of "the various operations of button making":

> It is really surprising how many persons are employed to make a single button—one makes one part, another another &c, not one of these could make a whole button—this, by the by, is a principal security against artificers being seduced into foreign countries. I saw the different operations in making plated goods, the laying the silver on the plates of copper. . . the silversmiths shop, where they were chasing a turin for the Empress of Russia—I have seen more elegant forms however—the making of the new machine for copying writings, for which Mr Watts, concerned with Mr Bolton, has a patent.[48]

Perhaps the young Russians were too taken with the techniques of producing fancy consumer goods, for on their return to London, the Russian ambassador Vorontsov took them in hand and wrote to the Russian authorities that "it would be of far greater use to our country if our arms factories were able first and foremost to produce what is essential rather than provide our fops with pretty outfits, highly finished swords, shining buckles, chains and similar items."[49] Surnin and Leont'ev were therefore placed with the leading London gun makers Nock and Egg.

It was obvious in speaking firstly of Korsakov and then of Shishorin and Sveshnikov how difficult it could be to learn the secrets of English manufacturers and craftsmen. There were strict laws forbidding the emigration of British specialists and the export of plant and machinery as opposed to finished goods. In 1771 the British ambassador in Petersburg expressed his concern over the activities of the Russian ambassador in London and of Baxter in particular with regard to enticing away masters such as Morgan,[50] and some years later Smirnov wrote to Petersburg that "the acts of Parliament which of late have been published, threaten too great punishments to ye emigrators & the parties concerned in it."[51] Nevertheless, the Russians enjoyed a fair degree of success, much to the annoyance of such as Samuel Garbett, who incensed above all by the defection of his former partner at Carron, Gascoigne, continually denounced to the British government any Russian attempts at seduction and resolutely closed the doors of his Birmingham factory to all foreign visitors.[52] Surnin and Leont'ev were therefore more than fortunate in gaining the confidence and trust of such leading gunsmiths as Nock and Egg. Henry Nock (1741-1804) was the outstanding gun maker of his time, "an engineer as well as an artist," who produced for the army what was "probably the first military musket ever made" and carried out numerous modifications and improvements on flintlocks and breechblocks for the Navy. He ran a shop at No. 10, Ludgate Street and a series of workshops in Whitechapel.[53] Durs Egg (1750-1834), a Swiss by origin, was not renowned for the same degree of inventiveness and skill Nock, but had government contracts for muskets and carbines and produced a large number of the previously standard Ferguson rifle.[54] In a report submitted to Catherine in 1792 Surnin spoke very highly of Nock, "an honest man, completely devoted to Russia," who "told me without the slightest evasion all the secrets of his trade and put me in charge of all his projects with the supervision of two hundred skilled apprentices." He frankly admitted that he was indebted to him "for all my success, for my visits to the most important factories, for information about and export of various useful machines which were of the utmost secrecy."[55] It is difficult to judge from the documents available what moved Nock to such dubious and patently treasonable activities: possibly Surnin had proved invaluable when Nock was endeavouring to meet deadlines for the delivery of his new rifle to the army;

possibly Nock received some financial inducements from the Russians, although his existing contracts with the British government and other business were enough to ensure his financial prosperity. At all events Nock provided a faithful friend when others denounced Surnin for his activities. Vorontsov described in a letter to Potemkin of August, 1791, how "as soon as they began to talk here about preparing the fleet for war against Russia, all the workmen began to be angry with him and voice their suspicions that he was living here in order to copy all the weapons for use against England to such an extent that he was forced to leave his master who had always acted in the most friendly way towards him."[56] As Vorontsov goes on to reveal, however, the suspicions of Surnin resulted from a denunciation from his companion Leont'ev to the Master General of Ordnance, the Duke of Richmond, which led to a search of Surnin's rooms and his close questioning. Nothing was found and Nock's testimony brought Surnin's release.

Leont'ev's action was the gesture of a man who had long since decided to remain in England and who was leading, according to the ambassador, "a dissolute life." He had apparently fallen in love with an Englishwoman, abandoned his master Egg, and was probably enjoying being "indépendent et mille fois plus heureux qu'à Toula," the last feared by Vorontsov as attractions which together with a fat salary might in turn seduce Surnin.[57] Surnin, however, did not disappoint him, and returned to Russia in the summer of 1791 with plans of various machines but also with machines smuggled out of England through the non-religious offices of the Rev. Smirnov.

Vorontsov could not praise Surnin enough for his irreproachable conduct and application and with the pride of an old soldier ("six years an army colonel"), he foresaw the great improvements which Surnin could introduce in Russian ordnance. His already much-quoted letter to Potemkin contrasts the excellence of Russian rifle barrels with the deficiencies in their working parts, particularly the breech. Surnin had acquired lathes which would enable him to produce these parts with such precision that they would be interchangeable for rifles of a like kind; in addition he knew the secrets of Nock's recently invented lock which was held together by a single screw and could be dismantled and re-assembled by an average soldier without difficulty. Surnin, the talented apprentice, was returning as a highly competent master, who should be rewarded "as an example for all those who, sent abroad to study, conduct themselves well, apply themselves to their tasks and return willingly to their homeland."[58] Inevitably, however, the rewards he received were meagre, the obstacles to his displaying his capabilities to the full were immense. In 1805 Vorontsov's son, Mikhail Semenovich, visited Surnin at Tula; his father noted "si on le laissait faire, il aurait mis notre fabrique d'armes sur le meilleur pied possible."[59] Surnin's achievements were, nevertheless, noteworthy.

Although he was appointed initially to supervise the building of a new arms factory in Olonets region, pressure from the governor-general of Tula province, Major-General M. N. Krechetnikov, and the director of the Tula works, S. N. Venitseev, eventually led to his secondment and ultimately permanent appointment at Tula. Full of what he had seen in Englnad, Surnin envisaged a major re-organization of the Tula works, which had made little if any progress during his long absence. In a long report dated 20 September/ 1 October 1793, to Platon Zubov, Catherine's new favourite, Surnin detailed the numerous deficiencies in the operations of the works, its hopelessly inefficient system, its antique machinery and inaccurate tools; he offered plans plans for new buildings, a re-organization of the workforce which would raise it from the level of a cottage industry, an outline of the new weapons to be produced.[60] In every area the example of England, the successes of Nock, provided the blueprints for action, the spur to emulation. Zubov was impressed and gave the go-ahead for Surnin's proposals and early the following year Surnin was appointed supervisor of weapon-production at Tula with a salary of 500 rubles. In 1795 he was admitted to the lowest rank in the Table of Ranks, that of ensign; by his death he had been advanced to the ninth rank in the civil list, that of titular counsellor.

Tula was not to be re-organized and re-built in a day, but Surnin worked steadily in the remaining fifteen years of his life towards his ideal of a modern factory with a skilled labour force, precision machinery, and products of high quality and performance. Of high priority was the need to produce rifles with interchangeable and easily assembled parts, and this became of even greater urgency in the reign of Paul, when the decision was made to equip the army with new rifles. Some 160 rifles of the new type were ready for trials in November, 1798, some four months after Paul's ukaz, but they failed to meet required standards and the experiment was switched to the smaller modern factory at Sestroretsk.[61] Undeterred, Surnin continued to strive for what was a major revolution in the running of the Tula works, which was to be effected fully only towards the end of Alexander's reign. Recognition for Surnin came from Alexander at the end of 1806 when he received a thousand rubles for "his outstanding efforts and zeal," following increased production of rifles for the war against France.[62]

Potemkin's experiment in sending two apprentices to England and Vorontsov's care in seeing that their attention was concentrated on the manufacture of guns had largely paid off. It seems that Leont'ev also returned to the fold and brought to bear his lesser but still important experience towards the end of the century. The Cambridge don, Edward Daniel Clarke, who visited Tula in June, 1800, spoke of meeting workmen 'purposely sent to England by the late Empress,"[63] and six years later Reginald Heber met and named Leont'ev, whom he called one of the overseers of the factory and a former apprentice of Nock [sic]. In a later letter he described him as "a very sensible plain man, who spoke English, and had served his apprenticeship in London."[64]

IV

The year before Surnin and Leont'ev came to London there had arrived
Lev Sabakin, a classic example of the Russian *samouchka*, or self-taught
mechanic. He was already in his thirty-ninth year and had come to the notice
of Catherine earlier in 1784 for a wall "astronomical" clock, which he had
made during his leisure hours from his work as a clerk in the Tver' criminal
court. Sabakin's emergence appears particularly striking because of our ignorance of his background and upbringing. He was apparently the son of a
peasant from a village near Tver', who at the age of thirty had become a
copyist in the office where he worked until he was sent to England to develop
his skills as a mechanic. In his service record (1802), Sabakin mentions that
his mechanical expertise had been exploited as part of his duties in Tver'.[65]
Catherine clearly recognized his potential, awarded him a thousand rubles for
his clock, which she took into the Hermitage, and sent him to England.

His first task was to learn English but within weeks he was also designing
his own steam pump. In December, 1784, Smirnov informed Samborskii
that "Mr Sobakin makes but slow progress in the English language," but
"his great Genius has lately contrived a kind of force pump which was shown
to H. E. Mr Simolin who desired Mr Sobakin to make a description of it &
promised to send it to His Ex. Count Besborodko."[66] Simolin, however, was
soon to leave London for a new appointment and it was left to the new
ambassador, Vorontsov, to send off Sabakin's drawings to Russia and seek
some financial reward for him from the empress. Sabakin was clearly a man
whom Vorontsov could respect for his skill and his devotion to Russia, as
his letter to Bezborodko makes clear: "This mechanic, despite the fact that
he is already over forty years of age, is unflagging in his study of the English
language and the basic principles of mathematics which are necessary to
read technical books which are all written here in a mathematical way. It
can only be regretted that he did not have the opportunity to receive a better
education in his birthplace, that is, in Staritsa; nevertheless, his tireless
application and zeal in acquiring knowledte about mechanics seem to promise
that in time he will acquire all that is necessary." Vorontsov noted with
approval that Sabakin was "more inclined to invent things which are useful
rather than amusing" and cited the examples of his steam engine and of a
pile-driving machine.[67] Sabakin had made a brass working model of his
steam engine which was demonstrated to leading English mechanics and a
drawing was shown to George III, who wanted to see the model working.
One of the men to see Sabakin's machine was Hyacinthe Magellan, who was
impressed by the simplicity of its design and undertook to get Smeaton's
view of a machine which he though could be introduced with great profit if
it were proved capable of adaptation for large-scale machines.[68] Unfortunately, the letters containing Smeaton's verdict have not been found,

neither have the drawing nor the model of Sabakin's machine. It is possible, however, that the drawing was reproduced in a work Sabakin published after his return to Russia.

A book which was of considerable importance for Sabakin's development was *Lectures on Select Subjects in Mechanics, Hydrostatics, Pneumatics and Optics* (1760; sixth ed., 1784) by James Ferguson, F.R.S. (1710-76), Boswell's "self-taught philosopher," who had enjoyed a considerable reputation both as a popular and popularizing lecturer, and as a prolific writer.[69] There was much in Ferguson's book to inform and instruct Sabakin, who also realized its potential usefulness as a textbook for other Russian mechanics. It seems probable that he began a translation during the latter part of his stay in England, for in October, 1786, Catherine ordered the book to be published at the expense of the government. The translation, which appeared from the press of the Mining Institute in 1787, was in fact a translation of only the first four and a half lectures in Ferguson's book.[70] The first three lectures provided a succinct exposition of the basic principles of physics, a theoretical course preparatory to examples of practical application, described in the fourth lecture. The fifth lecture, dealing with hydrostatic and hydraulic machines, was translated up to and including the section on pumps, but the final pages on water wheels was rejected. The omitted final six lectures were concerned with matters of optics, pneumatics and astronomy and were rejected as peripheral to Sabakin's main concern and interest, the steam engine. Sabakin soon realized that the work as published in Russia was, nevertheless, unsatisfactory, largely because it neglected important developments in the construction of steam engines which had taken place principally since Ferguson's death. He therefore decided to re-issue the translation with an added lecture of his own devisng, which would incorporate the present state of knowledge. Sabakin offered a comparison between the old type of engine, developed by Newcomen, and the new type, pioneered by Watt, he also provided two illustrations, which are considered by his biographer, F. N. Zagorskii, to be Sabakin's original variant on Watt's engine.[71] Sabakin's revised edition of Ferguson's work also appeared in 1787 and a separate edition of his own lecture on "fire machines" appeared the following year in Moscow.[72]

Apart from its undoubted importance as the first detailed discussion in Russian of the new steam engine, Sabakin's lecture is of interest for the information it gives of his movements in England. In his letter to Bezborodko of 19/30 December 1785, Vorontsov had mentioned his intention to send Sabakin to Edinburgh and he set off early in the New Year with Dr Terekhovskii. Ten years previously, Korsakov seems to have taken some nine days on the journey from London to Edinburgh and one of the places en route which took his particular attention was Newcastle with its thriving coal industry. He described a "fire-engine" which he saw there and it is probably the same engine which Sabakin mentions in his "Lecture" as working in a deep coal-mine near Newcastle and fed by three combined boilers. Sabakin does not allude to his activities in Scotland, but it is almost certain that it was to Professors Robison and Black that he had letters of introduction. Not only did both men have strong ties with Russia but both, particularly Black, had specialist knowledge of steam engines. It was Black's discovery of latent heat which was utilized by Watt when he was first attracted to the problem of steam engines at Glasgow in the 1760s and they had remained firm friends and constant correspondents ever since. Robison, it will be recalled, had attempted to enlist Watt into Russian service when he himself was secretary to Admiral Knowles in Petersburg in the early 1770s, after which an order was placed with the Carron factory for a steam engine to be installed at Cronstadt. By coincidence Sabakin was also in Edinburgh precisely at the time when Russians sent by Vorontsov were arranging for the departure for Russia of Charles Gascoigne, the former director of Carron.

From Edinburgh Sabakin journeyed south, inevitably towards Birmingham and a meeting with Boulton and Watt. In his "Lecture" Sabakin spoke of the construction of the new steam engine and of its wide application for any number of tasks; at Soho he saw an engine which "turned a great number of grindstones, lathes and several drills for boring large holes in various metal objects and so on." As was only to be expected, Sabakin encountered difficulties in seeing everything that was of interest but on the whole was very impressed by what he did see and by the hospitality accorded him by Boulton and Watt:

> all the works and manufactories are operated by machines and I heard indirectly that there are many machines which are found only there and are kept secret. I was also able to observe that with the recommendation obtained for me by my protector, His Excellency Count Semen Romanovich Vorontsov, they were more prepared to entertain me and take me through the gardens than through their works and factories and if through the latter, then, I expect, that they gave warning in advance what was secret and where I should not be taken. However, for my part I was quite satisfied, for I saw so many new and interesting things which I certainly would never have seen anywhere else. I must admit that on that occasion I had difficulty in deciding which of the machines I saw demanded the closest attention and above all, I was afraid that such attention might make them suspicious of me.[73]

Sabakin returned to Russia in the summer of 1786, a much more complete and informed mechanic than when he had left two years previously. His stay in Britain was of crucial importance in his development, giving him a chance to learn English and thereby to acquaint himself with technical works which were not available in Russian, allowing him to meet leading British engineers, factory-owners and scholars and to visit a number of factories and towns. In several ways he resembled Ferguson, whose works had such an appeal for him —a self-taught man with great natural gifts and "golden hands" who was given the chance to improve and add to his knowledge with the help of benefactors and able to pass on what he had learnt in published works. Not without reason Zagorskii suggests that an acquaintance with Ferguson's *An Easy Introduction to Astronomy, for Young Gentlemen and Ladies* (1768) prompted Sabakin to compose his *Maloe zdanie ili razgovory, kasaiushchiesia do astronomii, fisiki i mekhaniki . . . v pol'zu maloletnykh detei* ("The Small Building, or Dialogues about Astronomy, Physics and Mechanics . . . for Young Children," 1789) which presented in an easy and fairly palatable form the sort of basic scientific information of which such as Sabakin himself had been deprived as children. More direct evidence of what Sabakin considered noteworthy in England is contained in a series of small articles which he contributed to a journal of the Free Economic Society in 1788. In some twenty pages he covered the following varied topics: "English Steel in Birmingham," "A Notice about Fire-Engines in England," "On the Roads of England There Are No Wheel Tracks or Ruts," "The Particular Method of the English of Putting Money into Circulation," "Patriotic Societies in England," and "On the Manufacture of English Stone-Ware."[74]

In 1787 Sabakin at his own request returned to his native region to rejoin his family and to become the District Mechanic of Tver', a post which although rarely encountered in the eighteenth century, became characteristic for regions with developed or developing industrial enterprises in the nineteenth century. Sabakin's activities seem to have been principally in the field of instrument making. He constructed an apparatus for measuring the speed of ships, a new improved astronomical clock, an instrument for surveying, a weighing machine, and a machine for the rolling and winding of linens—all by 1800, and his efforts were acknowledged by considerable sums from the government, by modest advancement up the Table of Ranks and by election to the Free Economic Society.

The new century brought a change of appointment and an opportunity to display to greater effect his skills. His new position was mechanic to the Office of Main Administration of Factories in the Urals at Ekaterinburg and his responsibilities included the supervision of the mechanics and craftsmen working at the numerous factories, mines and dams in the region as well as the repair and renewal of plant. His own workshop was at the Ekaterinburg Mint where in the course of the five years up to his retirement in 1804 he produced an impressive variety of machines including a steam-engine and minting machinery which are of particular interest for possible English influences, as will be seen later. He himself gave particular significance to his instruction of craftsmen which included teaching them "how to make English instruments and apparatus which they did not know about."[75] Sabakin's retirement was not of his own seeking and therefore he was more than willing to accept an invitation from the head of the Goroblagodat' and Perm' factories, A. F. Deriabin, to continue his work. Sabakin worked a further six years in the Urals before following Deriabin to Petersburg. Despite his advanced years, he was patriotically to accept one more post, in 1812, at the Izevsk gun factory, and he died there the following year.

V

Sabakin's links with England are not exhausted by what has so far been recounted of his life and activities. He was one of the few Russians other than diplomats to make a second visit to England but the significance of that visit can only be appreciated in the wider context of the visits of other Russian specialists and mechanics, not least of whom was the previously mentioned Deriabin, in the period 1797-1802.

The problems of producing good coin and fine medals had attracted the attention of Peter the Great and the London Mint was one of the places which he had been anxious to visit in 1698, as was the Paris Mint during his later visit to France. His mechanic Nartov studied minting machines and processes in London and Paris. During the reign of Anna Ivanovna it was decided to send young medallists abroad with a view to improving their art and it seems that Ivan Levken (b. 1714) was sent to England in 1731 by his father, Johann Levken (or Leffken), an established foreign master at the Petersburg Mint.[76] Somewhat later, in 1748, an Englishman, Benjamin Scott, Jr. was invited to Russia, where he worked until 1761, training a new generation of talented Russian medallists.[77] The Mint was one of the first buildings which Peter had been anxious to see built within the Peter and Paul Fortress, and although over the years the machinery had been improved and replaced, by the reign of Catherine its performance left much to be desired. Early in 1796 approaches were made to Boulton through the Russian Consul, Alexander Baxter, about possible repairs to the existing machinery and the sending out of skilled workmen. Boulton had suggested that it would be difficult to find workmen willing to emigrate and that anyway "many Men may be found in St Petersburg or in H I M's foundries who are capable of making such repairs."[78] At the same time he took the opportunity of sending the empress examples of the coins and medals which he had himself minted and of proposing a new modern mint after his own design. In October, 1796, Vorontsov was informed that "Her Majesty has approved of the Plan proposed by Mr Boulton for erecting a Mint, and has granted a permission for the same to be erected upon the same Plan and with all that Machinery which he has represented as contributing so much towards carrying it into execution." However, she wished Boulton to supervise personally the installation of the machinery in St. Petersburg or, failing that, for "one or two well known to him and trusty persons, who being furnished with proper instructions, should come over here to superintend the Execution." At the same time, "for the better management of the machinery, thus to be made by Mr Boulton; and for the sake of acquiring a further knowledge in the money-making business, Her Majesty was pleased to order, that without delay proper persons should be appointed."[79]

Thus, towards the end of January, 1797, there arrived in Soho a group of five young Russians, led by Fedor Ivanovich Shlatter (or Schlatter), son of the former head of the Petersburg Assay Office, I. A. Schlatter, and recommended to Boulton by Smirnov as "a very good worthy Character & . . . perfectly well acquainted with every thing respecting the money Department in Russia."[80] His companions were Dmitrii Ovtsyn and Aleksei Izvol'skii, whose speciality was not indicated and who were merely said to have made "some progress in the English language," a Mr Reinhard, skilled in the making of stamps and dies, and F. W. Gass (or Hass), the son of the noted engraver at Petersburg, J. B. Gass.[81] The young Gass had himself worked at the Petersburg Mint since 1787 and had worked on a series of historical medals in the 1790s. Unfortunately, no sooner had the Russians arrived in Soho than they were recalled to Russia. Paul I was now on the throne and consistent with his intention to undo or do differently anything and everything instigated by his mother, he had vetoed the proposed mint. Informing Boulton of the tsar's decision on 6 February, Smirnov said that Vorontsov was writing to Petersburg to urge that the project be continued and suggested that the returning Shlatter be given plans and as much information as possible. Boulton had been much impressed by Shlatter during their short acquaintance and declared that "it is some satisfaction to me that I have had an opportunity of showing Mr Shlatter & Co. my Coining Mill & giving him Occular demonstration of all I said in my letter to your Excellency last year." The Russians had seen Boulton's laminating mill at Soho and one of the steam engines of the size and power which would be erected at St. Petersburg. If Paul were persuaded to reconsider, Shlatter should be sent back "as no person can be more proper for the business, nor any that I can open my bosom & my Machinery to, with more confidence & satisfaction to my Self."[82]

Vorontsov's arguments and Boulton's gifts had their effect. Shlatter and his companions left for Russia at the end of February, but by the end of June he was back once more in England, bearing a gold medal from Paul for Boulton and to await the arrival of a new group of workmen. It was this second group which was to include Sabakin, enlisted for his special knowledge of both minting machinery and steam engines. Shlatter, however, was not to carry out his duties for long. He remained in Birmingham for less than three months during which time he seems to have fallen into a state of hypochondria, which made him desperate to return to Russia. At the end of September he returned to London, from where Smirnov wrote to Boulton that "our friend Mr Shlatter, I am very sorry to say, is strangely altered. I agree perfectly with you in

the Idea, that his abstinence from wine and animal food, and his close application to study have greatly affected his spirits, which I hope is not past recovery. The Count and all other friends we have done everything to rouse him
a little, but he is grown so obstinate, from being the mildest and the most pliable man in the world, that he will not listen to any thing."[83] Shlatter soon
returned to Russia, leaving behind Sabakin's group which had eventually arrived in London after a hazardous journey and shipwreck.[84] Shlatter's responsibilities were assumed by Andrei Fedorovich Deriabin (1770-1820), who had
been sent to Europe the previous year by M. F. Soimonov, head of the Petersburg Mining Institute, of which Deriabin was an outstanding graduate. With
Sabakin were his elder son, Ivan L'vovich I (his second son bore the same first
name, hence Ivan I and II) and three young men called Tuganov, Grezin and
Lizel, an Austrian by birth. In a memorandum, dated 6 December 1797, Smirnov detailed the areas in which the men were to be instructed:

1. Mr Deriabin to be instructed in the mineralogical Part necessary for the
   mint, working mines, carting, melting, essaying metal, to prepare, flatten or roll the same &c &c and the whole process of the coinage
2. Messrs Sobakin in the mechanical part of it, viz to erect construct & to
   conduct the machinery &c
3. Mr Lizel, in Smith's business, making dies, tempering steel, and to arrange the metallic part of the machinery
4. Messrs Touganoff & Grezin making instruments for the mint & other
   kinds of work.[85]

The group arrived in Birmingham almost a year to the day after Shlatter's party and were lodged by Boulton in the same house as the others and been and
similar arrangements were made for them to learn some English. Of the six
men who came to Birmingham in January, 1798, three were to remain until
1802, while the other three left earlier for differing reasons.

The first to go was Deriabin, for whom the establishment of the mint had
not been the primary object of his European tour. His original brief had been
to acquaint himself with mining practices in Western Europe and prior to arriving in England he had travelled through various parts of Germany. Soon after his arrival in England he reported to his superior in Petersburg that during
his travels he had collected a rich mineral collection which he had decided to
present to the Mining Institute on his return and that during his stay in England he was hoping to remain in Birmingham only for some two months, acquainting himself with Boulton's plans for the Russian mint and with the
workings of his factories, but equally concerned with elaborating the itinerary
for his own extensive tour through England, Wales and Scotland. When he
had heard that one of the new group of Russians included "a miner," Boulton
had suggested to Smirnov that Cornwall was the obvious place to visit, and it
was to Cornwall that Deriabin made his way in April, 1798.[86] Since 1778
Boulton and Watt had effected a revolution in the Cornish tin and copper

mines by the introduction of their steam engines to pump away the water from considerable depths: by 1780 twenty of their engines were in operation there.[87] Both Boulton and Watt spent a considerable amount of time in the area and they were known inevitably to all the mine owners. Deriabin reaped the benefits of his acquaintance with Boulton in the form of letters of intro-duction throughout Cornwall—and not only Cornwall, but many other places along his route. The first letter from Deriabin to Boulton during his travels was sent from Carmarthen on 3 August and "the mineralogical traveller" deemed it his "duty to present to You my truest and most grateful thanks for the civilities I have received from your Friends."[88] From Cornwall Deriabin had gone to Bristol and thence to Wales. He had visited the copper works of a Mr Holbrook at Swansea and other works and mills in the district. From Car-marthen he intended to travel to Wrexham and then on to Liverpool and Man-chester and he appended a long list "of the places and Gentlemen You were so kind as to promise to write to," which included the looking-glass factory at Prescot, Glasgow and the Carron Works, Newcastle, Leeds, Sheffield, Rother-ham, Bakewell, and Derby. An urgent letter from Smirnov of 18 September requested a letter of introduction from Sir Joseph Banks which would allow Deriabin to visit his lead mine at Keswick.[89] Deriabin's next letter dates al-ready from May of the following year and is addressed to Matthew Robinson, Boulton's son. Deriabin had evidently finished his first tour towards the end of the previous year and had managed to pay a further visit to Cornwall where Boulton's son and the Boulton and Watt agent, Thomas Wilson, had looked after him. After a few days in London, he had paid a last visit to Birmingham before going on to Bakewell, which he had evidently missed on his first tour. In Soho "j'ai vu les machines nouvelles de la maison de la monnoie, toutes en mouvement. C'est un chef d'oeuvre de la machinerie. Les presses travaillent à merveille, et vraiment il n'y a rein plus à desirer."[90] On 5 July 1799 Deriabin set sail for Norway, where he was to spend a further few months of study be-fore arriving in Petersburg in November.

The son of a poor Siberian priest, Deriabin by his determination, undoubted ability and engaging personality made a notable career on his return to Russia. He had won many friends and protectors during his years abroad. Baron Grimm had recommended him to Vorontsov as "un sujet qui m'a paru rempli de zèle pour sa patrie et pour lequel la couronne n'aura pas à regretter les moyens qu'elle lui a fournis. Il me semble qu'il peut devenir un homme précieux pour la Russie, si l'on veut l'employer d'une manière convenable à son retour dans sa patrie."[91] He was indeed a man after Vorontsov's heart and the ambassa-dor was untiring in his efforts to impress on his influential friends back in Russia just how valuable Deriabin was.[92] In 1799 Deriabin was made an *Ober-bergmeister*, head of the department for the separation of gold from silver, with the rank of Court Counsellor; in 1802 he became a State Counsellor and head of the Blagodat' and Perm' mines and factories, in 1811 he was made

Director of the New Department for the Mints, Mines and Saltworks and head
of the Mining Cadet Corps. Throughout the reign of Alexander until his death
in 1820 Deriabin was involved in every important venture connected with
mining, displaying enormous flair and initiative as an enlightened administrator.

Shortly after his return, Deriabin prepared two long reports for his chief
Soimonov, entitled "A Description of the Smelting of Copper Ore in Reverberatory Furnaces in England" and "On Cladding or Strengthening with Stone
in Mines," which arose directly from what he had seen in England and there is
little doubt that his experiences here proved invaluable for his future work.[93]
He always retained the warmest memories of the hospitality of the Boultons,
as shown by a letter to Matthew Robinson Boulton in 1813, and in the years
when Boulton's workmen were working at the Mint in St Petersburg he was
always ready to help.

Two months after Deriabin left England he was followed by Sabakin, with
whom he was later to be closely associated. But if Deriabin left behind him
people who thought well of him, the same cannot be said of Sabakin. There is
no precise information about Sabakin's activities on his second visit to England,
but he seems to have remained for some eighteen months at Soho, closely
watching the preparation of the machinery destined for Russia and apparently
crossing swords with Boulton and his workmen. Boulton, referring in 1802 to
Sabakin's son as "a Man of not much intellectual Ability but . . . of a very affectionate Disposition", added that "I fear I cannot say so much of his Father";[94] that same year, one of Boulton's workmen in Petersburg, James Duncan, wrote that "We hear that Mr Sabacian is on his way from Siberia—Comeing to be along with us but we had much rather he had stayed there; as I ame
afraid we Can not agree Long with him hear."[95] Sabakin's mission was specifically "to inspect the lately arrived Boulton machines, so that, by taking
something from them, he can complete with greater success the steam engine
which he is making for the gold mines."[96] This is no further evidence to indicate what precisely Sabakin was anxious to learn but there is little doubt that
with regard both to steam engines and to the minting machinery which he invented at Ekaterinburg the achievements of Boulton and Watt proved indispensable.

Sabakin had left behind in England his elder son, who, he hoped, could gain
benefits from his stay in Britain other than those offered by Birmingham.
Shortly after his father's departure, Ivan was called to London by the Russian
ambassador, who "wished to send him to Scotland, there to attend Lectures
on Philosophy, Chemistry & whatever else you [Boulton] will advise him to
do in that way."[97] Boulton provided him with letters of introduction to his
friends Robison and Black and Sabakin went off to Scotland for a year, but
by the time he arrived in Edinburgh Black was dead. Sabakin appears in the
matriculation lists as enrolling for the course on chemistry under Black's suc-

cessor, Professor Thomas Hope. His name is next met with only in November, 1802, when he returned to Birmingham, after recovering from an illness. Sabakin had been periodically ill ever since his arrival in England and his condition now worsened considerably. By April, 1802, Boulton was writing: "I am sorry to say that poor Sabakin is too far gone in a Consumption ever to get to St Petersburgh,"[98] but he was insisting on making preparations to leave with his companions and Boulton's workmen. Boulton was, however, soon proved correct, for early in the morning of 5 April he died, "quite calm & easy, without a Groan."[99] He was buried in the graveyard of the local parish church. Two days later Grezin, who seems to have acquired a wife, and Lizel set out for Hull and Russia. The other Russian, Tuganov, had left the previous September "owing to the losses sustained in his Family."[100]

Boulton provided each of the Russians with a certificate of good behaviour, but also promised Smirnov "a separate & confidential Letter" with "my real opinion of each which will be a necessary Guide to you & such Ministers as will have the superior control of the Mint."[101] This private opinion soon followed.

I think Touganoff is an honest, tractable good dispositioned Man & capable of becoming a good Workman by Time and Experience & should be employed to assist the Men I have sent
Grezin is also an honest well-meaning Man, but doth not show any Signs of great Ability, or Activity, neither is he a capital Workman
Leizel is a better Workman, has more genius & better inventive Faculties than any of them & would be more likely to manage the mechanical Part of the Mint, he has a clearer Head and better Hands than either of the others.[102]

Lizel, the Austrian, worried Boulton, however, despite or rather because of his skill. He wrote again to Smirnov:

Liezel is by far the best workman of all the Russians but he is not open & communicative, & I fear has other objects in View besides & beyond the Russian Mint, for when he has been regaling himself amongst his Companions, & his heart a little expanded by Birmingham Ale, he has talked of going to Viena when the Russ Mint is finished, unless he is paid to his Satisfaction in Russia. I could not help viewing this as an ungenerous Idea when it is considered how kind & liberal he has been treated by the Russian Government at whose expence he has obtained all his knowledge. In regard to the Modells which Liezel has made: I know he made Mr Kakouskin (or some such Name) his Confidant I mean the Russian Workman who was some time in London working. I say he sent a part of his Modells by him such as of Steam Engine, a Coining press, & a modell of my Hydrolick Ram: but as Kakouskin's finances ran short he pawned them for £50 with a Woman he lodged with on Bank side in

the Borough. . . . These things I believe are not yet redeemed & I presume you may see them. If these things had been made to shew his supervisors in Russia as a proof of his application to the subject of his Mission I should have considered his Conduct as praiseworthy & I should
have had pleasure in assisting him. As you say these things have been
done without the knowledge of the Russian government I presume they
have been made with a view to *Viena.* . . .[103]

Before following this curious episode further, it is necessary to digress a little
to introduce the new Russian character mentioned in Boulton's account. Evstafii Kokushkin was an apprentice from Kronstadt who had been sent by the
Admiralty to England in 1794 to learn what he could about steam engines.[104]
It will be remembered that a steam engine ordered for Cronstadt by Admiral
Knowles had been set up by Carron workmen between 1774 and 1777. In
connection with the maintenance of that engine and to gain wider knowledge
of English achievements in the field other Russian apprentices had been sent
to England in the late 1770s: Roman Dmitrev was in England for about two
years from 1777 and was followed in 1779 by Fedor Borzov.[105] Kokushkin's
brief was of a similar nature, but he seems to have been generally inept and
frustrated in his attempts to gain useful information. He had been introduced
to Boulton in London by Smirnov in June, 1799, who mentioned "that there
are two or three Places near London, where there is some Machinery very
much worth seeing, but that the People belonging to the Inspection of it will
not shew it without your Permission."[106] In June the following year, he was
sent to Soho for a week for so, "if he has sense enough to see and comprehend
those things, which your Goodness will point out to him as useful."[107] Apparently during this visit he managed to act in a foolish fashion, for on 18 June
he was recalled to London on account of his "imprudence." It was at this time
that he became acquainted with Lizel and took away some of the models
which the Austrian had made. Smirnov tried very hard to placate Boulton, offering to retrieve the models in pawn if they were of value and could be sent
on to Russia with the other machinery, although he recollected that originally
Boulton had given the Russians "leave to make a model of every Part or of
the whole of the Steam-Engine."[108] Kokushkin was to re-appear on the scene
again in Petersburg, snooping around the English machinery, sketching the
machines and making himself a "plague" for the English workmen.[109]

On 12 July 1799 a public "Act to enable Matthew Boulton, Engineer, to
export the Machinery necessary for erecting a Mint in the Dominions of His
Imperial Majesty, the Emperor of all the Russias" (3 Georgii III, 1799, cap.
96) had been passed, and some of the machinery was sent to Hull to be shipped
to Petersburg, but a scare soon spread among Birmingham merchants and manufacturers that Boulton intended "to export all their tools, their inventions &
artists."[110] A petition was presented to Lord Grenville to stop Boulton but it

was unsuccessful, but it was only early in the reign of the new tsar, Alexander I, that the steam engines, minting presses and other machinery arrived in Russia. Boulton sent out four of his workmen, Duncan, Walker, Speedywell and Harley to supervise the installation of the machinery with, it was assumed, the help of the Soho-trained Russians. As it soon became apparent, this was mere wishful thinking. On 10 November 1802 Duncan wrote from St. Petersburg:

> I am sorry to inform you that poor Mr Grezen is like to be very badly off hear, on his arraival hear Count Vassilioff sent him to work in his old place again, to a manufactory of Surgents instruments where his Selery is only 100 Roubles per Year and must work from 6 in the morning to 9 at night too, and thro being so long in england he has almost forgot his own business, and expecting to be employed in the Mint business when he came hear, and now we wish very much to have him hear and find that he would be a useful hand for us in the work as well as speaking the Language, and we have applied to General Alabieff [A. B. Aliab'ev, President of the College of Mines] & to Count Vasillioff and lastly to Mr Novosiltsoff [N. N. Novosil'tsov] to get him away for us but they all have been against him and now we have very little hopes left of getting him at all, but he is very uncomfortable and unhappy where he is and wishes very much to come hear—Count Vasilioff was head manager of that place at the time he sent Greezen there but now it is one Count Cuchebey; and the reason why he will not let him off is because it has been represented to him that Greezen being lately come from England is capable of giving instructions to people and improving there boxes of Instruments.[111]

Grezin's expertise was thus being used by the Medical College, of which first Count A. I. Vasil'ev and then Count V. P. Kochubei was the head. Lizel at least was "employed at the bank mint in forgeing Dies," but not directly connected with the establishment of the new mint, while "Touganoff is employed in another Department in the manufacyture of surgical Instruments & could not be removed without considerable difficulty, these departmental divisions being frequently attended to with more minuteness than advantage."[112] This last observation came from Boulton's nephew, Zacchaeus Walker, a man of long experience who was in charge of operations at the Mint: his letters over the next few years reveal his frustrations at dealing with the Russian bureaucracy and the continued failure to gain the services of Grezin, Tuganov and Lizel. The Petersburg Mint was eventually finished and Boulton's machinery installed within a building designed by the Italian architect Antonio Porto, an excellent example of an industrial complex built in a strict Classical style which still graces the Peter and Paul fortress today; the Boulton machines performed their functions admirably for decades, but seemingly without the supervision at any stage of the Russians specially trained in Soho to maintain them.

VI

It has been possible on the basis of archival and published material to re-
trace the movements and illustrate the activities of such as Korsakov, the canal
engineer, Surnin, the Tula craftsman, Sabakin, the mechanic, Deriabin, the
mining specialist, and the men concerned with the mint, but there were other
apprentices and students in other fields of whom we have no more than a
passing glimpse, who seemingly came from nowhere and were lost without
trace on their return to Russia. Efrem Karamyshev was such a man.

Karamyshev is first mentioned in April, 1782, when Smirnov refers to the
lack of money from Petersburg to support him: "and what to do with him I
do not know for he only looses his time here for no profit to any Body."[113]
It seems likely that he had been sent to England by Potemkin, whose neglect
of the financial arrangement for his protégés was notorious. Karamyshev next
appears in August, 1784, when he and Ivan Sudakov, the man sent by Ivan
Chernyshev to study distilling, were introduced by Samborskii to Dr. Bryan
Higgins (1737-1820) with a view to studying chemistry with him.[114] Higgins,
a Doctor of Medicine from Leyden and one-time Professor of Chemistry at
Dublin, had in the preceding decade earned a considerable reputation as a lecturer in London. In 1774 he had established a school of practical chemistry
in Greek Street, Soho, for suitably qualified adults. In his original advertisement he described the three-month course, with lectures every other day,
which was to begin in November, 1775, for fifty gentlemen, paying ten guineas.
The lectures would take place in Higgins's laboratory and would be accompanied by practical demonstrations and discussions. The school continued until 1794 and the lectures have been said to represent "a notable advance on all
previous public lectures and in fact were a school of research which required
the active collaboration of the students," who included physicians, practical
chemists and manufacturers in their number.[115] Higgins agreed to take on
Karamyshev on virtually a full time basis for instruction in what was the Russian's particular field of study—the making of glass. In three letters in 1786-
87 Karamyshev describes the experiments which were conducted and Higgins's
"particular zeal and enthusiasm" in his instruction.[116] This relationship was,
however, to turn rapidly sour, because of Karamyshev's inability to pay Higgins. Higgins began to suspect that Karamyshev would attempt to leave England without paying the vast sum of £1000, which Higgins claimed was owing
to him. Poor Karamyshev was committed to the debtor's prison and Higgins
threatened to keep him there until he was paid in full. This was towards the
end of February, 1788, and on 4 May Smirnov reported that Karamyshev had
been released and was about to leave for Russia; Higgins had agreed to leave
the matter for Potemkin to settle, which presumably he did.[117] It is recorded
that Higgins paid a visit to Russia sometime between 1780 and 1790 at the invitation of the empress:[118] perhaps this was a palliative to Higgins after the

unpleasantness of the Karamyshev affair.

Among the other concerns said by the *Scots Magazine* to bring students to Britain was "merchandize" or commerce. Given the importance of Anglo-Russian trade, this was only to be expected. Catherine in fact herself took the initiative in this area, issuing an ukaz on 29 May 1766 (O.S.), in which the governor of the province of Archangel was ordered to find two merchants' sons of promise and good upbringing and aged between eleven and twelve for training in commerce in England.[119] Archangel itself had been a thriving port and trading centre for centuries and had a considerable number of foreign merchants based or trading there, prominent among whom were the English, particularly the leading Petersburg merchant William Gomm. Gomm, who had been in Russia since the late 1740s and had traded in the area for many years, was instrumental in creating the new port of Onega and had received special timber concessions from the Russian government in 1764. Gomm indeed may have suggested to the empress the value of training in England for young merchant sons; at all events his assistance was enlisted, once they were chosen. One of the boys chosen, eleven-year-old Stepan Bazhenin, was the son of an Archangel merchant Ivan Bazhenin, who was an associate of Gomm, and the other, Vasilii Nikolaevich Sveshnikov, was the son of a town "deputy." Sveshnikov was already fourteen, selected because of the lack of suitable younger candidates but possessing a smattering of German and some trading experience. After being seen by the empress, they were sent off to England at the end of July, 1766, with a stipend of 300 rubles a year for three years: they travelled out on a ship belonging to Gomm with letters of instruction for his brother, who was in charge of the London-end of the business. At the end of their stay William Gomm reported that they had "entièrement rempli les intentions avec les quelles il a plu à sa Majesté de les envoyer, étant en état, par moyen des connoissances qu'ils ont acquises, d'entrer dans un comptoir de Négociant et d'y profiter en tout ce que l'on pourroit leur enseigner."[120] From another source it is known that in London they had studied in a school rather than in a merchant's office: Sveshnikov had studied languages, mathematics and book-keeping, while the younger Bazhenin had concentrated simply on languages. On their return, they were given the choice of going to Archangel or joining an English commercial house in Petersburg. They chose the latter.[121]

Although trade with Russia was dominated by English merchants of the Russia company, Russian merchants were occasionally found in Britain and indeed a clause in the original Commercial Agreement of 1734 allowed them to become quasi-members of the Company. At different times during the century we find such merchants as Afanasii Shebonin and Artemii Novoselov in 1735, Erofei and Vasilii Karzhavin in 1753, Ivan Pastukhov in 1765, Semen Sidnev in 1799, carrying on their business, and men of the importance of Nikita Demidov, merchant and owner of numerous factories, whose own Grand Tour brought him to England in 1772 and 1773, were anxious to have some of their own employees trained in English commercial ways. In 1778 Demidov sent a young man by the name of Ivan Sherlaimov and in 1780, Nikolai Zubrilov to learn book-keeping and trade practices.[122]

With few exceptions, all the examples of the Russian specialists and apprentices in England examined in this chapter date from the reign of Catherine the Great. This was not only yet another reflection of the empress's own admiration for England but an inevitable recognition of England's pre-eminence at this period in all matters industrial and technological. For Russia itself, straining to develop its own resources and build up cadres of its own specialists, learning from the British was not merely a wish but a need. In certain instances the experiment of sending men to be trained in England was only of limited success, due sometimes to the limited potential of the people chosen but more often to the crass inefficiency of the Russian bureaucracy and the in-fighting between different departments; in other cases, the abilities of the men and the operations of chance, influential and/or enlightened patrons came together to product positive and important results. It is now time to turn from a consideration of men whose contribution was, to use the eighteenth-century distinction, "useful," to that of those whose aim was to make life "pleasant," to the painters, engravers, sculptors and men of letters.

1. Russian Ambassadors to England: Prince Antiokh Kantemir (1708-44)
   (Engraving by Joseph Wagner, 1738, after painting by Jacopo Amiconi);
   Count Ivan Grigor'evich Chernyshev (1726-97) (marble bust by Fedot
   Shubin, 1776); Ivan Matveevich Simolin (1720-99) (miniature by un-
   known artist); Count Semen Romanovich Vorontsov (1744-1837) (Oil
   painting by George Romney)

2. Father Andrei Afanas'evich Samborskii 91732-1815) (Oil painting by V. L. Borovikovskii)

3. Princess Ekaterina Romanovna Dashkova (1732-1815) with her son Pavel
   and daughter Anastas'ia (Unfinished engraving, 1777-78, by G. I. Skorodumov, after his own drawing)

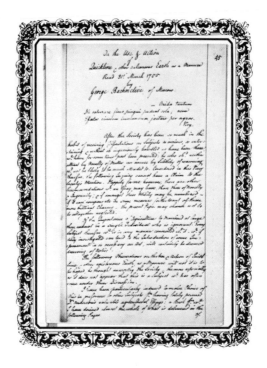

4. "On the Use & Action of Quicklime & other Calcareous Earth as a Manure," Paper read by Iurii Alekseevich Bakhmetev to the Natural History Society, Edinburgh, 31 March 1785

5. Admiral Nikolai Semenovich Mordvinov (1754-1845) (miniature by Charles Reichel, 1817) and his English wife Henrietta (née Cobley, 1764-1843) (miniature by unknown Russian artist)

6. Vasilii Petrovich Petrov (1736-99) (Engraving possibly by Filiter Stepanov)

7. The Palladian Bridge, or Siberian Gallery, in the grounds of Tsarskoe Selo.
   Designed by Vasilii Ivanovich Neelov (1722-82)

8. Gavriil Ivanovich Skorodumov (1755-92) (Self-portrait, watercolours, 1780s)

9. Prince Grigorii Grigor'evich Orlov (1734-83) (Oil painting by F. S. Roko-
tov, 1762-63)

10. Princess Dashkova's account of her visit to the West Country in 1770 published in 1775.

CHAPTER 8
"HERE THE ARTS FLOURISH"

In October, 1781, an English visitor to Matthew Boulton's Soho Works, proceeded to the silversmiths' shop, "where there were chazing a turin for the Empress of Russia," and commented "I have seen more elegant forms."[1] Catherine had become Boulton's customer ten years previously when she bought a consignment of vases and ormolu ware which Lord Cathcart had undertaken to show her, although she refused to be tempted by a "sidereal clock" which Boulton sent to Petersburg in 1776.[2] The wares of Boulton's friend and neighbour, Josiah Wedgwood, also made an impact: the purchase of the "Husk service" in 1770 was followed three years later by the special commission for the table and dessert service known as "the Frog."

Catherine's interest in the fine products of the Boulton and Wedgwood factories was an aspect of her general "collectomania." Her ambassadors and agents throughout Europe were instructed to be on the lookout for suitable collections of paintings and other works of art which would enhance the Hermitage: England, the home of many great collectors and of countless cultural kleptomaniacs who had indulged themselves on the "Grand Tour," proved a rich hunting-ground. Her most prized acquisition was the Houghton collection of paintings formed by Sir Robert Walpole and sold by his impecunious grandson in 1779. *Gentleman's Magazine* commenting on its sale to Catherine for £43,000, felt that it "ought to have been added to the Devonshire or Bedford collections: but is gone, if it survives the hazard of the sea or the risques of war, to assist the slow progress of the arts in the cold unripening regions of the North."[3] Catherine was a magpie, but a discriminating one, for the following year she turned down Lord Pembroke's offer of his collection of medals and of his mother-in-law, Lady Diana Beauclerk's library. James Harris, the British Ambassador, wrote that "medals are not to her Imp. Maj: taste,"[4] as indeed a former chaplain to the British community in Petersburg and medallist to the empress, the Rev. John Glen King, well knew. When King returned to the Russian capital in 1781 to sell his collection of medals, he found a buyer in Aleksandr Lanskoi, the current favourite.[5] Catherine did, however, have a particular liking for "pierres gravées." In 1780 she obtained through the agency of Princess Dashkova the collection of the British antiquary James Byers[6] and five years later that of Lord Algernon Percy.[7] The same year Count Vorontsov was requested to purchase the best pieces from the Duchess of Portland's collection.[8] In 1781 the Scottish portrait medallionist and reproducer of gem-stones, James Tassie, received an order from Catherine for a cabinet containing a full range of his gem-stone reproductions, which then numbered 6,076 items. The cabinet, consisting of 200 drawers with both intaglio and cameo casts of each items, was sent to Petersburg, together with a two-volume catalogue.[9] The Tassie reproductions included many from the gem-stones cut by the English masters William and Charles Brown. In 1786 Catherine began ordering gem-stones directly from the Browns who in the next decade supplied some 200 items, both intaglios and cameos, illustrating a wide range of themes from classical mythology, allegories and historical portraits, as well as a specially created Russian series.[10] A final important acquisition by Catherine in 1788 was the sculpture collection of Lyde Browne of Wimbledon, for which, however, she seems never to have paid in full.[11]

The Walpole collection had brought to Russia a mere three canvases by English artists: William Dobson's portrait of Abrahan van der Doort (1630s) and Sir Godfrey Kneller's portraits of Grinling Gibbons (1680s) and John Locke (1697). There was nothing from the eighteenth century until Catherine bought at about the same time three works by Joseph Wright of Derby, including "An Iron Forge." In 1785 Lord Carysfort, a friend and patron of Sir Joshua Reynolds, suggested to Catherine that contemporary English painting was poorly represented in the Hermitage: this prompted her commissioning from Reynolds a painting on a subject of his own choosing. His "Infant Hercules" was eventually sent off in 1789 with another painting, "Snake in the Grass," which he had completed for Potemkin.[12] Only one further painting by an English artist, Thomas Jones's "Landscape with Aeneas and Dido," was bought, but nothing by such as Gainsborough, Romney, Hogarth, West, or Lawrence, although attempts were made to bring the last painter to work in Russia. If Lawrence was unwilling to seek his fortune in Petersburg, other lesser known painters and engravers, such as Richard Brompton, Joseph Hearn, James Walker, John Atkinson and Edward Miles were, but an account of their activities is more apposite in the companion volume to this study. It is to their Russian counterparts who came to London that our attention might now be turned.

I

The Imperial Academy of Arts was founded in Petersburg in 1758 on the suggestion of Count Ivan Shuvalov, the Curator of the University of Moscow, which had been established but three years earlier. The Statues of the Academy were published only in the reign of Catherine, in 1764, in many cases confirming what had already been practised. The clauses regarding the possibilities of study abroad for outstanding graduates of the Academy read as follow:

The Academy is likewise allowed to send abroad, every three years, for further improvement in their art, twelve of the Artists who shall have obtained prizes, and to place them under the protection of the Imperial Ambassador in the place of their residence, taking care to recommend them to persons capable of forwarding them in their pursuits,

These artists are ordered to keep, and transmit to the Academy, a regular Journal of their studies and acquirements, and to inform the Academy, once in every four months, of their place of abode, their employments, and the most interesting objects of their notice. At the end of the term prescribed for their travels, they are to send one of their performances to the Academy, after which they shall recèive a sum sufficient for the expenses of their return, and the same certificate of liberty as above-mentioned, with regard to the exercise of their profession.

They shall likewise have a preference over others, in any competition for being elected Members of the Academy.[13]

In planning the new academy Shuvalov had turned to the Paris Académie Royale de Peinture et de Sculpture for advice and with an invitation for eminent French artists to go and teach in Russia, and it was to Paris that the first Russian students were sent to perfect their skills in painting and sculpture. In 1760 the painter A. P. Losenko and the architect V. I. Bazhenov began their studies in Paris and during the first decade of Catherine's reign the many Russians in France included the sculptors F. I. Shubin, F. G. Gordeev and I. V. Prokof'ev, the painter P. M. Grinev and the architect I. I. Ivanov. From Paris several of the students travelled to Rome, the great centre of inspiration for contemporary European art, and it was more by chance than design that one of them on his return journey paid a brief visit to England.

Fedot Ivanovich Shubin (1740-1805), the outstanding Russian sculptor of the eighteenth century, had first studied in Paris under Jean-Baptiste Pigalle from 1766 to 1770, before leaving for Rome. In Rome in 1772 he met Nikita Demidov, the rich industrialist and philanthropist, who was to become one of his patrons, and returned with him the following year to France and then to England. Shubin was in London only a matter of days in the beginning of July 1773 with time merely to see the sights.[14] He may well, however, have met the first two Russian graduates from the Academy of Arts sent specifically to study in England, who had arrived a few weeks earlier.

Both Gavriil Ivanovich Skorodumov (1755-92) and Mikhail Ivanovich Bel'skii (1753-94) were sons of artists: Skorodumov's father, Ivan Ivanovich, was a painter attached to the St. Petersburg Building Commission and Bel'-skii's, another Ivan Ivanovich (1719-95), had worked at Tsarskoe Selo since the early 1750s. Skorodumov, who at the age of nine had entered the Academy's *gymnasium*, opted to take courses in both engraving and painting in the Academy, while Bel'skii concentrated on painting. Both proved talented pupils and received prizes and medals for outstanding work during their courses. Skorodumov studied engraving under a number of teachers, principally under the French master Antoine Radig, and together with Bel'skii, painting under Losenko. Towards the end of 1772 both young artists received gold medals and the right to study abroad for three years. It was Skorodumov's skill as an engraver which persuaded the Academy to vary its usual practice of sending its students exclusively to Paris and Rome and select London as a particularly suitable centre. Skorodumov and Bel'skii set out in May, 1773, with a letter of recommendation from Vallin de la Motte, the Professor of Architecture, for the Russian ambassador in London, Count Musin-Pushkin, who was soon to place them in the schools of the Royal Academy.[15]

The Royal Academy was still in its infancy. It had been founded on 10 December 1768 by George III on lines proposed by Sir William Chambers, the Royal architect, and twenty one other prominent artists, who included Benjamin West, Nathaniel Dance, Paul Sandby, Angelica Kauffmann and Francesco Bartolozzi. The first president was Sir Joshua Reynolds, who gave his inaugural discourse on 2 January 1769, and Professors of Anatomy, Architecture, Painting and Perspective were appointed at the end of January, 1769, and totalled seventy seven in the first year. Among them were men who were later to be distinguished in various branches of the arts: Joseph Farington, James Tassie, Richard Cosway, John Flaxman, Thomas Banks, Pierre Falconet (son of the sculptor of the "Bronze Horseman" and himself later to work in Russia). Bel'skii and Skorodumov were admitted on 9 November 1773, by which time some 200 young men had studied or were studying at the Academy.[16] Nothing is known about the precise activities of the young Russians for virtually two years, but the first extant reports from Skorodumov to the Academy of Arts in the summer of 1775 suggest that they were dutifully following the courses stipulated by the Royal Academy. In July, 1775, he mentioned that "I am practising drawing from life and from paintings and statues and also particularly engraving from the paintings by various masters" and went on to name works by Angelica Kauffmann, Reynolds, West and Boucher.[17] The Royal Academy regulations of 1769 required students to attend both the plaster academy and the life room to practise their skills in drawing or modelling from plaster casts and living models. In common with long-standing custom, these classes were held in the evenings by candlelight to emphasize light and shade and throw forms into strong relief. The particular regulations for the life classes, which began at 6 p.m. in the winter and 4 p.m. in the summer, read as follows:

The Model shall be set by the Visitor and continue in the Attitude two Hours (by the Hour-Glass) exclusive of the Time required for resting. There shall be two different Models, each Week, each Model to sit three Nights.

While the Visitor is setting the Model, the Students shall draw Lots for their Places, of which they shall take Possession so soon as the Visitor hath set the Figure.

During the time the Model is sitting the Students shall remain quiet in their Places.

As soon as any Student hath done Drawing or Modeling, he shall put out his Candles, and while Drawing or Modeling, he shall be careful to keep them under the Bells.[18]

For the first two years, however, Skorodumov, if not Bel'skii, would have been allowed to draw only male figures, for "no Student under the Age of twenty, be admitted to draw after the Female Model, unless he be a married Man." The reverse was of course true for ladies, even if they were married and R.A., like Angelica Kauffmann and Mary Moser, as Zoffany's famous painting of the Academicians of 1771-72, makes clear. Zoffany's painting, as well as his unfinished canvas from the following year of the Professor of Anatomy, Dr. William Hunter, lecturing to students, provide an excellent illustration of the settings and personalities at the Royal Academy shortly before Skorodumov and Bel'skii arrived.[19] The students listening to Hunter have not been identified, but possibly in their number was the young Thomas Rowlandson, who is said to have later produced a sketch showing Skorodumov and his friends at a drawing class in the Academy.[20]

As further reports from Skorodumov indicate, he continued with drawing and engraving classes throughout the following year, when he pleaded severe rheumatism as the reason for not obeying instructions from the Academy of Arts to go to Paris to continue his studies.[21] A report in 1777 implies, however, other reasons why he was reluctant to leave London:

I have the honour to report to the Imperial Academy of Arts that the best engravers in Europe are to be found in London, namely F. Bartolozi in the historical genre, Woolet for landscapes as well as Vivares and several other skilful masters in their field of art whose works are found in every country. In painting Mr de Louter-Bourg is the best painter of historical and battle scenes in Europe and Mrs Angelica Kauffmann is an extremely skilled woman in the historical genre. The best English artists are the famous royal portrait painter Sir Joshua Renolds, Mr West, Mr Mortimer, N. Dance and Cipriaine. Here the arts flourish and artists are highly esteemed and greatly encouraged. English gentlemen are great connoisseurs and have their own collections, filled with the works of the Old Masters. Apart from the Royal Academy, there are a great number of schools where drawing and other skills are taught.[22]

Foreign artists figure prominently and it is with the names of two of them, the Italian engraver Francesco Bartolozzi (1727-1815) and the German painter Angelica Kauffmann (1741-1807), that Skorodumov's own had by that time become closely linked.

Bartolozzi had settled in London in 1764, two years before Angelica was persuaded to leave Rome for greener English pastures. Both were soon much courted and commisssioned by the English aristocracy and gentry and Angelica's fame was assured by the favour of Reynolds and by a portrait which he painted of her in 1769 and which was engraved by Bartolozzi. It was, however, for his engravings after paintings by Angelica that Bartolozzi is best known and the estimated eighty eight such productions testify to the fecundity and popularity of both painter and engraver. Angelica was much in demand as a portrait painter but her forte lay, as Skorodumov noted, in "historical" painting and it was her re-creations from Homer, her classical mythological scenes, her moral allegories which found favour with the engraver. She met the contemporary tastes for an idealized classical world fused with a morally edifying and frequently cloying sentimental treatment of themes popularized by eighteenth-century poets and prose writers. Although Angelica herself in the 1770s turned to etching, it was the method of stipple engraving brought to perfection by Bartolozzi which was to enhance the sentiment and mood of her painting. Bartolozzi had begun as a line engraver, using a technique employed since the fifteenth century and demanding great skill and precision, but switched to stipple engraving, in which an etching needle or special tool, known as a *mattoir*, was used to stipple dots over a grounded copper plate. It was the stipple method which Skorodumov, who had been trained in line engraving in Petersburg, adopted when he became a pupil of Bartolozzi in 1773.

Skorodumov was soon emulating his teacher not only in technique but also in his frequent copying of paintings by Angelica. He is commended by Tuer in his chapter on "Bartolozzi's Pupils" in his standard biography of Bartolozzi, where he says that "his prints possess considerable power and finish; good examples, more especially those after Angelica Kauffman, being prized by collectors,"[23] and he is listed among "the engravers who secured the copyright of her designs" in Gerard's word on Angelica.[24] Skorodumov began sending examples of his work to Petersburg from the end of 1775 and continued to do so until his return to Russia in 1782. It is calculated that he produced more than fifty engravings during his years in England, half of which were after Angelica and including such subjects as "Cupid's Revenge," "The Discovery of Achilles by Ulysses," "Sacrifice to Ceres," "Abelard and Eloisa Surprised by Fulbard," and "Justice," "Temperance," "Fortitude" and "Prudence" (the last four engravings all dedicated to Catherine II!). Skorodumov also produced engravings after paintings by Guido Reni, Loutherbourg, Maratti, and, interestingly for the combination of

English literary subjects and English painters, of "Clarissa Harlow," after Reynolds, and "The Parting of Romeo and Juliet," after Benjamin West.[25] The last engraving was published on 26 June 1775 and is mentioned in a letter by Skorodumov as executed "in the manner of red pencil,"[26] a reference to the red chalk method of engraving which was then all the rage in fashionable London society and was much encouraged by Angelica for engravings after her own designs.

Skorodumov's early years were plagued, as was seemingly inevitable with Russian students, by inadequate financial support from Petersburg,[27] although it might be noted that the Royal Academy provided free tuition for all its students. Skorodumov, however, had the unique opportunity of freeing himself from financial worry, when his talent was recognized and orders for his work began to come from English merchants as well as from visiting Russian aristocrats. If in 1776 he was requesting money from the Academy, in 1777 his letters speak of "a great many orders" and of visits from Princess Dashkova, who commissioned from him portraits of herself and of her family, and Count Pavel Sergeevich Potemkin, a cousin of Prince Potemkin.[28] In June, 1777, his official period of study came to an end, but Skorodumov was unwilling to return and the Academy seems not to have pursued the matter. His biographers offer no explanation, but it seems likely that Catherine herself may have given her blessing. Skorodumov gave Musin-Pushkin an engraving to present to the empress during the ambassador's visit to Petersburg in 1777. Musin-Pushkin wrote in September that the presentation was made by Count Orlov and the empress had ordered £200 to be sent to the engraver as a sign of her pleasure.[29] Two years later Skorodumov collected together many of the engravings which he had made in England and sent them in a specially prepared album to the empress. Catherine was therefore well acquainted with Skorodumov's work long before Baron Grimm met him in the summer of 1782 in Paris and recommended him to her. Skorodumov was invited to Petersburg to make engravings from paintings in the Hermitage and at the beginning of September he was back in Petersburg with a salary of 1200 rubles a year and 600 rubles for accommodation and the title of Imperial Engraver and keeper of engravings in the Hermitage. He was, as Grimm put it, "au comble de ses voeux"[30]—at least, for a time.

Skorodumov returned to Russia after nine years in England with a mastery of stipple engraving and of colour printing, with a valuable collection of plates, with a high regard for English cultural life and ways and acquaintance with some of the outstanding contemporary artists in Europe—and with an English wife. His wife's name was Mary and they were married in 1775 or 1776. Grimm provides the following characterization of her: "Il emmène avec lui sa femme, née en France et élevée en Angleterre. Elle est protestante et m'a paru une femme d'un vrai mérite. Il y a, je crois, huit ans qu'ils sont mariés. Il doit beaucoup à cette femme, parce qu'elle a eu des facilités par

ses protections de faire connaître les talens de son mari à qui, faute de protection, il aurait fallu bien de temps pour percer. Ils quittent un fort joli étab-
lissement en Angleterre. La femme peint la miniature et grave aussi."[31]
Nothing is known about her father or connections, but it should be noted
that she was only fifteen or sixteen when she married Skorodumov. Although
Grimm describes her as a miniaturist and engraver, no work seems to have
appeared under her name during her husband's lifetime. It is likely that she
developed her talents under her husband's direction and helped him in his
work in London. However, after Skorodumov's death in 1792, she married
the Russian painter M. M. Ivanov and at least three engravings under her new
name were published between 1795 and 1797. She died in 1827 and in
accordance with her will there was placed in her coffin a portrait of her
first husband painted apparently by Reynolds.[32]

Although Skorodumov was made an Academician of the Academy of Arts
in July, 1785, his career in Russia did not develop as he might have hoped
and expected. Catherine was soon expressing her annoyance to Grimm
about Skorodumov's idleness and what she evidently considered were un-
reasonable demands.[33] It seems obvious that Skorodumov found work in
Petersburg, and specifically work for the empress, uncongenial and restric-
tive. In this respect an account by the French traveller Fortia de Piles of his
visit to Skorodumov in 1791 is very revealing. Skorodumov, whom Piles
considered "plus connu en Angleterre que dans son propre pays," expressed
his dislike of working in the Hermitage, where possible visits by the empress
obliged him to dress correctly at all times and generally behave in a way
which, one must surmise, was so different from the life he had lived in
England. Piles nevertheless found Skorodumov at work on two major projects which were however left incomplete on his death the following year:
a huge engraving after a drawing by P. I. Sokolov of Falconet's Bronze
Horseman and a séries of animated scenes along the embankments of the
Neva.[34] Skorodumov in fact produced very little during the last decade of
his life in Petersburg: a handful of engraved portraits of Russian dignitaries,
an engraving of the death of Potemkin, seemingly only one engraving after
a painting in the Hermitage, a striking self-portrait in watercolour, etc.
There were indications of new projects and initiatives, a renewed interest
in painting but in general his fate seems to bear out the remarks made by
William Coxe in his *Travels* of 1784 (for which, incidentally, Skorodumov
provided two drawings of Russian types):

> The scholars, for the most part, make a considerable progress during
> their continuance in the academy, and many improve themselves
> abroad. It is remarkable, however, that the persons of the greatest
> merit often settle in other countries, or, if they return, soon sink
> into an indolence, which appears almost national. The cause of this

failure seems to proceed from the little encouragement which they receive from the nation in general. The sovereign may rear artists, like foreign plants in a hot bed, at a prodigious expense, and by constant cultivation, but unless the same care is continued when they are brought to maturity, they will sicken by neglect.[35]

In his last years Skorodumov took to drinking heavily and some of the reasons for this are suggested by the satirist Ivan Krylov in the character of Trudoliubov ("Workwilling"), a thinly veiled portrait of the artist, in his *Pochta dukhov* ("Spirits' Post," 1789).

> Rather than defend the advantages of my profession in my homeland I will leave at the first opportunity and return to England where they appreciate the value of my art and where I received for it a hundred times more 'than here, although I cannot see the slightest difference in my skill and this has saddened me to such an extent that I have given myself to drink without thinking about it. I know that it is inexcusable for a rational being, but what can I do when now that I have thought about it I have become an out-and-out drunkard. And so, dear Plutarez, if you want your son to be fortunate in one of the arts, then either send him to work abroad or tell him not to become involved, because here people do not respect artists or their work and admire only what is brought from abroad.[36]

If evidence of Skorodumov's activities in both England and Russia is comparatively rich, there is almost nothing about his companion Bel'skii. Bel'skii is known to have studied in Paris, under the famous painter Greuze, and later in Rome and probably left England in 1776 in accordance with the Academy's instructions, which Skorodumov found excuses to disobey. Bel'skii next appears only at the end of 1787 when he was made an associate of the Academy (*Naznachennyi*) on presentation of a portrait in oils of Count A. I. Musin-Pushkin. In the following year he completed a portrait of the composer D. S. Bortnianskii and at about the same time of the President of the Academy of Arts, Count I. I. Betskoi. Like Skorodumov, Bel'-skii died at an early age in 1794.[37]

The association of Russians with the Royal Academy does not, however, begin and end with the names of Skorodumov and Bel'skii, for shortly after they were enrolled, they were joined in April, 1774, by another Russian, Filiter Stepanov (1745?-97?), a man who, as it were, followed the advice of Coxe and Trudoliubov and settled in England to pursue his art. Almost everything about Stepanov is obscure and contradictory, beginning with the entry in the Royal Academy minutes. The register gives "Stepanoff," with the Christian name "Gertrude" added later in red ink, while the Council minutes state "Stepanoff, Geo: Burder." Stepanov's age is given as twenty-nine and the further information is given that he (or she) was a painter and was awarded a silver medal in 1775.[38] Filiter Stepanov was married to an English woman by the name of Gertrude and she was also a painter, but if the entry refers to her and not to her husband, then she would be the only female student admitted in the eighteenth century. Other sources, however, speak of Filiter Stepanov studying at the Academy and other evidence, such as the birth dates of her children, suggest that Gertrude was somewhat younger than her husband. But who was Stepanov, or Stephanoff? There exist at least two versions of his origins. Some accounts hold that he was "the eldest son of a Russian nobleman, . . . sent to this country in the last quarter of the eighteenth century, with others of his own rank, to be educated. He alone remained in England, where, having acquired a love for the fine arts, he settled in London to practise art as a profession."[39] More credible are the details provided by the Rector of the Academy of Arts, F. I. Iordan, who himself studied engraving in London between 1830 and 1834 and undoubtedly knew Stepanov's sons. According to him, Stepanov was a former serf by the name of Stepan who deserted his master during a visit to London.[40] At all events he studied together with Skorodumov and Bel'skii at the Academy and was later to show his abilities both as an engraver and a painter. Rovinskii gives details of seven engravings produced in the period 1778-93 and one of these, undated, of three cupids sharpening their arrows bears the details "Drawn and Engraved by Stepanof under the Direction of F. Bartolozzi R. A. Engraver to his Majesty."[41] His first engraving (1778) was a portrait of his fellow countryman, the poet Vasilii Petrov, who had studied a few years earlier in London, while the dating of the last three engravings (1791-93) makes nonsense of the usual English references to his suicide sometime before 1790.[42] Rovinskii who gives no date for his death produced an equally fanciful variant, according to which Stepanov went mad on the death of his wife and spent the next few years in an asylum. The actual year of Stepanov's death (1797), if not the circumstances, may be established from a letter from the Russian ambassador Vorontsov in February, 1798: "Je vous envoye en même tems un dessin pour une table, fait par madame Stépanoff, veuve d'un habile graveur et dessinateur russe qui a été établi à Londres et qui est mort l'année passée. Il a laissé deux fils et la femme qui est une femme de mérite et qui élève bien ses enfants. Elle dessine supérieurement bien les fleurs, donne des leçons dans ce genre de peinture et vit de cela honnêtement; elle envoye de ses dessins à l'Impératrice pour savoir si ce genre de peinture plaît à s.m.i. et si elle ne lui commanderait pas quelque ouvrage."[43]

Like Skorodumov, Stepanov was married to a talented artist in her own right and Gertrude Stepanov, who died in fact in 1808, exhibited paintings at the Royal Academy in 1783 and again in 1805. Her husband in addition to his work as an engraver also exhibited some six paintings at the Academy in 1778, 1779 and 1781, which included three female portraits and an historical subject.[44] Stepanov is also known to have painted a number of ceilings, to have produced stage scenery at the Opera House in the Haymarket and at the Circus in St. George's Fields and also to have made landscapes in the so-called "stained manner."[45] It was probably to Stepanov's essays in this last medium that Princess Dashkova was referring in a letter from Edinburgh in October 1778 when she wrote: "I hear great praise of the *Landskip* which our Russian is painting. Ask him to paint one for me, I'll certainly pay him for his trouble."[46] Stepanov was not, however, known in Russia other than to Russians who had met him in London, and all his work was produced in England and therefore he quite rightly finds a place in Redgrave's *Dictionary of Artists of the English School* alongside his wife and his son Francis (1789-1860), a prolific oil and water-colour painter, who also exhibited frequently at the Royal Academy and the Oil and Water-Colour Society.[47] Redgrave, however, overlooked Stepanov's elder son James (1788-1874), even more prolific and versatile, and his daughter, M. G., a painter of flowers like her mother.[48]

Skorodumov and Bel'skii—both sons of painters, Stepanov—the father of painters, but the account of Russian artists in England ends with a father and son, who were both architects and who came together to England in 1771. Vasilii Ivanovich Neelov (1722-82) was given the official title of "architect" in 1760, but had learned his trade on the job, employed as a workman since 1744 at Tsarskoe Selo, where Rastrelli was beginning to realize the great designs of the Empress Elizabeth. By 1770, after twenty-six years of unbroken service at Tsarskoe Selo, he knew the buildings and the gardens better than anyone and under Catherine he became responsible for a number of projects, although the period of his greatest activity came in the 1770s after his brief visit to England. Catherine's English tastes had found an immediate outlet in the re-planning of the park and buildings at Tsarskoe Selo and her conversion to the English style in landscape gardening finds its most eloquent expression in a letter to Voltaire in 1772: "J'aime à la folie présentement les jardins à l'anglaise, les lignes courbes, les pentes douces, les étangs en forme de lacs, les archipels en terre ferme, et j'ai un profond mépris pour les lignes droites, les allées jumelles. Je hais les fontaines qui donnent la torture à l'eau pour lui faire prendre un cours contraire à sa nature: les statues sont reléguées dans les galeries, les vestibules, etc.; en un mot, l'anglomanie domine ma plantomanie."[49] Her instructions to lay out an English garden at Tsarskoe Selo were issued in May 1770 and in the following months Neelov prepared a number of reports of proposed alterations to the paths and ponds and ground elevations, all aimed at producing a more "natural" effect.[50] He also drew up plans for new buildings in the grounds and modifications to existing ones. Catherine, however, was anxious that Neelov and his younger son Petr (1749-1848?) "should further improve their knowledge of architecture and inspect both old and most recent examples of buildings" and she sent them to England "for an unspecified period."[51]

The Neelovs arrived in London early in 1771 but Vasilii was to remain only six months: by the end of June he was back at Tsarskoe Selo, having left his son in the care of the Russian chaplain in London, Samborskii, to learn the language and further his architectural studies. Since Vasilii knew neither English nor French, he would have been dependent on Russians resident in London to escort him and in a letter written shortly after his return he mentions with appreciation members of the Embassy staff as well as Nikitin, the "Inspector" of the Russian students in Oxford.[52] This suggests that he had paid a visit to Oxford as part of a tour of the West of England which may have taken him to some of the finest cities and estates. In the absence of any evidence about what precisely he saw and did, one can only speculate that he may have been in Bath and Bristol, have seen Blenheim and Stowe, Wilton and Strawberry Hill. He had ample opportunity to acquaint himself with the work of such architects as George Dance, Nicholas Hawksmore, the Adam Brothers, and Sir William Chambers, and of the landscape gardeners Kent and Brown. Like other Russian travellers, he possibly went to Kew, Syon House, Osterley Park, Pope's Villa at Twickenham, Hampton Court, Windsor. Six months was indeed more than adequate for Neelov to see a great deal and to acquire design-books and other materials to help him in his future work. And it is the work which he completed during the decade after his return up to his death which is the most eloquent testimony to the usefulness of his visit.

Among the buildings which Neelov built during the 1770s were the Admiralty and Hermitage Kitchen (1772-75), the Large and Small Caprices (1770-72) and the Palladian Bridge (1771-76). Although the last and most graceful of these, the Palladian Bridge, reveals clearest of all its English inspiration, some Soviet scholars have seemed reluctant to acknowledge it. B. Vasil'ev in the one substantial article on the Neelovs states, after discussing the Admiralty and Hermitage Kitchen, that "all Neelov's buildings are distinguished by this originality and he cannot be charged with copying examples of Western European park architecture." He then continues: "This also applies to the Marble (Palladian) Bridge, the design and model of which were completed by the architect before his departure for England. Whereas in its English interpretation the Palladian Bridge at Stowe is extremely complicated in its details (particularly its roof), V. I. Neelov, taking into account the comparatively smaller dimensions of his bridge, resolves it in simple, laconic forms."[53] There is no evidence that Neelov designed his bridge before leaving for England; on the contrary, the document quoted by Vasil'ev in a note refers to the design and model of three smaller bridges across canals in the park.[54] The reference to Stowe is equally misleading, for the bridge there was a more complex and larger variant on the original English Palladian Bridge at Wilton, completed by Roger Morris in 1737. The Wilton bridge, on the other hand, is mentioned by A. N. Petrov in his recent book on the parks and palaces of Tsarskoe Selo, but he emphasizes non-existent differences, such as an alleged different number of supporting arches.[55] Both scholars ignore M. V. Alpatov's earlier admission that Neelov's bridge "was an exact copy of the Palladian Bridge" at Wilton.[56] Both bridges have the same number of arches, the same number of Ionic columns, the same form of balustrade, a very similar roof. Copy though it was, Neelov's bridge was a fitting embellishment to the Imperial park which could not have failed to find favour with Catherine. She may well have been equally satisfied with her architect's essays into other fashionable "English" styles.

The Hermitage Kitchen and the Admiralty are generally regarded as the first Russian examples of the pseudo-Gothic style and present a typical amalgam of features of classicism with the more obvious features of the baronial castle, English examples of which Catherine would have found among the numerous views on her Wedgwood "Frog" service which arrived at the end of 1774. Neelov would have seen both genuine and imitation Gothic in England, but although his buildings have inevitably features in common with English Gothic architecture, his inspiration, as scholars have suggested, was Dutch rather than English, shown above in the triangular crenellations of the flanking towers of the Admiralty and the central tower of the Kitchen.[57] English sources are more easily demonstrable in the case of Neelov's efforts at introducing Chinese buildings at Tsarskoe. The leading contribution to the popularity of architectural *chinoiserie* was made by Sir William Chambers, who twice visited China and produced two influential treatises: *Designs of Chinese Buildings, Furniture, Dresses, Machines, and Utensils. To which is annexed, a Description of their temples, houses, gardens etc.* (1757) and *A Dissertation on Oriental Gardening* (1772). In the interim he published his *Plans, Elevations, Sections, and Perspective Views of the Gardens and Buildings at Kew in Surry* (1763). Part of the appendix to Chamber's first work, "Of the Art of Laying Out Gardens Among the Chinese," appeared in a Russian translation in 1771 and it was probably parts of the same book that Catherine herself was translating and annotating "for builders of cottages on the Peterhof road" in 1773.[58] The previous year the Russian ambassador in London had been sent money "for the model of the Chinese building."[59] Possibly it was of Chambers's famous pagoda at Kew, which was also pictured in his Plans of 1763. At all events an imitation of the pagoda was included in the wooden model of the Chinese village which was constructed by the Italian architect Rinaldi with the probable assistance of Vasilii Neelov in the early 1770s. The pagoda was not built but Neelov began work on the village, although the final stages of construction were taken over by Charles Cameron, who arrived in Russia in 1779 and whose influence thereafter was to be dominant. Neelov was responsible for building the Large and Small Caprices, the first of which was a Chinese summerhouse on a wide arch spanning the road leading to the Great Palace. It was inspired by a print of an arch at Fukien which appeared in a Dutch work of 1670. It was to another print, but this time in an English work, William and John Halfpenny's *Rural Architecture in the Chinese Taste* (1750), that Neelov turned for his Cross Bridge, begun in 1776.[60] The name came from the four arches, two from each bank, which met in the middle to support a Chinese pavillion.

Helping his father in the late 1772 was Neelov's elder and younger son, Il'ia (1745-92), a graduate of the Academy of Arts who had trained later in Rome, but of Petr there was no sign. All that is known about Petr is contained in a previously unquoted letter from his father to Samborskii, dated 10/21 March 1773. It is one long plaint of self-pity and apprehension of what the Empress might say about the actions of his unworthy and sinful son: Petr had fallen in love with an English girl and was obviously proposing not to return to Russia.[61] Regrettably there is no end to the story. It has been suggested that Petr returned to Russia after four years in England, but only in 1794 does his name suddenly re-appear, when he was appointed architect at Tsarskoe Selo, succeeding his recently deceased brother. Over the next few years he was active in completing buildings which had been begun and repairing others, but apparently not designing any original works. His one distinction seems to have been to live to the ripe old age of ninety-nine.[62]

II

A British traveller in Russia noted that Catherine "knows the French Belles Lettres perfectly, and, anno 1786, was reading Shakespeare in the German translation."[63] The visual arts allowed Catherine direct acquaintance with British achievements, her lack of knowledge of the English language deprived her of similar opportunities in the field of literature. She depended, as did so many of her subjects, on French and German translations, but we know from her correspondence that she had read and liked novels by such as Richardson, Fielding and Sterne.[64] She referred to Sterne in particular on many occasions, and his influence has been detected, however distantly, on some of her own literary efforts.[65] Shakespeare she was wont to acknowledge openly as her mentor in the construction of dramatic works,[66] and she may indeed have seen in 1772 the first performance of a play by Shakespeare (*Othello*) in Russia: she had certainly seen, if not understood, the previous year performances in English by the same English troupe of John Home's *Douglas* and Nicholas Rowe's *Jane Shore*.[67]

Catherine as author and spectator was passionately interested in the theatre and, anxious to improve standards in the imperial companies, she had sent abroad in 1765 one of her outstanding actors "to see the English and French theatres" and to perfect his art.[68] Ivan Afanas'evich Dmitrevskii (1733-1821) had been a member of the Iaroslavl' troupe of the Volkov brothers which had been brought to Petersburg by the Empress Elizabeth in 1752; along with the most promising actors from the troupe he subsequently entered the Noble Cadet Corps and was to become a prominent actor of the "Russian Theatre" established by the empress in 1756 and headed by the famous playwright A. P. Sumarokov. By 1765 Dmitrevskii had a well-established reputation for his performances in Sumarokov's tragedies and other tragic and comic roles in both Russian and foreign plays. He was an actor in the grand declamatory mould of the French classical theatre and his visit to France gave him the opportunity to strengthen his technique at first hand and to meet leading actors. In Paris he became particularly friendly with the great actor of the Comédie Française, Le Kain, who was acquainted with David Garrick; it was Le Kain who was to escort him to London in March, 1766, with the intention of meeting the famed Englishman.

In later life Dmitrevskii was to regale listeners at literary salons and soirées with stories of his life in Paris and London and anecdotes of the famous actors and actresses he had met, embroidering the details, confusing the dates; those who recorded what he said also added their own inaccuracies and distortions to such an extent that later historians who probed the available facts and dates were inclined to see much of what he said, particularly about Garrick, apochryphal, and indeed to question whether he ever went to London.[69] The aged Dmitrevskii may well have got carried away, but he did not lie about his visit.

When Le Kain and Dmitrevskii arrived in London, Garrick himself was taking the waters at Bath and they were entertained in his absence by his brother George, who took them to performances at Drury Lane and to visit the Shakespeare Temple in the grounds of Garrick's villa Hampton House. (See the series of paintings in 1762 by Zoffany of the villa, temple and grounds.) Le Kain was obliged to return to Paris at the beginning of April and before he left, wrote to Garrick about "un bien-aimable Russe que j'ai amené avec moi en Angleterre, et dont je vous ai déjà fait le portrait: il reste ici pour vous voir, vous parler, vous entendre, et vous admirer."[70] Dmitrevskii was to remain in London until the end of June, a stay of three months during which he had ample time to get to know Garrick well, if not to see him perform in public (Garrick after his return from Bath on 1 May performed only once again that season). Dmitrevskii also undoubtedly had the opportunity to meet many of the leading theatrical and literary figures of the day. His presence in the London capital was announced in *The London Chronicle* for 17-19 April as follows: "Lately arrived in town from Petersburgh, being in his travels, by the order of her Imperial Majesty, the celebrated Mr Dmitriefskoy, the head manager and chief actor of the theatres of Russia."[71] Two months later Horace Walpole considered him newsworthy enough to mention in a letter to Sir Horace Mann: "We have a Russian Garrick here, the head of their theatre, and like Shakespeare, both actor and author. He has translated *Hamlet*, and it had been acted at Petersburg."[72] Walpole had mis-heard or been mis-informed—Dmitrevskii had not translated Shakespeare's play but had acted in Sumarokov's pseudo-classical variant via La Place—but his words testify nevertheless to the interest which Dmitrevskii's visit provoked. The Russian left London sometime in early June with a letter from Garrick to Le Kain, who replied on the twenty third of the same month, thanking Garrick for "L'accueil agréable que vous avez bien voulu faire à mon Russe policé; vos leçons, votre conversation, et vos talents, l'ont très instruit sur le genre de la declamation Anglaise, dont il n'avait aucune idée."[73] Dmitrevskii may not have done all the things he or others claimed that he had done in London, but there seems little doubt that Le Kain was expressing the Russian's real sense of gratitude to Garrick. Dmitrevskii later characterized Garrick as "a great man," who was "more a comedian than an actor, that is an imitator of nature in ordinary life," in contrast to Le Kain, who "created types of historical characters."[74] If Le Kain's style was nearer to Dmitrevskii's in tragic roles, Garrick's versatility and his skill in comedy may well also have left their imprint on the Russian. In 1767 Dmitrevskii was again sent to Europe, to recruit actors, but although he renewed his acquaintances in Paris, he did not cross the Channel for a second time.

Some six years after Dmitrevskii, another leading Russian dramatist paid a brief visit to London, not, however, to meet Garrick and frequent the theatres but to carry out Masonic business. In the early 1770s Ivan Elagin, Director of the Imperial Theatres and a playwright himself, was as much concerned with ensuring his eminence as Provincial Grand Master of Russia as with improving the state of the Russian theatre, and his secretary, Vladimir Ignat'evich Lukin (1737-94), soon to become Secretary to the Grand Provincial Lodge, was sent to London in 1772 to secure his superior's patents of office.[75] Lukin, a fertile dramatist who preferred to adapt mainly French plays to Russian manners rather than compose his own original works, had by then made his one, accidental contribution to furthering Russian exposure to English literature: his *Shchepetil'nik* ("The Trinket Seller," 1765) was an adaptation, via a French intermediary, of Robert Dodsley's *The Toy Shop* (1735).[76]

Lukin's visit to London coincided with the arrival of a Russian poet in search of less arcane knowledge. Vasilii Petrovich Petrov (1736-99), who was subsequently to style himself accurately and openly as "the pocket poet" (*karmannyi stikhotvorets*) of Catherine the Great, had come to the notice of the empress in 1766 for his "Oda na velikolepnyi karusel' " ("Ode on the Grand Carousel"), composed when he was a teacher of rhetoric and poetics at the Moscow Slavonic-Greek-Latin Academy. Summoned to Petersburg in 1768, Petrov was appointed a translator in the empress's office and made her private reader. His apparently long desired opportunity to travel abroad came four years later when Catherine made him guardian and companion to a young court page by the name of Galaktion Ivanovich Silov, who was to be sent to study in London.

Of Silov little in known. He is first mentioned by Catherine herself in a letter of 1768, where he is described as "the sprightly Cupid Galaktion,"[77] and he seems to have inspired much affection in the empress and some of her courtiers, and subsequently among members of the Russian colony in London. From his two extant letters to Catherine (1773), it appears that Silov was an orphan, but with brothers living in Moscow for whom he sought imperial protection.[78] In London he studied mathematics, a "wife" who "gives me no rest but a lot of headaches,"[79] and inevitably English, in which he soon became proficient enough to read with delight the works of Addison. "Your Addison" is referred to in one of the two verse epistles which Petrov wrote and dedicated to Silov during their stay in London; in addition to indicating that Silov, like Petrov himself, was of humble origins, they reveal the poet's role as Silov's mentor and his love for his protégé.[80] Both the mature poet (Petrov in 1772 was in his thirty-seventh year) and the young Silov (who seems to have been about sixteen) were not only handsome in appearance but also engaging personalities; Petrov, moreover, could not have failed to impress by his undoubted talent and erudition. There is ample evidence to show on what good terms they were with members of the Russian embassy, from the Ambassador Musin-Pushkin himself to such officials as the Tatishchev brothers and Mikhail Pleshcheev. They enjoyed the particular attention of the embassy chaplain Samborskii, whom Silov commended to the empress as "loved and respected by everyone for his virtues and attachment to Russia."[81] Among other Russians in England in the early 1770s Petrov became particularly close with three men who have already appeared in these pages, the two remaining students at Oxford, Nikitin, whom he had known since Moscow days, and Suvorov, and the future Admiral Mordvinov. all were to maintain contact after their return to Russia. The names of Petrov, Nikitin and Suvorov were to come together in a memorable way a few years later when on 17 November 1783 they were all made members of the newly formed "Russian Academy," and they were indeed united not only by friendship but by similar views on literature and language. With Mordvinov Petrov was on even friendlier terms, and remained so until his death. In 1796 the poet dedicated an ode ("Oda ego vysokoprevoskhoditel'-stvu . . . Nikolaiu Semenovichu Mordvinovu") to his friend, at a time when Mordvinov was being attacked and slandered by enemies in St. Petersburg. The following year, his troubles over and now raised to the rank of full admiral, Mordvinov decided to set up a printing press at Nikolaev with the help of the Moscow printer S. I. Selivanovskii who had been recommended by Petrov. One of the first productions from the press in 1798 was Petrov's ode on the coronation of Paul–a characteristic acknowledgement by Mordvinov of his gratitude and respect. The following year Petrov died but Mordvinov lived on for almost another fifty years, inspiring Pushkin also to address a poem to him, "Mordvinovu" (1827), which contined the line "ne votshche Petrov tebia liubil" ("Not without reason did Petrov love you").[82]

Up to this point the years Petrov spent in London have been seen as primarily important for his acquisition of often lifelong Russian friends and indeed he spent much of his time in the company of Russians. He was nonetheless manifestly interested in England, English literature and institutions and in making a circle of English acquaintances. Given his personality and interests this would present few difficulties and he had furthermore in Father Samborskii a friend with a remarkable range of English contacts. Five letters from Petrov to Samborskii are extant: from these and other sources some of Petrov's more interesting English acquaintances can be established.[83]

The first letter is of particular importance for revealing that Petrov availed himself of a unique opportunity to see more of Europe than England, an opportunity offered by one of the most exotic personalities of the age, Elizabeth Chudleigh, Duchess of Kingston (1720-88).[84] Shortly after the funeral of the Duke of Kingston, her second husband by a bigamous marriage, on 18 October 1773, the duchess decided to go to Rome, sailing up the Tiber in her own private yacht. In Rome she received a flattering reception, was frequently received by the Pope, Clement XIV, and feted by the cream of Italian society. Petrov's letter dates from 17 May 1774 during the duchess's return journey, which took them overland from Rome via Florence, Genoa, Antibes, Geneva (from where the letter was written), and Paris, which was reached in late June. They arrived in London only on 9 July, and by the beginning of August she had left again, just avoiding arrest on charges of bigamy and of course leaving Petrov behind in London, reunited with Silov. The duchess apparently had conceived a desire to learn Russian and Petrov had been introduced to her as an appropriate teacher by a longstanding friend of Samborskii, the Reverend John Forster (1697?-1781).

Forster was very much an original character, who had been keenly interested in Russia since his first visit there during the reign of Elizabeth, when he acted as private chaplain to the Earl of Hyndford, the British representative in St. Petersburg from 1744 to 1749. In the 1760s we find Forster acting for some time as tutor in history to a Russian nobleman in London by the name of Arsen'ev and telling him a story which was to be published in the *Public Ledger* of 25 October 1777, by which time Forster was again in Petersburg, where he was to remain until his death in June, 1781. Forster in the 1720s and 30s had been governor to Edward Wortley Montagu, and in 1777, a year after his former pupil's death, he claimed publicly authorship of *Reflections on the Rise and Fall of the Ancient Republics*, published under Montagu's name in 1759.[85] Undoubtedly Samborskii and Petrov were among the Russians who knew of his claim from their time in England, and Petrov was to see Forster frequently in Russia in the late 1770s, together with the Duchess of Kingston, whose chaplain Forster was.

Forster was known as "a sort of atheistic parson" to members of the Bentham family,[86] to whom he consistently introduced Russian friends in London during the 1760s-70s. Petrov was among them and Samuel and Jeremy Bentham made use of his nearness to the empress, on his appointment as her librarian on his return, in connection with their Russian projects and own subsequent visits to Russia. One other notable friend Petrov acquired was John Paradise, whose closeness to the Russian community has previously been noted. Paradise had many acquaintances among literary and scholarly circles.

Petrov was in England when much of interest and importance was taking place on the literary scene. Samuel Johnson, a close friend of Paradise, was at the height of his powers and influence. The famous "Club," founded in 1764, continued to be the meeting place of outstanding literary and cultural figures, such as James Boswell, Sir Joshua Reynolds, Oliver Goldsmith and Edmund Burke. Goldsmith, who was to die in 1774, continued to the end to write verse and prose and above all completed *She Stoops to Conquer* (1773), Burke was delivering in elegant prose his speeches in Parliament; Reynolds was in the middle of his presidential lectures to the Royal Academy. There were literary events which created considerable excitement in London and which could not have failed to interest Petrov. In 1773 James Macpherson published his "definitive" edition of the *Poems of Ossian*; the following year saw the publication of Lord Chesterfield's *Letters to His Son Philip Stanhope* and Thomas Warton brought out the first volume of his pioneering *History of English Poetry*.

The extent to which Petrov was influenced by what he saw, read and heard in England has been estimated by critics at all points between "great" and "insignificant."[87] In London he wrote a number of poems, epistles varying in tone from the intimate, the respectful and the satirical and including the two poems to Silov, one to Catherine and two to unnamed addressees, as well as a more formal ode "Na pobedu rossiiskogo voinstva" ("On the Victory of the Russian Armies"). In content they are concerned almost exclusively with Russian personalities and Russian subjects; in form they reveal a widening of Petrov's range beyond the ode. Although the influence of Pope has been detected, it is less an influence than an analogy; more interesting is the suggestion that Petrov's thought was "undoubtedly influenced by the sensualist philosophy of Locke."[88] Certainly one of Petrov's contemporaries, M. N. Murav'ev, declared that "it is noticeable in his way of thinking and feeling that he has lived in England," suggesting that he sacrificed sensibility to reason.[89] On firmer ground, another contemporary, the English chaplain in Petersburg William Tooke, wrote that "a long residence in England inspired him with a fondness for British literature, and animated him to the difficult undertaking of translating the Paradise Lost of Milton into his mother tongue; which, though in prose, has justly added to his reputation."[90] Petrov's prose translation of the first three books of Milton's epic, published in St. Petersburg in 1777, is the most obvious testimony to his interest in English literature and his command of the English language. In his dedication to Prince P. I. Repnin, he writes: "Bored with rhymes in Virgil, I rest with prose in Milton. And where could I drown more fittingly the cares which oppress me as a mortal than in Milton's hell? With this poet it is pleasanter to wander through the underworld than with others through Elysium. Afflicted by blindness, he knew how to benefit from his darkness. He is strong, when he soars above the stars, he is even stronger, when he descends into the valley. Hell is the land of his imagination."[91]

Petrov and Silov saw little of England apart from the capital. In September 1774 Silov wrote to the empress, asking for permission to stay longer, "to study more, and then to travel through England, visiting various mills and factories, and among other notable things, your beloved gardens"; hitherto they had lived "more like hermits than travellers to foreign parts."[92] It seems unlikely that they received permission and they started back to Russia that autumn, travelling via France and Germany. En route Silov died,[93] and a saddened Petrov arrived alone in Petersburg early in 1775. After his appointment as Catherine's librarian, he remained at court until 1780, when he retired to his estate, from which he emerged to spend his winters in Moscow. His love and knowledge of the English language he was to impart to his son Iason,[94] and his continuing interest in English literature is evident in his requests for books from Samborskii in London. In his retirement one non-literary aspect of English influence manifested itself. In a biographical memoir of his father, Iason Petrov wrote that "as a relaxation from his scholarly pursuits he devoted himself to agriculture, in the perfecting of which he followed in many respects the English, sending orders for their agricultural implements."[95] In this he was a true disciple of Samborskii.

Petrov was neither the first nor the last Russian poet to visit England in the eighteenth century. The most famous of course was Prince Kantemir, whose poetry was published posthumously in London in 1749, although in a French rather than an English translation. Also attached to the Russian embassy at a later date and in a post markedly inferior to that of ambassador was Andrian Illarionovich Dubrovskii (b. 1732). Like Petrov a former student of the Moscow Slavonic-Greek-Latin Academy, he was even more a representative of the "Lomonosov school" not only by the nature of his poetry but by his personal contacts with Lomonosov at the Academy in the 1750s. Dubrovskii wrote a number of satirical and didactic poems, some original, others translated, which were published in *Ezhemesiachnye sochineniia* ("Monthly Compositions") in 1755 and 1756, and reflected Lomonosov's own work as both teacher and poet. Although his best known piece, "Na osleplenie strastiami" ("On Blindness from the Passions," 1755), has been compared both for its ideas and poetic expression with such works by Lomonosov as his "Pis'mo o pol'ze stekla" ("Epistle on the Use of Glass"),[96] it might well have suggested analogies with the work of Pope and Locke, as did poems by Petrov in a similar vein, had it been written during or after his stay in England rather than earlier. However it is inter esting to note that Dubrovskii undoubtedly knew Pope's *Essay on Man* in the 1750s: his friend from Moscow days and in Petersburg and Lomonosov's favourite pupil at the Academy was Nikolai Popovskii, who produced his noted translation of Pope's poem (from the French version) in 1754.[95] Dubrovskii, who succeeded Popovskii as teacher of Latin at the Academy gymnasium when the latter moved to Moscow in 1755 to become a professor at the new university, soon became friendly with the Vorontsov family, particularly with the young Semen, whom he accompanied on a journey through southern Russia in 1759-60. It was under Semen's elder brother Aleksandr that Dubrovskii served, after his transfer to the College of Foreign Affairs, first in Vienna and then in London. Dubrovskii was in England between 1762 and 1764, but his few letters from this period reveal little, except that with regard to his knowledge of English, "je la possède autant qu'il faut pour demander les choses nécessaires, mais pour soutenir un dis cours, j'y renonce."[98] He soon moved with Vorontsov to the Hague, where he was to remain as an embassy translator into the 1770s.

As far as one can judge from the scant evidence, England and English literature made little impact on Dubrovskii. Indeed, the only Russian to wax lyrical after a sojourn in England seems to have been Samborskii's protégé Dzhunkovskii, who devoted the opening stanzas of his long descriptive poem *Aleksandrova* (1793) to a eulogy of Albion.

By white shores embraced you stand,
Albion, amidst the roaring seas.
Around sail rich ships,
A throne is raised to Neptune;
In its cities flourish minds, sciences.
Hands, tireless in the fields,
Are guided by skill and respect nature,
Everywhere greatness in seen alongside simplicity,
Pleasantness lives with, befriends utility,
Thus all the works of centuries are enjoyed.[99]

In some respects it might seem unfortunate to end a chapter in which the activities of Russian artists, architects, dramatists and poets have been surveyed with lines of such poetic mediocrity. It is, however, the general sentiment, echoing the words of Skorodumov which gave the chapter its title that excuses the recalling.

CHAPTER 9
RUSSIANS ON THE GRAND TOUR

The tourist was hardly a creation of the eighteenth century, as Professor John Hale was the most recent but far from the first to point out.[1] Renaissance Italy knew the breed and so did Shakespeare's England and Cervantes' Spain: if Shakespeare's Portia ridiculed the young Englishman who "bought his doublet in Italy, his round hose in France, his bonnet in Germany, and his behaviour everywhere," Cervantes' Man of Glass and other heroes were inclined to stress the educational benefits of a tour of the Italian cities. With the latter view the redoubtable Dr Johnson would have concurred: "a man who has not been in Italy is always conscious of an inferiority, from not having seen what it is expected a man should see. The grand object of travelling is to see the shores of the Mediterranean."[2] Although the term itself was borrowed from the French and used already in the seventeenth century in print in Richard Lassels' *Voyage of Italy* (1670), the Grand Tour is primarily associated both with the English and with the eighteenth century. The cities of Italy, particularly Rome and Naples with nearby Herculaneum and Pompeii, Goethe's infinite delight-affording disaster, were the magnet, but there were fascinating permutations on the route there and back for the tourist. The cities and roads of France, Switzerland, Germany, Austria, and the Low Countries saw ever increasing crowds of travellers as the century grew old, and in 1785 there were, according to the estimate given to Edward Gibbon,[3] some 45,000 English on the Continent. By that time new horizons were beckoning the jaded and/or intrepid English traveller and the Northern Tour or Circuit—Scandinavia, Poland, Russia—began to exercise its attraction, justifying Menshikov's prediction that "Petersbourg should become another Venice, to see which Foreigners would travel thither purely out of Curiosity."[4] The English tourist was everywhere, but the disease was contagious and such as the French and the Germans had long been infected. So too were to be the Russians, once they were given the opportunity.

This opportunity came in 1762 with the one major decree of Peter III's short reign, freeing the Russian gentry from obligatory state service, allowing them to retire to their country estates and to travel abroad without hindrance. The phenomenon of the Russian Grand Tourist in Europe is characteristic of the Age of Catherine the Great, but towards the end of Elizabeth's reign enough aristocrats were able to leave Russia for reasons of official business, study or health to form little national groups in The Hague or in Paris, such as A. R. Vorontsov describes in 1759.[5] French police reports on the liaisons of rich

Russians, such as Prince Andrei Belosel'skii, Buturlins, Golitsyns, Saltykovs, Razumovskiis, Kurakins and Shuvalovs, with French actresses and singers and amusing and sordid details of their financial transactions, for enticement and escape, show that by the very early 1760s Russia was doing its utmost to catch up with the West in some of its least praiseworthy aspects.[6] Curiously enough, a Russian in Paris, squandering his family fortune as he goes from one mistress to another, became the subject of an English satirical piece, allegedly an auto-biographical confession and published in 1792. "Adventures of a Russian Gentleman at Paris, Narrated by Himself" was given an eloquent epigraph—"Send a fool to France, and he will return a greater fool"—and its application to English "men of fashion" was hammered home in a preface,[7] but it might well have found a place in one of Nikolai Novikov's famous satirical journals of the early 1770s, where the evils of xenomania were relentlessly attacked. In his first journal, *Truten'* ("The Drone," 1769), Novikov had castigated just such a returning fool in a mock news item: "A young Russian piglet, who has been travelling in foreign parts for the enlightenment of his mind and who, having duly profited, has returned a perfect swine, may be seen free of charge on many streets in this city."[8] The satirical shafts of Russian journalists, poets and dramatists were largely directed against Gallomania, against the *petimetry* ("petits maîtres"), who, like Denis Fonvizin's Ivanushka, regretted their bodies were born in Russia but knew their souls belonged to France, against the invasion of the Russian language by French words and of the Russian market by French gewgaws and fashions. The Russians thus made common cause with a host of European writers and artists who exercised their pens and brushes throughout the century with portrayals of the absurdities of their travelling contemporaries.

A reluctant traveller himself in the early days of Catherine's reign and then later ambassador in Venice, where he had ample opportunity to view his fellow-countrymen in their assault on Italy,[9] Count Semen Vorontsov was little disposed by his own pronounced Gallophobia to view the antics of Russians in France with approval. From London, he thundered against "des petits maîtres, des fats, des rimailleurs français, qui se faisaient gloire d'avoir rempli quelques pages de leur plate versification dans le Mercure de France, tandis qu'ils ne savaient ni parler, ni écrire dans leur propre langue, et qui, portant l'uniforme et se disant au service militaire, n'avaient pas honte de rester à Paris, tandis que leur Patrie gémissait sous le poids d'une double guerre."[10] This outburst dates from 1792 and although provoked by one specific person whom he does not name but who is easily identifiable, it is made applicable to almost all "nos jeunes seigneurs, que j'ai vu depuis 9 ans que je suis employé hors de ma Patrie." More and more of these Russian Frenchmen had been making their way across the Channel to England. Anglomania was for many of them simply a side effect of Gallomania, an enthusiasm for "blessed Albion" excited by the French themselves.

The dangers, real and imagined, of an excessive attachment to things English had indeed been long anticipated by Russian observers. As early as February, 1758, Petersburg audiences had greeted warmly an operatic version of Goldoni's play *La Ritornata di Londra*, which ridiculed the vogue for English fashions.[11] Somewhat later, Prince M. M. Shcherbatov, that humourless and bilious critic of the "new" Russian aristocracy, also located the beginnings of the English infection in the last years of the reign of Elizabeth. He attacked Count Petr Shuvalov for being the first to buy highly expensive English horses to pull his carriage and took Countess Anna Vorontsova, the wife of the grand chancellor, to task for her addiction to English beer.[12] Novikov, very sensitive to changes in fashion, was by the time of his third journal, *Zhivopisets* ("The Painter"), published in 1772, highlighting the swing from France to England in the following cautionary passage: "We have become accustomed to adopting greedily everything from foreigners, but unfortunately we frequently only adopt their vices. For instance, when the French were in fashion, our intercourse with them left us only with flippancy, inconstancy, foppery, freedom in manners which exceeded all bounds of decency, as well as many other vices. The French have been replaced by the English: now men and women are falling over themselves to adopt something from the English; everything English now seems to us good, charming, and everything enchants us."[13] The cult of things English gained momentum with a small but influential section of the upper classes. Admiration for English workmanship was high and demand for English products great. The merchant houses imported a vast range of goods, "English shops" were opened in Petersburg, and the hard-pressed Russian chaplains in London spent much time fulfilling the commissions of Russian noblemen, who of course were quick to follow the imperial example. The *Morning Chronicle* reported on 31 July 1783, for instance: "a very commodious travelling-coach, of an uncommon size, and containing a variety of conveniences, is just finished by Hatchett of Long Acre for the Empress of Russia."[14] By 1800, the Cambridge don, Edward Daniel Clarke, could suggest with some complacency that the Russians "entertain extravagant notions of the wealth and happiness of Englishmen; and they have good reason to do so; since whatever they possess useful or estimable comes to them from England. Books, maps, prints, furniture, clothing, hardware of all kinds, horses, carriages, hats, leather, medicine, almost every article of convenience, comfort, or luxury, must be derived from England, or it is of no estimation."[15]

The general condition of Anglomania was well enough defined by the end of the eighteenth century and specific "carriers" were identified with ease. Although the label of *Angloman* ("Anglomaniac") was worn willingly by the embassy official and littérateur M. I. Pleshcheev as early as the 1770s, it was generally later used against others for ridicule. The word itself appears in N. Ianovskii's *Novyi slovotolkovatel'* ("New Dictionary") of 1803, defined as "a person who is astonished by, and imitates to ludicrous excess, everything that is done in England."[16] Examples of the type began to appear in the literature and memoirs of the period. Zhikharev's diaries offer, for instance, from the 1790s the joint master of the Moscow hunt, N. M. Gusiatnikov, "a very great Anglomaniac and a very precise gentleman," with his English hounds and English hunters, and V. A. Vikulin, known as "the Hamburg Gazette," "who was in raptures about anything which merely smacked of England and the English."[17] Anglomania, Anglophobia; realm of folly, rule of reason: a Russian visitor to London in 1789 attempted to discriminate. Close to Novikov's views he suggested that "Russians, our countrymen, who for a century have continually adopted everything from others, have also adopted the general fashion to be *à l'anglaise*," but his own attitude is that of the intelligent observer of customs, habits and institutions, intent on providing information "instructive for our fellow-countrymen."[18] What he saw generally confirmed his love and respect for England and his impressions became one of the very few personal accounts of England to be published in Russia in the eighteenth century. But Anglophiles or Anglomaniacs or simply curious, an impressive number of titled and landed Russians descended on London in the last decades of the century.

To provide even approximate figures for the number of Russians visiting London as part of a Grand Tour is not possible. All that may be said is that the names of about 100 people who come more or less within that category may be established by searching through published sources, such as the Vorontsov and Kurakin archives, and unpublished ones, among which the Samborskii archive is of prime importance. Given that the Samborskii and Vorontsov archives between them cover most but not all of the years of the reigns of Catherine and Paul, certain conclusions might be reached: the vast majority of the visitors came during the 1770s and 1780s, the middle decades of Catherine's reign, when European interest in England was at a height, and ending with the French Revolution, when the numbers of Russians touring Europe in general sharply and understandably declined; the tourists in the main represented, not unexpectedly, the foremost and richest families in Russia. More surprising, however, are the identities of many of the visitors, few of whom are recognized as having had direct acquaintance with England and fewer still about whom anything relating to their visits has been published. In their number were such as Princes Dashkova, who has already loomed large in these pages; two former "favourites," Orlov and Ermolov; one imperial bastard, Bobrinskoi; the last Hetman of the Cossacks, Razumovskii, and, later, some of his sons; the future "man of 1812," Kutuzov, recovering from a serious would received in the Russo-Turkish war; numerous members of the fabulously rich Demidov clan; leading aristocrats from the Russian "Burke": Iusupov, Kurakin, Rumiantsevs, Rostopchin, Repnin, Sheremetev, Stroganov, Viazemskii and gaggles of Golitsyns and Gagarins. Some left almost no trace of their visit, others wrote their own memorials in the form of letters and diaries which have been preserved, still others, because of their eminence or notoriety, had their passage recorded in the English newspapers and journals of the period.

Almost vying with each other for pride of place in the last of these categories, as they had earlier for the affections of their sovereign, were Princess
Dashkova and Prince Grigorii Orlov, whose reputations as fellow-conspirators
of Catherine in the overthrow of her husband and as something worse in his
subsequent demise had long preceded them to England. It is on their frequently colourful adventures in Britain that attention will now be focussed.

II

The passionate friendship between the two Catherines, the young new empress and the even younger new princess, was quick to cool in the early years
of the new reign. The empress was irritated by Dashkova's exaggerated role as
her most resourceful and effective supporter, and the princess resentful of the
greater influence with the empress that Orlov was not slow to reveal. Widowed
in 1764 at the age of twenty-one, Dashkova the following year moved to Moscow to begin a life of seclusion and strict economy. However, a desire to travel
and thoughts of a European education for her children induced her to set out
from Russia at the end of 1769 on a tour which would take her overland
through Prussia to Berlin, then on to Spa, from where she would make her
way to England. Although years before she had confided in an English ambassador to Petersburg: "Why was I not born an Englishwoman? How I adore
the freedom and spirit of that Nation!"[19] and that love had been nourished
by the positive reports from her brother, Aleksandr, during his own ambassadorship in London, it seems unlikely that she would have gone on to England
on this first European tour if she had not made a number of new and important acquaintances during her stay in Spa. There she met in particular two Irish-
women, Mrs Catherine Hamilton, daughter of the Bishop of Tuam and the
widow of an Irish rector, and Mrs Elizabeth Morgan, daughter of the Irish
Attorney-General, both of whom were to become close and treasured friends.
In addition she met Dr John Hinchcliffe, Bishop of Peterborough, whose services she was later to enlist as a translator for a sermon on the Russian naval
triumph at Chesme and whose recommendation of Westminster School, of
which he had earlier been the headmaster, as a suitable place for her son she
was bent on pursuing when she left for London at the end of September,
1770.

Styling herself Mme. Mikhalkova after the *incognito* fashion initiated by
Peter the Great and imitated by endless travelling Russians in the 1770s-80s
who thought their eminence deserved it, Dashkova with her two children and
their governess Miss P. F. Kamenskaia settled in rooms in the Gentlemen's
hotel, began a hectic round of social calls and prepared for a fortnight's excursion to the West of England. Her diary for 14 October records visits paid to
her during the day by the famous Corsican patriot General Paoli, by a Mr
Fitzgerald, who took her off to inspect the museum of the Society of Arts,

by a Mrs Jones and her aunt, with whom she left to call on Mrs Noel, and later
Lady Spencer, and a dinner with the Russian Ambassador Musin-Pushkin and
his wife.[20]

Early the next morning, Princess Dashkova, with her daughter, Miss Kamenskaia and a cousin Ivan Alekseevich Vorontsov, who had been attached to
the Russian Embassy in London in the 1750s, set off from the capital on a
tour which was to take her to Guildford, Portsmouth, Southampton, Salisbury
and so to Bath. From Bath an excursion was made to Bristol, and from Bath
she returned to London via Woodstock, Oxford, Windsor and Hampton Court.
Five years later she was to publish a description of that journey, which was
the first account of its kind ever to appear in Russia, clearly conveying her
enthusiasm for every aspect of English life, for the beauty of country towns
and private estates with their magnificent gardens and grounds, for buildings
and institutions. She visited the estates of Lord Clive at Claremont, Sir William
Hamilton at Cobham, Lord Weymouth at Longleat, Lord Pembroke at Wilton
and the Duke of Marlborough at Blenheim; she described in great detail the
cathedral at Salisbury ("an enormous Gothic building, remarkable only for its
antiquity") and Stonehenge ("the ruins of the ancient temple of the Druids");
she was in and out museums and shops and factories. The two places where
she stayed the longest and to which she devoted most space were Bath and
Oxford. Her days in Bath were full of visits to the Pump Room, to concerts,
to soirées, and the pages reflect a typical cross section of the fashionable society of the time: Lady Kerry, the Duchess of Portland, the Duke of Northumberland, her friend the Bishop of Peterborough, and famous Dr Lister, and
a former Russian embassy official, Theodore Luders, who was living in retirement in the city. Here are her first impressions of the Pump Room:

> . . . we entered the room where the hot water fountains are and found
> such a multitude of people that only with difficulty could we make our
> way through to the pump. After we had drunk a glass of the water (al-
> though its taste is somewhat sulphurous, it is less revolting than the
> water at Aachen), we went to look at the baths, which are alongside the
> main room and the people bathing can be seen from its windows. Men
> and women are also mixed together and are dressed in yellow flannel
> garments with hats made from oilskin on their heads. Up to their necks
> in the water so that just their heads are visible, they follow each other
> round in a circle.[21]

Her visit to Oxford, where, as was noted in an earlier chapter, she met the
group of young Russians studying at the university, was marked by the special
attentions of the Dean of Christ Church, William Markham, who gave her a
conducted tour of his college on her first afternoon. The following day he
took her to see a number of other colleges, which, she observed, gave different names to their heads—Master, Provost, Warden, Principal and Rector, "al-

though they mean the same thing," and to buildings of the university such as the Sheldonian, the Ashmolean Museum, the Clarendon Press and the Bodleian Library, where she inspected Russian manuscripts. Her tour was so tiring and her subsequent dinner in the Dean's rooms in Christ Church so satisfying that she was glad to retire "to the embrace of Morpheus."[22]

Back in London in the evening of 29 October, she was to spend a further two weeks or so in England and give the highly curious Horace Walpole the opportunity to inspect her at the Duchess of Northumberland's:

> Well! I have seen Princess Daschioff, and she is well worth seeing—not for her person, though for an absolute Tartar she is not ugly; her smile is pleasing, but her eyes have a very Cataline fierceness. Her behaviour is extraordinarily frank and easy. She talks on all subjects, and not ill nor with striking pedantry, and is very quick and very animated. She puts herself above all attention to dress and everything feminine, and yet sings tenderly and agreeably with a pretty voice. She and a Russian lady that accompanies her sung two songs of the people who are all musical; one was grave, the other lively but with very tender turns, and both resembling extremely the Venetian barcaroles. She speaks English a little, understands it easily; French is very familiar to her and she knows Latin.[23]

After mentioning her exchange with a woman after attending a meeting of Quakers as an "instance of her quickness and parts," he offers the verdict that "she is a very singular personage." By the time he was to see her again towards the end of her second visit to England, his enthusiasm had considerably abated. In the interim Dashkova had continued her travels, becoming extremely close with Diderot in Paris before travelling south with her Irish friends to Aix-en-Provence, and, in the following spring, to Switzerland and a meeting with Voltaire at Ferney. Dashkova was back in Russia early in 1773, but soon planning and again strictly economising for a return to Britain and the entry of her son into Edinburgh University.

In October, 1776, she was again in London, no longer incognito, but enjoying all the recognition which her reputation and rank brought her. She and her son and her daughter, now Mme. Sherbinina, but already estranged from her husband, were presented at Court, and pursued an active social life. On 3 October, for instance, she "was in the stage-box at Drury-lane theatre, and drew the eyes of the whole audience upon her," while she, it is hoped, was following the fortunes of Nicholas Rowe's *The Fair Penitent*.[24] About the middle of November she and her family began their journey to Scotland, which was broken by a stay at Easton Maudit in Northamptonshire, the home of her friends the Duke and Duchess of Sussex, where she met the Irishman Edward Wilmot, with whose daughters, first Martha (1775-1873), then Catherine (d. 1824), her own last years were to be so closely linked. From Northampton-

shire, Dashkova went northwards, staying again with an old friend, the Duke
of Northumberland, at Alnwick Castle, before arriving in Edinburgh to begin
the stay of some two and a half years, the "academic" concerns of which have
already been described in Chapter 5. However, from the point of view of "tourism," these years also have their interest.

During the summer vacation of 1777 Dashkova took her son and daughter
on a fortnight's tour of the Scottish Highlands. Unlike the journal of her first
tour in 1770, Dashkova's account of the Highlands was never published but is
preserved in a copy made by Martha Wilmot in 1804 from Dashkova's own
copy of the original which she had sent to her friend Mrs Morgan in the form
of a letter.[25] Once again, however, it is a unique document, describing parts
of Britain not known to have been visited by any other Russian visitors in the
eighteenth or, as far as I know, nineteenth centuries. The first day, however,
took them to the Clyde-Forth Canal and the ironworks at Carron, places which
had been inspected only shortly before by the practised eye of the engineer
officer Nikolai Korsakov, but the following day, 26 August, saw them arrive
in Perth and already "Nature begins to change her appearance towards the
terrible and arid," opined the princess in one of her few sentences of English
in an otherwise French text. After visiting the estate of the Duke of Atholl at
Dunkeld and waxing lyrical with an appropriate quotation from Pope, they
journeyed on to Taymouth Castle, where the aged but active Lord Breadalbane
was to be their host for four days, firing off a twenty-four gun salute in their
honour and producing a piper, "habillé et armé, comme l'étoient ancienne-
ment les montagnards." From Taymouth they went across to Inverary with
wretched inns en route, and then through Glen Coe to Dumbarton, where her
son received the freedom of the town, an honour which Edinburgh was also
to bestow on him later and one which at least two other Russians in the eighteenth century, Korsakov and Pavel Grigor'ev Demidov (1738-1821), had already received from Glasgow. They arrived back in Edinburgh on 7 March after a tour which left the princess with lasting memories of the beauty of the
countryside, of the mountains and the lochs, particularly Loch Lomond, but
equally with impressions of the poverty and hardship of the lives of many of
the inhabitants, of the squalor of some of the inns and of the lack of taste she
detected in the buildings of the "Seigneurs."

It was a tour she was not to repeat, for her ill-health obliged her the following summer to take the waters at Buxton and Matlock and to bathe in the
sea at Scarborough, where she was glimpsed by Judith, Lady Milbanke, who
found her a "very extraordinary Character" and "of a strong Masculine Spirit
which I should guess was the case from her Appearance."[26] After her son's
graduation, however, she was able to undertake one further and long-desired
tour, to Ireland, to enjoy the company of her closest friends Mrs Hamilton
and Mrs Morgan. The diary of this tour, unlike those of the previous two, has
been lost, but her memoirs give some idea of what she did, whom she saw,

and of her enthusiasm for a stay in Dublin, which "even now seems like a happy dream which lasted a whole year," and for its society, "distinguished by its elegance, its wit and its manners, and enlivened by that frankness which comes naturally to the Irish."[27] She first went north to Antrim and the Giant's Causeway and then settled in Dublin for many months. Pre-eminent among the new friends she made was Lady Arabella Denny, noted blue-stocking and philanthropist, who managed among other things to appeal to Dashkova's penchant for music. Dashkova provided a setting for four voices for a favourite hymn of Lady Denny's which was sung in church "in the presence of a numerous congregation drawn by curiosity to hear what a Russian bear could have composed." (Incidentally, the previous year, "the Russian bear" had been in correspondence with David Garrick, sending him a piece she had composed and which he had had performed to the rapture of a "small audience."[28]) Towards the end of her stay, Dashkova travelled west to Kilkenny and Killarney and then down to Cork and Limerick. Dashkova may not have been the first Russian in Ireland in the eighteenth century—no less a figure than Ivan Shuvalov, for instance, had been in Dublin in February, 1764,[29] but she certainly saw more and stayed longer than any. She sailed from Ireland in May, 1780, and landed at Holyhead, which meant that she was able to have a brief look at Wales with its "many most romantic places" on her journey to London.

Her memoirs at this point mention a further gracious reception by George III and Queen Caroline and visits to various "royal castles" and great houses but make no reference to the momentous events in London in early June, 1780, the Gordon Riots, with which her own name was then frequently associated, not least by Horace Walpole. During the night of 2-3 June rioters sacked the chapel of the Sardinian ambassador, the Marchese di Cordon, in Duke Street, Lincoln's Inn Fields, and among the thirteen men apprehended at the scene was a Russian officer. Within hours of "the outrage at Cordon's," Walpole informed the countess of Upper Ossory that "one person seized is a Russian officer who had the impudence to claim acquaintance with the Sardinian minister and desired to be released. Cordon replied, 'Oui, Monsieur je vous connaissais, mais je ne vous connais plus.' I do not know whether he is an associate of Thalestris [Dashkova], who seems to have snuffed a revolution in the wind."[30] By the following week he had no doubts: "That Scythian heroine the Princess Daskiou is here, her natural brother Rantzau was taken in Mons. Cordon's chapel, and was reclaimed by Simonin [the Russian minister, Simolin], and released; *she* herself on Wednesday, *I know* sent Lord Ashburnham word that his house was marked for destruction, merciful tigress! it is proof that he is not an Emperor."[31] Despite Walpole's insinuations, it was mere chance, however, that Dashkova and her family should have returned to London precisely at a time when her half-brother had arrived from Russia, apparently as a diplomatic courier. Rantzau was in fact Aleksandr Romanovich Rontsov, the illegitimate son of Dashkova's father by his English mistress Mrs

Elizabeth Brockett, and his involvement in the riots was a source of embarrassment not only for members of his family but also for the Russian government, which received an official complaint. Catherine did not hide her own displeasure at the incident and told the British ambassador in Petersburg that: "she was sorry, she said, her Minister had applied in his behalf and most sincerely wished we had brought him to his trial. That in any country whatsoever, a stranger concerned in an insurrection deserved no mercy but in a country like ours, where the laws were so mild and so wisely administered, he was doubly culpable. She added, that though he had escaped justice in England it awaited him here, and that it would meet him the moment he set foot in her Empire."[32] Further dispatches related that Rontsov had been apprehended on his return and had been interrogated, but "nothing appears from his examination but much folly, and a strong disposition to riot and mischief."[33] It was said that the empress intended to send him to Siberia, but the exact punishment he received is not known. It is likely that he was merely confined to his estate of Medushi near Oranienbaum, where he was certainly to be found a few years later.[34]

Dashkova meanwhile continued her sight-seeing and excursions. She descended later in June on Strawberry Hill with "her horde of Tartars," but Walpole "kept out of sight, having nothing to regale her but one old horse."[35] She made a second excursion to Bath and Bristol at the end of July and left England for the last time in August. After two more years on the Continent she returned in 1782 to Russia and to a few years of renewed intimacy with the empress. In the last years of Catherine's reign, when once again misunderstanding between them arose, she retired to her estate at Troitskoe, putting into practice her enthusiasm for the English garden. Later, offering her brother Aleksandr advice on the laying out of the grounds at his estate of Andreevskoe, she was to style herself "your English gardener."[36] Her memories of Britain and her correspondence with friends sustained her through many periods of despair and disillusionment, and without hesitation she responded to her friend Mrs Morgan's suggestion that Martha Wilmot should spend some time with her at Troitskoe. The companionship afforded by Martha and, later, also by her sister Catherine, brought her a great deal of joy in her later years and it was at Martha's insistence that she began in February, 1804, the memoirs which are perhaps her most enduring monument.[37]

III

Prince Grigorii Grigor'evich Orlov's visit to England came in the interval between the two visits by Princess Dashkova, the first of which it resembled in its duration and the nature of things done and places seen. However, unlike Dashkova, Orlov arrived with full splendour and publicity. Horace Walpole was on this occasion well prepared for Orlov's visit by his friend, Sir Horace

Mann, who described his departure from Florence en route for England and added: "Shan't you be curious to see a man who has set a great Princess on a throne and has governed her despotically and her whole empire so long, now sent to foreign parts to recover his vigour! "[38] Walpole's amusing response came on 14 November: "Orlow the Great, or rather the Big, is here; and as proud of his infamous diamonds as the Duchess of Kingston herself. He dances gigantic dances, and makes gigantic love; but no conquests yet. He has quitted his post with honour, for the Empress has appointed two to supply his functions—I suppose they are Gog and Magog. Orlow talks an infinite deal of nonsense; but parts are not necessary to a royal favourite or to an assassin."[39] By that time Orlov had been in England some six weeks and many of the most interesting and amusing incidents of his visit had already taken place.

Ever since the events of 1762 European interest in the quintet of Orlov brothers had been enormous and the varied activities of four of them, if not of the eldest Ivan, in the intervening years had been such as to be the stuff of gossip even in England. Although Counts Aleksei (1737-1808) and Fedor (1741-96) intended to visit England in 1768, they were obliged to change their plans by the outbreak of the new Russo-Turkish war. Aleksei as the Russian commander-in-chief was to earn fame and the extra handle to his name of Chesmenskii (passed to his illegitimate son who was later to study at Cambridge) and probably to conceive at that time his oft expressed love for the British, not least for the skill of the British officers which had helped ensure his victory. A sympathetic account of Aleksei and his brother soon appeared in the *Scots Mazazine*, written by "Dr Blay, his body physician, an Englishman,"[40] and many other details about the Orlovs filtered through to the highest levels of British society, as the youngest brother, Vladimir (1743-1831), discovered on speaking with George III on his visit to London in 1772.[41] Vladimir, the youngest of the brothers, the "academic," who had spent three years as a student at Leipzig, where he mixed with the likes of Haller and Gottsched, returned to Russia in 1766 to be appointed Director of the Academy of Sciences at the age of twenty-three. He accompanied Catherine on her trip down the Volga the following year, contributing chapter 15 to the joint aristocratic translation of Marmontel's *Vélisaire*. By 1771 his health had deteriorated and he decided on a tour of the spas of Europe. He was in England from early October, 1772, and 18 February 1773, spending two months of that time taking the waters at Bath but also visiting Windsor and Oxford, but more unusually Derby and Manchester. His travel diary is among the tersest of documents but his enthusiasm for English industrial achievements, for the beauty of the gardens, for the workings of parliament and his courteous reception in the highest society is very apparent.[42] Certainly, the highest society was well prepared to receive his brother less than three years later.

Grigorii Orlov arrived in London on 29 September 1775, but within days left for a tour, described in the *Daily Advertiser* as follows: "After seeing two

days' races at Newmarket, his Highness visited Wobourn-Abbey, Stowe, Blenheim, and Oxford; and, before he returns to town, he purposes seeing Bath,
Salisbury, Winchester, Portsmouth, Payne's hill, etc."[43] On 25 October he
was presented at Court, "dressed in scarlet, faced with black velvet, gold buttons, and buff waistcoat, the uniform of the Russian Artillery, of which he is
Grand Master, the first military post in that Empire; he had on the blue ribbon, the order of St. Andrew, his star, cross, and epaulet, were of most superb
brilliants; and the portrait of the Empress, which he wears as Her Majesty's
Adjutant General, is set round with brilliants."[44] The fame of his diamonds
spread quickly and led two evenings later to a celebrated incident. Among the
crowds milling around the prince as he left Covent Garden after seeing a performance of *The Merchant of Venice* was one George Barrington, later to be
hailed as "the prince of pickpockets" and transported to Botany Bay. Barrington managed to relieve the prince of a gold snuff-box, studded with diamonds
and valued, according to the conflicting reports, between £10,000 and £40,000;
the prince, however, realized his loss immediately and was able to grab hold
of Barrington, who was then arrested by two constables, but not before he
had managed to slip the snuff-box back in Orlov's waistcoat. Barrington duly
appeared before the famous magistrate, blind Sir John Fielding, but was released for lack of evidence and Orlov's unwillingness to prosecute.[45] The incident was eventually reported back to a delighted Catherine who commented
"Je savais bien qu'en Angleterre on rendrait justice au prince Orloff; son histoire avec le filoux au sortir de la comédie m'a beaucoup amusée."[46]

Undeterred, a "brilliant" Orlov continued his social round and is caught
once more for posterity by the pen of the incomparable Fanny Burney at a
musical evening in St Martin's Street arranged at the request of a family friend,
Dr John Glen King, formerly English Chaplain in St Petersburg, who wished
the prince to hear Fanny's brother Charles Rousseau and his wife Esther perform their celebrated duets. It was attended by "a most superb party of company," which included the Dean of Winchester, Emma, Lady Edgecumbe,
James "Hermes" Harris, scholarly father of the future British ambassador to
Russia, Mr Bruce Brudenell, his brother Lord Bruce, Charles Boone and Anthony Chamier, both Members of Parliament. The prince's entry was delayed
by his attendance first at dinner with Lord Buckingham and then at Lady Harrington's rout, but at last he arrived: "Enter His Highness Prince Orlof. This
prince is of a prodigious stature, something resembling Mr Bruce. He is handsome, tall, fat, upright, and *magnifique*. His dress was superb. . . . His air and
address were gracious and condescending; and he seemed to have a very agreeable share of drollery in his composition."[47] A duet by the Burneys and the
information that the performers were married allowed Orlov his *bon mot*—
"s'ils sont aussi d'accord en toutes autres choses qu'en la Musique, il faut qu'ils
soient bien heureux" and a Russian nobleman who accompanied him to add
"Dis is so pretty as ever I heard in my life." Lady Edgecumbe was introduced

to the prince and "entered into an absolute flirtation with him" and he was soon induced to remove the picture of the empress from around his neck for general inspection. "He was very facetious upon this occasion, and declared that, if they wished the *ladies* might *strip him entirely!*" The evening was a great success, and the prince and his diamonds were to be much in demand during his remaining weeks in London, giving Mrs Boscawen, another noted gossip, her chance to see him at the house of the Portuguese minister and find his height "*Patagonian*, his diamonds *Mogulian*, their quantity immense indeed."[48] Orlov sailed from Portsmouth on 12 December 1775 and arrived back in St. Petersburg in February. He was eventually to receive permission from Catherine to marry his beautiful young cousin Ekaterina Nikolaevna Zinov'eva, and enjoy a few happy years before her death in Lausanne in June, 1781, at the age of twenty-three brought him to madness.

Orlov's visit was the most spectacular of all those connected with the most eminent personalities of Catherine's court; certainly, when another of her discarded favourites visited England in 1787 English interest in him was minimal. Aleksei Petrovich Ermolov (1754-1834) was briefly in favour in 1785-86 and took the customary tour when he lost it. Semen Vorontsov found him "un fort bon homme, très-peu instruit, mais assez modeste," who caused him but one moment of acute embarrassment by his insistence on being presented at court. "Le roi, quelque temps après cette présentation, avait voulu plaisanter avec moi sur son compte; mais j'ai fait semblant de ne pas comprendre et j'ai pris un air si sérieux que je l'ai dégouté et l'ai forcé de changer de discours; mais je sais qu'avec d'autres, lui et sa chère epouse, qui est fort méchante, ils se sont moqués de monsieur Ermolow et de l'Impératrice. Le roi a surtout trouvé ridicule que dans deux ans, sans servir, on puisse devenir chez nous de sergent général-major."[49]

Further embarrassment for Vorontsov came later the same year with the arrival of Count Aleksei Grigor'evich Bobrinskoi (1762-1813), the son of Catherine and Orlov. The family coat-of-arms was to bear the motto "Bogu slava, zhizn' tebe" ("Glory to God, life to thee"), said to have been the words uttered by his mother at the moment of his birth, but Catherine's maternal feelings of gratitude on that occasion were subsequently to be sorely tried by her son's antics and actions. Bobrinskoi was educated at the Cadet Corps in Petersburg from 1774 until 1782, when he began the years of foreign travel which were to take him out of sight but not out of mind of the empress. They were years when he was allowed to indulge the worst sides of his character, when he contracted huge and lasting debts, and when he lacked the strict control which his youth and inexperience demanded. He travelled widely through Poland, Prussia, Austria, Italy and France and his diaries clearly reveal the sort of undisciplined existence to which he quickly became accustomed. A typical entry for 1 December 1783, when he was in Vienna, reads: "I went to play billiards and lost 120, which was quite a considerable sum, and before that I had lost 69. I played for about four hours. At dinner I asked my companions what they had seen of interest. Whereupon Bushuev began to say that the officer who had accompanied them was very displeased by my absence and that it was bad of me not to see things which people had been paid to show us and that if I had been in Russia, I would not have been so remiss. All this was said in a most unpleasant tone of voice."[50] Bobrinskoi, however, seems not to have left any record of his stay in London, and it is in the memoirs of a young officer who arrived as a diplomatic courier at about the same time that a further glimpse of his activities may be discovered. Count Evgraf Fedorovich Komarovskii (b. 1769) recalls how early one morning Bobrinskoi burst into his room and implored him to accompany him to Paris for a few days "because a certain acquaintance of his had left for there suddenly and he could not live without her."[51] Komarovskii was able to find a suitable excuse and Bobrinskoi left alone. A letter of Baron Grimm in Paris to Semen Vorontsov provides further details: "J'ai été informé qu'il a passé ici trois jours, il y a quelques semaines, chez une fille qui s'est donné le nom d'Elliot, qui l'avait suivi à Londres et qui en était revenue 24 heures avant lui. Il s'est tenu dans le plus grand incognito et est retourné à Londres à franc étrier. Suivant mes notions, il a dit à cette fille qu'il reviendrait et qu'il la menerait en Italie."[52] By that time, however, plans were afoot to inveigle Bobrinskoi back to Russia by encouraging his expressed wish of joining the Russian forces engaged with the Swedes. Vorontsov received money to pay off the most pressing of his debts and Bobrinskoi was sent back to Russia early in March, 1788. At Riga he was detained and then escorted to his estate of Bobriki near Revel, "there to live until his debts were paid."[53] There he was to remain until the end of Catherine's reign, but from his half-brother, the new Emperor Paul, he was to receive many favours, promotion to major-general, the title of count and some public responsibilities. He was by then married, to an Ungern-Sternberg, and soon sired a family whose descendants after the 1917 Revolution were to find themselves again in London and in permanent exile.[54]

IV

Although the visits of Princess Dashkova and Prince Orlov have been treated in some detail, it would be both tedious and repetitive to follow so closely the movements of other tourists, whose impact on English society was less spectacular and whose adventures less noteworthy. Nevertheless, there exists an interesting and considerable corpus of travel impressions, both published and archival, which on the one hand gives the lie to the suggestion made by the compilers of an anthology of foreigners' impressions of England that "most studies of England written in a foreign language have been translated at one time or another" and on the other, provides additional material for such a study as that of *Travellers in Eighteenth-Century England*, the author of which was unaware of any possible Russian contribution.[55] The most famous of Russian eighteenth-century accounts and the only one to be translated into English, soon after its appearance and again in recent years, is N. M. Karamzin's *Pis'ma russkogo puteshestvennika* ("Letters of a Russian Traveller"), which describes his visit to London in 1790. Princess Dashkova's journals, both published, in Russian, and unpublished, in French, have already been exploited, and mention has been made of both Count Vladimir Orlov's and Count Komarovskii's brief memoirs relating to 1772-73 and 1787-88 respectively. Additionally, among printed sources in either journal or book form there are, with an indication of the period to which they relate, Prince Aleksandr Borisovich Kurakin's *Souvenirs de voyage en Hollande et en Angleterre*, 1771-72, Nikita Akinfievich Demidov's *Zhurnal puteshestviia* ("Journal of a Journey"), 1772-73, Vasilii Nikolaevich Zinov'ev's letters, 1786-87, an anonymous "Rossiianin v Anglii" ("A Russian in England"), 1789-91, and Petr Ivanovich Makarov's letters bearing the same title, 1795. Finally, there are two anonymous diaries in Soviet archives, dating from 1758 and 1783.[56] It is from such accounts that a more general picture of Russian responses to aspects of English society, institutions and achievements may be drawn.

Many Russian visitors did not stray far from London, to Greenwich or to Richmond, or to Windsor at most, but for many others the route to the west proved the most popular, with Bath as its pivot: some went directly, others preferred to make a longer, circular route, which would take in Portsmouth and Southampton and Salisbury and on the return journey, Oxford. Others still were more adventurous and contrived to journey north, to Yorkshire and in some cases, to Scotland. Two of the most interesting tours, both described in some detail, are by Kurakin and Zinov'ev. Aleksandr Kurakin (1752-1818), a descendant of Peter's ambassador to England and one of the most famous members of his family in his own right, known later as "le prince superbe," was accompanied by two other young aristocrats who had studied with him at Leyden University, Count Nikolai Petrovich Sheremetev (1751-1809), and Prince Gavriil Petrovich Gagarin (1745-1808), and his tutor Karl-Heinrich Saldern. The trio of princes, advised by the Russian minister to discard their travelling names of Borisov, Meshcherinov and Penzin "dans un pays où les titres ne sont rien," headed first for Cambridge and then via Stamford and Grantham, through Nottinghamshire, to Leeds, "petite ville dans l'Yorckshire." From Leeds they went across to Manchester and then down to Buxton and Castleton. They then visited in succession Derby, Lichfield, Birmingham, Worcester, Gloucester, and reached Bristol, their furthest point west, before turning to Bath and returning eventually to London by the familiar route via Oxford. Zinov'ev (1755-1827), educated at Leipzig University, translator and author, related both to Semen Vorontsov and to Grigorii Orlov, with whom he had come to England in 1775,[57] returned in 1786 to spend six months in London before beginning one of the longest

of tours around Britain. He made first for Oxford and then proceeded to War-
wick and Birmingham; passing through Burton, where the ale comes from and
noting that "it is all shipped to us from Hull," he followed Kurakin's route in
reverse, Derby-Matlock-Leeds. Heading north, he stayed three days in York,
before crossing two days later into Scotland and making for Edinburgh. After
a week in the Scottish capital, enjoying the company of Robertson, Adam
Smith and Lord Monboddo, he went across to Glasgow and then down the
west coast to Manchester and Liverpool, continuing via Shrewsbury, Hereford
and Bristol to Bath. Journeys such as made by Kurakin and Zinov'ev were also
made by Prince Andrei Ivanovich Viazemskii (1754-1807), by the young
Counts Razumovskii and by the anonymous "Rossiianin," although only in
the last case does the account exist to flesh out the surviving itineraries.[58]

The various accounts provide *en somme* fascinating glimpses of a large
number of provincial towns where the tourist's eyes were as likely to be attracted by factories and machinery as by historical monuments and natural
beauties. This was obviously so of the rapidly growing but in many cases still
comparatively small northern industrial towns of Sheffield, Leeds, Newcastle,
Manchester, and Liverpool. Zinov'ev found Sheffield "much begrimed, like
the majority of its inhabitants, with soot and coal," and noted that it already
had "45,000 inhabitants, increased daily by people leaving nearby villages."
In Leeds he inspected coal mines and declared that coal was one of the main
reasons for England's wealth; later, in Manchester and visiting the mills, he
found another reason in the English ability to "use wheels instead of people
and thus become the manufacturer for the whole world."[59] Kurakin visited
the same towns, commenting on machines and factories, but was impressed
above all by the Bridgewater Canal, which "je conseille à tout étranger de ne
point quitter l'Angleterre sans l'aller voir."[60]

Even more than the cities, towns and villages, the country estates consistently attracted Russian visitors. After visiting in quick succession the Nottinghamshire great houses of Clumber Park, Thoresby, Welbeck, and Worksop, belonging to the Dukes of Newcastle, Kingston, Portland, and Norfolk respectively, Prince Kurakin commented:

Toutes ces campagnes sont magnifiques. Il est bon de savoir que c'est
dans leurs terres que les seigneurs anglais font le plus de dépenses. C'est
là qu'ils vivent conformément à leur rang et à leurs richesses et qu'ils
restent pendant huit mois de l'annee. . . . La chase et la promenade sont
leurs principaux amusements. Certains jours de la semaine, ils tiennent
table ouverte. Alors toute la noblesse des environs est la bienvenue chez
eux. Ils ne se contentent pas de vivre avec leur famille, ils aiment encore à
s'entourer d'un cercle d'amis choisis. En outre, ils ont toujours, en cas
de visites étrangères, un grand nombre de chambres toutes prêtes à rece-
voir les personnes qui pourraient venir à l'improviste. Ils regardent l'hos-
pitalité comme une grande vertu, et elle n'est nulle part plus en honneur

que chez eux. Ils l'exercent non-seulement à l'égard de leurs compatriotes, mais encore vis-à-vis des étrangers qui se rendent en foule chez eux, poussés par le double motif et de satisfaire leur curiosité et de connaître d'une manière approfondie les moeurs et les usages du pays, connaissance que les livres ne peuvent donner qu'imparfaitement et qui ne peut s'acquérir qu'en observant sur les lieux mêmes.[61]

Visiting great houses had become an established habit by the last decades of the century, and if the owners did not have the modern habit of charging, they already in some cases had set open-days and issued a limited number of passes for visitors. This was certainly the case at Wilton, where many Russians went on their way to Bath, and Horace Walpole instituted the same thing at Strawberry Hill. His visitors' book for 1784-96, prefaced by his instructions for obtaining tickets, has been published in the Yale edition of his correspondence and reveals the names of Countess Ekaterina Petrovna Shuvalova (July 1786), Count Semen Vorontsov (on three occasions in 1787-89), Prince Boris Vladimirovich Golitsyn (August 1789) and Grigorii Aleksandrovich Demidov with another Russian, probably Karamzin (August 1790).[62] Somewhat earlier, in May, 1776, we find Walpole noting testily: "I must seal my letter, and leave my blue room to be seen by Prince Yuzupoff [Nikolai Borisovich Iusupov (1750-1831)], who sent for a card of admission. We have a torrent of foreigners in England, and unfortunately they are all sent hither, but then they comprehend nothing, and are gone in half an hour."[63] The comments of similar owners of great houses are not known, but Russians descended on their homes, when they were in residence, or in their absence making do with conversation with the domestics or such as the gardener at Blenheim, a favourite haunt, who regaled them with the drinking powess of "le comte Ouronsou" and his memories of the Demidovs and the Orlovs.[64] The accounts contain descriptions of houses such as Burleigh, Wentworth, Harewood, Studely Park, Chatsworth, Kedleston and many others in the Midlands and the North, and almost every one that fell on the various routes to and from Bath.

If the magnificence of one house after another, of its furniture and paintings made its impact, the beauty of the estates proved overwhelming. The enthusiasm of Catherine for "le jardin anglais," the visit of her architect and gardener from Tsarskoe Selo, Neelov, have already been noted, but many of the Russian nobility had the opportunity to see for themselves what variety and beauty had been achieved on countless English estates and many had the means and the wish to imitate what they saw after their return to Russia. Dashkova was far from an isolated example: Vladimir Orlov, who noted in his diary: "in their design the attempt is made to imitate nature and conceal the work that is necessary and frequently greater than in regular gardens; in these gardens everything is spread around—here a wood, here, a shrubbery, here, flowers, here, a pond," spent much time and effort after his withdrawal from public life on his own English garden at Otrada;[65] Pavel Grigor'evich Demidov

(1738-1821), scholar and collector, "who had been long enough in England to speak and write the language, has adorned his country seat at Sivorik [near Petersburg] with four extensive contiguous gardens, in as many varieties of the English stile, to suit the size, ornaments, furniture, and water of four houses placed at proper distances; where he entertains his friends in a stile correspondent to the comparative magnificence or simplicity of the seat and gardens, table service, and everything else in character, from silver down to white stone ware";[66] as early as 1764 Ivan Shuvalov was writing to Count M. L. Vorontsov: "The gardens are beautiful, in a taste completely distinct from all others. When I return, I will give you an idea of how you can lay one out at Kimora [an estate on the Volga in Tver' province]: the whole art is in being close to nature. I think that this is the best way."[67] Prince Ivan Tufiakin came to England in 1771, with money provided by the empress "pour se perfectionner dans l'architecture et dans la distribution des jardins,"[68] but where and if he put his knowledge of the English garden to good effect in Russia is not known, or whether he managed to visit Claremont, Pains Hill, Wilton, Leasowes, Stowe, Hagley, Blenheim and the numerous other great gardens where fellow-countrymen were to be found. Not all the Russians agreed on which gardens were the most successful: Blenheim brought universal praise and Zinov'ev was moved to say: "I have rarely seen anything which pleased me more; the garden is for me even better than the house, and so fine that, despite my propensity to criticize, I can only praise it";[69] Stowe, "ce superbe parc," was justly praised, but Lord Lyttleton's Hagley showed "little art," according to Vladimir Orlov, but "fixed the attention" of Kurakin, who found it different from other gardens he had seen by its sanded walks, its cascades and cottages.[70] Kurakin saw perhaps more great houses and gardens than any other visitor, and the effect of the Nottinghamshire parks moved him to pen "quelques réflexions sur le goût des Anglais quant au jardinage," which include the following: "Tout est bizarre et conforme au goût étrange qu'ils ont adopté. Ce ne sont partout que de vastes prairies où se trouvent parsemés des collines, des bosquets, des parterres de fleurs, des champs, des groupes d'arbres, des arbres isolés ou, quelquefois, des monuments en pierre d'une architecture antique. Lorsque l'on parcourt ces promenades, on est frappé sans contredit de la nouveauté du spectacle. A chaque pas, la scène varie. Tout est contraste."[71] On the whole, Kurakin's admiration is somewhat begrudging; his later diaries from France reveal that he is more at ease with the regular garden, as he is with the more decorous French theatre. Not so the young ardently Anglophile visitor of 1783: "Voyez ce que peut l'homme, dont la génie libre ne connaît pas les entaves du despotisme et de la tyrannie! Il embellit de mille facons la nature, quelquefois même ingrate, et jouit ainsi de son existence."[72]

The Russian tourists have so far been followed on their excursions outside London, but it was first and foremost the English capital which had beckoned them and where they spent most, and in many cases, all of their time. What they saw is essentially what is still *de rigueur* for the visitor from the provinces or from abroad: the royal palaces and parks, Parliament, Westminster Abbey, St Paul's, the Tower, the British Museum, but in addition eighteenth-century London offered a whole series of attractions which are no more: the Vauxhall Gardens, improved and re-opened in 1752, receiving its first recorded Russian visitors in 1758 and described by Karamzin in 1790 as "a beautiful evening resort, worthy of an intelligent and rich people"; its rival Ranelagh, "where fashionable London society gathers on summer evenings to listen to music and to stroll about";[73] more dubiously, Bedlam, with a whole range of unfortunates to be inspected by permission of the obliging custodians, or Newgate, and the chance of a hanging at nearby Tyburn.[74] There was much to enthuse about in the city: several travellers commented on the street lights which seemed to illuminate the whole city, others, on the well-constructed pavements and streets, and one noted "une chose qui me plaît beaucoup est que les noms des rues et des places sont marquées à chaque maison qui fait coin et comme toutes les maisons sont numerotées, il n'y a rien de plus aisé que de trouver quelqu'un."[75] The shops were well-stocked, everything gave an impression of tidiness, order and well-being. "L'utilité, la solidité et la beauté sont les trois points auxquels les artistes de ce pays s'attachent. Je les ai vu réunis dans le magazin d'un meunisier."[76] It was difficult not to be overwhelmed by favourable impressions. Makarov conceded that "Travel dispels prejudices. A Russian who has never left his country is sure that Petersburg is the most beautiful city in the world. I also thought this, but London has made me change my mind."[77] Karamzin, after enumerating the various attractive features, opined that "all this forms an indescribably pleasing picture, and you keep repeating a hundred times, 'London is beautiful'," and another Russian conceded that "j'ai vu presque toutes les villes de L'Europe, mais London seule m'a étonné."[78]

There were, of course, aspects not so much of the appearance of the city—although the comment on the overhanging fog was almost universal—as of the life that was lived within it which brought murmurs of disapproval, and, for one notable phenomenon, attracted glances of scandalized fascination. Beggars there were in droves, and thieves and robbers operated seemingly at will in the city and in the countryside—Komarovskii was indeed robbed by a highwayman on his way to London and seems glad to have had the experience![79] But it was the "priestesses of Venus," in Makarov's coy term, whose activities exercised the descriptive powers of the Russian diarists. Makarov indeed devoted no less than eight of the fifty pages of his London diary to would-be poetic eulogies of the physical beauty of London prostitutes, especially of what he called "the particular class" which frequented the London theatres, to his own encounter with a young seventeen-year-old beauty in St James's Park, and to comparative costs of the London brothels. The experiences of the anonymous visitor of 1783 began already in Rochester, where only with

difficulty could he prevent himself from weakening before the charms of another seventeen-year-old; in London, he too discovered that "le théâtre est le
champ de bataille des filles du monde," and more than once returned to the
subject in his diary. A later tourist was more censorious, noting the high incidence of venereal disease.[80]

The fascination with the prostitute was, however, merely an element in a
unanimous accolade for the beauty of Englishwomen who seemed to offer
such a contrast with women on the Continent by their fresh and clear com-
plexions, their natural elegance, and additionally by their conduct both in society and within the family, by their intelligence and willingness to discuss
books and politics, and not least by their fidelity to their native tongue. Kurakin, whose *voyage à Cythère* began on the ferry boat, quickly confessed his
devotion to "le beau sexe":

> Ma naïveté ne me permet pas de se taire. J'épanche volontiers mon coeur
> sur un sujet dont il est trop pénétré. Les femmes y ont, sans contredit,
> toutes les qualités qui constituent la beauté. Leur teint ressemble à de
> l'albâtre, leurs joues vermeilles et leurs lèvres de corail appellent le baiser.
> Ajoutez-y beaucoup d'entrain dans le caractère, de la gaieté dans la
> conversation et un grand penchant au plaisir. Peu d'entre elles parlent le
> français et même lorsqu'elles le comprennent, elles effectent de s'en
> tenir à l'idiome de leurs pays.[81]

Englishmen inspired somewhat different reactions. They were to be respected for their honesty and reliability, but they tended to be unsociable towards
foreigners. "Not to be born an Englishman and to be an honest man seems to
them an incomprehensible contradiction. Thinking in this fashion, they receive
a foreigner coldly, with a look of contempt, with an obvious desire to avoid
getting to know him." Makarov conceded, nevertheless, that once a friend, an
Englishman proved a good friend. Others found them taciturn, thoughtful,
gloomy, and their tendencies towards melancholy, suicide and madness very
apparent. Kurakin, however, saw "franchise" and "humanité" basic to the
English character, and added, "l'Anglais est loin d'être aussi brutal qu'on le
dépeint ordinairement," but "ses passions sont violentes, et la raison a rare-
ment de l'empire sur elles."[82]

Such cautionary notes did not stop Kurakin and others from forming an
overwhelmingly positive impression of England. In a letter written in March,
1772, Kurakin summed up:

> Nous sommes déjà sur notre départ. Je dois avouer que c'est pas sans re-
> gret que je quitte Londres. On nous y comblait de politesse, et nous vi-
> vions très contents, après nous être un peu accoutumés aux moeurs et à
> la facon de vivre de la nation. J'aurais toujours regretté de n'avoir pas
> vu l'Angleterre de mes propres yeux. On débite sur ce beau pays tant de

contes, qu'il est presque impossible de ne pas s'en laisser séduire; mais à
présent je sais du moins à quoi m'en tenir, et je puis apprécier plus au
juste le prix de tout ce que je serais dans le cas d'en entendre dire. De
tous les peuples qui habitent sur notre globe, les Anglais sont à ce que
je crois les plus heureux et les plus à envier. Non soumis à la volonte ar-
bitraire ou plutôt au caprice d'un seul, ils n'obéissent qu'à des lois dictés
par la sagesse même, et que forme la seule uniformité. Leur vie ne peut
devenir la victime des passions vicieuses d'un troisième: leurs biens sont
à l'abri de toute violence. Leurs actions sont spontanées et absolument
libres d'une gêne odieuse. Ils n'ont rien à craindre ni de la disgrace du
souverain, ni de la haine des ministres et des courtisans: leur excellente
Constitution est l'égide redoutable qui les garantit de toute injustice.
Ils n'ont enfin qu'à jouir de leur existence, chacun selon son bon plaisir
et sa fantaisie; mais la plupart n'en jouissent pourtant qu'en gens sensés
qui connaissent et le but de celui qui les a crées, et jusqu'où s'étend la
chaîne de leurs devoirs envers eux-mêmes et envers les autres. Je suis si
pénétré de cette situation que, si je n'étais attaché à ma patrie par des
liens aussi indissolubles, et ayant à choisir en même temps le pays auquel je devrais consacrer et ma vie et mes travaux, l'Angleterre serait
sans aucun doute celui que je choisirais par affection autant que par
conviction.[83]

It is a reaction which it is difficult to match as a sustained statement but not
as an expression of enthusiasm. One after another, diarists speak of the Eng-
ligh as the nation they love above all others, stressing particularly the public
spirit and institutions as well as "la liberté civile." For several, "c'est sa constitution qui determine son caractère, et c'est celui ce qui le porte à une bien-
veillance universelle, propre à rassurer tous les espirits."[84]

It is easy to suggest that favourable impressions notwithstanding, it was for
the majority of tourists a case of "out of sight, out of mind," once they had
returned to Russia; it is equally easy to point to elegant carriages, leather
goods, English-style clothes as the evidence of the superficial nature of the
impact of England on the privileged classes. It is much more difficult to trace
ways in which experiences of life and society in England affected and changed
people's attitudes and actions. Nevertheless for the diarists at least it is clear
that the recognition of English achievements in cultural, political and social
life did not give rise to feelings of frustration and discontent; on the contrary,
they seemed encouraged to voice high-minded thoughts about the improvements and advances possible in a Russia ruled by a well-intentioned empress.
"The beautiful beginnings of Alexander's days," when esteem for England
could be seen in its most influential manifestations, were both a climax and a
renewal of ideals nourished in the 1770s and 1780s.

CHAPTER 10
A LOVE AFFAIR WITH ENGLAND: N. M. KARAMZIN

Across the pages of this book have flitted innumerable Russians united by the accident of their having visited Great Britain in some capacity in the course of the eighteenth century. In some cases their names are well enough known to anyone with a sound knowledge of eighteenth-century Russian history; in other cases they are recognized perhaps only by specialists in certain areas and disciplines (e.g., diplomacy, technology, literature); others still are as obscure as a mere mention in a previously unpublished letter or diary can make them. In the vast majority of cases the English "episode" in their lives has not called for particular attention, but with the otherwise well-documented life, the significance of the episode can perhaps be appreciated, whereas at times the episode is all and gains its meaning only as a piece in a general jig-saw or in the context of a general trend or development. To have the evidence to trace throughout an individual's life its English element is indeed a rarity. It therefore seemed fitting to offer as a concluding chapter a detailed study of a man whose long career as an author and journalist allowed him to record his attitudes to many aspects of English life and culture and whose literary eminence has led scholars to preserve and assess all manner of information about his life and activities.

Nikolai Mikhailovich Karamzin (1766-1826), prose artist, poet, translator, editor of two important literary journals and, finally, eminent historian, came from modest gentry stock in the Simbirsk region by the Volga. At the age of eleven and already with some knowledge of French and German, he was sent to a Moscow boarding school run by one of the Moscow University professors, the German J. M. Schaden, whose influence on his moral, religious and literary development was to be considerable. It is with Schaden's school that Karamzin associated his first interest in England, which apparently found expression in his organizing feasts for his schoolfriends to celebrate victories by the British admirals during the American War of Independence.[1] More importantly, he began to learn English and possibly to gain his first impressions of English literature, which was to vie for precedence with German and French in his reading in the eight years between his leaving Schaden's school and his departure on his extensive European travels in May, 1789.

It was in 1783, during a brief period of service in a guards regiment in St. Petersburg, that Karamzin made his literary début as a translator from German. It was, however, in connection with an unpublished piece from the previous year that there is the first mention of an English literary work known to

Karamzin: he received as payment for his translation a copy of the Russian version of Fielding's *Tom Jones*.[2] After his retirement and return to Simbirsk on the death of his father, Karamzin began to read widely if "without discrimination,"[3] combining an enthusiasm for such lesser works of Voltaire as "Le Taureau blanc" with an absorption in Edward Young's *The Complaint, or Night Thoughts on Life, Death and Immortality* and a passion for Shakespeare. A friend commented in 1785 that all the Moscow presses would soon be "engaged on the printing of the *Russian Shakespeare*," and asked in ironic wonder: "What is there missing on the subject of literature? Everything is there! You write about translations, about your own works, about Shakespeare, about Voltaire's unjust criticism [of Shakespeare], as well as about coffee and tobacco."[4]

Karamzin's life began to show more shape and purpose with his move to Moscow in July, 1785, to join the Friendly Learned Society (*Druzheskoe uchenoe obshchestvo*), formed in 1781 to promote the translating and publishing enterprises of the Moscow Freemasons, headed by the famous publisher N. I. Novikov. Karamzin had joined a masonic Lodge in Simbirsk and in Moscow he was soon to be transformed into "a pious student of wisdom, with a burning eagerness for self-perfection."[5] He found himself in a company of fine, enquiring, and frequently tormented minds, who looked for spiritual nourishment to German and English authors rather than to the French, seeing in the former "true philosophers" who emphasized the primacy of the heart over the reason and in the latter merely cynical, rationalist *philosophes*. For the Moscow Masons England was an outstanding example of national enlightenment, a country where the inhabitants, irrespective of class or wealth, enjoyed the fruits of true philosophy and literature and lived in peace. The English were enlightened because they knew how to live in harmony with themselves. Self-knowledge, basic to all masonic teaching, was above all knowledge of the workings of the human heart which led to delight in God's world and compassion for one's fellow men. In literature this aim, they believed, was nobly served by such English writers as Shakespeare and Milton, Pope and Young, Thomson and Sterne. Among Karamzin's closest friends among the Masons were A. M. Kutuzov, who published his translation of Young's *Night Thoughts* in 1785, and I. P. Turgenev, translator of John Mason's *On Self-Knowledge* (1783), and Karamzin was soon to make his own considerable contribution to the fund of translated English literature.

In 1787 a significant milestone in Russia's slow journey to awareness of Shakespeare was reached with the publication of Karamzin's version of *Julius Caesar*: it was in prose, but literal and from the English original, and preceded by an introduction in which Shakespeare's genius as a playwright but above all as an interpreter of the passions and observer of the human heart was extolled: "Few writers penetrated so deeply into human nature as did Shakespeare; few knew so well the most secret springs within a man, his innermost impulses, the difference of each passion, each temperament and each form of life as did this astonishing Artist."[6] Karamzin ranked Milton, Young and Thomson among the few poets who manifested to advantage Shakespeare's influence, and these three names, along with those of Shakespeare and the Scottish bard Ossian, appear in his early poetic manifesto "Poeziia" ("Poetry," composed in 1787, published in 1792) under the banner "Britannia is the mother of the greatest poets."[7] James Thomson's *The Seasons* was held in particular esteem by the young Karamzin, who produced a prose version of the poem in that same productive year of 1787 as well as, a little later, verse translations of the concluding "Hymn" and inset tale "Lavinia." These were all published in *Detskoe chtenie dlia serdtsa i razuma* ("Children's Reading for the Heart and Mind"), a journal issued as a free supplement to Novikov's *Moskovskie vedomosti* ("Moscow News") and of which Karamzin had become joint editor in 1787. Both in his translated and original work for the journal Karamzin gave clear notice of his fascination with England but perhaps nowhere more so than in his tale "Pustynnik" ("The Recluse," 1788).[8]

The hero of the story, the "recluse," is a German living in Switzerland who relates the story of his life to a young English traveller by the name of Davis. At every stage the story reflects the youthful Karamzin's dreams and emotions and in particular his vision of England and the English, nourished completely by his reading. The crucial part of the story, the sad love affair of the young German with a young English noblewomen, who dies two years after their marriage in childbirth, is set in England, where the German, accompanied by his mentor, Professor L* from Leipzig University, arrives in the course of his European travels. His response to England coincides with all we know of Karamzin's own enthusiasm: "From my childhood I have loved England. . . . Here is a land which industry has brought to the highest degree of political perfection! What abundance there is here! What contented calm is depicted on the face of every peasant, assured of sufficient food!" The professor echoes him, describing England as: "one of the most perfect political societies. It owes its prosperity to the wisdom of its lawgivers, who knowing the nature of man, have been able to instil in the hearts of their fellow-citizens a desire for work, guaranteeing generous rewards. The spirit of industry, the spirit of competition has enriched England with many great discoveries, for which the whole of mankind is indebted with its gratitude. Here commerce flourishes; but its flower would soon fade if the spirit of national industry ceased to give it life."[9] Two years after publishing his tale, Karamzin himself arrived at Dover and exclaimed, according to the account which appeared in 1794: "I am in England, that land which in my childhood I loved with such passion and which for the character of its inhabitants and the degree of national enlightenment is certainly one of the first states in Europe."[10] In another passage, published somewhat later, he again recalled his childish expectations: "There was a time when having met almost no Englishmen, I was enraptured by them and imagined England to be the country most attractive to my heart. . . . It seemed to me that to be brave was to be English, magnanimous also, sensitive also, a real man also. Novels, if I'm not mistaken, were the main source for such an opinion."[11] The reading of English novels, of Fielding and Richardson, certainly inspired him in the delineation of the characters in "The Recluse": the family of Lord R*—his wife, Lady R*, their son, Sir Charles, and their daughter Sophie, embody, however weakly, the virtues and, in the case of Lord R*, the idiosyncracies he associated with the English.

Karamzin's love of English literature and England was at a peak during his four years with the Moscow Masons. He was anxious now only to travel through Europe, to meet the famous scholars and writers whose works he knew so well and to see the noted cities and beauty spots of which he had read. Travel had become, in his own words, "a necessity of the soul."[12] He set out in May 1789, travelling through Germany, Switzerland and France, and arrived in England in early June 1790. The record of his travels was to be published as *Pis'ma russkogo puteshestvennika* ("Letters of a Russian Traveller"), one of the first Russian works in prose of any distinction, but one to be used with some caution in the present context. The complete text of "Letters" was published only in 1801; in the preceding decade the sections dealing with Germany and Switzerland had been published in full, but by no means all of the French section; of his adventures in England there had appeared in 1794 a mere ten pages describing his arrival at Dover and journey to London. There is little doubt that the English letters, if they had ever been written in their entirety in the early 1790s, were considerably amended and added to before their publication. They differ sharply in character from those written about Germany or Switzerland or indeed about France. The latter have a freshness and immediacy singularly lacking in most of the English letters, which frequently take the form of essays on aspects of English life, institutions and literature. Nevertheless, many of the views and ideas expressed in the English letters represent the Karamzin of 1789-90, and can be verified by reference to other works published by him in the early 1790s, particularly his influential journal *Moskovskii zhurnal* ("Moscow Journal," 1791-92).

Unlike the letters and diaries used to illuminate the activities of other Russians in Great Britain, Karamzin's "letters" were consciously prepared for publication in imitation or emulation of the travelogue of such as Laurence Sterne or C. P. Moritz.[13] Although he presents them as real letters, his "Letters" were independent of the few extant letters which he sent to friends during his travels. Indeed only one such letter survives from the English period, which indicates that Karamzin arrived in England at the very beginning of June, 1790, and not in the middle of July as he would have us believe from his published work. From another source it is known that he arrived back in Russia in August and not in September, as indicated in "Letters."[14] Whatever the reasons were for the "careless" dating in the published work, Karamzin was however, in England for a period of a little over two months in the summer of 1790, and on the basis of that stay he presented the Russian reading public with the sort of personal and informed comment on England–and Europe in general– which it had hitherto so conspicuously lacked. Karamzin himself noted in 1797: "Cet ouvrage doit en partie son succès à la nouveauté du sujet pour les lecteurs russes. Depuis assez longtems nos compatriotes voyagent dans les pays étrangers; mais aucun d'eux, jusqu'à présent, ne s'est avisé de la faire sa plume à la main. L'auteur de ces lettres a eu le premier cette idée, et il a parfaitement réussi à intéresser le public."[15] In its turn, "Letters" became the first Russian prose work to be widely known abroad. The British press first carried notices of the German translation from which the English version was duly made and published in 1803 to a mixed critical reception. It earned a virulent dismissal from Henry Brougham in the *Edinburgh Review*, but other journals, such as the *Anti-Jacobin* and the *Monthly Review* sprang to Karamzin's defence, if at times for reasons rather more political than literary.[16] Karamzin's comments on England, however, were generally seen as immature and superficial, when not simply "erroneous"; they were attributable to his youth and his association only with members of the Russian Embassy.

The reviewer of the *Annual Register* felt that Karamzin seemed "least to have naturalised himself in our country" and Brougham found him "apparently so much exhausted with his previous delights, that he can scarcely enjoy himself at all."[17] They were both reacting to Karamzin's expressions of disappointment and disillusionment when reality, as he perceived it at least, fell far short of his keen expectations. He had been completely enchanted by France and the French and had left Paris with reluctance. Sailing from London, he admits that "I would come to England again with pleasure, but I leave it without regret." As for Englishmen, "Now I have seen Englishmen at close quarters, I do justice to them, I praise them–but my praise is as cold as they are themselves."[18] Englishwomen are a different matter: "the women are all enchanting and divine: their form, their faces, their dress, their movements, are all true copies from the Graces; and they are all, he tells us, without either 'powder or *paint*'," but as the reviewer cynically goes on to point out, "under this last impression he must indeed have given our fair countrywomen credit for the most exquisite natural rouge that nature ever bestowed on the female race. We may safely conclude, however, that the dye is not yet so thickly laid on but it may deceive a foreigner."[19] It was not so much deceiving foreigners as despising them which Karamzin found characteristic of the English: foreigners were seen as "some sort of imperfect, pitiful people. 'Don't touch him', they say in the street, 'he's a foreigner–which means 'He's a poor man or an infant'." As Yorick himself opined, "they order this matter better in France," and it is no surprise to find Karamzin reflecting that "I wish to live and die in my dear homeland; but after Russia there is no country more attractive to me than France, where a foreigner frequently forgets that he is not among his own people."[20] In London Karamzin mainly consorted with his own, with members of the embassy—and hidden under initials in "Letters" are the Rev. Smirnov, his brother Ivan, V. F. Malinovskii, Ambassador Vorontsov—, and with other Russians on the Grand Tour, such as Pavel Demidov with whom he visited Strawberry Hill and sampled the delights of Ranelagh and Vauxhall. He lived in London as a tourist, saw the sights in and around London (venturing no further than Windsor), observed as closely and as widely as he could in a brief visit and wrote afterwards about his experiences as honestly as his literary sensibilities, his changing views and Russian conditions allowed. "Letters" can best be appreciated as part and parcel of an ongoing statement about England from the 1790s into the nineteenth century.

Within a few months of his return to Russia Karamzin began publication of his monthly "Moscow Journal," of which his letters from Germany and Switzerland but not of England were an integral part. Nevertheless English literature and culture occupied a prominent place in its pages. Indeed, a quotation in English of a line by Pope, "Pleasures are ever in our hands or eyes," served as the epigraph to the first part of the journal. Karamzin's liking for Pope was a reflection of his preference for moral philosophy, conveyed attractively in poetic form. During his stay in England Karamzin had dutifully visited Pope's house at Twickenham and picked a sprig from the willow tree by which the poet used to sit. He also visited Windsor and was guided in his enthusiastic response by appropriate readings from the poet's "Windsor-Forest."

Pope, whose "Universal Prayer" Karamzin had incidentally translated before his travels, belonged to the great and glorious past of English literature which Karamzin revered. No less a disappointment than real Englishmen was the contemporary English literary scene: "Modern English literature does not merit the slightest attention: here they are writing now only the most mediocre novels, and there is not a single good poet. Young, the threat to the happy and the comfort to the unfortunate, and Sterne, the original painter of sensibility, closed the phalanx of immortal British authors."[21] These lines conclude an inset essay in "Letters" in which he had extolled Thomson as the father of "descriptive poetry," singled out Milton's description of Paradise and Dryden's "Ode to Music" as the summits of English poetic achievement and paid homage to Shakespeare as England's *only* dramatic poet, believing that his successors merely exhibited his bombast without his genius. Finding nothing of merit in English comedy—and, as he reveals elsewhere, having no understanding of English humour, he saw England's great literary achievement in the eighteenth century in its array of novelists and historians.

Pre-eminent among the novelists for Karamzin, as is evident everywhere in his other writings, were Fielding, Richardson and Sterne. In the "Moscow Journal" Karamzin reviewed a Russian translation of Richardson's *Clarissa*, noting that the novelist was "a skilful painter of the moral nature of man" and that his works contained "the best philosophy of life, presented in the most attractive way."[22] Karamzin was particularly enthusiastic about Richardson's ability to fill eight volumes with descriptions of everyday life and masterful delineation of character. It was precisely to the Englishman's ability to make the everyday interesting that Karamzin referred in his preface to the 1797 edition of "Letters," where he defended himself against criticism of his own work: "Much is unimportant, trivial—I agree; but if we read without boredom in Richardson's and Fielding's novels that, for instance, Grandison drinks tea twice a day with dear Miss Byron, that Tom Jones slept exactly seven hours in some village inn, then why not forgive the Traveller some trifling details?"[23] In his letters from London Karamzin suggested that the two English novelists taught the French and the Germans how to write novels that were "like a history of life" and reports a conversation with a servant girl at his lodgings on Oxford Street who knew her novels and vastly preferred Lovelace to Grandison, to the Russian's alleged bewilderment.[24] However much Karamzin enjoyed the work of Richardson and Fielding it was to the playful and sentimental Sterne that he gave the palm and the compliment of imitation. Karamzin's debt to Sterne was noted by contemporary English reviewers of "Letters," where the Russian was guided to the "correct" response to touching scenes and situation. In some of his original stories, Karamzin also attempted to imitate Sterne's narrative manner and exploitation of form. In the 'Moscow Journal' Karamzin published translations from both *Sentimental Journey* and *Tristram Shandy*, together with a veritable paean to "Incomparable Sterne": "In what learned university were you taught to feel so tenderly? What rhetoric revealed to you the secret of touching with two words the most delicate fibres of our hearts? What musician commands the sounds of his strings as skilfully as you command our feelings?"[25]

If Sterne (d. 1768) was the last of the great novelists and Young (d. 1765) was the last of the great poets, Karamzin in the early 1790s was still prepared to detect signs of a revival. He might still with approval publish in May 1791 an item from an English source deploring the low level of contemporary poetry, but the following year he reviewed the *Dramatik Sketches of the Ancient Northern Mithology* by the little known Norwich poet Frank Sayers and *Anna St Ives*, a new novel by Thomas Holcroft. "It is long since the British Muse produced anything worthy of note. It seemed that with Shakespeare, Milton, Pope, Gay and others, long since dead, all the poetic fire of Albion had been exhausted. People wrote and wrote in a pure style—but nowhere was there spirit of life." But Sayers is the new hope: "In his work we see a rich imagination, natural simplicity, Ossianic painting and the flowers of Greece."[26] As for Holcroft, here was a novelist excelling Richardson, for he avoided his "coldness." Holcroft "writes as though inspired, like a poet" and engages the reader's attention by completely credible adventures and by characters worthy of Shakespeare. "Thus English literature again rises. Sayers and Holcroft have appeared on the scene, and the public crowns them with laurels."[27] Within a few years Karamzin was to regret his enthusiasm and the review of Holcroft which had begun with the words "a rare novel" (*roman, kakikh malo*) was replaced in the second edition of the journal in 1803 by the cryptic dismissal "a weak, run-of-the-mill novel" (*roman, kakikh mnogo*).[28] The bleak picture was thus re-established, in accord with the essay in "Letters" and the verdict in his new journal, *Vestnik Evropy* ("Messenger of Europe," 1802): "Englishmen can now only boast of the number and not of the gifts of their writers; they have not even a single second-class author."[29]

One of the distinctive features of the "Moscow Journal" had been its "miscellany" section. His mixture of literary anecdotes, sad and amusing stories, and news items of cultural and scientific interest, written in his engaging and elegant style, produced a favourable response from the reading public, and in 1795 the publishers of the "Moscow News" persuaded him to contribute a regular column in a similar vein. In his introductory note, Karamzin states that apart from notices of new English and German publications he would provide "characteristic features from the London News."[30] Over the years, in the "Moscow Journal," "Moscow News," and later in "Messenger of Europe," Karamzin published anecdotes about Dr. Johnson, Oliver Goldsmith, Shakespeare, Pope, Milton, Swift, Bacon and other English writers; he described such things as the witches' ducking-stool at Kingston-on-Thames and wrote of the longevity of various Englishmen, including one who married Oliver Cromwell's daughter and lived to the age of 139. Karamzin was always fascinated with the English character and with the amazing eccentrics who seemingly abounded in our island. In his review of Richardson's *Clarissa* he suggested that the abundance of good English novels was attributable to the fact that "they [the English] have more originality in their customs, more interesting characters."[31] He wrote a whole essay in "Letters" on the "numerous English singularities, which would be called madness in any other place, but here are called merely *whim*" and are a product of the notorious English spleen. After providing various examples, he asserted that "Englishmen, in a moral sense, grow like wild oaks at the will of fate, and although they are all of one species, they are all different: and it was left to Fielding not to invent characters for his novels but merely to note and describe them."[32] In the opening letters of England published in 1794, he immediately presented his theories on English spleen and solemnly attributed it to the roast beef that thickened the blood and made the English melancholic, phlegmatic and suicidal, conditions not improved by constant mist from the sea and thick coal smoke. Within a page he was relating the story of an English lord who shot himself shortly after his marriage. The "Moscow Journal" had presented pen-pictures of arrogant and eccentric Englishmen abroad in the letters from Germany and France, and anecdotes elsewhere in the same journal offered Karamzin's readers an English miser, a collector of suppressed books, a misguided joker, and the writer Butler, starving to death through a misplaced sense of pride. In "Messenger of Europe" there were to follow stories about a young Englishman who shot himself because he was so happy, and a whole cluster of anecdotes showing the English at their strangest. Particularly revealing is the note on English character that was to find peculiar development in European literature of the following decades: "The crowd was obscenely delighted by the execution of the unfortunate man—and not only the mob, because curious people paid up to twenty guineas for a place in those houses from which the gallows were visible!"[33] The companion piece to this is Karamzin's physiognomical observations: "I also looked at Englishmen, whose faces can be divided into three types—the morose, the good-natured and the bestial. I swear to you that nowhere have I chanced to see so many of the last type as here. I am sure that Hogarth painted from nature."[34]

The "Messenger of Europe," Karamzin's last journal, in general reveals new emphases and pre-occupations in his attitude towards England. Karamzin's lack of sympathy for the English character, which dates from the time of his travels, did not prevent him from appreciating the achievements of English "enlightenment." Throughout the 1790s Karamzin had been a constant apologist of the value of the arts and sciences, of progress in all peaceful forms of human endeavour. Among the names of European writers, philosophers and scientists that abound in his essays and even his fiction and poetry, those of Bacon, Locke, Hobbes and Newton appear frequently. In his passionate refutation (1793) of Rousseau's attack on the sciences, he massed examples of European "Enlighteners" to support his creed that "enlightenment is the palladium of good manners."[35] Enlightenment implied the ability of a people to live in harmony and enjoy the fruits of true philosophy, scientific advancement, general literacy, to be free from fear and oppression, confident in the rule of law and justice and never chasing the chimera of equality. Karamzin was thus at some pains to separate social institutions from political forms, believing that the former could be brought to perfection without tampering with the time-hallowed system of government. "Not the constitution, but the enlightenment of the English is their true palladium," Karamzin asserted,[36] and although one might have thought the constitution to be a fruit of English enlightenment, he endeavoured to show how politicians were able to play with the constitutional forms and dupe the electorate. It was in the respect for family life that Karamzin preferred to locate true enlightenment, although there were many things which earned his praise and led him to exclaim: "There is much that is good in England; and best of all are the social institutions which show the virtuous wisdom of the government. *Salus publica* is truly its device. Englishmen should love their country."[37] Similarly, Russians living under the beneficient reign of Alexander I should love their own country for its own new and wise institutions. Karamzin was continually looking for constructive analogies between

Russian and European experience, conducting a political and social assessment in which features worthy of Russian imitation or indeed rejection were emphasized. His journal signalled an absorbing stage in the development of Russian national self-consciousness. In another essay he commented that the English were famed for their patriotism because of their almost total concern only with themselves—an insight which had led him from his earlier cospomolitanism to proud patriotism. The attitude of the English to their native language, their unwillingness to speak any other, was also naturally a challenge to Russians to be as proud of their own. The pages of the "Messenger of Europe" provided a mine of information on English life: he published accounts of institutions and acts of public service and courage, and almost all were matched in subsequent issues by articles or "letters to the editor" containing tales of virtuous peasants, intellectually-minded gentry, military valour, philanthropic actions and agricultural expertise in Russia.

The "Messenger of Europe" was divided into two main sections, "Literature and Miscellany" and "Politics," and despite Karamzin's expressed hope that the latter would "not be very rich or interesting for the sake of Europe,"[38] it was. Karamzin spoke as a Russian confident of the important role his country had to play in the destiny of Europe. His concern for peace and established order in Europe lent pathos to his political commentary on affairs in England and France; it enabled him to criticize arbitrary actions on both sides and formed the link between his admiration for Napoleon as a great man, set on restoring order to France, and his love of England for its enlightenment. In one of his "News and Comment" articles he summed this up as "in the one we are curious to know national affairs and in the other, the actions of Consul Bonaparte."[39] He provided a continuous review of the political scene which changed rapidly during the two years of his editorship (1802-03), from the days of the Peace of Amiens, when he praised the English for their generosity towards the defeated French, to the time when in 1803 Britain mobilized and war threatened. He reported parliamentary debates and elections, took malicious delight in exposing the scurrilous nature of the English press in their slander of Napoleon, but he was not slow to reprimand the French when they did the same against England. Karamzin in 1803 still clung to his admiration for Napoleon, but at the same time his concern for England grew. Under the impression of a patriotic gesture by the English ministers, Addington and Pelham, to make way for Pitt, if the good of England demanded such a man in her hour of trial, he wrote perhaps his most moving tribute to England:

Such admissions are touching, magnanimous, and recall the most famous epochs of the ancient republics. In England the homeland is not a word but a thing, and love for it is not a figure of speech but a feeling. We as yet do not know what will happen in France, but we have seen for a long time what is in England, and we must desire, for the happiness of the world and posterity, for the progress of civic life and all that is truly human in people, that the Genius of Albion long, long will preserve the prosperity of this wonderful island.[40]

The final number of the "Messenger of Europe" under Karamzin's editorship announced his appointment as "Imperial Historiographer" and the beginning of his work on a history of Russia which was to occupy the last twenty-two years of his life and remain incomplete at his death. In his development from an author of sentimental fiction to patriotic historian the example of England again played its role, and Karamzin joined in the general European admiration for the skill and method of British historians. "Letters" contain several deliberations on the meaning of history, and more particularly, on the tasks confronting the historian of Russia. In his noted defence of Peter the Great against the criticisms of the French historian Levesque, he began by listing the names of historians whose example was to be followed: "Tacitus, Hume, Robertson, Gibbon—these are the models!"[41] The three Britons were names in his essay on English literature, where after speaking of the great English novelists, he continued: "Robertson, Hume, Gibbon gave to history all the attractiveness of an absorbing novel by their intelligent placing of action, vividness of adventures and characters, ideas and style. After Thucydides and Tacitus no one can compare with the Historical Triumvirate of Britain."[42] During the difficult years of Paul's reign, when Karamzin wrote little original work and was concerned principally with translations, the works of British historians occupied a prominent place in the required reading he set himself: "If Providence spares me; if what is more frightening for me than death does not happen [an allusion to his fears of blindness], I will concern myself with history. I will begin with Gillies; then I will read Ferguson, Gibbon, Robertson—read with attention and make notes."[43]

It was, however, David Hume who provided Karamzin with most intellectual and artistic stimulus, and to whom he most frequently alluded. In a poem from as early as 1790 he recommended Hume and Plutarch to the budding historian,[44] and in a letter from London, he described his recent reading of Hume, when his imagination was filled with scenes of violence and bloodshed from English history—"Who could love the English after reading their history?"[45] Yet it was a further indication of English enlightenment that ordinary tradesmen apparently read and reflected on Hume's work. In later years it was almost exclusively to Hume (of British historians) that Karamzin referred in his correspondence and writings. In the early stages of his own work of his history, he noted the need to compare what Hume wrote "about the customs and laws of the Saxons at the beginning of his second volume."[46] In 1812 during the critical days of Napoleon's advance on Moscow, he spent his time "reading Hume on *the origin of ideas*."[47] Subsequently Karamzin came to regard Hume's writings as cold and dry since he considered them lacking in the enthusiasm and emotion required of a true historian of one's people. In the introduction (1818) to his own "History of the Russian State" (*Istoriia Gosudarstva Rossiiskogo*) he suggested that Hume was "a historian whom we would call the most perfect of the Moderns, if he did not shun England so excessively, did not compliment himself so much on his impartiality and hereby make his fine work so cold."[48]

British influences were clearly central to Karamzin's development throughout his life. His interests were not of course restricted to England, or indeed to England, France and Germany. What made his attention to England important, however, was the significance which he himself gave to English literature and life. England was for him the home of much that was vital to the development of European civilisation in the eighteenth and nineteenth centuries and it was to England that he turned when he needed examples of national enlightenment and wise institutions. What began as youthful Anglomania soon became increasingly moderated, particularly after his first-hand acquaintance with England and Englishmen. English arrogance and patriotism led him to initiate a calculated programme of providing evidence of Russian moral and intellectual equality with the West. Alexander and the new Russia of the nineteenth century allowed him to view French and English political upheavals with confidence and often superiority. Finally the example of British historians and their efforts to make the history of their homeland known and appreciated by their compatriots moved Karamzin to emulation on behalf of Russia. Although Karamzin lived throughout the first quarter of the nineteenth century, his view of England changed little in his later years. There is little evidence that he followed the fortunes of English literature into the Romantic era—apart from two interesting instances. A reading of Byron's *Don Juan* did nothing to change his poor opinion of contemporary (i.e., post-Young!) English poetry,[49] but at least he found a worthy successor to such as Fielding and Sterne in Sir Walter Scott, whose novels he read to his family and whose influence indeed has been detected on the narrative style of his own "History."[50] Karamzin's initial Anglomania had become a balanced Anglophilia, and his work and thought provide an interesting chapter in the reception of English culture at the turn of the eighteenth century.

CONCLUSION

Shortly after publishing in 1958 his invaluable pioneering study entitled *Britain's Discovery of Russia 1553-1815* M. S. Anderson wrote an article in which he attempted to trace "Some British Influences on Russian Intellectual Life and Society in the 18th Century."[1] In the main he used materials which he had gathered for his earlier book but moved his emphasis from questions of British reception and assimilation of information about Russia, its geography, history, government, people and culture to consideration of ways in which the British through their literature, scientific achievements, technical expertise as well as their presence in Russia contributed to that country's development throughout the eighteenth century. Anderson's article provoked the Soviet scholar V. M. Vazhinskii to a vitriolic, at times hysterical review in which he accused Anderson of distortion and of an attempt "to hide his real aims under the mask of scholarly objectivity."[2] Vazhinskii, not unexpectedly, used the very few facts at his own disposal to exaggerate Russia's independent growth and the extent to which it was able to influence and instruct the West. If Anderson is to be criticized, however, it is for attempting to do too much in too little space and perhaps above all, for not knowing quite enough about a subject of which the ramifications are endless. One area in particular which receives a minimum of attention is that to which the whole of this book is devoted, the presence of Russians in Great Britain in the eighteenth century and the direct influence and impact which their sojourn had upon their lives and careers.

It is to be hoped that the evidence of the preceding chapters largely speaks for itself. Anglo-Russian relations in the eighteenth century may now be seen as far from circumscribed by the widely acknowledged and obvious areas of diplomacy and commerce: agriculture, mathematics, navigation, ship-building, medicine, law, canal-building, gun-making, production of all manner of machines and instruments, engraving, painting, literature, landscape gardening, architecture are just some of the ways in which Britain provided examples for Russians to follow. Of course only one side of the picture of Anglo-Russian intercourse has been shown and the very significant activities and presence of the British in Russia are still to be described in a second volume. Furthermore, concentration on the British contribution or influence in various fields has meant that the frequently wider context has had to be ignored: the great and the at times but not always greater contributions made by France, Germany and Italy, as well as the importance of native Russian traditions and achievements (should the likes of Mr. Vazhinskii think that these have been overlooked) would be given their due prominence, were the aim of this study a thorough-going investigation of Russia's relations with Europe in the eighteenth century.

Although there seems little point in reiterating here the findings of each chapter with regard to particular activities indulged in by Russians in England, there remain certain general conclusions to be made and certain threads to be drawn. Establishing that the number of Russians who visited England in the course of the century was far in excess of what had hitherto been supposed has led in turn to the discovering of a great variety in the nature of their activities; at the same time, the numbers involved confirm that the graph of Russian presence in England shows a marked decline after the reign of Peter throughout the 1730s, 40s and 50s and that only with the accession of Catherine II is there a steeply rising upward curve, although the true extent of activity in the last four decades of the century may only now be fully appreciated. Despite the interest which the early contacts may hold, they are but a prelude to the reign of Catherine which in so many respects provides a distinctive high point in the whole history of Anglo-Russian relations. Only from the 1760s is there any sense of real interchange, a flow not only from England to Russia of British merchants, specialists and tourists but also from Russia to England of Russians representing different strata of society and pursuing a wide variety of interests, professions and commissions. In this development it is clear that the empress herself played a decisive role.

By numerous statements and actions favouring and distinguishing the British, by her respect for their attainments as legislators, merchants, entrepreneurs, landscape gardeners and indeed as doctors, by generally complimentary references and inferences in her influential *Nakaz*, Catherine gave direction and substance to an emerging Anglophilia among, initially, the upper classes of society. "The Briton is loyal and steadfast" proclaimed a poet, who was well acquainted with Catherine's *Nakaz* and who had worked as a secretary to the Legislative Commission it was intended to instruct,[3] and the *Nakaz* might be seen to have influenced or confirmed some of the new forms Anglo-Russian interchange assumed in the 1760s and 70s. Many of the later clauses of the *Nakaz* speak of the benefits to the State of thriving agriculture, manufacturing, "mechanics" and trade,[4] and precisely in these areas English expertise was able to make a significant contribution. Catherine herself sponsored young men who went to England to study commerce and agriculture or to pursue courses at Oxford and she encouraged institutions such as the Academy of Sciences and the Academy of Arts to send their own apprentices and students. Catherine's example was quickly followed by influential members of her court, representing some of the most prominent and powerful families in Russia. Potemkin, the Orlovs, the Vorontsovs, the Chernyshevs, the Kurakins all looked to England with respect and enthusiasm and at one time or another sent young men to England for training in various fields.

Tourists and diplomats apart, the majority of the men coming to Britain in the eighteenth century were, in the description of the *Nakaz*, of "the Middling sort . . . from which great Advantages accrue to the State," including "all those who being neither Nobles, nor Peasants are employed in Arts, Sciences, Navigation, Trade and Manufactures."[5] They were the sons of officials in the lower ranks, graduates of schools and seminaries, members of what was later to become known as the "raznochintsy" intelligentsia. In the ranks of Russians in Britain in the last decades of the eighteenth century seminarists in particular loom large, and above all, seminarists of Ukrainian extraction.[6] If the students sent by Catherine to Oxford in 1765 were all recruited from seminaries in Great Russia, the students selected a decade later to study agriculture came principally from the Ukraine. The reason for this and indeed for the high incidence of Ukrainians thereafter as students, as *tserkovniki* and as officials in the Embassy is not difficult to establish. For a hundred years from the death of Kassano in 1746 until the death of Smirnov in 1840 the Embassy church was headed by Ukrainians, among whom Samborskii played the most decisive role in the early years of Catherine's reign. If Samborskii and the man he groomed as his successor, Smirnov, combined a devotion to the church with a passion for agriculture, many of the young men whom they were instrumental in bringing to England returned to Russia to serve the State in purely secular fields, as teachers, as "professors of agriculture," as doctors, as civil servants.

By the time Samborskii himself returned to Russia for good and became closely connected with the imperial family, the Ukrainian star was very much in the ascendant in Petersburg and men such as Bezborodko and Zavadovskii occupied positions of enormous influence.[7] The links with Britain continued to be very strong not only through the offices of Samborskii and his contacts with Smirnov but also through Bezborodko's and Zavadovskii's friendship with that other crucial figure in Anglo-Russian relations from the 1780s, Count Semen Vorontsov. Vorontsov lived and worked for the rest of his life in close harmony with Smirnov and his embassy not only shows a whole line of Ukrainians among its minor long-serving officials but also among its temporary attached "gentlemen" such as Kochubei.

Vorontsov became a familiar and respected figure in English high society long before his daughter's marriage put a final seal on his family's bond with the English aristocracy, but his circle of acquaintances might be seen as exceptionally wide rather than as exceptional, for contacts with London, if not English, society at all levels were far more developed than is generally suspected. If the Russian has always been a rare visitor to certain parts of the country, in London in the 1770s and 80s in particular he became a far more common phenomenon. The diaries and correspondence of both English and Russians reveal the presence of Russians at social gatherings, theatres, country houses: Dashkova and Grigorii Orlov received particular attention, but other visiting Russians were widely received. Contacts between the English and Russian nobility were made not only in London but also in such places as Paris and Spa; in addition, greater numbers of Englishmen were visiting Russia and were pleased to return hospitality to their former hosts or to their friends who arrived in London with letters of recommendation. Similar webs of acquaintances were established between merchants, professional men and scholars; although the Bentham family had specific reasons for cultivating Russians in England, their correspondence nevertheless shows the sort of contacts which were being fostered. Samborskii, Smirnov and the Russian Consul Baxter, as well as such a well-connected man as John Paradise, were very active in introducing Russians to Englishmen in appropriate fields, and Englishmen, not perhaps unaware of the advantages to their personal fortunes Catherine's Russia might offer, responded in the main with courtesy and help.

Mention might be made here of another characteristic form of intercourse at this period, which at its best was "classless": Freemasonry. Masonic links between England and Russia are said to date back to the visit of Peter the Great in 1698, when the tsar was allegedly initiated into the secrets of the Craft by Sir Christopher Wren. The British nevertheless were closely connected with the establishment of Freemasonry in Russia in the 1730s and 40s when first a Captain John Philipps and then the much more famous General James Keith became Provincial Grand Masters. It was, however, during the reign of Catherine that Freemasonry became truly fashionable and the number of Lodges and Masons increased rapidly. The overall picture is one of extraordinary confusion and prolonged ferment from the 1770s until the closure of the Lodges in 1794 by order of an empress suspicious of their political allegiances, but the role and influence of English Freemasonry is confined largely to the early 1770s. In 1771 an English Lodge "Perfect Union" was erected in Petersburg and comprised mainly British residents in the Russian capital but also some other foreigners and a few Russians. It was the first Lodge in Russia to be warranted by the Grand Lodge of England, which soon issued warrants to five other Lodges.[8] In 1772 a Russian, Ivan Perfil'evich Elagin, was made Provincial Grand Master and it was in connection with his dealings with the Grand Lodge in London that the first evidence of Russian masonic activity in England is found. Early that same year, Elagin's secretary, the dramatist Vladimir Ignat'evich Lukin, was sent, as has been described earlier, to London to secure Elagin's patents of office. The only other direct evidence of a Russian Mason sent from Russia to London on masonic business dates from 1774, when Ivan Vasil'evich Raznotovskii, a member of the "Urania" Lodge, arrived with letters of introduction to the "Somerset" Lodge.[9] On the other hand, Russians were admitted both as visitors and as full members of English Lodges, as happened at the "Arthur" Lodge in Oxford with the students Nikitin and Suvorov and the visiting engineer officer Nikolai Korsakov. However, although numerous prominent Russian Masons visited England throughout Catherine's reign,[10] their involvement with English Lodges must remain a matter of conjecture, except in the case of Mordvinov, who in 1778 wrote from Petersburg to Samborskii asking him to send on his insignia "of Royal Archer" which he had left behind.[11]

The name of Mordvinov suggests a more obvious sort of Anglo-Russian bond, that of marriage, although Mordvinov, it is true, found his English wife not in England but in Italy. It was in Italy too that Prince A. I. Viazemskii (1754-1807), shortly after a visit to England in 1783, fell in love with an Irishwoman, Eugenie Quinn (née O'Reilly), and ran away with her.[12] But other Russians found their brides in England—Samborskii, Chichagov, Petr Vasil'evich Kapnist (d. 1826),[13] Skorodumov, the mechanic Grezin, as well as Filiter Stepanov, the former serf turned engraver, and Fedor Ushakov, the former serf turned barber, who both settled in England.[14] The numbers are small, but the real significance lies, in three cases at least, in the establishing of Anglo-Russian households back in Russia, which became meeting-places for Russian Anglophiles and resident and visiting Englishmen: such were the houses of the Samborskiis in Petersburg, the Mordvinovs in Nikolaev and the Viazemskiis in Moscow.[15]

The English language was never widely known in eighteenth-century Russia, ceding pride of place first to German and then, with the reign of Elizabeth, to French. The French language and French culture dominated Russian upper-class society way into the nineteenth century, surviving with ease periods when Russo-French political relations were at a low ebb, particularly during the years following the French Revolution and the Napoleonic invasion,[16] but the slow progress made by English is not without interest and significance, as M. P. Alekseev demonstrated in his important essay of 1944.[17] The present study does not merely add to the list of English-speaking Russians in the eighteenth century but specifically highlights the role Russians who had been in England were able to play in spreading knowledge of the language and culture.

Outside the British community itself, the Russian navy was the most important repository of the English language throughout the century. Respect for the British navy and the constant influx of British naval officers into Russian service had their complementary manifestation in the number of Russians sent to serve in England and on British ships. These Russian seamen and officers formed by far the largest category of Russians with first-hand experience of England and inevitable exposure to the language, which many of them came to speak well and to use in other ways. The Naval Cadet Corps, first at Petersburg and then at Cronstadt, was one of the few institutions where English was taught and it employed at various times a number of men who had originally gone to England as *tserkovniki* or students—Permskii and Zhdanov, former *tserkovniki*, both taught English at the Corps when it was in Petersburg and produced grammars and dictionaries, and Suvorov and Nikitin, the Oxford graduates, taught English and other subjects at Cronstadt. The Corps also had teachers in other fields who had been in England—Krivov and Chetverikov in the reign of Elizabeth, and Greben-shchikov at the end of the century after his return from Cambridge. Vying with Cronstadt in the 1790s as a home of English speakers was Nikolaev, where Suvorov became teacher of English to the cadets at the School of Navigation. Nikolaev under Mordvinov attracted English-trained specialists in other fields, agriculturists like Livanov and mechanics like Shishorin. Naval establishments apart, Moscow University was the only other major centre where English was taught[18] and here again it was a Russian who had been to England, Desnitskii, who was responsible for the teaching. In 1784 the teaching of English language and English literature passed to an English-man, John Baily,[19] who three years earlier had schooled Daniil Pischekov, shortly to leave for Edinburgh University, in English pronunciation. Pische-kov himself, incidentally, taught English to the sons of Russian merchants in Petersburg.[20]

Russians who had been in England made an even greater contribution as translators of works from English on all manner of subjects—agriculture, navigation, hydrology, jurisprudence, history, travel and exploration, mech-anics, *belles lettres*. To the names of Permskii, Zhdanov, Desnitskii, Nikitin, and Suvorov, who were active as translators as well as teachers, might be added those of Samborskii, Mikhail Pleshcheev, Sergei Pleshcheev, Ivan Cherkasov, Lev Sabakin, Ivan Tatishchev, Petrov, Kolmakov, Karamzin, who were among the few able to translate works directly from the English origin-als rather than via French or German versions, which was more often the case. Some of these men also produced translations for restricted circulation which were never published: such were the translations of *An Estimate of the Comparative Strength of Great Britain* . . . (1794) prepared by Nikitin and Suvorov for the empress, and of English diplomatic papers by Ivan Tatishchev for the College of Foreign Affairs;[21] in addition, English works on naviga-tion, shipbuilding and other maritime subjects were produced by such as Krivov, Chetverikov and other seamen and apprentices down the century.

The translation, in the sense of transference, of English works to Russia was effected in other ways. It was Vorontsov who had sent to the empress the work translated in 1794 by Suvorov and Nikitin, and he and first Sam-borskii, then Smirnov, continually sent to Russia works which their cor-respondents had specifically requested or which they considered interesting or useful. Thus we find Vorontsov sending Adam Smith's *Wealth of Nations* to his brother, Mordvinov asking Samborskii for books on agriculture and Freemasonry, Samborskii after his return to Russian requesting Smirnov to send him religious and travel works, and Count Vasilii Meshcherskii needing Richardson's *History of Sir Charles Grandison*.[22] It may also be assumed that many of the Russian visitors also took back with them for their own private libraries English works on many subjects.

The reading of English works in the original or in Russian translation was one obvious way in which an awareness of England, its culture, traditions and history was stimulated in Russia and an image of the Englishman, complementing, indeed contradicting that suggested by the flesh-and-blood representatives on the streets of Petersburg and Moscow, was formed. Interest in England was sustained by articles and works coming from other non-English sources, particularly translations from German or French. At the same time English influences manifested themselves in original Russian works, where it is no longer a question of translation but of the sometimes naive, frequently critical assimilation and dissemination of ideas and attitudes. To restrict examples to writers who had been to England, one might point to such as Desnitskii and, to a far lesser degree, Tret'iakov in the fields of jurisprudence and economics, to Livanov and Komov in agriculture, to Sabakin in mechanics, to Karamzin in literature and history.

Russians visiting England were with few exceptions students in the best sense. They came to learn and to gain practical experience, prompted by their own or their masters' desire to dispense ultimately with foreigners in positions of influence in Russia and to create cadres of Russian specialists in all fields. Not in all cases did Russia receive its expected benefits, but the English-influenced contribution to eighteeth-century Russian advances on many fronts was considerable and generally positive. In some cases it might well have been greater if Russia had been geared to make the most of what its students had learned. In connection with the subsequent careers of a number of young Russians who returned from England (and to be fair, not only from England) it is clear that bureaucratic inefficiency, vested interests and sheer stupidity prevented talents from being used to the full and led to the abuse of potential and the squandering of opportunities. A colourful contemporary English assessment of the situation came from one of Matthew Boulton's mechanics who went to Russia in 1802 with the Mint machinery and was witness to the fate of the Soho-trained Russian workmen:

> I have insisted as far as providence and decorum would admit with the Court in their not sending any more Slaves of the Crown, as numerous Precedents in this Country prove the improbability of their ever doing much good—not that a great deal of ingenuity may not exist amongst many of them:—it would be a libel on human nature to suppose the contrary; but even during the enlightened Reign of Catherine herself, after sending many of them abroad as Painters, Architects etc. at an expense of several Hundred Sterling individually per Annum, on their return, these unfortunate people were invariably forced into the service of the Crown again at paltry Salaries of a four hundred Rubles, and soon degenerating into misanthropy and dejection, applied to the Whiskey-bottle for consolation and fell the early Victims of disappointed Hope.[23]

Nevertheless, an awareness of the losses and mismanagements which such an autocratic state as Russia made almost inevitable should not obscure the very real gains accruing to Russia from the exposure to England of an increasing number of its servants in the eighteenth century. Kantemir, Musin-Pushkin, Aleksandr and Semen Vorontsov; Samborskii and Smirnov; Malinovskii, Longinov and Kochubei; Livanov and Komov; G. F. Müller, Desnitskii, Nikitin and Suvorov; Surnin, Sabakin and Deriabin; Skorodumov and Neelov; Mordvinov, Sergei Pleshcheev, Chichagov, Kruzenshtern and Lisianskii; Petrov, Dmitrevskii and Karamzin; Dashkova, Orlov, Kurakin and Novosil'-tsev; these are but some thirty names from the several hundred which appear in the checklist for whom a residence in England was a significant event in their lives and who served Russia in various yet important ways. The reign of Alexander I is traditionally seen as the great period of Russian Anglomania for which the preceding century provided, in Alekseev's term, "the historical roots";[24] and it is certainly true that England became to a much greater extent the object of a cult or "mania" among wider sections of the upper classes and that English "ideas" were to the fore because of the influence and interests of people close to the emperor, such as the "Young Friends," the Vorontsov brothers and Mordvinov. It was also a time when people who had been in England such as Deriabin, Murav'ev, Dzhunkovskii, Longinov, Malinovskii, to name but a few, occupied positions of importance and made their most valuable contributions. But the significance of the eighteenth century and of the reign of Catherine in particular should not therefore be minimized or its distinctive character overlooked. The study of direct Russian knowledge of England in the eighteenth century reveals that it was not as isolated and largely upper-class a phenomenon as is usually suggested on the basis of very restricted and fragmentary evidence: during the reign of Catherine it was already a question of blossom and not merely of roots, of Anglophilia largely based on personal experience rather than of a widespread Anglomania.

ERRATUM

On pp. 62 and 141-42 it was tentatively suggested that Dr. D. S. Samoilovich paid a visit to Britain in 1783. A recently discovered document reveals, however, that he was ultimately prevented from doing so.

NOTES

NOTES TO INTRODUCTION, pages 1-4

1. Ia. S. Lur'e, " 'Otkrytie Anglii' russkimi v nachale XVI v.," *Geograficheskii sbornik*, III, *Istoriia geograficheskikh znanii i geograficheskikh otkrytii* (Moscow-Leningrad, 1954), 185-87.

2. M. P. Alekseev, "K voprosu ob anglo-russkikh otnosheniiakh pri Iaroslave Mudrom," *Nauchnyi biulleten' Leningradskogo gos. universiteta*, no. 4 (1945), 31-33.

3. Joseph Jacobs, "The First Russian in England," *The Academy*, XXXIV, no. 868 (22 December 1888), 404-05. I am grateful to Professor Rodney Needham of All Souls College, Oxford for this reference.

4. M. P. Alekseev, "Shekspir i russkoe gosudarstvo XVI-XVII vv.," in *Shekspir i russkaia kul'tura* (Moscow-Leningrad, 1965), pp. 784-805.

5. Leo Loewenson, "Escaped Russian Slaves in England in the 17th Century," *Slavonic and East European Review*, XLII (1964), 427-29.

6. B. Alexandrenko, "The First Russian Students in England," *The Academy*, XXXVI, no. 918 (7 December 1889), 372.

7. W. R. Morfill, citing Walker's *Sufferings of the Clergy*, in his *Russia* (2nd edition, London, 1891), p. 98.

8. *Ibid.*, pp. 98-99; N. V. Golitsyn, "Nauchno-obrazovatel'nye snosheniia Rossii s Zapadom v nachale XVII v.," *Chteniia v Imperatorskom Obshchestve istorii i drevnostei rossiiskikh pri Moskovskom universitete*, no. 4, section III, *Issledovaniia* (1898), 3-18.

9. Golitsyn, pp. 19-20.

10. See M. M. Bogoslovskii, *Petr I*, II (Moscow, 1941), 293-389; A. I. Andreev, "Petr I v Anglii v 1698 g.," in *Petr Velikii: sbornik statei* (Moscow-Leningrad, 1947), pp. 63-103; Leo Loewenson, "Some Details of Peter the Great's Stay in England in 1698: Neglected English Material," *SEER*, XL, no. 95 (1962), 431-43.

11. See my "British Awareness of Russian Culture (1698-1801)," forthcoming in *Canadian-American Slavic Studies*, XIII (1979).

NOTES TO CHAPTER 1, pages 5-34

1. D. S. Likhachev (ed.), *Puteshestviia russkikh poslov XVI-XVII vv.* (Moscow-Leningrad, 1954); N. N. Bantysh-Kamenskii, *Obzor vneshnikh snoshenii Rossii,* I (Moscow, 1894), 91-123; N. Charykov, *Posol'stvo v Angliiu dvorianina Grigoriia Mikulina v 1600 i 1601* (Moscow, 1876); A. Lodyzhenskii, "Russkoe posol'stvo v Angliiu v 1662," *Istoricheskii vestnik,* III, no. 11 (1880), 433-53; Z. I. Roginskii, *London 1645-1646 godov. Novye istochniki o poezdke gontsa Gerasima Semenovicha Dokhturova v Angliiu* (Iaroslavl', 1959); N. E. Evans, "The Meeting of the Russian and Scottish Ambassadors in London in 1601," *Slavonic and East European Review,* LV (1977), 516-28.

2. Quoted in V. N. Aleksandrenko, *Russkie diplomaticheskie agenty v Londone v XVIII veke,* I (Warsaw, 1897), 4, note 2. Aleksandrenko's two-volume work of analysis and documents is the indispensable source for the activities of Russian diplomats in England. See also V. Timiriazev, "Russkie diplomaty XVIII stoletiia v Anglii," *Istoricheskii vestnik,* LXXII (1898), 243-66, 567-81.

3. See Aleksandrenko, *Russkie agenty,* I, 214-23; II, 7-18.

4. Ivan Afanas'ev in 1719 and Mikhail Tatishchev in 1768: *Ibid.,* I, 409-10.

5. *Arkhiv kn. F. A. Kurakina,* I (Spb., 1890), 101-240. See A. Brikner, "Russkii turist v Zapadnoi Evrope v nachale XVIII veka," *Russkoe obozrenie,* I (1892), 5-38.

6. *Arkhiv Kurakina,* I, 145-6; II (1891), 340-54; III (1892), 207-18, 257-302; IV (Saratov, 1893), 210-424.

7. *Ibid.,* IV, 35-36.

8. *The Muscovite,* no. 1 (Wed. 5 May 1714), 1. See Iu. D. Levin, "Angliiskii zhurnal 'Moskovit' (1714)," in Iu. D. Levin and K. I. Rovda (eds.), *Vospriiatie russkoi kul'tury na Zapade* (Leningrad, 1975), pp. 7-23.

9. The best discussion of the fluctuations of Anglo-Russian diplomacy and of the general British reaction not only at this period but throughout the century is provided by M. S. Anderson, *Britain's Discovery of Russia, 1553-1815* (London, 1958), pp. 49-214.

10. *The Memorial of M. Bestuschef, His Czarish Majesties Resident in London presented October 17, 1720, to the Court of Great Britain, being a reply to the two Answers given by the British and Brunswick Minister to a former Memorial presented by the Resident Wesselofski* (London, 1721).

11. *A Memorial Presented to His Britannick Majesty, by Monsieur Wesselowsky, Minister from His Czarish Majesty* (London, 1717), p. 8.

12. *A Memorial Presented to the King of Great-Britain, by Mr. Wesselofski, the Czar's Resident at London, on the 14th of December, 1719* (London, 1720).

13. Professor Alexandrenko, "Peter the Great's Minister in England," *Proceedings of the Anglo-Russian Literary Society,* no. 9 (1895), 38-41; Aleksandrenko, *Russkie agenty,* II, 24-34; V. N. Aleksandrenko (ed.), *Reliatsii kn. A. D. Kantemira iz Londona (1732-1733 g.),* I (Moscow, 1892), 118-20.

14. *Sbornik Imperatorskogo Russkogo istoricheskogo obshchestva,* LXVI (Spb., 1889), 408.

15. Further dispatches are found in *Chteniia v Imperatorskom Obshchestve istorii i drevnostei rossiiskikh,* III, sect. 1 (1892), 1-262.

16. Quoted in Aleksandrenko, *Russkie agenty,* I, 385, note 3. During a short visit to Paris in August 1736, Kantemir wrote: "Je suis peu satisfait de medecin de ce pays comme du pays même. Le seul profit que je tire de mon voyage est de m'avoir détrompé de la grande idée que j'avois de cette ville et de ses habitans." (Bodleian Library, Oxford, Zamboni Papers, Ms. Rawl. letters 126, f. 551v.)

17. Aleksandrenko, *Reliatsii*, pp. 1, 5, 7. (The English text was published in the *Daily Journal*, no. 4250 (31 August 1734).)

18. *Ibid.*, pp. 8-9.

19. Aleksandrenko, *Russkie agenty*, II, 65-66, 70-74.

20. For detailed discussions of Kantemir's life in London, see R. J. Morda Evans, "Antiokh Kantemir: A Study of His Literary, Political and Social Life in England, 1732-1738," Unpublished Ph.D. thesis, University of London, 1959; Helmut Grasshoff, *Antioch Dmitrievič Kantemir und Westeuropa* (Berlin, 1966), pp. 90-160.

21. L. N. Maikov, "Materialy dlia biografii kn. A. D. Kantemira," *Sbornik Otdeleniia russkogo iazyka i slovesnosti Imper. Akademii Nauk*, LXXIII (1903), 108.

22. On the Kantemir-Rolli links, see Valentin Boss, "Kantemir and Rolli-Milton's *Il Paradiso Perduto*," *Slavic Review*, XXI (1962), 441-54. See also generally George E. Dorris, *Paoli Rolli and the Italian Circle in London 1715-1744* (The Hague-Paris, 1967).

23. *Satyres du Prince Cantemir, traduites du russe en français; avec l'histoire de sa vie*, I (London, 1750), xlvii-xlviii.

24. Aleksandrenko, *Russkie agenty*, I, 384; Evans, *op. cit.*, pp. 145-48.

25. See in particular Valentin Boss, *Newton and Russia: The Early Influence, 1698-1796* (Cambridge, Mass., 1972), pp. 116-27. Also Maikov, *op. cit.*, p. 110.

26. Quoted from Algarotti's preface to the 1739 edition of his *Newtonianismo* by Evans, *op. cit.*, p. 209. Also Boss, p. 126.

27. *Satyres du Prince Cantemir*, pp. li-lii. The history translated from the Latin by an English vicar, Nicholas Tindal, appeared as *The History of the Growth and Decay of the Othman Empire* (London, 1734).

28. Quoted by B. Alexandenko, "A Russian Ambassador in England in the Reign of George II," *The Academy*, no. 900 (3 August 1889), 72.

29. *Russkii biograficheskii slovar'*, vol. Shchapov-Iushnevskii (Spb., 1912), 98-100.

30. Bodleian Library, Ms. Rawl. letters 128, ff. 158a-180 (Naryshkin); ff. 239a-245a (Shcherbatov). See on Naryshkin, *RBS*, vol. Naake-Nakenskii-Nikolai Nikolaevich (Spb., 1914), 97-98.

31. According to the nomination, dated 10 December 1747, the day after the signing of the Anglo-Russian treaty, Chernyshev himself "desired to be offered a Candidate": Royal Society Minute Books, Ms I, 329, f. 361

32. Aleksandrenko, *Russkie agenty*, I, 344.

33. *Ibid.*, II, 83-92. On Chernyshev's career generally, see *RBS*, vol. Chaadaev-Shvitkov (1905), 327-30.

34. Macartney to Sir Andrew Mitchell, quoted in Helen Robbins, *Our First Ambassador to China*, I (London, 1908), 18.

35. Prince M. M. Shcherbatov, *On the Corruption of Morals in Russia*, edited and translated by A. Lentin (Cambridge, 1969), p. 194.

36. See Earl of Ilchester and Mrs Langford-Brooke, *The Life of Sir Charles Hanbury-Williams, Poet, Wit and Dramatist* (London, 1929), particularly Chapter XVI.

37. *SRIO*, XII (1873), 382.

38. *Ibid.*, LXXXVII, 349; 300.

39. Quoted in Anderson, *op. cit.*, p. 131, n. 1.

40. Earl of Ilchester, *The Home of the Hollands 1605-1820* (London, 1937), pp. 117-18.

41. Quoted in Aleksandrenko, *Russkie agenty*, I, 62-63, n. 6.

42. On Vorontsov generally, see Jules S. Zimmerman, "Alexander Romanovich Vorontsov, Eighteenth-Century Enlightened Russian Statesman, 1741-1805," Ph.D. thesis, City University of New York, 1975. There is little discussion of Vorontsov's time in London.

43. *Arkhiv kniazia Vorontsova*, 40 vols. (Spb., 1870-95) V, 145; Aleksandrenko, *Russkie agenty*, I, 344.

44. *AKV*, IX, 40.

45. Letter from Duke of Buckinghamshire to Lady Suffolk, 13 September 1762, in Lewis Melville, *Lady Suffolk and Her Circle* (London, 1924), pp. 271-72.

46. Letter to the Duke of Newcastle, 9 April 1764, in Aleksandrenko, *Russkie agenty*, II, 101.

47. *AKV*, XXXI, 438-41.

48. *AKV*, IX, 47, 54, 86. It is also interesting to note that Vorontsov's name is found among the list of subscribers (3 sets) to the 1763 edition of John Bell's *Travels in Russia*.

49. The words of A. R. Vorontsov in 1758: Aleksandrenko, *Russkie agenty*, I, 37, no. 1.

50. *Ibid.*, p. 38.

51. *SRIO*, XII, (1873), 297-99. Cf. a similarly scathing attack by Prince M. M. Shcherbatov in his *On the Corruption of Morals, op. cit.*, pp. 204-06.

52. *SRIO*, XII, 380.

53. *Journal intime du Chevalier de Corberon*, II (Paris, 1901), 183.

54. W. S. Lewis (ed.), *Horace Walpole's Correspondence*, XXIII (London, 1967), 125. Other comments by Walpole on Chernyshev, *ibid.*, pp. 75-76, 116.

55. *Ibid.*, p. 127. See "Account of the dispute between two illustrious foreigners at Court last Monday," *St James's Chronicle*, 8-10 June 1769. For Count Panin's reply to Chernyshev's report of the incident, see *SRIO*, LXXXVII (1893), 465-67; for the French version of the affair, see *ibid.*, CXLI (1913), 576.

56. *SRIO*, XIX (1876), 45.

57. *Ibid.*, XII, 299-300.

58. *The Letters and Journals of Lady Mary Coke*, II (Bath, 1970), 417.

59. Elizabeth Craven, *Journey through the Crimea to Constantinople* (London, 1789), p. 127. Cf. *Memoirs of the Margravine of Anspach*, I (Paris, 1826), 100.

60. [Lionel Colmore], *Letters from the Continent* (London, 1812), pp. 96-97.

61. Aleksandrenko, *Russkie agenty*, II, 178-79.

62. *Ibid.*, II, 41-2, 387-90. Texts of reports in *ibid.*, II, 112-28, 155-57, 161-65, 176-82.

63. *Ibid.*, II, 166-75.

64. *Ibid.*, II, 195-96.

65. *Scots Magazine*, LII (March 1782), 123. See generally Isabel de Madariaga, *Britain, Russia and the Armed Neutrality of 1780* (London, 1962).

66. Aleksandrenko, *Russkie agenty*, I, 291; II, 216-17.

67. Lenin Library, Moscow, Fond 183, Inostrannaia literatura, no. 1673, ff. 95v., 110.

68. *AKV*, IX, 92; Aleksandrenko, *Russkie agenty*, I, 51, n. 2.

69. Aleksandrenko, *Russkie agenty*, I, 444-47.

70. *Memoirs of Catherine the Great*, translated by Moura Budberg (London, 1955), p. 262.

71. *AKV*, VIII (1876), 3.

72. *Ibid.*, p. 2.

73. *Ibid.*, p. 17.

74. Marchioness of Londonderry and H. M. Hyde (eds.), *The Russian Journals of Martha and Catherine Wilmot 1803-1808* (London, 1934), p. 9.

75. *AKV*, IX, 104.

76. *Ibid.*, XVII, 118. Cf. *Ibid.*, XVIII, 302.

77. *Ibid.*, XXXI, 438.

78. *Ibid.*, XVIII, 25.

79. *Ibid.*, IX, 40.

80. *Ibid.*, p. 41.

81. *Ibid.*, VIII, 25.

82. *Ibid.*, p. 18.

83. Aleksandrenko, *Russkie agenty*, I, 287.

84. *AKV*, IX, 181. On his brother's relations with A. N. Radishchev, see Zimmerman, *op. cit.*, pp. 111-34.

85. Anderson, *op. cit.*, p. 167. For other analyses of the crisis, see E. Shteinberg, "S. R. Vorontsov i anglo-russkie otnosheniia na rubezhe XVIII i XIX vekov," *Istoricheskii zhurnal*, nos. 11-12 (1943), 34-40; James Walton Marcum, "Semen R. Vorontsov: Minister to the Court of St. James's for Catherine II, 1785-1796," Ph.D. thesis, University of North Carolina, 1970; Lester Jay Humphreys, "The Vorontsov Family: Russian Nobility in a Century of Change, 1725-1825," Ph.D. thesis, University of Pennsylvania, 1969, pp. 169-86.

86. *Norwich Mercury*, no. 2096 (Saturday 30 April 1791). See also C. A. Jewson, *Jacobin City* (Glasgow and London, 1975), pp. 25-26.

87. *AKV*, VIII, 22.

88. *Ibid.*, 22-23.

89. On these personalities, see in particular Gleb Struve, "John Paradise–Friend of Doctor Johnson, American Citizen and Russian 'Agent'," *Virginia Magazine of History and Biography*, LVII (October 1949), 365-70.

90. Aleksandrenko, *Russkie agenty*, I, 72, n. 1.

91. *AKV*, XXII, 535.

92. Aleksandrenko, *Russkie agenty*, II, 296.

93. *AKV*, XX, 475.

94. *Ibid.*, XVII, 254.

95. For much fascinating detail on the Vorontsov family fortunes in England, see Gleb Struve, "An Anglo-Russian Medley: Woronzows, Pembrokes, Nicolays and Others," *California Slavic Studies*, V (1970), 93-136.

96. Aleksandrenko, *Russkie agenty*, I, 396-401. See also the letter from V. P. Kochubei to Vorontsov, 10/21 November 1798: *AKV*, XVIII, 180.

97. Aleksandrenko, *Russkie agenty*, I, 401-05.

98. *AKV*, IX, 59. Cf. *ibid.*, p. 406; XX, 23. His letters to Vorontsov from Copenhagen over the years 1800-04 are in *ibid.*, XX, 411-56.

99. Lenin Library, Fond 183, no. 1673, f. 18.

100. Aleksandrenko, *Russkie agenty*, I, 410.

101. W. F. Reddaway (ed.), *Documents of Catherine the Great* (Cambridge, 1931), p. XXXI. The title of the English translation reads: *The Grand Instructions to the Commissioners Appointed to Frame a New Code of Laws for the Russian Empire* (1768). Tatishchev received ten guineas from the Russia Company to which he presented a copy in 1769: Guildhall Library, London, Mss. 17741/7, f. 275.

102. Timothy L. S. Sprigge (ed.), *Correspondence of Jeremy Bentham*, I (London, 1968), 122-24. (Thomas Bray (1656-1730) was founder of what became the S.P.C.K.)

103. *Ibid.*, II, 99.

104. John Bowring (ed.), *The Works of Jeremy Bentham*, X (Edinburgh, 1843), 67.

105. *Correspondence of Jeremy Bentham*, II, 101.

106. Evgenii, *Slovar' russkikh svetskikh pisatelei, sootechestvennikov i chuzhestrantsev, pisavshikh v Rossii*, II (Moscow, 1845), 203-04.

107. *AKV*, XXX, 391.

108. V. F. Malinovskii, *Izbrannye obshchestvenno-politicheskie sochineniia* (Moscow, 1958), p. 50.

109. In the introduction to the Soviet edition of Malinovskii's work (p. 27), E. A. Arab-Ogly discusses without enthusiasm the possibility of his acquaintance with Bentham's treatise (published only in 1843, but written in the late 1780s) in manuscript, but is unaware of the close contacts existing between the Benthams and Russians in England. Another work on a similar theme which is of interest for its Anglo-Russian aspect is the anonymous *Lasting Peace to Europe: the Dream of an Ancient Cosmopolite Dedicated to . . . the Empress of Russia* (London, 1781).

110. Malinovskii, *Izbrannye sochineniia*, pp. 144-45. On Malinovskii's own family life, see the interesting memoirs of his son-in-law, Baron A. E. Rozen, *Zapiski dekabrista* (Spb., 1907), pp. 36-38.

111. *Ibid.*, pp. 102-03. Looking for the "progressive" elements in Malinovskii's ideas, Soviet scholars tend to compare him with Radishchev. A much more interesting comparison is with the views of N. M. Karamzin, whom Malinovskii met in London in 1790.

112. On Malinovskii and Pushkin, specifically their ideas on "peace," see M. P. Alekseev, "Pushkin i problema 'vechnogo mira'," in his *Pushkin: sravnitel'no-istoricheskie issledovaniia* (Leningrad, 1972), pp. 192-97.

113. Kochubei's unpublished diary covering his movements during the second half of 1789 is in Pushkin House, Leningrad, Fond 93, Sobranie P. Ia. Dashkova, op. 2, no. 122. He was frequently in the company of Frederick, Lord North (1766-1827), visiting with him a number of towns and estates in Kent. Kochubei then spent several months in Portsmouth, studying navigation.

114. *AKV*, IX, 415.

115. *Ibid.*, p. 416. The complete texts are pp. 415-21. Cf. *ibid.*, pp. 245-46; XXII, 502. Letters from Kochubei to Vorontsov, *ibid.*, XVIII, 1-295.

116. F. F. Vigel', *Zapiski*, I (Moscow, 1928), 151. See generally on Kochubei, N. Chechulin, "Kochubei, Viktor Pavlovich," in *RBS*, vol. Knappe-Kiukhel'beker, 365-82; Patricia Kennedy Grimsted, *The Foreign Ministers of Alexander I* (Berkeley and Los Angeles, 1969), pp. 80-91.

1. "Kratkoe opisanie ob osnovanii Grecheskoi tserkvi v Londone," printed in V. N. Aleksandrenko, *Russkie diplomaticheskie agenty v Londone v XVIII v.*, II (Warsaw, 1897), 37-52. This document, together with Aleksandrenko's chapter on the Embassy church in Vol. I, 411-36, is the basic source for the early history of the church.

2. The first Greek church in London was built in 1677 in Hog Lane (Charing Cross Road), but was closed by royal command in 1684. Services were conducted by a Greek bishop, Joseph Georgirenes: *Ibid.*, I, 412.

3. *Ibid.*, pp. 413-14.

4. *Ibid.*, p. 424.

5. *Ibid.*, p. 418.

6. *Ibid.*, II, 93-94.

7. *Ibid.*, I, 417.

8. Pushkin House, Leningrad, Fond 620, Arkhiv A. A. Samborskogo, ed. khr. 157, no. 6, f. 11.

9. *Ibid.*, no. 7, f. 13.

10. *Arkhiv kniazia Vorontsova*, XXVIII (Moscow, 1883), 70-71.

11. Pushkin House, Leningrad, Arkhiv N. M. Longinova, ed. khr. 23736, no. 6, f. 14.

12. Aleksandrenko, *Russkie agenty*, I, 420, n. 2.

13. *Ibid.*, II, 94.

14. *Ibid.*, I, 422, n. 1. This episode in the unfortunate Diakovskii's biography was unknown to N. I. Petrov, who wrote that nothing was known of the last thirty years of his life. Diakovskii was the author of a number of sermons and a treatise on the composition of sermons during his years at Kiev. See N. P. [N. I. Petrov], "Ieromonakh Efrem Diakovskii, kievskii gomilet i propovednik vtoroi poloviny XVIII veka," *Trudy Kievskoi dukhovnoi akademii*, no. 7 (1893), 437-72.

15. Aleksandrenko, *Russkie agenty*, I, 430.

16. *O zhizni protoiereia A. A. Samborskogo* (Spb., 1888), p. 6. This rare work, printed in only 100 copies, contains many inaccuracies, as do all the published accounts of Samborskii's life; it is valuable above all for its documents (pp. 23-72), which include Samborskii's diary for 1768-69.

17. On Samborskii and Smirnov and their relations with the Paradises and Ludwells, see Glev Struve, "Dva pravoslavnykh anglichanina v XVIII v.," *Novoe russkoe slovo*, 28 August 1949; "John Paradise—Friend of Doctor Johnson, American Citizen and 'Russian Agent'," *Virginia Magazine of History and Biography*, LVII, no. 4 (1949), 355-75.

18. On North, see Struve's first article in note 17.

19. From Samborskii's diary in *O zhizni Samborskogo*, *op. cit.*, pp. 24-26.

20. N. Barsov, "Samborskii, Andrei Afanas'evich," *Russkii biograficheskii slovar'*, vol. Sabaneev-Smyslov (Spb., 1904), 148.

21. Lenin Library, Moscow, Fond 41, Bulgakovy, karton 129, ed. kh. 27, no. 3, ff. 5-5v.; no. 5, ff. 9v.-11.

22. Fond 620, ed. khr. 141, no. 5, f. 5v.

23. *The Morning Chronicle, and London Advertiser*, No. 4432, 31 July 1783.

24. *Correspondence of Jeremy Bentham*, II (London, 1968), 208.

25. *Ibid.*, II (London, 1971), 150.

26. Fond 620, ed. khr. 76, ff. 1-1v.

27. See Baron A. E. Rozen, *Zapiski dekabrista* (Spb., 1907), pp. 36-39.

28. Dzhunkovskii's letters to Samborskii from England are in Fond 620, ed. khr. 99 and 100.

29. *AKV*, XXIV (Moscow, 1880), 218-20.

30. *O zhizni Samborskogo, op. cit.*, p. 10.

31. *Russkaia starina*, XVI (1876), 13.

32. W. Tooke, *The Life of Catharine II*, III (Dublin 1800), 84.

33. Three letters from Planta on his sister's behalf are in the Speranskii archive in the Saltykov-Shchedrin Library, Leningrad, Fond 731, no. 2323, ff. 1-5v. See also Marc Raeff, *Michael Speransky: Statesman of Imperial Russia, 1772-1839* (The Hague, 1957), pp. 18-19.

34. M. I. Pyliaev, *Zabytoe proshloe okrestnostei Peterburga* (Spb., 1889), p. 2.

35. See my "Dzhunkovskii's *Aleksandrova*: Putting Samborskii in the Picture," *Study Group on Eighteenth-Century Russia Newsletter*, No. 3 (1975), 22-29.

36. *Aleksandrova, uveselitel'nyi sad ego imperatorskogo vysochestva blagoverennogo gosudaria i velikogo kniazia Aleksandra Pavlovicha* (Spb., 1793), pp. 1, 9.

37. Fond 620, ed. khr. 61, no. 2.

38. *Russkii biograficheskii slovar'*, vol. Sabaneev-Smyslov, 148.

39. *Ibid.*

40. *Gentleman's Magazine*, New Series XIV (1840), 103.

41. "Londonskii sviashchennik Ia. I. Smirnov," *Russkii arkhiv*, XVII, pt. 1 (1879), 356.

42. "Zapiski grafa E. F. Komarovskogo," *Osmnadtsatyi vek*, I (2nd ed., M., 1869), 389-99.

43. *Moskovskii Merkurii*, I, no. 1 (1803), 29-31.

44. *The Russian Journals of Martha and Catherine Wilmot, 1803-1808*, edited by the Marchioness of Londonderry and H. M. Hyde (London, 1934), p. 10.

45. *Progulka za granitsu Pavlom Sumarokovym*, III (Spb., 1821), 26.

46. *Khronika russkogo: Dnevniki (1825-1826 gg.)* (M.-L., 1964), pp. 395-407.

47. "Zapiski rektora i professora Imperatorskoi Akademii Khudozhestv Fedora Ivanovicha Iordana, 1800-1833 gg.," *Russkaia starina* (May 1891), p. 321.

48. *Putevye pis'ma iz Anglii, Germanii i Frantsii*, I (Spb., 1839), 174.

49. *AKV*, XXII (Moscow, 1878), 184.

50. "Dokumenty o zhizni i tvorchestve Gerasima Stepanovicha Lebedeva 1796-1817 gg.," *Russko-indiiskie otnosheniia v XVIII v.* (M., 1965), pp. 488-91.

51. *AKV*, XXX (Moscow, 1881), 252.

52. *Ibid.*, IX, 465-66.

53. Smirnov's role is discussed in detail in my "Yakov Smirnov—A Russian Priest of Many Parts," *Oxford Slavonic Papers*, N.S. VIII (1975), 37-52.

54. *Russkii arkhiv*, XVII, pt. 1 (1879), 356; Aleksandrenko, *Russkie agenty*, II, 294.

55. Aleksandrenko, *Russkie agenty*, II, 279-81.

56. *Ibid.*, p. 284.

57. *Ibid.* (Smirnov's reports have not been published.)

58. *AKV*, II, 466.

59. *Ibid.*, p. 472.

60. Aleksandrenko, *Russkie agenty*, II, 277-78.

61. *AKV*, IX, 488.

62. *Ibid.*, XVIII, 251.

63. Arkhiv N. M. Longinova, ed. khr. 23737, no. 15, f. 40v.

64. *The Autobiography of Arthur Young, with Selections from His Correspondence*, edited by M. Betham-Edwards (London, 1898), p. 387.

65. *AKV*, XX, 469.

66. *Sbornik materialov dlia istorii Imperatorskoi S.—Peterburgskoi Akademii khudo-zhestv*, edited by P. N. Petrov, II (Spb., 1865), 109-10.

67. Saltykov-Shchedrin Library, Leningrad, Fond 542, Oleniny, ed. khr. 300, no. 5, ff. 9-9v. Smirnov in 1823 was also attempting to get engravings from the Society of Antiquaries of the Bayeux Tapestries. As he notes, "large bodies move slowly" (*ibid.*, f. 9v.) and this order was completed only in 1826.

68. *Zapiski, mneniia i perepiska Admirala A. S. Shishkova*, II (Spb., 1870), 401-02.

69. Guildhall Library, London, Russia Company Court Minute Books, Mss. 11741/9, f. 189.

70. *Histoire de l'Empire de Russie sous la règne de Catherine*, traduite de l'anglais par M. S. . . . avec les corrections de M. Imirnove [sic] et revue par M. Leclerc, 6 vols. (Paris, 1801).

71. *Ode to Her Imperial Majesty Catherine the Great, Presented by the Chief National School at St. Petersburg* (London, 1815).

72. M. Ia. Moroshkin, *Iezuity v Rossii s tsarstvovaniia Ekateriny II i do nashego vremeni*, II (Spb., 1870), 21.

73. Aleksandrenko, *Russkie agenty*, I, 407, n. 3.

74. Fond 620, ed. khr. 133, f. 1.

75. Arkhiv N. M. Longinova, ed. kh. 23742, no. 19, f. 52.

76. Aleksandrenko, *Russkie agenty*, I, 422, n. 2; 424, n. 1; 435-6, n. 2.

77. *Ibid.*, p. 424, n. 1.

78. *Ibid.*, pp. 406-07.

79. *Prakticheskaia angliskaia grammatika* (Spb., 1766), pp. 180-92. On Permskii, see *Opyt istoricheskogo slovaria o rossiiskikh pisateliakh* (1772) in N. I. Novikov, *Izbrannye sochineniia* (M. -L., 1951), p. 334; M. P. Alekseev, "Angliiskii iazyk v Rossii i russkii iazyk v Anglii," *Uchenye zapiski Leningradskogo gos. universiteta*, No. 72 (1944) seriia filologicheskikh nauk, vypusk 9, 90; M. M. Shtrange, *Demokraticheskaia intelligentsiia Rossii b XVIII vede* (M., 1965), pp. 82-83.

80. *A New Dictionary English and Russian* (Spb., 1784), dedication. The work is unpaginated. On Zhdanov, see Alekseev, *op. cit.*, p. 91; N. M. Ispolatov, "Pervye anglo-russkie slovari v Rossii," *Vestnik Leningradskogo universiteta*, no. 20 (1971), 135-37.

81. V. P. Semennikov, *Sobranie staraiushcheesia o perevode inostrannykh knig, uchrezhdennoe Ekaterinoi II, 1768-1783 gg.* (Spb., 1913), pp. 80-81.

82. On Kolmakov, see *Russkii biograficheskii slovar'*, vol. Knappe-Kiukhel'beker (Spb., 1903), 73; V. A. Bochkarev, *Russkaia istoricheskaia dramaturgiia* (Kuibishev, 1959), pp. 354-57; *Shekspir i russkaia kul'tura*, edited by M. P. Alekseev (M. -L., 1965), pp. 48-49.

83. Fond 620, ed. khr. 103, f. lv.

84. Erik Amburger, *Geschichte der Behördenorganisation Russlands von Peter dem Grossen bis 1917* (Leiden, 1966), pp. 84, 87. Many details about Longinov's career after his return to Russia are found in his archive, particularly in the 159 letters which Smirnov sent to him over the period 1807-39.

85. Alexander Soumarokove, *Demetrius the Impostor; A Tragedy* (London, 1806), pp. vi-vii.

86. On Evstav'ev, see M. P. Alekseev, "A. G. Evstaf'ev—russko-amerikanskii pisatel' nachala XIX veka," *Nauchnyi biulleten' LGU*, no. 8 (1946), 22-27; Dieter Boden, *Das Amerikabild in russischen Schrifttum zum Ende des 19 Jahrhunderts* (Hamburg, 1968), pp. 74-75; A. G. Cross, "Russkoe posol'stvo v Londone i znakomstvo anglichan s russkoi literaturoi v nachale XIX veka," in *Sravnitel'noe izuchenie literatur* (Leningrad, 1976), pp. 99-107.

NOTES TO CHAPTER 3, pages 57-91

1. William Coxe, *Travels in Poland, Russia, Sweden, and Denmark*, II (London, 1784), 151.

2. A. I. Pashkov (ed.), *A History of Russian Economic Thought: Ninth through Eighteenth Centuries*, trans. John M. Letiche (Berkeley and Los Angeles, 1964), pp. 376-78.

3. J. A. Prescott, "The Russian Free (Imperial) Economic Society, 1765-1917," *Journal of the Royal Society of Arts* (December 1965), 33-37; (December 1967), 68-70. It is interesting to note that Sievers' role is ignored by V. Oreshkin in his *Vol'noe ekonomicheskoe obshchestvo v Rossii 1765-1917* (Moscow, 1963), pp. 16-19.

4. The translation is Prescott's (pp. 69-70) from K. L. Blum, *Ein russischer Statts-mann. Des Grafen J. J. Sievers' Denwürdigkeiten zur Geschichte Russlands*, I (Heidel-berg, 1857), 187-89.

5. D. G. C. Allan, *William Shipley: Founder of the Royal Society of Arts* (London, 1968), pp. 40-57.

6. *Transactions of the Society of Arts*, XVI (1798), 339-60.

7. See my "Early Contacts of the Society of Arts with Russia: I–Corresponding Members in Russia," *Journal of the Royal Society of Arts* (March 1976), 204-07.

8. Coxe, II, 153-54.

9. *Annals of Agriculture and Other Useful Arts*, II (1784), 233-54.

10. On Young, see: John G. Gazley, *The Life of Arthur Young 1741-1820* (Phila-delphia, 1973).

11. *The Autobiography of Arthur Young, with Selections from His Correspondnece*, edted by M. Betham-Edwards (London, 1895), pp. 66-67.

12. *On the Husbandry of Three Celebrated British Farmers, Messrs Bakewell, Arbuth-not, and Ducket: being a lecture read to the Board of Agriculture, on Thursday, June 6, 1811, by the Secretary of the Board* (London, 1811), pp. 27-8.

13. Pushkin House, Leningrad, Fond 620, Arkhiv A. A. Samborskogo, ed. khr. 61, no. 24, f. 29v.

14. *Ibid.*, no. 51, ff. 68-68v.

15. V. P. Gur'ianov, *Ivan Mikhailovich Komov. Ego zhizn' i deiatel'nost'* (Moscow, 1953), pp. 47-48.

16. *Dokumenty i materialy po istorii Moskovskogo universiteta vtoroi poloviny XVIII veka*, edited by N. A. Penchko, III (Moscow, 1963), 460-61.

17. *Russkii biograficheskii slovar'*, vol. Zhabokritskii-Ziablovskii (Spb., 1916), 321.

18. Gur'ianov, *Komov*, pp. 11-45.

19. Fond 620, ed. khr. 176, no. 2, ff. 2-2v.

20. *Ibid.*, no. 4, f. 4.

21. *Arkhiv kniazia F. A. Kurakina*, IX (Saratov, 1902), 438-39.

22. *Correspondence of Jeremy Bentham*, edited by Timothy L. S. Sprigge, II (London, 1968), 209.

23. *Ibid.*, p. 225.

24. Fond 620, ed. khr. 52, ff. [1-13].

25. *Ibid.*, ed. khr. 61, no. 1, ff. 1-1v.

26. *Ibid.*, f. 2.

27. Coxe, II, 153.

28. *Correspondence of Jeremy Bentham*, II, 393.

29. *Annals of Agriculture*, II, 242.

30. *Autobiography of Arthur Young*, p. 125.

31. *Ibid.*
32. Fond 620, ed. khr. 52, f.[12].
33. *Ibid.*, ed. khr. 157, no. 2, f.3.
34. *Ibid.*
35. *Autobiography of Arthur Young*, p. 124.
36. Fond 620, ed. khr. 61, no. 1, f. 1.
37. *Letters and Papers on Agriculture, Planting, etc.* selected from the correspondence book of the Society instituted of Bath for the Encouragement of Agriculture, Arts, Manufactures and Commerce, II (1783), 3.
38. Fond 620, ed. khr. 157, no. 4, f. 5.
39. 'Primechaniia Rossiiskikh byvshikh v Anglii uchenikov zemledeliia, v 1786 [sic] godu', *Khozaistvennye zapiski,* VI (1814), 22–60.
40. Gur'ianov, *Komov,* p. 50.
41. *Ibid.*, pp. 50-51.
42. I. M. Komov, *O zemledelii* (Moscow, 1788), pp. 209-10. It was probably during this trip that he met Young for the first time.
43. Bath Public Library, Ms. R69/12675, B920. I am grateful to Mr. T. Fawcett of the University of East Anglia for bringing Rack's journal to my attention.
44. Bodleian Library, Oxford, Library Records, L. P. Admissions, e. 2, f. 45v.
45. Komov, *O zemledelii*, p. 18.
46. Gur'ianov, *Komov*, pp. 53-54.
47. *Ibid.*, p. 56.
48. *Ibid.*, pp. 56-65.
49. "Ob otdelenii kosteria ot pshenitsy i rzhi semennoi, i o predokhranenii pshenitsy ot golovni," *Prodolzhenie trudov Vol'nogo Ekonomicheskogo obshchestva,* VII (1787), 39-47.
50. Gur'ianov, *Komov,* p. 60.
51. N. Stelletskii, "Protoierei A. A. Samborskii (Zakonouchitel' Imperatora Aleksandra I)," *Trudy Kievskoi dukhovnoi akademii,* no. 10 (October 1896), 191-92.
52. *Sbornik Imperatorskogo Russkogo istoricheskogo obshchestva,* XXVII (Spb., 1880), 357.
53. I. I. Nazarenko, "Professor M. G. Livanov–vospitannik Moskovskogo universiteta. Razvedka nedr na iuge Rossii v XVIIIv.," *Istoriia geologicheskikh nauk v Moskovskom universitete,* edited by D. I. Gordeev (Moscow, 1962), pp. 45-60.
54. E. I. Druzhinina, *Severnoe Prichernomor'e v 1775-1800* (Moscow, 1959), p. 134.
55. Fond 620, ed. khr. 119, no. 2, f. 3.
56. *Ibid.*, ed. khr. 127, no. 8, f. 13v. Italicized words were in English in the original.
57. *Ibid.*, ed. khr. 119, no. 4, f. 6v.
58. *Ibid.*, no. 5, f. 8v. As we shall see, however, Mordvinov was still very much involved with agricultural improvements.
59. *Ibid.*, no. 6, f. 10.
60. *Autobiography of Arthur Young*, p. 102.
61. *Annals of Agriculture,* II (1784), 252-54.
62. Fond 620, ed. khr. 157, no. 4, f. 5v.
63. *Ibid.*, no. 11, f. 20.
64. *Annals of Agriculture,* VI (1786), 482-83. Cf. H. Cecil Pawson, *Robert Bakewell: Pioneer Livestock Breeder* (London, 1957), p. 88.
65. Lenin Library, Moscow, Fond 313, Fedorov, No. 25, "Zhurnal Ivana Sudakova v bytnosti evo v Anglii, dlia primechaniia ekonomicheskikh i protchikh, do Zemledeliia kasaiushchikhsia nadobnostei," III, ff. 5-51.
66. *Ibid.*, I, ff. 27-36.

67. Druzhinina, *Severnoe Prichernomor'e*, p. 134, note 157.

68. Ian R. Christie, "Samuel Bentham and the Western Colony at Krichev, 1784-1787," *Slavonic and East European Review*, XLVIII, no. 111 (1970), 241-42.

69. "Ob uvol'nenii iz Morskogo vedomostva chernomorskikh admiralteiskikh selenii," *Morskoi sbornik*, XLVIII, no. 111 (1970), 241-42.

70. Fond 620, ed. khr. 127, no. 6, f. 9; no. 8, f. 13v.

71. *Ibid.*, ed. khr. 119, no. 5, f. 8.

72. *Ibid.*, ed. khr. 127, no. 14, f. 21.

73. V. Veshniakov, "Ekspeditsiia Gosudarstvennogo khozaistva (1797-1803 gg.)," *Russkaia starina*, CVIII (1901), 406.

74. Fond 620, ed. khr. 127, no. 2, f. 3v.

75. *Ibid.*, no. 3, ff. 4-4v.

76. *Ibid.*, no. 4, f. 6.

77. Christie, "Samuel Bentham . . . ," p. 242.

78. Fond 620, ed. khr. 127, no. 7, f. 11v.

79. *Arkhiv kniazia Viazemskogo. Kniaz' Andrei Ivanovich Viazemskii* (Spb., 1881), p. 161.

80. Fond 620, ed. khr. 166, no. 4, f. 5v.

81. Lenin Library, Moscow, Fond 93/II, Dostoevskii F., karton 9, ed. khr. 122.

82. 'Zhurnal Ivana Sudakova', *op. cit.*, I, f. 3. Subsequent references in the text are by volume and page.

83. Fond 620, ed. khr. 157, no. 6, f. 10v.

84. See my "Early Contacts of the Society of Arts with Russia, III: The Visit of a Russian Serf," *Journal of the Royal Society of Arts* (May 1976), 374-76.

85. Fond 620, ed. kh. 100, nos. 1-10.

86. On Dzhunkovskii's career, see D. P. Priklonskii, *Biografiia tainogo sovetnika Stepana Semenovicha Dzhunkovskogo chlena i nepremennogo sekretaria Vol'nogo Ekonomicheskogo obshchestva* (Spb., 1840).

87. *Communications to the Board of Agriculture, on Subjects Relative to the Husbandry, and Internal Improvement of the Country*, I (2nd edition, London, 1804), 329-47. See my "'Zamechaniia' Sera Dzhona Sinklera o Rossi," *XVIII vek*, X (Leningrad, 1975), 160-68.

88. *SRIO*, XLIV (Spb., 1885), 606-07.

89. *Travels in Poland, Russia, Sweden, and Denmark*, II, 212.

90. *Journal of the Royal Society of Arts* (December 1965), 70.

91. Fond 620, ed. khr. 127, no. 14, f. 21.

92. The dedication and foreword occupy 24 unnumbered pages.

93. *Opisanie prakticheskogo aglinskogo zemledeliia, sobrannoe iz raznykh Anglinskikh Pisatelei* (Moscow, 1781), pp. 6, 7.

94. *Svodnyi katalog russkoi knigi XVIII veka*, III (Moscow, 1966), 84, no. 6268.

95. M. P. Alekseev, "K 'Opisaniiu moego vladeniia'," in *Radishchev: Sbornik statei* (Leningrad, 1950), pp. 281-85.

96. K. V. Sivkov, "Voprosy sel'skogo khozaistva v russkikh zhurnalakh poslednei treti XVIII veka," *Materialy po istorii zemledeliia SSSR*, I (Moscow, 1952), 594-95.

97. *Trudy Vol'nogo obshchestva sorevnovatelei prosveshcheniia i blagotvoreniia*, I, no. 1 (1818), 137.

98. *O zemledelii, skotovodstve i ptitsevodstve* (Nikolaev, 1797), p. 147.

99. I. F. Kopyl, "Iz istorii russkoi agronomii XVIII v. (I. M. Komov o zemledelii)," *Materialy po istorii sel'skogo khozaistva i krest'ianstva*, VII (Moscow, 1969), 89. For Komov's article, see note 49.

100. *O zemledelii* (Moscow, 1788), p. 27.

101. *Ibid.*, pp. 17-19.

102. Sivkov, *op. cit.*, pp. 601-02.

103. V. S. Lekhnovich, "K istorii kul'tury kartofelia v Rossii," *Materialy po istorii zemledeliia SSSR* II (Moscow-Leningrad 1956), 284. The Senate published an instruction on potato-growing in 1765, *Nastavlenie o razvedenii zemlianykh iablok, potetes imianuemykh*. See *Svodnyi katalog*, II, 283, no. 4479.

104. *O zemledelii*, pp. 232-37.

105. *O zemledelii, skotovodstve i ptitsevodstve*, p. 138.

106. *Ibid.*, pp. 10, 13, 15-16, 43, 70, 87, 93, 125, 130-31, 138.

107. *O zemledelii*, p. 22.

108. *O zemledelii, skotovodstve i ptitsevodstve*, dedication and preface unnumbered.

109. Fond 620, ed. khr. 119, no. 4, ff. 6v.-7.

110. *Trudy VEO*, XXXVI (1788), 133-51.

111. *Khozaistvennye zapiski VEO*, II (1812), 1-41, V (1814), 65-78. Cf. Komov, *O zemledelii*, pp. 153-57 and Livanov, *O zemledelii, skotovodstve i ptitsevodstve*, p. 23.

112. *Prodolzhenie trudov VEO*, IX (1789), 172-83.

113. Sivkov, *op. cit.*, pp. 581-83. See also the basic work on the subject, Michel Confino, *Systèmes agraires et progrès agricole: l'assolement triennial en Russie aux XVIIIe-XIXe siècles* (Paris and The Hague, 1969).

114. Cf. V. Veshniakov, "Ekspeditsiia gosudarstvennogo khozaistva (1797-1803gg.)," *Russkaia starina*, CVIII (1901), 195-202, 403-22. This is the basic source of information on the Bureau.

115. See the lists in Fond 620, ed. khr. 195, no. 5, f. 5; no. 10, f. 11.

116. *Ibid.*, ed. khr. 61, no. 24, f. 31.

117. *Trudy Kievskoi dukhovnoi akademii*, no. 12 (1896), 515.

118. British Library, Add. Mss. 35128, f. 469.

119. *Ibid.*, f. 468.

120. *Ibid.*, f. 488.

121. *Ibid.*, ff. 496-97; 35129, ff. 158-59; *Autobiography of Arthur Young*, pp. 387, 401.

122. *Autobiography of Arthur Young*, p. 402.

123. *Ibid.*, pp. 402-10, 428-32; British Library, Add. Mss. 35129, ff. 194, 219, 254, 366-67; 35130, f. 110; 35133, f. 129. See also *The Russian Journals of Martha and Catherine Wilmot, 1803-1808* (London, 1934), pp. 215, 264.

124. Saltykov-Shchedrin Library, Leningrad, Fond 603, Poltoratskii, S. D., no. 248, f. 13v.

125. *Ibid.*, no. 309, f. 1.

126. N. S. Trusova and O. A. Bliumfel'd, "Iz istorii vozniknoveniia i nachal'noi deiatel'nosti Moskovskogo obshchestva sel'skogo khozaistva (1820-1830 gg.)," *Materialy po istorii sel'skogo khozaistva i krest'ianstva SSSR*, III (Moscow, 1959), 282-83.

127. Fond 603, Poltoratskii, S. D., no. 248, f. 11.

128. *Ibid.*, f. 14v.

129. The fullest account of the dispute is in Confino, *op. cit.*, pp. 242-47.

130. In November 1817 the Grand Duke Mikhail Pavlovich toured Poltoratskii's farm at Avchurino and G. A. Glinka gave a glowing account of Poltoratskii's achievements in his report to the Empress Mariia Fedorovna: *Russkii arkhiv*, XV, book 2, no. 7 (1877), 249-50.

NOTES TO CHAPTER 4, pages 92-121

1. *Scots Magazine*, XXXIII (1771), 598.

2. Leo Loewenson, "Some Details of Peter the Great's Stay in England in 1698: Neglected English Material," *Slavonic and East European Review*, XL. No. 95 (1962), 442. 442.

3. Narcissus Luttrell, *A Brief Historical Relation of State Affairs from September 1678 to April 1714* (Oxford, 1857), 368. Quoted in Loewenson, p. 442.

4. "Puteshestvie odnoi Rossiiskoi znatnoi Gospozhi, po nekotorym Aglinskim provintsiiam," *Opyt trudov Vol'nogo Rossiiskogo Sobraniia*, II (Moscow, 1775), 136.

5. [John Barrow], *A Memoir of the Life of Peter the Great* (London. 1832), p. 88; A. I. Andreev, "Petr I v Anglii v 1698 g.," in *Petr Velikii: sbornik statei* (Moscow-Leningrad, 1947), pp. 80-81. Also on Postnikov, see Iser Steiman, "P. V. Posnikov: A Russian Pioneer in Physiology," *Canadian Slavonic Papers*, VII (1965), 63-70. Steiman gives different birth and death dates: 1673-1716.

6. *Arkhiv kniazia F. A. Kurakina*, IV (Saratov, 1893), 36.

7. Bodleian Library, Oxford, Library Records L. P. Admissions, e.2, f.24v. I am also indebted to Mr J. S. G. Simmons for these references from the Bodleian Library records.

8. On Müller, see: Jakob Staehlin, *Original Anecdotes of Peter the Great* (London, 1788), pp. 430-31; Eduard Winter, *Halle als Ausgangspunkt der deutschen Russlandkunde im 18. Jahrhundert* (Berlin, 1953), pp. 85, 99, 102, 104, 124, 207-08; P. N. Berkov, "Deutsch-russische kulturelle Beziehungen im 18. Jahrhundert," *Wissenschaftliche Annalen*, VI, no. 10 (1957), 695.

9. On Blumentrost, see M. I. Pyliaev, *Zabytoe proshloe okrestnostei Peterburga* (Spb., 1889), pp. 215-20; *Istoriia Akademii Nauk SSSR*, I (Moscow-Leningrad, 1958), 31-36, 44-47, 145.

10. M. I. Radovskii, *Iz istorii anglo-russkikh nauchynkh sviazei* (Moscow-Leningrad, 1961), pp. 58-60.

11. L. P. Admissions, e.2, f.32.

12. "Otchet, podnesennyi Petru Velikomu ot bibliotekaria Shumakera o zagranichnom ego puteshestvii v 1721-22 godakh," in P. P. Pekarskii, *Nauka i literatura v Rossii pri Petre Velikom*, I (Spb., 1862), 533-58.

13. *Oxford in 1710. From the Travels of Zacharias Conrad von Uffenbach*, edited by W. H. Quarrell and W. J. C. Quarrell (Oxford, 1928), pp. 14-15.

14. L. P. Admissions, e.2, f.36v; *Istoriia Akademii Nauk SSSR*, I, 453.

15. Radovskii, *op. cit.*, pp. 116-21. See also Iu. Kh. Kopelevich, "Pervaia zagranichnaia komandirovka peterburgskogo akademika (iz zapisod G. F. Millera o ego puteshestvii 1730-1731 gg.)," *Voprosy istorii estestvoznaniia i tekhniki*, no. 2 (1793), 47-52.

16. Radovskii, pp. 138-43.

17. *Ibid.*, p. 142.

18. R. T. Gunther, *Early Science in Oxford*, XI (Oxford, 1937), 398.

19. It is possible that the three young brothers Pavel, Petr and Aleksandr (surname unknown), whose manuscript diary covering the first part of their stay in London to the end of 1758 is extant, are the students in question: Library of the Academy of Sciences, Leningrad, "Zhurnal puteshestviia po Evrope v 1758," Ms. no. 16.14.32.

20. F. Veselago, *Ocherki istorii morskogo kadetskogo korpusa* (Spb., 1852), pp. 103-07.

21. M. I. Sukhomlinov, *Materialy dlia istorii Imperatorskoi Akademii Nauk*, IX (Spb., 1897), 611, 693.

22. Gunther, I (1923), pp. 201-02.

23. *A New and General Biographical Dictionary*, III (London 1798), 48.

24. There exists a letter in English, dated Cambridge, 14 September 1747, which Kostiurin sent to Rev. Johns of Limpsfield, Surrey, whom he had recently visited, and in which he discusses the types of grouse found in Russia: Norfolk Record Office, Ms. WKC 7/42, 404 x 2.

25. L. P. Admissions, e.2, f.43.

26. *Opyt trudov Vol'nogo Rossiiskogo Sobraniia*, II, 257-61.

27. See *Shekspir i russkaia kul'tura*, edited by M. P. Alekseev (Moscow-Leningrad, 1965), pp. 51-53.

28. *Opyt trudov*, III (1776), 1-39. Cf. Pushkin's foreword to Chapter I of *Evgenii Onegin* (1825) and his letter to Prince P. A. Viazemskii on 13 July of the same year: *Pushkin on Literature*, translated and edited by Tatiana Wolff (London, 1971), pp. 78, 154.

29. *Opyt trudov*, III, 72-74.

30. *Jackson's Oxford Journal*, no. 532, 9 July 1763, p. [3].

31. "Proekt bogoslovskogo fakul'teta pri Ekaterine II," *Vestnik Evropy*, VI, no. 11 (1873), 301; V. N. Aleksandrenko, "Iz zhizni russkikh studentov v Oksforde v tsarstvovanie Ekateriny II," *Zhurnal Ministerstva narodnogo prosveshcheniia*, CCLXXXV, no. 1, section 2 (1893), 1.

32. Nicholas Hans, "Russian Students at Leyden in the 18th Century," *SEER*, XXXV, no. 85 (1957), 553; "Dumaresq, Brown and Some Early Educational Projects of Catherine II," *ibid.*, XL (1961), 229-35.

33. *Vestnik Evropy*, VI (1873), 313-16.

34. V. N. Aleksandrenko, *Russkie diplomaticheskie agenty v Londone v XVIII v.*, II (Warsaw, 1897), 105.

35. *Ibid.*, pp. 106-11.

36. *Ibid.*, I, 271-72.

37. V. Z. Dzhincharadze, "Iz istorii russko-angliiskikh kul'turnykh otnoshenii v 18 veke," *Vestnik istorii mirovoi kul'tury*, V (Sept.-Oct. 1960), 72.

38. U. A. Chancellor Court Papers, bundle 109 (1774-77), deposition of Basil Nikitin. The Rev. Mr. Stubbs in question would seem to be John Stubb (b. 1735?): John Foster, *Alumni Oxonienses*, IV (Oxford 1888), 1369.

39. *Vestnik Evropy* VI (1873), 308.

40. A. D. Godley, *Oxford in the Eighteenth Century* (London, 1908), p. 198; *Woodforde at Oxford 1759-1776*, edited by W. N. Hargreaves-Mawdsley, (Oxford, 1969), p. xv.

41. *Opyt trudov*, II, 135.

42. Godley, p. 130.

43. John Richard Green and Geo. Roberson, *Studies in Oxford History, Chiefly in the Eighteenth Century* (Oxford, 1901), p. 53.

44. Aleksandrenko, *Diplomaticheskie agenty*, II, 138.

46. *Ibid.*, p. 142.

47. *Ibid.*, p. 153.

48. *Ibid.*, p. 164.

49. Pushkin House, Leningrad, Fond 620, Arkhiv Samborskogo, ed. khr. 134, no. 1, f.1.

50. Entries in Minute Book of the Chancellor's Court, Hyp. A. 61 (1763-1780), for 24 June, 8, 15 July, 4, 11, 25 November, 2, 16 December 1774, 20, 27 January, 3, 10, 13, 17, 24 February, 10 March, 1775.

51. *Woodforde at Oxford*, pp. 274-75.

52. Deposition of Robert Pepall, Butler of Merton, 8 February 1775.

53. From the three long undated and unfoliated depositions of Nikitin to the Court.

54. Aleksandrenko, *Diplomaticheskie agenty*, II, 143.

55. Godley, p. 57.

56. Bukhovetskii as early as 1766 rebelled against the need to study theology and despite Musin-Pushkin's remonstrances was allowed to study "history, geography, mathematics and similar sciences, which are necessary and useful in every calling and position": Aleksandrenko, *Diplomaticheskie agenty*, I, 271-72.

57. M. I. Sukhomlinov, "Istoriia Rossiiskoi Akademii," *Sbornik Otdeleniia russkogo iazyka i slovesnosti*, XXII (Spb., 1881), 17-18.

58. Godley, p. 40.

59. Christopher Wordsworth, *Scholae Academicae: Some Account of Studies at the English Universities in the Eighteenth Century* (Cambridge 1877) p. 222, n. 3.

60. *A Catalogue of All Graduates in the University of Oxford* (Oxford, 1851), p. 482. Nikitin in his own service record gives the year as 1771, which all Russian accounts have adopted.

61. *Uchenaia korrespondentsiia Akademii Nauk* (Moscow-Leningrad, 1937), pp. 86, 88, 92, 100, 105, 106, 108, 150.

62. *Biograficheskii ocherk grafa Vladimira Grigor'evicha Orlova*, I (Spb., 1878), 162-63.

63. *Philosophical Transactions*, LIX (1770), 181; Gunther, II, 87. Hornsby also published papers concerned with the transit in *Philosophical Transactions*, LIII (1763), LV (1765) and LXIII (1773).

64. Gunther, XI, 407.

65. Aleksandrenko, "Iz zhizni russkikh studentov," p. 14.

66. Gunther, I, p. 203.

67. Aleksandrenko, "Iz zhizni russkikh studentov," p. 14.

68. *Ibid.*, pp. 10-11.

69. Sukhomlinov, XXII, 300, 302.

70. Aleksandrenko, *Russkie diplomaticheskie agenty*, II, 186.

71. *Woodforde in Oxford*, p. 286.

72. *Ibid.*, p. 217.

73. *Ibid.*, p. 274.

74. *Ibid.*, pp. 277, 278, 286.

75. *Transactions of the Quaruor Coronati Lodge*, XXII (1909), 173.

76. King's College Library, Aberdeen, Beattie Mss., C. 28.

77. *Letters of Richard Radcliffe and John James of Queen's College, Oxford, 1755-83*, (Oxford, 1888), pp. 93-4.

78. *James Beattie's London Diary, 1773*, edited by Ralph S. Walker (Aberdeen, 1946), p. 67.

79. *Transactions of the Quaruor Coronati Lodge*, XXII, 152.

80. Lenin Library, Moscow, Fond 137, Korsakovy, papka 2, ed. khr. 12, ff. 47v-48. Williamson moved to London in 1783 and tutored a number of Russians in geometry and earned the tribute from the Russian ambassador as "un des meilleurs commentateurs d'Euclide": *Arkhiv kniazia Vorontsova*, IX (Moscow, 1876), 116.

81. *Elements of Plane and Spherical Trigonometry*, p. i.

82. Williamson's *Elements of Euclid* was published at the Clarendon Press in 1781.

83. F. Petrushevskii, quoted by V. V. Bobynin in "Nikitin, Vasilii Nikitich," *Russkii biograficheskii slovar'*, XI (Reprint: New York, 1962), 316.

84. *Vestnik Evropy* (1873) p. 309.

85. Sukhomlinov, "Istoriia Rossiiskoi Akademii," XI, 298-99; *Russkii biograficheskii slovar'*, X, 159.

86. *Life of Reginald Heber*, I, (London, 1830), 179.

87. S. Smirnov, *Istoriia Troitskoi lavrskoi seminarii* (Moscow, 1867), pp. 397, 506.

88. *Vestnik Evropy* VI (1873) 315-16.

89. Information in a letter from Dr. R. P. Bartlett of the University of Keele.

90. Sukhomlinov, "Istoriia Rossiiskoi Akademii," XXII, 19.

91. *Ibid.*, pp. 199-301 (for Nikitin), 301-05 (for Suvorov).

92. *Ibid.*, pp. 14-15.

93. *Ibid.*, pp. 20-21.

94. Fond 620, Arkhiv Samborskogo, ed. khr. 134, no. 3, ff. 3-4.

95. *AKV*, IX, 408-09. F. U. T. Aepinus was head of the Cipher Department in the College of Foreign Affairs: see R. W. Home, "Science as a Career: The Case of F. U. T. Aepinus," *SEER*, LI, no. 122 (1973), 92.

96. Al. Sokolov, "Prokhor Ignat'evich Suvorov, uchitel' morskogo korpusa i shtur- manskogo uchilishcha v Nikolaeve," *Morskoi sbornik,* XXIV, no. 10, *Smes'* (1856), 29-32.

97. This aspect of his activities is studied in my "Printing at Nikolaev, 1798-1803," *Transactions of the Cambridge Bibliographical Society*, VI, part 3 (1974), 149-57.

98. Sukhomlinov "Istoriia Rossiiskoi Akademii," XXII, 305.

99. *Arkhiv Grafov Mordvinovykh*, IV (Spb., 1902), 276-79, 280-82.

100. Sukhomlinov "Istoriia Rossiiskoi Akademii," XXII, 305.

101. *Arkhiv kniazia F. A. Kurakina*, VII (Saratov, 1898), 155. In later years he was known for the generous treatment of his peasants as "the liberal lord." His son, by his second marriage, was the famous reformer Aleksandr Koshelev, on whom N. Koliupanov, *Biografiia Aleksandra Ivanovicha Kosheleva* (Moscow, 1889-92).

102. *Ibid.*, V (1894), 408.

103. Lenin Library, Moscow, Fond 183, No. 1673, f. 87v.

104. *Ibid.*, f. 88v.

105. L. P. Admissions, e.2, f. 45v.

106. John Parkinson, *A Tour of Russia, Siberia and the Crimea, 1792-1794* (London, 1971), p. 142.

107. *Russkii biograficheskii slovar'*, vol. Chaadaev-Shvitkov (Spb, 1905), 167-69; 173-74; P. N. Berkov, *Istoriia russkoi zhurnalistiki XVIII veka* (M.-L., 1952), p. 99.

108. John Forster, *The Life and Adventures of Oliver Goldsmith* (London 1848), p. 701.

109. *The Despatches and Correspondence of John, Second Earl of Buckinghamshire*, edited by A. Collyer, II (London, 1902), 198-99.

110. F. A. Biuler, "Dva epizoda iz tsarstvovaniia Ekateriny II," *Russkii vestnik*, LXXXV, no. 1 (1870), 40-59.

111. Catherine asked Cherkasov in 1767 to obtain from the Earl of Buckinghamshire a copy of *The Declaration of Rights* (1688) and to provide a French translation: *Russkii vestnik*, LXXXV, no. 3, 186.

112. Berkov, *Istoriia russkoi zhurnalistiki*, p. 99.

113. *Henry, Elizabeth and George*, edited by Lord Herbert (London, 1989), p. 279. A short biographical sketch of Chesmenskii is to be found in *Russkii biograficheskii slovar'*, vol. Chaadaev-Shvitkov, 360-61.

114. *Diaries and Correspondence of James Harris, First Earl of Malmesbury*, I (London, 1844), 233-34.

115. *Henry, Elizabeth and George*, p. 153.

116. *Ibid.*, p. 393. See also pp. 201, 349, 362, 368, 370 412 and *Pembroke Papers (1780-1794)*, edited by Lord Herbert (London, 1950), pp. 41-42, 46.

117. S. P. Zhikharev, *Zapiski sovremennika* (Moscow-Leningrad, 1955), p. 205. See also pp. 57-58, 160, 424, 727-28.

118. Dzhincharadze, *op. cit.*, p. 73.

119. John Peile, *Biographical Register of Christ's College 1505-1905*, II (Cambridge, 1913), p. 322; Fond 620, Arkhiv Samborskogo, ed. khr 100, no. 5, f. 9.

120. D. A. Winstanley, *Unreformed Cambridge* (Cambridge, 1935), pp. 131-32.

121. Henry Gunning, *Reminiscences of the University, Town and County of Cambridge, from the Year 1780*, I (London, 1854), 8.

122. *Ibid.*, pp. 11-12.

123. *Ibid.*, p. 17.

124. *Ibid.*, p. 19.

125. Veselago, *Ocherk istorii morskogo kadetskogo korpusa*, p. 177.

1. D. A. Winstanley, *Unreformed Cambridge* (Cambridge, 1935), p. 210.

2. V. N. Aleksandrenko, *Russkie diplomaticheskie agenty v Londone v XVIII v.*, I (Warsaw, 1897), 271.

3. Cf. Davis D. McElroy, *Scotland's Age of Improvement: A Survey of Eighteenth-Century Clubs and Societies* (Pullman, Wash., 1969). McElroy also mentions (pp. 162-63) Professor Simson's Friday Club which included Smith and other professors among its members.

4. Lenin Libarry, Moscow, Fond 137, Korsakovy, papka 2, ed. khr. 12, f. 48v.

5. Quoted in Henry Grey Graham, *The Social Life of Scotland in the Eighteenth Century* (London, 1964), p. 455, note 3.

6. W. R. Scott, *Adam Smith as Student and Professor* (Glasgow, 1937), pp. 158-59.

7. *Arkhiv kniazia Vorontsova*, V (Moscow, 1872), 107.

8. Scott, *op. cit.*, p. 159.

9. *Dokumenty i materialy po istorii Moskovskogo universiteta utoroi poloviny XVIII veka* edited by N. A. Penchko, II (Moscow, 1962), 52.

10. N. A. Penchko, "Vydaiushchiesea vospitanniki Moseovskogo universiteta v ino-strannykh universitetakh (1758-1771 gg.)," *Istoricheskii arkhiv*, no. 2 (1956), 167-69. 69.

11. *Dokumenty i materialy*, III, 422.

12. N. A. Penchko, *op. cit.*, p. 168.

13. A. H. Brown, "Adam Smith's First Russian Followers," in Andrew S. Skinner and Thomas Wilson (eds.), *Essays on Adam Smith* (Oxford, 1975), p. 252.

14. Brown suggests from the internal evidence of Desnitskii's later work that he attended Millar's lectures on Scottish law as well as on civil, i.e., Roman law. (*Ibid.*, p. 253). The evidence is in Penchko, *op. cit.*, p. 171.

15. Brown, *op. cit.*, p. 259.

16. Eric Robinson (ed.), *Partners in Science: Letters of James Watt and Joseph Black* (London, 1970), p. 84. The Russians also knew Watt from his time as instrument-maker to the University. See Brown, *op. cit.*, pp. 254-55.

17. Penchko, *op. cit.*, p. 170.

18. Brown, *op. cit.*, p. 252.

19. *Ibid.*, p. 255.

20. Penchko, *op. cit.*, p. 172.

21. *Ibid.*,

22. The whole incident has been reconstructed by Brown, *op. cit.*, pp. 256-59.

23. *Ibid.*, p. 259. The entry is somewhat puzzling. Were their theses on the passages from Justinian's *Pandects* read to the Faculty in February 1766 merely "specimens of their knowledge in the Civil Law" or the "Theses" which they were still apparently expected to defend in public?

24. *Dokumenty i materialy*, III, 119.

25. *Ibid.*, pp. 56-73.

26. "S. E. Desnitsky, Adam Smith, and the *Nakaz* of Catherine II," *Oxford Slavonic Papers*, NS VII (1974), 42-59.

27. Marc Raeff, "The Empress and the Vinerian Professor: Catherine II's Projects of Government Reforms and Blackstone's *Commentaries*," *Ibid.*, pp. 18-41.

28. *Dokumenty i materialy*, III, pp. 124, 426.

29. "S. E. Desnitskii i I. A. Tret'iakov v Glazgovskom universitete (1761-1767)," *Vestnik Moskovskogo universiteta*, no. 4 (1969), 84-88.

30. "Adam Smith's First Russian Disciple," *SEER*, XLV (1967), 424-38.

31. "Adam Smith and His Russian Admirers of the Eighteenth Century," in Scott, *op. cit.*, p. 425.

32. It is possible that another young Russian, P. I. Bogdanovich (d. 1803) studied briefly at Glasgow in the late 1760s, according to I. F. Martynov of the Department of Manuscripts and Rare Books in the Libaray of the Academy of Sciences, Leningrad. Martynov did not discover this information in time to include it in his "Knigoizdatel' literator i bibliograf XVIII veka Petr Ivanovich Bogdanovich," *Kniga*, XXI (1970), 89-105. Bogdanovich was at Leipzig University in 1765 and afterwards in Holland. He returned to Russia in 1771.

33. Quoted in McElroy, *op. cit*l, p. 71.

34. Fond 137, Korsakovy, papka 2, ed. khr. 12, f. 8.

35. "Rossiianin v Anglii. Otryvki iz pisem odnogo puteshestvennika," *Priiatnoe i poleznoe preprovozhdenie vremeni*, XI (1796), 362.

36. *Materialy dlia istorii russkogo flota*, edited by F. Veselago, XII (Spb., 1886), 232.

37. *Ibid*.

38. "Matriculation Roll of the University of Edinburgh–Arts–Law–Divinity." Transcribed by Dr. Alexander Morgan (1933-34), University of Edinburgh Library, I, f. 335; II, ff. 342-43, 345-46, 353, 356, 365.

39. *Correspondence of Jeremy Bentham*, II (London, 1968), 230.

40. *Scots Magazine*, XXXIX (October 1777), 562. On Greig, see my "Samuel Greig, Catherine the Great's Scottish Admiral," *Mariner's Mirror*, LX, no. 3 (1974), 251-66.

41. Eric Robinson, *Partners in Science*, p. 385. See also pp. 347, 382. The translation, however, seems never to have been published.

42. Tira Sokolovskaia, "O masonstve v prezhnem russkom flote," *More*, no. 8 (1907), 216-52; A. G. Cross, "British Freemasons in Russia during the Reign of Catherine the Great," *Oxford Slavonic Papers*, NS. IV (1971), 49, 58-59. Prokhor Zhdanov was also a member of the Lodge.

43. *The Russian Journals of Martha and Catherine Wilmot*, edited by the Marchioness of Londonderry and H. M. Hyde (London, 1934), p. 50.

44. National Library of Scotland, Ms. 3942, ff. 269-70, 281-82, 287.

45. *Ibid.*, ff. 281v.-282v. An English translation of this letter was published in *Memoirs of the Princess Daschkow*, translated by Mrs. Bradford, II (London, 1894), pp. 117-20. A French translation from this English version and by now far from the original appeared in *Mémoires de la Princesse Daschkoff*, translated by Pascal Pontremoli (Paris, 1966), pp. 288-91.

46. *Horace Walpole's Correspondence*, edited by W. S. Lewis, XXIX (London, 1955), 59.

47. Edinburgh University Library, Ms. Gen. 873/II, f. 90.

48. *Ibid.*, f. 92.

49. H. Montgomery Hyde, *The Empress Catherine and Princess Dashkov* (London, 1935), p. 148.

50. *The Memoirs of Princess Dashkov*, translated and edited by Kyril Fitzlyon (London, 1958), pp. 148-49.

51. *Ibid.*, p. 147.

52. Edinburgh University Library, College Minutes 1733-1790, ff. 286-87.

53. *Memoirs of Princess Dashkov*, p. 149.

54. *Sochineniia Dolgorukogo*, II (Spb., 1849), 539.

55. *Scots Magazine*, XLI (July 1779), 398.

56. Edinburgh University Library, Ms. Da. 1. 30/7. See my "Edinburgh University's Cabinet of Russian Medals," *Study Group on Eighteenth-Century Russia Newsletter*, no. 1 (1973), 27-28.

57. *Memoirs of the Princess Daschkow* II (1840), 135-36...

58. B. L. Modzalevskii, *Spisok chlenov Imp. Akademii Nauk* (Spb., 1908), p. 135.

59. Edinburgh University Library, Ms. Gen. 873/III, ff. 36-38.

60. Thomas Thomson, *History of the Royal Society* (London, 1812), p. LVII.

61. *Correspondence of Jeremy Bentham*, III (London, 1971), 480.

62. *Russian Journals of Martha and Catherine Wilmot*, p. 277.

63. Pushkin House, Leningrad, Fond 620, Arkhiv A. A. Samborskogo, ed. khr. 177, no. 44, f. 60.

64. *Ibid.*, ed. khr. 92, no. 7, f. 12.

65. *Ibid.*, no. 4, f. 6.

66. *Ibid.*, no. 7, ff. 11-11v.

67. Hermann was later Professor of Law at the University of Strasbourg. Documents relating to Hermann's lawsuit are found in *ibid.*, ed. khr. 201, nos. 1-3.

68. *Ibid.*, ed. khr. 170, no. 1, f.1.

69. John Howard, *The State of the Prisons* (London, 1929), pp. 148-49. Howard notes that in July 1779 there were thirteen debtors and nine felons in the Tolbrook.

70. Fond 620, ed. khr. 117, no. 1, f.1.

71. *Iroi-komicheskaia poema*, edited by B. Tomashevskii (Leningrad, 1933), pp. 267-71.

72. Georg fon-Gel'big, *Russkie izbranniki*, translated by V. A. Vil'basov (Berlin, 1900), p. 488.

73. *Russkaia starina*, CLIII (February 1913), 409-10.

74. Fond 620, ed. khr. 92, no. 4, f. 6v.

75. *Ibid.*, no. 7, f. 12.

76. Information in a letter from Mr. R. N. Smart, the Muniments Room, University of St. Andrews.

77. Graham, *Social Life of Scotland*, p. 482, n. 3.

78. *Laws of the Royal Physical Society* (Edinburgh, 1819), p. 38.

79. Details of Zverev's subsequent career in Russia are found in *Russkii biograficheskii slovar'*, vol. Zhabokritskii-Ziablovskii (Spb., 1916), 321; L. F. Zmeev, *Russkie vrachi pisateli*, I (Spb., 1886), 116.

80. Tatiana Bakounine, *Répertoire biographique des frans-maçons russes* (Paris, 1967), pp. 620-21.

81. *Arkhiv grafov Mordvinovykh*, IV (Spb., 1902), 375.

82. *The Diary of Sylas Neville 1767-1788* (London, 1950), p. 198.

83. *Ibid.*, p. 214.

84. *Ibid.*, p. 219. Italinskii was obviously much impressed by Dr. Black's lectures and asked Neville to send him a scribe's copy of lecture notes, which he did for a cost of £5 15s: Neville Papers, Norfolk Record Office, MC 7/4, 395 x 1, ff. 35-37, 80-82.

85. Letter to Samborskii from Gdansk, 9/20 August 1776: Fond 620, ed. khr. 107, no. 1, f. lv. Italinskii's interest in Beccaria was not known to previous scholars. See T. Cizova, "Beccaria in Russia," *SEER*, XL (1962), 384-408; Franco Venturi, "Cesare Beccaria and Legal Reform," in his *Italy and the Enlightenment* (London, 1972), pp. 160-62.

86. The main but far from reliable sources on Italinskii are Zmeev, I, 130; *Russkii biograficheckii slovar'*, vol. Ibak-Kliucharev, 151-52; *AKV*, XX (Moscow, 1881), 262 (and twenty letters to Vorontsov, 1787-1806, pp. 263-314).

87. *Nauchnoe nasledstvo*, II (Moscow, 1951), 446.

88. Both Shumlianski and Terekhovskii figure in Zmeev and *Russkii biograficheskii slovar'*, but the account which supersedes all others on Shumlianskii (and to some degree on Terekhovskii) is S. L. Sobol', "Osnovopolozhnik otechestvennoi gistologii A. M. Shumlianskii (1748-1795)," the introductory essay (pp. 401-31) to the publication of Shumlianskii's archive, cited in the preceding note.

89. *AKV*, IX (Moscow, 1876), 65. See also *ibid.*, XII, 26; XIII, 103.

90. *Laws of the Society instituted at Edinburgh MDCCLXXXII, for the investigation of Natural History* (Edinburgh, 1803), p. 21; "Obligation Book of the Edinburgh Medical Society" (Edinburgh University Library Ms.), unfoliated.

91. C. P. Finlayson, "Records of Medical and Scientific Societies in Scotland," *Bibliothek*, I, no. 2 (1958), 17.

92. *Laws of the Society*, p. 33. In addition to Bakhmetev, ordinary members of the Society included Mikhail Stepanov and Pavel Bakunin (pp. 27, 28).

93. Edinburgh University Library, Mss. Papers of the Natural History Society, IV, 45-9, 124-31.

94. *AKV*, XIII, 105; XVI, 198.

95. Information from Mr. R. N. Smart (see note 76).

96. Edinburgh University Library, Mss. 873/II, f. 279-279v.; 873/III, f. 38v.

97. Zmeev, I, 18.

98. Fond 620, ed. khr. 142, no. 1, f.1.

99. *Ibid.*, nos. 1-4; ed. khr. 157, no. 2, f. 3v. These letters help to correct gaps and inaccuracies in Zmeev's account of Pischekov's career.

100. Information in letter from Mr. C. A. McLaren, Archivist in the Library of the University of Aberdeen.

101. *Gentleman's Magazine*, LVI, pt. 1 (1786), 130-31.

102. *Prodolzhenie trudov Vol'nogo ekonomicheskogo obshchestva*, VII (1787), 1-13.

103. Zmeev, I, pt. 2 (1886), 61. See also S. M. Grombakh, *Russkaia meditsinskaia literatura XVIII veka* (Moscow, 1953), pp. 70, 164 on Pischekov's publications.

104. *Transactions of the Royal Society of Edinburgh*, I (1788), 80. Two letters from Grimm to Catherine II in 1782 and 1783 speak of Samoilovich's proposed visit to England: *Sbornik Imp. Russkogo istoricheskogo obshchestva*, XLIV (1885), 299-300, 312-13.

105. His son writes in a manuscript biographical account that "following his bent for knowledge, he went to Scotland, heard the lectures of the best professors in Edinburgh and completed his education": Saltykov-Shchedrin Library, Leningrad, Fond 603, Poltoratskii, S. D., no. 248, f. 13v.

106. M. I. Pyliaev, *Zamechatel'nye chudaki i originaly* (Spb., 1898), pp. 225-26. His information is taken from a contemporary source, "Zapiski grafa E. F. Komarovskogo," *Osmnadtsatyi vek*, I (2nd edition, 1869), 403.

107. *AKV*, XXII, 527. See *ibid.*, passim.

108. Alexander Vucinich, *Science in Russian Culture* (London, 1965), p. 143.

109. *Laws of the Society*, p. 28; Mss. Papers of the Natural History Society, VI, 213-17.

110. *Archaelogia Scotica*, III (1831), appendix, p. 82.

111. *Istoriia Akademii Nauk SSSR*, I (Moscow-Leningrad, 1958), 324-26.

112. Modzalevskii, *Spisok chlenov*, pp. 131, 77.

113. On Rogerson, see my "John Rogerson: Physician to Catherine the Great," *Canadian Slavic Studies*, IV (1970), 594-601.

114. See the two letters from Rogerson to Robertson, 1/21 August 1773 and 20 September/1 October 1776, in the National Library of Scotland, Mss. 3942, ff. 139, 277.

115. V. P. Semennikov, *Sobranie staraiushcheesia o perevode inostrannykh knig, uchrezhdennoe Ekaterinoi II. 1768-1783 gg.* (Spb., 1913), pp. 55-56, 71.

116. *Svodnyi katalog russkoi knigi grazhdanskoi pechati XVIII veka,* I (Moscow, 1963), 108, nos. 607-09.

117. "Rossiianin v Anglii," *Priiatnoe i poleznoe priprovozhdenie vremeni,* XI (1796), 364-65.

118. See Alekseev's article in Scott, *op. cit.,* pp. 424-31.

119. "Zhurnal puteshestviia V. N. Zinov'eva po Germanii, Italii, Frantsii i Anglii v 1784-1788 gg.," *Russkaia starina,* XXIII (1878), 436.

120. *Ibid.,* pp. 434-35.

121. See in addition to Alekseev's article, Georg Sacke, "Der Einfluss Englands auf die politische Ideologie der Russischen Gesellschaft in der 2. Hälfte des XVIII. Jahrhunderts," *Archiv für Kulturgeschichte,* XXX (1941), 85-105.

122. "Tra Scozia e Russia: Un dibattito settecentesco sul feudalismo," *Rossiia-Rusia,* I (1974), 9-40.

123. For a brief account of some of the Scottish doctors, see my "The British in Catherine's Russia: A Preliminary Survey," in J. G. Garrard (ed.), *The Eighteenth Century in Russia* (Oxford, 1973), pp. 252-55.

NOTES TO CHAPTER 6, pages 146-73

1. N. G. Ustrialov in his *Istoriia tsarstvovaniia Petra Velikogo*, II (Spb., 1858), appendex XVII, no. 8, 505-07, gives a list of the fifty *stol'niki* sent abroad in 1697 to acquire naval skills, of whom twenty-two were designated for Holland and England. Although most historians have assumed that a group did go to England, there is absolutedly no supporting evidence.

2. L. N. Maikov (ed.), *Rasskazy Nartova o Petre Velikom* (Spb., 1891), p. 10.

3. British Library Add. Mss. 28092, f. 53. Quoted by Bernard Pool, "Peter the Great on the Thames," *Mariner's Mirror*, LIX, no. 1 (1973), 11-12.

4. This information was kindly communicated to me by Dr. W. F. Ryan from Admiralty Office Minute Books and is included in a forthcoming article in the *Slavonic and East European Review*. The two Russians named are Gavrila Kobylin and Aleksei Petelin.

5. *Sbornik Imperatorskogo Russkogo istoricheskogo obshchestva*, XXXIX (Spb., 1884), 46. See also pp. 66-68, 113-16. (Hereafter *SRIO*.)

6. *Materialy dlia istorii russkogo flota*, III (Spb., 1866), 22-23. (Hereafter *Materialy*.)

7. *SRIO*, XXXIX, 112.

8. *Ibid.*, p. 294. The lists of the "navigators" are found in *Materialy*, III, 14-15 and in Whitworth's papers, British Library, Add. Mss. 37, 355, ff. 155, 401.

9. See N. Hans, "The Moscow School of Mathematics and Navigation (1701)," *Slavonic and East European Review*, XXIX (1951), 532-36; F. Veselago, *Ocherk istorii morskogo kadetskogo korpusa* (Spb., 1852), pp. 5-8, 98-102.

10. Max J. Okenfuss, "Russian Students in Europe in the Age of Peter the Great," in J. G. Garrard (ed.), *The Eighteenth Century in Russia* (Oxford, 1973), pp. 131-45.

11. V. Z. Dzhincharadze, "Iz istorii russko-angliiskikh kul'turnykh otnoshenii v 18 veke," *Vestnik istorii mirovoi kul'tury*, V (September-October, 1960), 70.

12. *Ibid.*, pp. 70-71.

13. The lists are given in *Materialy*, III, 14-17, 20-22.

14. *Ibid.*, pp. 18-20.

15. *Ibid.*, p. 34.

16. *SRIO*, XXXIX, 177.

17. *Materialy* III, 41, 55, 38. See also *Arkhiv kniazia F. A. Kurakina* V (Saratov, 1894), 205, 223.

18. *Materialy*, III, 41, 38-93.

19. *Ibid.*, pp. 51-52.

20. *Ibid.*, p. 24.

21. *SRIO*, XXXIX, 177. See also on the Naryshkins, *ibid.*, pp. 31-32, 100, 137-38, 156, 159-60, 166, 173-74, 176-78.

22. *Materialy*, III, 37, 38.

23. *Ibid.*, pp. 36-41.

24. *Ibid.*, pp. 82-84.

25. *Ibid.*, pp. 88, 53, 65, 114. On his career, see F. Veselago (ed.), *Obshchii morskoi spisok*, I (Spb., 1885), 14-15. (Hereafter *OMS*.)

26. *Materialy*, III, 53.

27. Cyprian A. G. Bridge, *History of the Russian Fleet During the Reign of Peter the Great* (London, 1899), pp. 102-03. (Bridge was unaware of the author's identity.)

28. N. N., *Truth is but Truth, as it is Timed!* (London, 1719), p. 7.

29. See Okenfuss, *op. cit.*, pp. 132-33.

30. *OMS*, I, 380 (Turchaninov); 316-17 (Rameikov); 380-81 (Urusov).

31. Dzhincharadze, p. 71; *OMS*, I, 419. On Saltykov, see *OMS*, I, 331-32.

32. *OMS*, I, 150-51.

33. *Ibid*., pp. 167-68 (Kalmykov); 105-06 (Golovnin); 156-58 (Zotov).

34. Okenfuss, *op. cit*., p. 144. On the Naryshkins' careers, see *OMS*, I, 274-75.

35. *Materialy*, III, 54.

36. *Ibid*., pp. 109-11.

37. Dzhincharadze, p. 71-72.

38. Veselago, *Ocherk*, p. 76.

39. *Russkii biograficheskii slovar'*, vol. Shchapov-Iushnevskii (Spb., 1906), 98.

40. Dzhincharadze, pp. 72, 71.

41. *SRIO*, X (1876), 28.

42. *Materialy*, XI (1886), 40-43.

43. *Arkhiv kniazia Vorontsova*, XXXIV (1888), 287.

44. *Materialy*, XI, 48-50. *Calendar of Home Office Papers 1760-1765* (London, 1878), p. 270.

45. *Materialy*, XI, 607; *OMS*, II (1885), 70.

46. *Materialy*, XI, 1-2, 607; *OMS*, II, 81-82.

47. *OMS*, II, 52-53 (Borisov); 184-87 (Kozlianinov); 240-41 (Lupandin); 456-59 (Khanykov). See also *Materialy*, XI, 49-50, 199, 217-19, 492-93, 605-06. For some contemporary English comments on Khanykov, see *The Russian Journals of Martha and Catherine Wilmot 1803-1808* (London, 1934), pp. 21, 381; William Tooke, *Life of Catharine II*, III (5th ed., Dublin, 1800), 280; George Forster, *Journey from Bengal to England*, II (London, 1798), 264.

48. *OMS*, IV (1890), 572-73; *RBS*, vol. Plavil'shchikov-Primo (1905), 113-15; N. P. Nikitin, *Otechestvennye ekonomiko-geografy XVIII-XIX vv*. (Moscow, 1959), pp. 99-102; *Materialy*, XI, 213, 607, 609.

49. *AKV*, XXII (1881), 54.

50. Andrew Swinton, *Travels into Norway, Denmark and Russia* (London, 1792), p. 486. Pleshcheev was friendly with many Englishmen, particularly with the Benthams. He even hoped at one time that his sister would marry Samuel Bentham. See *Correspondence of Jeremy Bentham*, II-III (London, 1968-71), passim.

51. *Materialy*, XI, 607.

52. *OMS*, II, 120.

53. *Russkaia starina* (May 1897), pp. 414-16.

54. *OMS*, IV, 406-08; J. L. Cranmer-Byng, "Russian and British Interests in the Far East," *Canadian Slavonic Papers*, X (1968), 364; Christopher Lloyd and R. C. Anderson (eds.), *A Memoir of James Trevenen* (London, 1959), passim.

55. *Arkhiv grafov Mordvinovykh*, I (Spb., 1901), 190.

56. *Autobiography of Benjamin Robert Haydon* (Oxford, 1927), p. 5.

57. *Travels in Various Countries of Europe, Asia, and Africa*, I (London, 1810). On Mordvinov at Nikolaev, see my "Printing at Nikolaev, 1798-1803," *Transactions of the Cambridge Bibliographical Society*, VI (1974), 149-57.

58. F. F. Vigel', *Zapiski*, I (Moscow, 1928), 158-59.

59. The major sources for Mordvinov, in addition to the family archive, are V. S. Ikonnikov, *Graf N. S. Mordvinov* (Spb., 1873); N. N. Mordvinova, *Vospominaniia ob admirale grafe N. S. Mordvinove* (Spb., 1873); *OMS*, IV, 393-95. References to the Mordvinovs are found in the accounts of several English travellers to Russia at the end of the eighteenth century (Elizabeth, Lady Craven; John Parkinson; Samuel Bentham; Maria Guthrie).

60. *Correspondence of Jeremy Bentham*, II, 218-19. See also *ibid*., pp. 220-21, 231, 311, 490, 491; III, 5, 19.

61. *OMS*, IV, 263-65.

62. *Materialy*, XI, 217, 449, 456, 475, 481, 617, 631; XII, 199, 223, 284, 320, 436, 460, 728; XIII, 46, 136; XV (1893), 184, 283.

63. *Correspondence of Jeremy Bentham*, II, 111.

64. *Ibid.*, pp. 208-09.

65. *Ibid.*, p. 228.

66. *Ibid.* Cf. *ibid.*, pp. 220-21, 222. For identity of Kutygin, see *Materialy*, XII, 343.

67. There are futher references to Kutygin's work back in Russia in 1788 and 1789 in *Materialy*, XIII, 450-51, 658.

68. *AKV*, IX, 116.

69. *Ibid.*, XIX (1881), 374-76, 391-94; Lenin Library, Moscow, Fond 313, Fedorov, No. 25, 'Zhurnal Ivana Sudakova', III, f. 76; *Laws of the Society . . . for the Investigation of Natural History* (Edinburgh, 1803), p. 27.

70. Jeremy Bentham's comments to Samuel about what should be the aims of Russian shipbuilders in England: *Correspondence of Jeremy Bentham*, II, 210.

71. *Materialy*, XIV, 576-77. See *ibid.*, XIII, 133; XIV, 528, 562 (Pospelov); XIII, 162 (Kanaev); XIII, 442, 444, 451; XIV, 528 (Masal'skii).

72. *Arkhiv grafov Mordvinovykh*, III (1902), 284-85. In 1799 Kurepanov also sent drawings of several ships, including H. M. S. *Victory: Materialy* XIV (1902), 360.

73. *AKV*, IX, 73. Cf. *ibid.*, 115-16, 178, 416; XX (1881), 14-15.

74. *Zapiski grafa E. F. Komarovskogo* (Moscow, 1914), p. 21.

75. *AKV*, IX, 178.

76. *Ibid.*, p. 198.

77. *Arkhiv grafov Mordvinovykh*, III, 338.

78. *AKV*, XXVIII (1883), 146-47; *Materialy*, XIV, 439-40; *Arkhiv grafov Mordvinovykh*, III, 338-40.

79. *AKV*, XVIII, 87-88.

80. Quoted by Eunice H. Turner, "The Russian Squadron with Admiral Duncan's North Sea Fleet, 1795-1800," *Mariner's Mirror*, XLIX (1963), 215. In addition to the sources used by Mrs. Turner, one should also consult the correspondence of Sir Evan Nepean, Secretary to the Admiralty, with the Rev. Smirnov and others: National Maritime Museum, Greenwich, Mss. AGC/M/2, 38/MS/9295-1-11.

81. William Hunter, *A Short View of the Political Situation of the Northern Powers* (London, 1801), p. 46.

82. On this aspect, see P. K. Crimmin, "Victualling the Russian Fleet in 1795-6," *Mariner's Mirror*, LI (1965), 172.

83. Turner, *op. cit.*, pp. 218-19. Blane had received a gold medal from Catherine in 1786 for his book *Observations on the Diseases incident to Seamen*; in 1799 he received another from Paul for a later work. See National Maritime Museum, BLA/50 and BLA/52.

84. See the Duncan papers in the National Maritime Museum, DUN/16, nos. 1-23.

85. The main sources used for the account of Chichagov's life are his letters to Vorontsov, *AKV*, XIX, 1-278, the *Mémoires de l'amiral Paul Tchitchagoff* (Paris, 1909) and *RBS*, vol. Chaadaev-Shvitkov (1905), 420-26.

86. *AKV*, XIX, 122. On Gur'ev, see *ibid.*, pp. 42-43, 122-23 and Alexander Vucnich, *Science in Russian Culture* (London, 1965), pp. 150, 189, 199, 203-05.

87. *AKV*, XIX, 34-36.

88. *Ibid.*, p. 15.

89. *Ibid.*, p. 20-21.

90. Vigel', *Zapiski*, I, 152.

91. *AKV*, XIX, 43.

92. *Ibid.*, p. 173.

93. The opening lines of "Shchuka i kot" in the translation by Bernard Pares, *Russian Fables of Ivan Krylov* (London, 1942), p. 21.

94. *AKV*, XIX, 122.

95. *Ibid.*, p. 241. He was particularly irritated by the constraints on freedom imposed by customs, passports and the Aliens Bill.

96. *OMS*, III, 281-82; D. Kobeko, *Tsesarevich Pavel Petrovich (1754-1796)* (2nd ed., Spb., 1883), pp. 67-69. As a schoolboy, Velikii had made a modest contribution to Anglo-Russian literary history by the translation of a story by Dr. Johnson: Iu. D. Levin, "Kto avtor 'vostochnoi' povesti 'Obidag'?," *Izvestiia Akademii Nauk SSSR*, Seriia literatury i iazyka, XXV (1966), 431-33.

97. Urey Lisianky, *A Voyage round the World, in the Years 1803, 4, 5, & 6; performed by order of His Imperial Majesty Alexander the First, Emperor of Russia, in the Ship Neva* (London, 1814), pp. xvii-xviii.

98. *Ibid.*, p. xix; *Voyage round the World, in the Years 1803, 1804, 1805, and 1806, by order of His Imperial Majesty Alexander the First, on board the Ships Nadeshda and Neva, under the Command of Captain A. J. von Krusenstern*, I (London, 1813), XXIV.

99. Lisiansky, pp. xiv-xv.

100. In addition to the accounts cited above, the following sources were used for describing the careers of the two circumnavigators: Charlotte Bernhardi, *Memoir of the Celebrated Admiral Adam John de Krusenstern, the First Russian Circumnavigator* (London, 1867); V. Nozikov, *Russian Voyages round the World* (London, 1945); V. V. Nevskii, *Pervoe puteshestvie rossiian vokrug sveta* (Moscow, 1951); V. S. Lupach, *I. F. Kruzenshtern i Iu. F. Lisianskii* (Moscow, 1953). Lisianskii left three extensive journals of his visits to England in 1793-1800 and 1813-14, which are in the Naval Museum Archive (TsVMM) in Leningrad and have never been published.

101. *Arkhiv grafov Mordvinovykh*, III, 339-44; Lenin Library, Moscow, Fond 533, kollektsiia E. V. Puzitskogo, Book 2, no. 20.

102. "Opyt o Velikobritanii i posledstvennyia razsuzhdeniia," *Severnyi vestnik*, V (Spb., 1805), 150-56, 247-60. On Murav'ev's literary activities, see Iu. D. Levin, "Angliiskaia poeziia i literatura russkogo sentimentalizma," in M. P. Alekseev (ed.), *Ot klassitsizma k romantizmu* (Leningrad, 1970), pp. 244-45. Otherwise on Murav'ev see 'Bumagi Nikolaia Nazar'evicha Murav'eva', *Sbornik Novgorodskogo obshchestva liubitelei drevnostei*, II (Novgorod, 1909), i-iv, 1-53. Mention is made here (p. 26) of an unpublished diary which Murav'ev kept during his years in England.

103. *AKV*, XXVIII, 146-47; *The Despatches and Letters of Vice-Admiral Lord Viscount Nelson*, V (London, 1844), 448; S. I. Unkovskii, "Zapiski moriaka," Lenin Library, Moscow, Fond 261, izdatel'stvo Sabashnikovykh, karton 20, ed. khr. 1; V. M. Golovnin, *Sochineniia* (Moscow-Leningrad, 1949), pp. 5-7.

104. *AKV*, XIX, 112; William Hunter, *A Sketch of the Political State of Europe at the Beginning of February 1805* (London, 1805), pp. 142-3; M. S. Anderson, "Great Britain and the Growth of the Russian Navy in the Eighteenth Century," *Mariner's Mirror*, XLII (1956), 145-46.

105. *AKV*, XIX, 154.

NOTES TO CHAPTER 7, pages 174-208

1. *Scots Magazine*, XLIII (November 1781), 601.

2. John Phillips, *A Treatise on Inland Navigation* (London, 1785), p. viii.

3. See R. P. Bartlett, "The Recruitment of Foreign Canal Engineers for Russia under Catherine II," *Study Group on Eighteenth-Century Russia Newsletter*, no. 4 (1976), 43-48.

4. Lenin Library, Moscow, Fond 137, Korsakovy, papka 2, no. 12. All the folio references in the text are to this item. The quotations reproduce the spelling and mistakes in the French original. A somewhat wider study of Korsakov's activities is provided by my "A Russian Engineer in Eighteenth-Century Britain: The Journal of N. I. Korsakov, 1776-7," *Slavonic and East European Review*, LV (1977), 1-20.

5. Virtually nothing more is known about Babichev, except for the fact that soon after his return to Russia he published at the press of the Engineer Cadet Corps his translation of Nivelle de la Chaussée's *Ecole des amis*. See *Svodnyi katalog russkoi knigi XVIII veka*, II (Moscow, 1964), 124, no. 3489.

6. See V. N. Aleksandrenko, *Russkie diplomaticheskie agenty v Londone v XVIII v.*, II (Warsaw, 1897), 166-75.

7. Fond 137, papka 70, no. 5.

8. Jean Lindsay, *The Canals of Scotland* (Newton Abbot, 1968), pp. 15-26.

9. Bartlett, *op. cit.*, pp. 46-48.

10. Lindsay, *op. cit.*, p. 24.

11. See my "The British in Catherine's Russia," in J. G. Garrard (ed.), *The Eighteenth-Century in Russia* (Oxford, 1973), pp. 260-61.

12. Hugh Malet, *The Canal Duke: A Biography of Francis 3rd Duke of Bridgewater* (Dawlish and London, 1961), p. 87.

13. Eliza Meteyard, *The Life of Josiah Wedgwood*, II (London, 1866), pp. 273 ff.

14. See the photograph in Malet, *op. cit.*, facing p. 88.

15. See Nicholas Goodison, *Ormolu: The Work of Matthew Boulton* (London, 1974), passim.

16. See Chapter V; also Archibald Brown, "S. E. Desnitskii i I. A. Tret'iakov v Glazgovskom universitete (1761-1769)," *Vestnik Moskovskogo universiteta*, no. 4 (1969), 78-79.

17. Eric Robinson and Douglas McKie (eds.), *Partners in Science: Letters of James Watt and Joseph Black* (London, 1970), p. 24.

18. Eric Robinson, "The Transference of British Technology to Russia, 1760-1820: A Preliminary Enquiry," in Barrie M. Ratcliffe (ed.), *Great Britain and Her World 1750-1914: Essays in Honour of W. D. Henderson* (Manchester, 1975), p. 7.

19. Letter from James Williamson, 12 July 1777: Fond 137, papka 74, no. 26.

20. Letter from I. I. Komov, 8 February 1782: Fond 137, papka 95, no. 21.

21. E. I. Druzhinina, *Severnoe Prichernomor'e v 1775-1800 gg.* (Moscow, 1959), p. 143.

22. *Ibid.*, p. 138.

23. *The Correspondence of Jeremy Bentham*, III (London, 1971), 282.

24. Elizabeth, Lady Craven, *A Journey through the Crimea to Constantinople* (Dublin, 1789), p. 208.

25. *Ibid.*, p. 211.

26. *Ibid.*, p. 212. There is much information about Korsakov in Kherson in 1786-87 in *Archivo del general Miranda*, Viajes, II (Caracas, 1929), 202 ff.

27. Fond 137, papka 115, no. 34.

28. British Library, Add. Ms. 33540, f. 489.

29. See B. Hollingsworth, "John Phillips, Canal Enthusiast in Russia, 1783-5," *Study Group on Eighteenth-Century Russia Newsletter*, no. 1 (1973), 36-40.

30. *Arkhiv kniazia Vorontsova*, XX (Spb., 1881), 473-74.

31. See Nicholas Hans, "The Moscow School of Mathematics and Navigation (1701)," *SEER*, XXIX (1950-51), 532-36; Valentin Boss, *Newton and Russia: The Early Influence, 1698-1796* (Cambridge, Mass., 1972), pp. 78-84.

32. A massive contribution in this area of research has been made by V. L. Chenakal. See his "Zerkal'nye teleskopy Vil'iama Gershelia v Rossii," *Istoriko-astronomicheskie issledovaniia*, IV (Moscow, 1958), 253-340; "Dzhems Short i russkaia astronomiia XVIII v.," *ibid.*, V (1959), 3-82; "Astronomicheskie instrumenty Dzhona Berda v Rossii XVIII v.," *ibid.*, VI (1960), 53-119; "Astronomical Instruments of John Rowley in Eighteenth-Century Russia," *Journal for the History of Astronomy*, III (1972), 199-35.

33. "John Bradley and His Sundials," *Journal for the History of Astronomy*, IV (1973), 162. Cf. Morgan's contract of 1771: P.R.O., SP 91/88, ff. 289-90.

34. *Protokoly zasedanii konferentsii Imperatorskoi Akademii Nauk*, III (Spb., 1900), 567.

35. The three principal secondary sources on Nartov are A. S. Britkin and S. S. Vidonov, *Vydaiushchiisia mashinostroitel' XVIII veka A. K. Nartov* (Moscow, 1950); V. V. Danilevskii, *Nartov i "Iasnoe zrelishche mashin"* (Moscow-Leningrad, 1958) and F. N. Zagorskii, *Andrei Konstaninovich Nartov, 1693-1756* (Leningrad, 1969).

36. L. N. Maikov, *Rasskazy Nartova o Petre Velikom* (Spb., 1891), p. 60.

37. Danilevskii, *op. cit.*, pp. 49-50.

38. The full text of the letter is given in Zagorskii, *op. cit.*, pp. 20-21.

39. S. L. Sobol', *Istoriia mikroskopa i mikroskopicheskie issledovaniia v Rossii v XVIII veke* (Moscow-Leningrad, 1949), pp. 167-68. On Adams and Cuff, see E. G. R. Taylor, *The Mathematical Practitioners of Hanoverian England 1714-1840* (Cambridge, 1966), pp. 152, 154-55. An engraving of Cuff's microscope after a Russian work of 1755 is in Sobol', p. 457.

40. V. L. Chenakal, 'Dzhems Short', pp. 40-43.

41. *Protokoly zasedanii Akademii Nauk*, III, 566-67. See also p. 772.

42. N. I. Nevskaya, "Correspondence between Astronomers," in S. C. Korneyev (ed.), *USSR Academy of Sciences: Scientific Relations with Great Britain* (Moscow, 1977), p. 195. On McCulloch, see Taylor *op. cit.*, p. 319.

43. V. L. Chenakal, *Watchmakers and Clockmakers in Russia 1400-1850* (London, 1972), pp. 54, 56. For Morgan, see *ibid.*, p. 43.

44. P. N. Petrov (ed.), *Sbornik materialov dlia istorii Imperatorskoi S. -Peterburgskoi Akademii Khudozhestv za sto let ee suschestvovaniia*, I (Spb., 1864), 282-83.

45. See V. Ashurkov, *Oruzheinogo dela nadziratel': Zhizn' i deiatel'nost' tul'skogo mekhanika Alekseia Surnina (1767-1811 gg.)* (Tula, 1969), pp. 39-44.

46. *Ibid.*, p. 8.

47. "Zhurnal puteshestviia V. N. Zinov'eva po Germanii, Italii, Frantsii i Anglii v 1784-1788 gg.," *Russkaia starina*, XXIII (1878), 430.

48. *The Diary of Sylas Neville 1767-1788* (London, 1950), p. 280.

49. Ashurkov, *op. cit.*, p. 11.

50. P.R.O. SP91/88, f. 284.

51. Pushkin House, Leningrad, Fond 620, Arkhiv A. A. Samborskogo, ed. khr. 157, no. 5, f. 7-7v.

52. *Russkaia starina*, XXIII, 429-30. See Robinson, "Transference," pp. 8-10.

53. Howard L. Blackmore, *British Military Firearms 1650-1850* (London, 1961), pp. 90-110.

54. H. C. B. Rogers, *Weapons of the British Soldier* (London, 1972), p. 121.

55. Quoted in Ashurkov, *op. cit.*, pp. 13, 16-17.

56. *Ibid.*, pp. 57-58.

57. *AKV*, IX (1876), 179.

58. Ashurkov, p. 57.

59. *AKV*, XVII (1880), 106.

60. Ashurkov, pp. 59-63.

61. *Ibid.*, p. 34.

62. *Ibid.*, p. 36.

63. Edward Daniel Clarke, *Travels in Various Countries of Europe Asia and Africa*, I (4th edition, London, 1816), 238. Clarke gave a characteristically negative picture of Tula workmanship which he found in every respect inferior to English.

64. *Life of Reginald Heber D.D., Lord Bishop of Calcutta*, I (London, 1830), pp. 203, 224.

65. This document is reproduced in F. N. Zagorskii, *L. F. Sabakin, mekhanik XVIII veka* (Moscow-Leningrad, 1963), pp. 77-78.

66. Arkhiv Samborskogo, Fond 620, ed. khr. 157, no. 6, ff. 10v.-11.

67. *AKV*, XVI (1880), 196-97.

68. Letter of Magellan to J. A. Euler, 18 November 1785, quoted in Zagorskii, *Sabakin*, pp. 18-19.

69. See Taylor, *Mathematical Practitioners*, pp. 176-77.

70. *Lektsii o raznykh predmetakh kasaiushchikhsia do mekhaniki, gidravliki i gik-rostatitiki . . .* (Spb., 1787); *Svodnyi katalog*, III, 298, no. 7764.

71. Zagorskii, *Sabakin*, pp. 22-32.

72. *Pribavlenie k Fergusovym lektsiiam, soderzhashchee v sebe o ognennykh ma-shinakh* (Moscow, 1788); *Svodnyi katalog*, III, 82, no. 6253.

73. *Ibid.*, pp. 330-31.

74. Zagorskii, *Sabakin*, pp. 34, 36.

75. *Ibid.*, p. 64.

76. E. S. Shchukina, *Medal'ernoe iskusstvo v Rossii XVIII veka* (Leningrad, 1962), p. 55.

77. A. A. Sivers, "Medal'er Ben'iamin Skott," *Izvestiia GAIMK*, V (1927), 157-78. This Scott was possibly the son of Benjamin Scott, instrument maker, mentioned earlier, who died in 1751.

78. Matthew Boulton Papers, Birmingham Reference Library, Russian Mint Box II, letter of Boulton to Baxter, 15 August 1796. My thanks are due to Mr. J. N. Wharton, Secretary to the Matthew Boulton Trust, for permission to quote from the Boulton papers, on which the following account is principally based. These papers have also been used by E. Robinson in his article, 'The Transference of British Technology', but his account, particularly with regard to some of the Russian workmen, is confused and not without major errors.

79. Russian Mint Box I. Translation of letter from Count A. N. Samoilov to S. R. Vorontsov, 10/21 October 1796, supplied to Boulton by Russian Embassy in London.

80. Russian Mint Box II, Ia. Smirnov to Boulton, 20 January 1797, f. 1.

81. Russian Mint Box II, Samoilov to Vorontsov, f. 2v. On Gass, father and son, see Shchukina, *op. cit.*, pp. 95-96.

82. Russian Mint Box II, Copy of letter from Boulton to Vorontsov, 26 February 1797, ff. 2-4.

83. Russian Mint Box II, Smirnov to Boulton, 8 October 1797, f. 1v.

84. Zagorskii, *Sabakin*, p. 37. Zagorskii has no other information to offer about Sabakin's second trip to England.

85. Russian Mint Box I, Smirnov to Boulton, 6 December 1797, f. 1.

86. L. A. Gol'denberg, *Mikhail Fedorovich Soimonov (1730-1804)* (Moscow, 1973), p. 87.

87. H. W. Dickinson, *Matthew Boulton* (Cambridge, 1937), pp. 94-95.

88. Matthew Boulton Papers, Box D2, no. 4, f. 1.

89. Russian Mint Box II, Smirnov to Boulton, 18 September 1798, f. 1.

90. Box D2, no. 8, Deriabin to M. R. Robinson, 17 May 1799, ff. 1-1v.

91. *AKV*, XX (1881), 327.

92. *Ibid.*, VIII (1876), 266; SVIII, 452. On Deriabin generally, see *Russkii biograficheskii slovar'*, vol. Dabelov-Diad'kovskii (Spb., 1905), 327-29. Deriabin was elected a Corresponding Member of the Royal Society of Arts in 1804.

93. Gol'denberg, *Soimonov*, pp. 87-88.

94. Russian Mint Box I, copy of letter from Boulton to Smirnov, 11 April 1802, ff. 1-2.

95. *Ibid.*, Duncan to Boulton, 10 November 1802, f. 2.

96. Zagorskii, *Sabakin*, p. 47.

97. Russian Mint Box II, Smirnov to Boulton, 19 September 1799, f. 2v.

98. Russian Mint Box I, copy of letter from Boulton to Smirnov, 8 April 1802, ff. 1-2.

99. *Ibid.*, copy of letter from Boulton to Smirnov, 15 April 1802, f. 1.

100. *Ibid.*, Smirnov to Boulton, 3 September 1801, f. 1.

101. *Ibid.*, copy of letter from Boulton to Smirnov, 8 April 1802, f. 2.

102. *Ibid.*, copy of letter from Boulton to Smirnov, 17 April 1802, f. 1.

103. *Ibid.*, copy of letter from Boulton to Smirnov, 18 April 1802, ff. 1-2.

104. P. P. Zabarinskii, *Pervye "ognevye" mashiny v Kronshtadtskom portu* (Moscow-Leningrad, 1936), pp. 141-44.

105. *Ibid.*, pp. 132-37, 162-66; P. P. Zabarinskij, "The Earliest News of Watt's Steam Engine to Reach Russia," *Transactions of the Newcomen Society for the Study of English History of Technology*, XVI (1935-36), 60-62.

106. Russian Mint Box I, Smirnov to Boulton, 16 June 1799, f. 1.

107. Russian Mint Box II, Smirnov to Boulton, 4 June 1800, f. 1.

108. Russian Mint Box I, Smirnov to Boulton, 12 April 1802, ff. 2-2v.; 21 April 1802, ff. 1-1v.

109. *Ibid.*, Zacchaeus Walker to Boulton, 4/16 October 1804, ff. 2-2v.; 5/17 November 1804, ff. 1v.-1.

110. Matthew Boulton Papers, D2, no. 10, Boulton to Deriabin, 9 July 1800, f. 1v.

111. Russian Mint Box I, Duncan to Boulton, 10 November 1802, f. 2.

112. *Ibid.*, Z. Walker to Boulton, f. 1v.

113. Fond 620, Arkhiv Samborskogo, ed. khr. 157, no. 3, f. 3.

114. Lenin Library, Moscow, Fond 313, Sobranie A. K. Fedorova, no. 25, Zhurnal Ivana Sudakova, I, f. 53v.

115. Nicholas Hans, *New Trends in Education in the Eighteenth Century* (London, 1951), pp. 149-50.

116. Fond 620, ed. khr. 108, nos. 1-3.

117. *Ibid.*, ed. khr. 157, no. 20, ff. 35-6; no. 21, ff. 37-37v.

118. *Dictionary of National Biography*, IX (London, 1908), 818.

119. A. Podvysotskii, "Otpravka kupecheskikh synovei v Angliiu (1766 g.)," *Russkaia starina*, XIII (1875), 437-39.

120. N. N. Firsov, *Pravitel'stvo i obshchestvo* (Kazan', 1902), p. 354.

121. Letter of G. N. Teplov to E. A. Golovtsyn, Governor of Archangel Province: Podvysotskii, *op. cit.*, p. 439. Given the remarks on the lack of trained and educated

merchants in the Archangel "Instruction" to Catherine's Legislative Assembly in 1767, it is to be hoped that eventually they returned to their home town. See Paul Dukes, *Catherine the Great and the Russian Nobility: A Study Based on the Materials of the Legislative Commission of 1767* (Cambridge, 1967), pp. 197-98.

122. Fond 620, ed. khr. 94, no. 5, f. 7v.; no. 6, f. 9.

1. *The Diary of Sylas Neville 1767-1788* (London, 1950), p. 280.
2. Nicholas Goodison, *Ormolu: The Work of Matthew Boulton* (London, 1974), pp. 122-23.
3. *Gentleman's Magazine*, XLIX (1779), 270-71.
4. Lord Herbert (ed.), *The Pembroke Papers (1780-1794)* (London, 1950), p. 22.
5. William Tooke, *The Life of Catharine II*, III (5th ed., Dublin, 1800), 66-67.
6. *The Memoirs of Princess Dashkov*, trans. by Kyril Fitzlyon (London, 1958), p. 176.
7. *Sbornik Imperatorskogo Russkogo istoricheskogo obshchestva*, XXIII (Spb., 1878), 328-29, 384, 387, 413.
8. *Arkhiv kniazia Vorontsova*, XIII (Moscow, 1879), 102.
9. Iu. O. Kogan, "Kabinet slepkov Dzheimsa Tassi v Ermitazhe," *Trudy Gos. Ermitazha*, XIV (1973), 82-96.
10. Iu. O. Kogan, *Reznye kamni Uil'iama i Charl'za Braunov: katalog vystavki* (Leningrad, 1976), pp. 5-17.
11. James Dallaway, *Anecdotes of the Arts in England* (London, 1800), p. 389.
12. Frederick W. Hilles, "Sir Joshua and the Empress Catherine," in *Eighteenth-Century Studies in Honor of Donald F. Hyde* (New York, 1970), pp. 267-77.
13. Prince Hoare, *Extracts from a Correspondence with the Academies of Vienna & St Petersburg* (London, 1802), p. 46. In 1801 Prince Hoare, Secretary for Foreign Correspondence to the Royal Academy, had contacted his opposite number in Russia, A. Labzin, about establishing regular correspondence between the two Academies.
14. O. P. Lazareva, *Russkii skul'ptor Fedot Shubin* (Moscow, 1965), pp. 26-27. In Rome Shubin's work had apparently impressed the Duke of Gloucester who ordered marble copies of the busts of Counts Aleksei and Fedor Orlov (*ibid.*, p. 24).
15. A. A. Trubnikov, "Graver Skorodumov pensioner Akademii," *Russkii bibliofil*, no. 3 (1916), 77.
16. Sidney C. Hutchinson, "The Royal Academy Schools, 1768-1830," *Walpole Society*, XXXVIII (1962), 140.
17. G. N. Komelova, "Russkii graver Gavriil Ivanovich Skorodumov, 1755-1792," *Trudy Gos. Ermitazha*, XV (Leningrad, 1974), 41.
18. Hutchinson, *op. cit.*, pp. 128-29.
19. Mary Webster, *Johan Zoffany 1733-1810* (London, 1977), pp. 57-58.
20. E. Nekrasova, *Gavrila Ivanovich Skorodumov 1755-1792* (Moscow, 1954), p. 11.
21. Trubnikov, *op. cit.*, pp. 79-80. Skorodumov apparently had spent two months in Paris in 1774 "pour visiter les ouvrages qui peuve [sic] m'être utile" (*ibid.*, p. 79).
22. *Ibid.*, p. 81. Skorodumov's spelling of the artists is retained. The lesser known artists are William Wollett, Thomas Vivares, Philippe Loutherbourg, John Mortimer, Giovanni Cipriani.
23. Andrew W. Tuer, *Bartolozzi and His Work*, II (London, 1881), 65.
24. Frances A. Gerard, *Angelica Kauffmann: A Biography* (London, 1892), p. 127. His name is given here as Scorodorf.
25. The most detailed and complete listings of Skorodumov's work as an engraver are found in D. A. Rovinskii, *Podrobnyi slovar' russkikh graverov XVI-XIVvv.*, II (Spb., 1895), cols. 889-922 and V. Ia. Adariukov, *Graviury G. I. Skorodumova: Katalog vystavki* (Moscow, 1927).
26. Trubnikov, *op. cit.*, p. 79.

27. The Russian ambassador wrote to the Academy of Arts that Skorodumov and Bel'skii arrived in clothes which were very old and which they had outgrown and asked for more money for them. They were told that "since they are artists, they must expect that the small allowance granted them should oblige them to greater industry and economy" (Adariukov, *op. cit.,* p. 8).

28. Trubnikov, *op. cit.,* p. 80; Komelova, *op. cit.,* p. 41.

29. Pushkin House, Leningrad, Fond 620, Arkhiv A. A. Samborskogo, ed. khr. 130, no. 2, f. 2; ed. khr. 135, no. 1, f.1.

30. *SRIO,* XLIV (1885), 233.

31. *Ibid.,* p. 256.

32. Rovinski, *op. cit.,* I, cols. 384-85.

33. *SRIO,* XXIII (1884), 260-61, 284.

34. *Voyage de deux Français en Allemagne, Danemarck, Suède, Russie et Pologne, fait en 1790-1792,* III (Paris, 1796), 197-99.

35. *Travels into Poland, Russia, Sweden, and Denmark,* II (London, 1784), 150.

36. I. A. Krylov, *Sochineniia,* I (Moscow, 1945), 73-74.

37. P. N. Petrov (ed.), *Sbornik materialov dlia istorii Imperatorskoi S. -Peterburgskoi Akademii Khudozhestv za sto let ee sushchestvovaniia,* I (Spb., 1864), 126, 132, 133, 296, 297; *Khudozhniki narodov SSR. Biobibliograficheskii slovar',* I (Moscow, 1970), 352.

38. Hutchinson, *op. cit.,* p. 140.

39. John Lewis Roget, *History of the "Old Water Colour" Society,* I (London, 1891), 382.

40. Rovinskii, *op. cit.,* II, col. 971.

41. *Ibid.,* col. 972.

42. Cf. Edward Edwards, *Anecdotes of Painters* (London, 1808), p. 176.

43. *AKV,* XXII, 509.

44. Algernon Graves, *The Royal Academy of Arts: A Complete Dictionary of Contributors and Their Work from its Foundation in 1769 to 1904,* VII (London, 1906), 247. 247.

45. Roget, *op. cit.,* I, 382; Edwards, *op. cit.*

46. Fond 620, Arkhiv A. A. Samborskogo, ed. khr. 92, no. 7, f. 12.

47. Samuel Redgrave, *A Dictionary of Artists of the English School* (2nd ed., London, p. 412.

48. See Graves, *op. cit.,* VII, 249; *Bryan's Biographical Dictionary of Painters and Engravers,* V (New ed., London, 1905), 124. The work of the Stepanov brothers is discussed at length in Roget, *op. cit.,* I, 382-83, 532-34; II, 148-50. See also on Francis Stepanov, A. I. Turgenev, *Khronika russkogo* (Moscow-Leningrad, 1964), pp. 419, 421.

49. *SRIO,* XIII.

50. B. Vasil'ev, "Arkhitektory Neelovy," *Arkhitekturnoe nasledstvo,* IV (1953), 77-78.

51. Il'ia Iakovkin, *Istoriia Sela Tsarskogo,* III (Spb., 1831), 82.

52. Fond 620, ed. khr. 132, no. 1, f. 2.

53. Vasil'ev, *op. cit.,* p. 77.

54. *Ibid.,* p. 79, note 15.

55. A. N. Petrov, *Pushkin: dvortsy i parki* (Leningrad, 1969), pp. 79, 128.

56. M. V. Alpatov, "Kameron i angliiskii klassitsizm," *Doklady i soobshcheniia filologicheskogo fakul'teta Moskovskogo universiteta,* I (1946), 55.

57. Petrov, *op. cit.,* pp. 71-72.

58. E. P. Shchukina, " 'Natural'nyi sad' russkoi usad'by v kontse XVIII v.," in *Russkoe iskusstvo XVIII veka: materialy i issledovaniia (Moscow,* 1973), p. 114.

59. Petrov, *op. cit.*, p. 131, note 17.

60. *Ibid.*, p. 97. Audrey Kennett, in her *The Palaces of Leningrad* (London, 1973), p. 140, is somewhat confused about the Halfpennys and their book, as indeed she is earlier about the Neelovs.

61. Fond 620, ed. khr. 132, no. 2.

62. Vasil'ev, *op. cit.*, pp. 86-89.

63. [Sir John Sinclair], *General Observations Regarding the Present State of the Russian Empire* (London, 1787), pp. 22-23.

64. *SRIO*, XXIII, 208 (Fielding and Richardson), 72, 131, 135-36, 152, 156, *passim* (Sterne).

65. By G. Gukovskii, on her *Byli i nebylitsy*, in *Istoriia russkoi literatury*, IV, pt. 2 (Moscow-Leningrad, 1947), 374.

66. As her contemporary British translator, Matthew Guthrie, noted about her *Nachal'noe upravlenie Olega* (1790): "As to the composition of her opera, the imperial author herself announces in an advertisement, that she had taken all the licence and latitude of our own Shakespeare, with regard to time, place, and even chronology in some instances. . . . (British Library Add. Mss. 14390, f. 364).

67. See my "Mr Fisher's Company of English Actors in Eighteenth-Century Petersburg," *Study Group on Eighteenth-Century Russia Newsletter*, no. 4 (1976), 49-56.

68. S. Poroshin, *Zapiski* (Spb., 1881), p. 383.

69. See in particular V. N. Vsevolodskii-Gerngross, *I. A. Dmitrevskoi* (Berlin, 1923), pp. 24-33.

70. James Boaden, *The Private Correspondence of David Garrick*, II (London, 1832), 474. First quoted by B. Malnick, "David Garrick and The Russian Theatre," *Modern Language Review*, L (1955), 173. Neither Ms. Malnick nor M. P. Alekseev, who found her suggestion that Dmitrevskii was the Russian in question "very plausible" (*Shekspir i russkaia kul'tura* (Moscow-Leningrad, 1965), p. 57, n. 50), knew of the further evidence cited below.

71. *London Chronicle*, XIX (17-19 April 1766), 370.

72. Letter of 9 June 1766: W. S. Lewis (ed.), *Horace Walpole's Correspondence*, XXII (London 1960), 426.

73. Boaden, *op. cit.*, II, 483.

74. S. P. Zhikharev, *Zapiski sovremennika* (Moscow-Leningrad, 1955), p. 309.

75. See my "British Freemasons in Russia during the Reign of Catherine the Great," *Oxford Slavonic Papers*, NS IV (1971), 48.

76. See H. McLean, "The Adventures of an English Comedy in Eighteenth-Century Russia: Dodsley's *Toy Shop* and Lukin's *Ščepetil'nik*," in *American Contributions to the Fifth International Congress of Slavists, Sofiia, September 1963*, II: *Literary Contributions* (The Hague, 1963), pp. 201-12.

77. Letter to Count Ivan Chernyshev: *Russkii arkhiv*, no. 9 (1871), 1321.

78. I. Shliapkin, "Vasilii Petrovich Petrov, 'karmannyi' stikhotvorets Ekateriny II (1763-1799). (Po novym dannym)," *Istoricheskii vestnik*, XXII, no. 11 (1885), 390.

79. *Ibid.*

80. "Shchastlivoe ditia neznatnogo ottsa" and "Tak, Silov! rassvelo, vosprianem oto sna." Both poems are most readily available in S. A. Vengerov (ed.), *Russkaia poeziia*, vyp. 2 (Spb., 1893), 420-24.

81. *Istoricheskii vestnik, loc. cit.*

82. See my "Printing at Nikolaev, 1798-1803," *Transactions of the Cambridge Bibliographical Society*, VI (1974), 149-57 and Iu. Stennik, "Stikhotvorenie A. S. Pushkina 'Mordvinovu'," *Russkaia literatura*, no. 3 (1965), 172-81.

83. The originals are in the Samborskii archive, Fond 620, ed. khr. 141, no. 5, ff. 1-5v. They have been printed as an appendix to my article "Vasilii Petrov v Anglii (1772-1774)," *XVIII vek*, XI (Leningrad, 1976), 243-45.

84. See my "The Duchess of Kingston in Russia," *History Today*, XXVII (1977), 390-95.

85. *The Diary of Sylas Neville 1767-1788* (London, 1950), pp. 31-32; Jonathan Spurling, *Edward Wortley Montagu 1713-1776: The Man in the Iron Mask* (London, 1954), pp. 40-47, 148-49.

86. John Bowring (ed.), *The Works of Jeremy Bentham*, X (Edinburgh, 1843), 67.

87. Compare L. G. Barag "O lomonosovskoi shkole v russkoi poezii XVIII veka (Vasilii Petrov)," *Uchenye zapiski kafedry literatury i iazyka Minskogo ped. instituta*, I (1940), 79; G. A. Gukovskii, "Petrov," in *Istoriia russkoi literatury*, IV (Moscow-Leningrad, 1947), 354; *Poety XVIII veka*, I (Leningrad, 1972), 321.

88. Barag, *loc. cit.*

89. *Sochineniia Murav'eva*, II (Spb., 1847), 379.

90. *Life of Catharine II*, III (5th ed., Dublin, 1800), 325.

91. *Poteriannyi rai poema Ioanna Mil'tona. Perevedena s Anglinskogo* (Spb., 1777), pp. [ii-iii].

92. "Dva pis'ma k Imperatritse Ekaterine Velikoi," *Bibliograficheskie zapiski*, I (1858), 530.

93. The only source of information on Silov's death is an undated letter from Mordvinov to Samborskii: Fond 620, ed. khr. 127, no. 18, ff. 25-6. See *XVIII vek*, XI, 234-35.

94. Iason, who later became Professor of Botany and Pharmocology at the Petersburg Medico-Surgical Academy, translated a poem by Derzhavin into English and sent it for publication to Semen Vorontsov in London in 1814: *Sochineniia Derzhavina*, VI (Spb., 1876), 328, 338.

95. "Zhizn' Vasiliia Petrovicha Petrova," *Trudy Vol'nogo obshchestva sorevnovatelei prosveshcheniia i blagotvoreniia*, I (1818), 137.

96. A. I. Dudenkova, "Poema A. Dubrovskogo 'Na osleplenie strastiami'," *XVIII vek*, III (Moscow-Leningrad, 1958), 463-70.

97. L. B. Modzalevskii, "Lomonosov i ego uchenik Popovskii," *Ibid.*, pp. 111-69.

98. *AKV*, XXXIV (1888), 289. There are five letters from Dubrovskii to S. R. Vorontsov from London between 17/28 December 1762 and 21 October 11 November 1763 (*Ibid.*, pp. 284-90). Dubrovskii's service in London has not been noted by his biographers: Vengerov, *Russkaia poeziia*, vyp. 6 (1897), 141-42; E. S. Kuliabko, *M. V. Lomonosov i uchebnaia deiatel'nost' Peterburgskoi Akademii Nauk* (Moscow-Leningrad, 1962), pp. 147-48.

99. *Aleksandrova, uveselitel'nyi sad ego imperatorskogo vysochestva ... Aleksandra Pavlovicha* (Spb., 1793), p. 1. See my "Dzhunkovskii's *Aleksandrova*: Putting Samborskii in the Picture," *Study Group on Eighteenth-Century Russia Newsletter*, 3 (1975), 22-29.

1. "Tourism in the Renaissance," B.B.C. Radio 3 talk, 21 February 1978. Cf. Clare Howard, *English Travellers of the Renaissance* (London, 1914); John Stoye, *English Travellers Abroad 1604-1667* (London, 1952).

2. Chartres Biron (ed.), *"Sir," Said Dr Johnson*— (London, 1932), p. 132.

3. Christopher Hibbert, *The Grand Tour* (London, 1969), p. 25. On the Grand Tour also see William Edward Mead, *The Grand Tour in the Eighteenth Century* (Boston and New York, 1914); R. S. Lambert (ed.), *Grand Tour: A Journey in the Tracks of the Age of Aristocracy* (London, 1935); *The Age of the Grand Tour*, introduction by Anthony Burgess (London, 1967).

4. [F. C. Weber], *The Present State of Russia*, I (London, 1723), 190.

5. *Russkii arkhiv*, book 1 (1883), 278-84.

6. V. Vereshchagin, "Russkie v Parizhe pri Liudovike XV," *Russkii bibliofil*, no. 3 (1916), 68-74.

7. *The Bee*, IX (1792), 264. The Preface was omitted when the piece was published earlier in the year. See *ibid.*, pp. 142-46.

8. P. N. Berkov (ed.), *Satiricheskie zhurnaly N. I. Novikova* (Moscow-Leningrad, 1951), p. 63.

9. For some discussion of Russians in Italy in the eighteenth century, see Ettore Lo Gatto, *Russi in Italia dal secolo XVII ad oggi* (Rome, 1971); for Russians in France, see Léonce Pingaud, *Les Français en Russie et les russes en France* (Paris, 1886) and Emile Haumant, *La Culture française en Russie (1700-1900)* (2nd ed., Paris, 1913).

10. *Arkhiv kniazia Vorontsova*, IX (Moscow, 1876), 417.

11. P. N. Petrov, *Istoriia Sankt Peterburga* (Spb., 1885), pp. 587-88; R. M. Gorokhova, "Dramaturgiia Gol'doni v Rossii XVIII veka," in M. P. Alekseev (ed.), *Epokha Prosveshcheniia* (Leningrad, 1967), p. 311.

12. M. M. Shcherbatov, *On the Corruption of Morals in Russia*, edited and translated by A. Lentin (Cambridge, 1969), pp. 222, 224.

13. *Satiricheskie zhurnaly Novikova*, pp. 328-29.

14. *Morning Chronicle and London Advertiser*, Thursday 31 July 1783.

15. *Travels in Various Countries of Europe, Asia and Africa*, I (London, 1810), 90.

16. Quoted by M. P. Alekseev, "Angliiskii iazyk v Rossii i russkii iazyk v Anglii," *Uchenye zapiski LGU*, no. 72, seriia filologicheskikh nauk, vyp. 9 (1944), 96. Alekseev's article is required reading for all interested in Anglo-Russian cultural relations over four centuries.

17. S. P. Zhikharev, *Zapiski sovremennika* (Moscow-Leningrad, 1958), pp. 244-45, 339.

18. "Rossiianin v Anglii," *Poleznoe i priiatnoe preprovozhdenie vremeni*, IX (1796), 65, 57.

19. Quoted in H. M. Hyde, *The Empress Catherine and the Princess Dashkov* (London, 1935), p. 107. This remains the most detailed life of Dashkova available in English.

20. "Puteshestvie odnoi Rossiiskoi znatnoi Gospozhi, po nekotorym Aglinskim provintsiiam," *Opyt trudov Vol'nogo rossiiskogo sobraniia*, II (1775), 108-09. The complete text covers pp. 105-44.

21. *Ibid.*, p. 121.

22. *Ibid.*, pp. 133-41.

23. *Horace Walpole's Correspondence*, edited by W. S. Lewis, XXIII (London, 1967), 248-49.

24. *London Chronicle*, XL (3-5 October 1776), 335. The play Dashkova saw has been established from *The London Stage*, part V (Carbondale, 1968), 22.

25. This journal, unlike the journal of 1770, was used by H. M. Hyde in his study, pp. 140-47. Mr. Hyde was kind enough to give me a copy of a typescript from the French original (now in the possession of a descendant of the Wilmots) and it is from this that I quote.

26. Malcolm Elwin, *The Noels and the Milbankes* (London, 1967), p. 122.

27. Kyril Fitzlyon (ed. and trans.), *The Memoirs of Princess Dashkov* (London, 1958), pp. 149-50.

28. Garrick's letter of 3 May, 1778 was printed in *The Memoirs of Princess Daschaw*, edited from the originals by Mrs. W. Bradford [i.e. Martha Wilmot], II (London, 1840), 136-37. Dashkova's overlooked original letter to Garrick is to be found in James Boaden, *The Private Correspondence of David Garrick*, II (London, 1832), 314.

29. *AKV*, VI (1873), 300.

30. *Horace Walpole's Correspondence*, XXXIII, 179.

31. *Ibid.*, XXIX, 59-60.

32. *Diaries and Correspondence of James Harris, First Earl of Malmesbury*, I (London, 1844), 323-24.

33. *Ibid.*, p. 330.

34. A detailed discussion of this incident, using other contemporary sources and newspapers, is found in my "A Russian in the Gordon Riots," *Study Group on Eighteenth-Century Russia Newsletter*, no. 1 (1973), 29-36.

35. *Horace Walpole's Correspondence*, XXXIII, 203.

36. *AKV*, XXI, 408-10.

37. A vivid record of Dashkova's final years is contained in H. M. Hyde and Marchioness of Londonderry (eds.), *The Russian Journals of Martha and Catherine Wilmot (1803-1808)* (London, 1934).

38. *Horace Walpole's Correspondence*, XXIV, 114.

39. *Ibid.*, pp. 143-44.

40. *Scots Magazine*, XXII (December 1770), 661. Cf. *Diaries and Correspondence of James Harris*, I, 210, 386-87; William Coxe, *Travels into Poland, Russia, Sweden and Denmark*, I (London, 1792), 379.

41. Vladimir Orlov-Davydov, *Biograficheskii ocherk grafa Vladimira Grigor'evicha Orlova*, I (Spb., 1878), 261.

42. For excerpts from his diary, see *ibid.*, pp. 249-62.

43. *Daily Advertiser*, 19 October 1775.

44. *London Chronicle*, XXXVIII, No. 2947 (26-28 October 1775), 410.

45. *Ibid.*, no. 2948 (28-31 October), 423; no. 2949 (31 October-2 November), 430. See Richard S. Lambert, *The Prince of Pickpockets: A Study of George Barrington Who Left His Country for His Country's Good* (London, 1930), pp. 53-56. The play Orlov saw has been established from *The London Stage*, part IV, p. 1923.

46. *Sbornik Imperatorskogo Russkogo istoricheskogo obshchestva*, XXVII (Spb., 1880), 54. Cf. *Ibid.*, p; 67.

47. Annie Raine Ellis (ed.), *The Early Diary of Francis Burney 1768-1778*, II (London, 1913), 109. The twice-told account of the evening occupies pp. 98-121. Cf *Letters of the 1st Earl of Malmesbury*, I (London, 1880), 330 (Letter of James Harris to his son).

48. *Ibid.*, p. 110, note 1.

49. *AKV*, IX, 110. Cf. *ibid.*, p. 71; XII, 45.

50. *Russkii arkhiv*, book III (1877), 158.

51. *Zapiski grafa E. F. Komarovskogo* (Moscow, 1914), p. 22. Further references to Bobrinskoi on pp. 17-18.

52. *AKV*, XII (1887), 56-57.

53. *SRIO*, XXVII (1880), 404 (Catherine to Pavel Petrovich). See for other material, *ibid.*, p. 405; *AKV*, XII, 52-58; XXVIII (1883), 76.

54. See generally David Geoffrey Williamson, *The Counts Bobrinskoy. A Genealogy* (Edgware, 1962); P. Bartenev, "Graf Aleksei Grigor'evich Bobrinskoi i ego bumagi," *Russkii arkhiv*, book III (1876), 5-12.

55. Harry Ballam and Roy Lewis, *The Visitor's Book: England and the English as Others Have Seen Them A.D. 1500 to 1900* (London, 1950), p. 13; Rosamund Bayne-Powell, *Travellers in Eighteenth-Century England* (London, 1951).

56. The details of the English sections of the works not hitherto cited in this chapter are as follows: N. M. Karamzin, *Izbrannye sochineniia*, I (Moscow-Leningrad, 1964), 513-97 (Hereafter Karamzin); *Arkhiv kniazia F. A. Kurakina*, V (Saratov, 1894), 376-425; VI (1896), 205-39 (Kurakin); *Zhurnal puteshestviia . . . Nikity Akinfievicha Demidova po inostrannym gosudarstvam* (Moscow, 1786), pp. 46-59, 151-56 (Demidov); "Zhurnal puteshestviia V. N. Zinov'eva po Germanii, Italii, Frantsii i Anglii v 1784-1788 gg.," *Russkaia starina*, XXXIII (1878), 421-40, 593-98 (Zinov'ev); "Rossiianin v Anglii," *Priiatnoe i poleznoe preprovozhdenie vremeni*, IX (1796), 56-63, 65-71, 97-107; XI, 11-14, 61-72, 97-101, 145-48, 209-19, 321-32, 356-67, 381-95, 403-10 (Rossiianin); *Sochineniia i perevody Petra Makarova*, II (2nd edition, Moscow, 1817), 5-50 (Makarov); "Zhurnal puteshestviia po Evrope v 1758 g.," Library of the Academy of Sciences, Leningrad, Ms. 16. 14. 32, ff. 159-89 v. (*Zhurnal* (1758); "Putevye zapiski russkogo vo vremia puteshestviia po Anglii v 1783 g.," Lenin Library, Moscow, Fond 183 (Inostrannaia literatura), Ms. N1673, ff. 1-125 (Anon 1783).

57. *London Chronicle*, XXXVIII, no. 2947 (26-28 October 1775), p. 10 ("the Chambellan, Mr. de Zirowiew"). See also *Russkaia starina*, XXXIII (1878), 614. Zinov'ev was probably the Russian gentleman whose name Fanny Burney could not remember.

58. Viazemskii, father of Pushkin's close friend, was in England in 1783. See *Arkhiv kniazia Viazemskogo. Kniaz' Andrei Ivanovich Viazemskii* (Spb., 1881), Ch. 7 "Puteshestvie kniazia Andreia Ivanovicha za granitsu," espec. pp. LVII-LIX. Later in Italy Viazemskii met, ran away with, and later married an Irishwoman called Eugenie Quinn (née O'Reilly). The three eldest Razumovskii brothers, Aleksei, Petr and Andrei (of Razumovsky quartet fame), visited England in 1768-69 with their tutor Ludwig Heinrich von Nicolay. See A. A. Vasil'chikov, *Semeistvo Razumovskikh*, II (Spb., 1880), 14-15. Their father's hitherto unknown visit was in 1766. See letter of Musin-Pushkin to Duke of Newcastle, 24 October 1766, British Library, Add. Mss. 33070, f. 425v.

59. Zinov'ev, pp. 423, 424, 427, 437.

60. Kurakin, V, 400.

61. *Ibid.*, p. 384.

62. *Horace Walpole's Correspondence*, XII (1944), 226, 228, 234.

63. *Ibid.*, XXVIII (1955), 269. Iusupov, fabulously rich, great collector of books, paintings and women, arrived in London on 19 March 1776 and was presented at Court the following day (*Public Advertiser*, 22 March 1776). His visit to London was celebrated by Pushkin in a famous poem "K vel'mozhe."

64. Anon (1783), f. 81.

65. *Biograficheskii ocherk grafa V. G. Orlova*, I, 263; II, 1-4.

66. *The Bee*, IX (1792), 156-57.

67. *AKV*, VI, 304.

68. Kurakin, V, 341.

69. Zinov'ev, p. 429. Cf. *Biograficheskii ocherk*, I, 256-57.

70. Anon (1783), f. 77v.; *Biograficheskii ocherk*, I, 257; Kurakin, V, 404.

71. Kurakin, V, 395.

72. Anon (1783), f. 27v.

73. *Zhurnal* (1758), ff. 161-162v.; Karamzin, I, 557, 565. Cf. Anon (1783), ff. 10-10v. (Ranelagh), 13-13v. (Vauxhall); Demidov, pp. 54-55 (Vauxhall).

74. Kurakin, V, 421 (Newgate); Karamzin, I, 533-34 (Newgate), 536-38 (Bedlam).

75. Makarov, pp. 10 (streets). Kurakin, V, 378 (lighting), 423-24 (streets); Karamzin, I, 520, 528 (streets), 522 (lighting); Anon (1783), f. 23 (street names).

76. Anon (1783), f. 23.

77. Makarov, p. 12.

78. Karamzin, I, 520; Anon (1783), f. 9v.

79. Komarovskii, pp. 14-15. Cf. Makarov, pp. 24-26 (thieves); Rossiianin, IX, 68-69 (beggars); Karamzin, I, 562 (thieves).

80. Makarov, pp. 50-57; Anon (1783), ff. 5v.-6, 12, 120; Rossiianin, IX, 70.

81. Kurakin, V, 385. Cf. Zinov'ev, p. 428; Rossiianin, IX, 66-67; Karamzin, I, 515, 530-31.

82. Makarov, pp. 43-44; Kurakin, V, 385. Cf. Anon (1783), f.4; Zinov'ev, p. 437; Rossiianin, IX, 65-66, 215; Karamzin, I, 518, 524.

83. Kurakin, VI, 332-33 (letter to Nikita Panin).

84. Anon (1783), ff. 121v.-122. Cf. Rossiianin, IX, 57, 60-61, X, 215; Zinov'ev, p. 438; *AKV*, VIII, 341 (Count F. V. Rostopchin).

1. N. M. Karamzin, *Sochineniia*, II (Spb., 1848), 773.
2. I. I. Dmitriev, *Sochineniia*, II (Spb., 1895), 24.
3. *Ibid.*, p. 26.
4. "Pis'ma Aleksandra Andreevicha Petrova k Karamzinu," *Russkii arkhiv* (1863), p. 889.
5. Dmitriev, *op. cit.*, p. 26.
6. *Iulii Tsezar', tragediia Villiama Shekespira* (Moscow, 1787), p. 4.
7. N. M. Karamzin, *Polnoe sobranie stikhotvorenii* (Moscow-Leningrad, 1966), p. 61.
8. An analysis of this tale and arguments for its attribution to Karamzin are given in my "Karamzin's First Short Story?," in Lyman H. Legters (ed.), *Russia: Essays in History and Literature* (Leiden, 1972), pp. 38-55.
9. *Detskoe chtenie dlia serdtsa i razuma*, XV (1788), 41-42.
10. Karamzin, *Sochineniia*, II, 659.
11. *Ibid.*, p. 773.
12. *Ibid.*, III, 363.
13. A Russian traveller in England in 1795 was subsequently moved to publish his own letters under the influence of Karamzin. See P. I. Makarov, "Pis'ma iz Londona," in his *Sochineniia i perevody*, II, pt. 3 (2nd ed.: Moscow, 1817), 5-50.
14. *Pis'ma N. M. Karamzina k I. I. Dmitrievu* (Spb., 1866), pp. 13-14; Ia. L. Barskov, *Perepiska moskovskikh masonov XVIII-go veka* (Petrograd, 1915), p. 30.
15. *Spectateur du Nord*, no. 4 (October 1797), 58.
16. See my *N. M. Karamzin: A Study of His Literary Career* (Carbondale, 1971), pp. 93-95.
17. *Annual Register, or General Repository . . . for the Year 1803* (1804), 302; *Edinburgh Review*, III (January 1804), 327.
18. Karamzin, *Sochineniia*, II, 782, 773.
19. *Annual Register, loc. cit.*
20. Karamzin, *Sochineniia*, II, 780.
21. *Ibid.*, 749.
22. *Moskovskii zhurnal*, IV (October 1791), 108-09.
23. *Pis'ma russkogo puteshestvennika*, I (Moscow, 1797), vi.
24. Karamzin, *Sochineniia*, II, 749, 679.
25. *Moskovskii zhurnal*, V (February 1792), 233-34.
26. *Ibid.*, VI (May 1792), 214-15.
27. *Ibid.*, VII (August 1792), 256-57.
28. *Ibid.*, VII (2nd edition: Moscow, 1803), 261.
29. *Vestnik Evropy*, II (March 1802), 56.
30. "Smes' k Moskovskim Vedomostiam 1795 goda. Otryvki, original'nye i perevodnye N. M. Karamzinym," *Moskvitianin*, no. 3 (1854), 47.
31. *Moskovskii zhurnal*, IV (October 1791), 110.
32. Karamzin, *Sochineniia*, II, 780-82.
33. *Vestnik Evropy*, II (February 1802), 91-92. Cf. Mario Praz, *The Romantic Agony* (London, 1960), p. 462.
34. Karamzin, *Sochineniia*, II, 674.
35. *Ibid.*, III, 399.
36. *Ibid.*, II, 779.
37. *Ibid.*, 723.
38. *Vestnik Evropy*, I (January 1802), 8.

39. *Ibid.*, IV (August 1802), 329.

40. *Ibid.*, IX (May 1803), 74.

41. Karamzin, *Sochineniia*, II, 511.

42. *Ibid.*, p. 749.

43. *Neizdannye sochineniia i perepiska Nikolaia Mikhailovicha Karamzina* (Spb., 1862), p. 203.

44. "Fillide," *Polnoe sobranie stikhotvorenii*, p. 367.

45. Karamzin, *Sochineniia*, II, 706.

46. *Neizdannye sochineniia*, p. 211.

47. *Pis'ma Karamzina k Dmitrievu, op. cit.*, p. 165.

48. *Istoriia Gosudarstva Rossiskogo*, I (Spb., 1830), xix. Cf. his remarks on Hume in 1824: *Russkaia starina*, LXVII (1890), 453.

49. *Pis'ma N. M. Karamzina k kniaziu P. A. Viazemskomu* (Spb., 1897), p. 159.

50. *Pis'ma Karamzina k Dmitrievu*, pp. 356, 399, 408. See G. A. Gukovskii, "Karamzin," in *Istoriia russkoi literatury*, V (Moscow-Leningrad, 1941), 98.

1. *Slavonic and East European Review*, XXXIX (1960), 148-63.
2. *Voprosy istorii*, no. 12 (1961), 183.
3. V. I. Maikov, "Elisei, ili razdrazhennyi Vakkh" (1771), *Izbrannye sochineniia* (Moscow-Leningrad, 1966), p. 105.
4. *Catherine the Great's Instruction (Nakaz) to the Legislative Commission*, edited by Paul Dukes (Newtonville, Mass., 1977), pp. 81-85, clauses 294-302, 312-28.
5. *Ibid.*, p. 92, clause 378. (The translation was made in the eighteenth century for the former English Ambassador to Russia, Sir George Macartney.)
6. For an important recent study of the role of the specifically Russian seminaries, see Gregory L. Freeze, *The Russian Levites: Parish Clergy in the Eighteenth Century* (Cambridge, Mass., 1977), pp. 78-106.
7. See D. B. Saunders, "The Political and Cultural Impact of the Ukraine on Great Russia, c. 1775-c. 1835," Unpublished D. Phil. thesis, Oxford University, 1979.
8. See my "British Freemasons in Russia during the Reign of Catherine the Great," *Oxford Slavonic Papers*, NS IV (1971), 43-62.
9. G. V. Vernadskii, *Russkoe masonstvo v tsarstvovanie Ekateriny II* (Petrograd, 1917), p. 19, note 5.
10. At least four of Catherine's ambassadors were Masons: Alexander and Semen Vorontsov, Ivan Chernyshev and Musin-Pushkin. Other leading Masons included Prince A. A. Cherkasskii, Prince G. P. Gagarin and Zinov'ev. Zinov'ev was closely involved in England with the notorious Saint-Martin. See M. Matter, *Saint-Martin le philosophe inconnu* (Paris, 1862), pp. 134 ff. (a very confused account) and Zinov'ev's own memoirs.
11. Pushkin House, Leningrad, Fond 620, Arkhiv A. A. Samborskogo, ed. khr. 127, f. 6v. Cf. his reference in an earlier letter to his gold compasses and a book called *The Ruband* (f. 4v.).
12. *Russkii arkhiv*, pt. 3 (1877), 159; *Arkhiv kniazia A. I. Viazemskogo* (Spb., 1881), pp. iii-xxiii. Viazemskii's travel diary breaks off just before his visit to England but a list of the people in Britain to whom he had letters of recommendation is given on pp. lviii-lix.
13. The brother of the dramatist and poet Vasilii Kapnist. On Petr Kapnist and his English wife (née Housman), see "Vospominaniia S. V. Skalon (urozhdennoi Kapnist)," *Istoricheskii vestnik*, XLIV, no. 5 (1891), 349-52.
14. Stepanov and Ushakov (on whom see N. M. Karamzin, *Izbrannye sochineniia*, I [Moscow-Leningrad, 1964], 569) were two of a very small number of Russians electing to remain in England. Another was Petr Dement'ev (d. 1756), an Old Believer who set up as a watchmaker in London (see Iu. Ia. Kogan, *Ocherki po istorii russkoi ateisticheskoi mysli XVIIIv*. (Moscow, 1962), p. 107).
15. See P. A. Viazemskii, "Dopotopnaia ili dopozharnaia Moskva," in his *Polnoe sobranie sochinenii*, VII (Spb., 1882), 110-11.
16. For the most recent contribution to the question of French, see D. K. Zhanne, "Frantsuzskii iazyk v Rossii XVIII v. kak obshchestvennoe iavlenie," *Vestnik Moskovskogo universiteta*, Seriia filologiia, no. 1 (1978), 62-70.
17. M. P. Alekseev, "Angliiskii iazyk v Rossii i russkii iazyk v Anglii," *Uchenye zapiski LGU*, No. 72, Seriia filologicheskikh nauk, vyp. 9 (1944), 77-137.
18. Some English teaching was also available at the *gimnazium* of the Academy of Sciences. See T. A. Lukina, *Ivan Ivanovich Lepekhin* (Moscow-Leningrad, 1965), pp. 155 ff.

19. On Bailey, see *Biograficheskii slovar' professorov i prepodavatelei Imperatorskogo Moskovskogo Universiteta*, I (Moscow, 1855), 90-91. The same source (pp. 362-64) indicates that for a short time in 1757-58 English was offered by a J. J. Rost.

20. Fond 620, ed. khr. 142, f. 4.

21. *Ibid.*, ed. khr. 160, f. 1; *Arkhiv kniazia Vorontsova*, XXX (Moscow, 1884), 409-12.

22. Fond 620, ed. khr. 27, ff. 3v., 4v.; ed. khr. 157, f. 26; ed. khr. 123, f. lv.

23. Birmingham Reference Libraries, Matthew Boulton Papers, Russian Mint Book I, Letter from Z. Walker to M. Boulton, 25 October 1803, f. lv.

24. Alekseev, *op. cit.*, p. 96.

SELECT BIBLIOGRAPHY

Precise details of the hundreds of works I have consulted and used in the preparation of this study are included in the end-notes. It would be pointless to reproduce them here, particularly as many provided merely a single quotation or reference. I have therefore limited myself to listing those works, both primary and secondary, which have the widest relevance to the topic in general.

Primary sources, published and unpublished
Aleksandrenko, V. N., *Russkie diplomaticheskie agenty v Londone v XVIII v.*, II (*Materialy*) (Warsaw, 1897)
Correspondence of Jeremy Bentham, edited by Timothy L. S. Sprigge (vol. I) and Ian R. Christie (vols. II-III), I-III (London, 1968-71) (Continuing)
Matthew Boulton Papers, Birmingham Reference Library, Birmingham
Arkhiv kniazia F. A. Kurakina, 10 vols. (Spb., and Saratov, 1890-1902)
Materialy dlia istorii russkogo flota, edited by S. I. Elagin, F. F. Veselago and S. F. Ogorodnikov, 17 vols. (Spb., 1865-1904)
Arkhiv grafov Mordvinovykh, 10 vols. (Spb., 1901-3)
Arkhiv A. A. Samborskogo, Fond 620, Institute of Russian Literature (Pushkin House), Leningrad
Sbornik Imperatorskogo Russkogo istoricheskogo obshchestva, 148 vols. (Spb.-Petrograd, 1867-1916)
Arkhiv kniazia Vorontsova, 40 vols. (Moscow, 1870-95)
Horace Walpole's Correspondence, edited by W. S. Lewis, 39 vols. (London, 1937-1974) (Continuing)

Secondary sources
Aleksandrenko, V. N., *Russkie diplomaticheskie agenty v Londone v XVIII v.*, I (Warsaw, 1897)
Alekseev, M. P., "Angliiskii iazyk v Rossii i russkii iazyk v Anglii," *Uchenye zapiski Leningradskogo gos. universiteta*, no. 72, seriia filologicheskikh nauk, vyp. 9 (1944), 77-137
Anderson, M. S., *Britain's Discovery of Russia 1553-1815* (London, 1958)
Anderson, M. S., "Great Britain and the Growth of the Russian Navy in the Eighteenth Century," *Mariner's Mirror*, XLII (1956), 132-46
Bantysh-Kamenskii, N. N., *Obzor vneshnikh snoshenii Rossii po 1800 god*, I (Moscow, 1894)
Cross, A. G., *Anglo-Russian Relations in the Eighteenth Century. Catalogue of an Exhibition* (Norwich, 1977)

Cross, A. G., (ed.), *Great Britain and Russia in the Eighteenth Century. Contacts and Comparisons* (Newtonville, Mass., 1979)

Dzhincharadze, V. Z., "Iz istorii russko-angliiskikh kul'turnykh otnoshenii v 18 veke," *Vestnik istorii mirovoi kul'tury*, V (Sept.-Oct. 1960), 63-76

Nikiforov, L. A., *Russko-angliiskie otnosheniia pri Petre I* (Moscow, 1950)

Obshchii morskoi spisok, edited by F. Veselago *et al.*, 13 pts. (Spb., 1885-1907)

Radovskii, M. I., *Iz istorii anglo-russkikh nauchnykh sviazei* (Moscow-Leningrad, 1961)

Robinson, Eric, "The Transference of British Technology to Russia 1760-1820: A Preliminary Enquiry," in Barrie M. Ratcliffe (ed.), *Great Britain and Her World, 1750-1914: Essays in Honour of W. O. Henderson* (Manchester, 1975), pp. 1-26.

Russkii biograficheskii slovar', 25 vols. (Spb. and Moscow, 1896-1916)

CHECKLIST OF RUSSIANS IN GREAT BRITAIN 1700-1800

Listed here in alphabetical order are the names of all the Russians (in the widest sense, including one or two foreigners in Russian service) known to have visited Great Britain in the eighteenth century. The names are accompanied, where possible, by an indication (sometimes very approximate) of the period spent in Britain and of their general area of specialization or interest at the time (e.g., navy, embassy, merchant, tourist). Omissions are inevitable and, in an exercise of this magnitude, I trust, excusable. Specifically excluded are members of Peter the Great's "Great Embassy" of 1698.

ABERNIBESOV, Konon Antonovich	Navy	1793-98
AFANAS'EV, Ivan	Embassy	1718-30s
AFANAS'EV, –	Shipbuilding	1776-
AKIMOV, Pavel	Navy	1796-97
ALEKSEEV, Aleksei	Navy	1706-
ALEKSEEV, Iakov	Shipbuilding	1716
ALISOV, Prokhor Ivanovich	Navy	1762-5/1769
AMOSOV, Vasilii	Shipbuilding	1797
ANGERSTEIN, John Julius (1735-1823)	Emigré	1750-1823
ANICHKOV, Gavriil Fedorovich (1773-1805)	Navy	1797-1802
ANIKIEV, Nazar	Shipbuilding	1716
ANTUF'EV, Mikhail (d. 1727)	Navy	1706-13
APLECHEEV, Petr Andreevich	Navy	1797-1802
APRAKSIN, Count Aleksandr Petrovich (d. 1725)	Navy	1709-16
APRELEV, –	Navy	1779
ARSEN'EV, –	Tourist	1768

B

BABARYKIN, Andrei Artem'evich (d. 1765)	Navy	1762-65
BABENKOV, Sergei	Navy	1763-69
BABICHEV, Prince Dmitrii Grigor'evich	Engineer	1774? -76
BAKBORODIN, Andrei	Shipbuilding	1716
BAKHMETEV, Iurii Alekseevich	Student	1776-87
BAKLANOVSKII, Semen	Shipbuilding	1715-
BAKUNIN, Ivan	Student	1780s

BAKUNIN, Pavel Petrovich (1762-1805)	Student	1785-87
BALABIN, Petr Ivanovich	Student	1784-90
BALDIN, - (d. 1804)	Ambassador's servant	1785-1804
BARATYNSKII, Bogdan Andreevich	Navy	1795-96
BARATYNSKII, Il'ia Andreevich (d. 1817)	Navy	1795-98
BARKHATOV (KIRILOV), Sila (d. 1763)	Church	-1763
BASHILOV, Dmitrii (d. 1724)	Navy	1707-13
BASILEVICH, Grigorii Ivanovich (1759-1802)	Student	1778
BASILEVICH, - (brother of above)	Student	1778
BASKAKOV, Mikhail Ivanovich	Navy	1793-99
BATURIN, Evgraf Petrovich	Tourist	1766
BAZHENIN, Stepan Ivanovich	Commerce	1766-69
BEITON, Aleksei	Riding Master	1792-93
BELIAEV, Nikolai Ivanovich	Student	1774-77
BEL'SKII, Mikhail Ivanovich	Painter	1773-78?
BELOSEL'SKII, Prince Aleksandr Mikhailovich (1752-1809)	Embassy	1768
BELOSEL'SKII, Prince Andrei Mikhailovich	Embassy	1752
BERGSDORF, -	Tourist	1785
BERING, Iakov (d. 1794)	Navy	1793-94
BESSONOV, Ivan	Navy	1706 -
BESSONOV, Ivan	Shipbuilding	1715 -
BESTUZHEV, Dmitrii (d. 1739)	Navy	1711-13
BESTUZHEV-RIUMIN, Count Mikhail Petrovich (1688-1760)	Embassy	1720
BEZOBRAZOV, -	Mechanic	1719
BIBIKOV, Gavrila Il'ich (d. 1812)	Tourist	1776
BIBIKOV, -	Courier	1780s
BLUMENTROST, Lavrentii Lavrent'evich (1692-1755)	Student	1709
BOBRINSKOI, Count Aleksei Grigor'evich	Tourist	1787-88
BOGDANOVICH, Petr Ivanovich (1756-1803)	Student	1760s
BOKOV, Stepan	Shipbuilding	1716-
BORISOV, Ivan Antonovich (1729-90)	Navy	1763-65
BORZOV, Fedor Prokof'evich	Mechanic	1779-83
BUKHOVETSKII, Aleksandr Sergeevich	Student	1765-72
BYKOV, Danilo	Navy	1706-
BYKOV, Mikhail Fedorovich	Student	1765-71

C

CHAADAEV, Fedor Vasil'evich	Navy	1708-16
CHEBOTAEV, Rodion	Shipbuilding	1715-
CHEBOTAEV, Vasilii	Shipbuilding	1715-
CHERENKOVSKII, Maksim	Church	-1755
CHERKASOV, Baron Aleksandr Ivanovich (1728-88)	Student	1742-47, 1752-56
CHERKASOV, Ivan Ivanovich (1732-1811)	Student	1742-56
CHERKASSKII, Prince Aleksei Aleksandrovich	Tourist	1783
CHERNYSHEV, Count Ivan Grigor'evich (1726-97)	Diplomat	1768
CHERNYSHEV, Count Petr Grigor'evich (1762-73)	Diplomat	1746-55
CHERNYSHEVA, Countess	Diplomat's wife	1768
CHERNYSHEVA (later SALTYKOVA), Dar'ia Petrovna (1738-1802)	Diplomat's family	1746-55
CHERNYSHEVA, Countess Ekaterina Andeeevna (1715-79)	Diplomat's wife	1746-55
CHERNYSHEVA (later GOLITSYNA), Natal'ia Petrovna (1741-1837)	Diplomat's family	1746-55, 1788-89
CHERTKOV, Aleksei (d. 1737)	Navy	1711-13
CHESMENSKII, Aleksandr Alekseevich (1763-1820)	Student	1779-80
CHETVERIKOV, Mikhail	Navy	1746-48
CHICHAGOV, Pavel Vasil'evich (1767-1849)	Navy	1792-93, 1796, 1798-1800
CHICHAGOV, Vasilii Iakovlevich (1726-1809)	Navy	c. 1740
CHICHAGOV, Vasilii Vasil'evich	Navy	1792-93
CHIZHOV, Nikolai Galaktionovich (1731-67)	Instrument maker	1759-60
CZARTORYSKI, Adam (1770-1861)	Tourist	1780?

D

DANILOV, Naum	Navy	1707-11
DANILOV, Stepan	Navy	1706-
DASHKOV, Prince Pavel Mikhailovich (1763-1807)	Student	1770, 1776-80

DASHKOVA (later SHCHERBININA), Anastas'ia Mikhailovna	Tourist	1770, 1776-80
DASHKOVA, Princess Ekaterina Romanovna (1743-1810)	Tourist	1770, 1776-80
DEMENT'EV, Petr (d. 1756)	Merchant	1756
DEM'IANOV, Iakov	Navy	1793-98
DEMIDOV, Grigorii Aleksandrovich (1765-1827)	Student	1790-92
DEMIDOV, Nikita Akinfievich (1724-89)	Tourist	1772, 1773
DEMIDOV, Pavel Grigor'evich (1738-1821)	Student	1760s
DEMIDOV, Prokofii Akinfievich (1710-86)	Tourist	1770
DERIABIN, Andrei Fedorovich (1770-1820)	Mining Engineer	1796-99
DESNITSKII, Semen Efimovich (d. 1789)	Student	1761-67
D'IAKOVSKII, Efrem (1727?-95)	Church	1765-67
DIUZHAKOV-	Courier	1789
DMITREV, Roman	Mechanic	1777-79
DMITREVSKII, Ivan Afanas'evich (1734-1821)	Actor	1766
DOLGORUKOV, Prince Vasilii Vasil'evich (1752-1812)	Tourist	1772?
DOLGORUKOV, Prince Vladimir Vladimirovich	Navy	1708-13
DROZHDIN, Matvei	Shipbuilding	1715-
DUBASOV, Fedor (d. 1773)	Navy	1762-66
DUBROVSKII, Andreian Illarionovich (1732-80's)	Embassy	1762-64
DURASOV-	Tourist?	1777
DZHUNKOVSKII, Stepan Semenovich (1762-1839)	Student	1784-92

E

EFREMOV, Filip Sergeevich	In transit	1783
EMIN, Fedor Aleksandrovich (1735?-70)	In transit	1761
ERMOLOV, Aleksei Petrovich (1754-1834)	Tourist	1787
EVSTAV'EV, Aleksei Grigor'evich (1779-1857)	Church	1798-1807

F

FEDOROV, Ivan	Navy	1707-
FLECHER (FLEICHER),-	Embassy	1786-87
FLOROV, Petr	Navy	1706-

G

GAGARIN, Prince Aleksei Matveevich	Navy	1708-
GAGARIN, Prince Gavriil Petrovich (1745-1807)	Tourist	1771
GAGARIN, Prince Ivan	Navy	1763-69
GAGARIN, Prince Petr	Embassy	1773-84
GAGARIN, Prince Sergei Sergeevich	Tourist	1772
GALIN, Aleksandr (Ivanovich?)	Riding Master	1792-93
GASS, F. W. (b. 1769)	Medallist	1797
GENNADII, Archimandrite (d. 1737)	Church	1712-37
GEZEL', Lorens	Navy	1766-69
GLEBOV, Ivan Alekseevich	Tourist	1776
GOLITSYN, Prince Aleksandr Mikhailovich (1723-1807)	Diplomat	1755-62
GOLITSYN, Aleksei Borisovich (1732-92)	Tourist	1787
GOLITSYN, Boris Vladimirovich (1769-1813)	Tourist	1789
GOLITSYN, Dmitrii Vladimirovich (1771-1844)	Tourist	1789
GOLITSYN, Prince Mikhail	Tourist	1780s
GOLITSYN, Sergei Mikhailovich	Embassy	1758
GOLITSYN, Prince Vasilii Vasil'evich	Navy	1710
GOLITSYN, Vladimir Borisovich (1731-98)	Tourist	1788-89
GOLOSTENOV, Fedor Alekseevich (d. 1801)	Navy	1797-1801
GOLOVIN, Count Aleksandr Fedorovich	Navy	1708
GOLOVIN, Fedor	Navy	1707-13
GOLOVIN, Count Nikolai Fedorovich (d. 1745)	Navy	1708-17
GOLOVKIN, Count -	Tourist	1786
GOLOVKINA, Countess -	Tourist	1786
GOLOVNIN, Vasilii Mikhailovich (1776-)	Navy	1797-98, 1802-06
GREBENSHCHIKOV, Ivan Ivanoyich	Student	1785-89
GREBNITSKII, Stepan	Agriculture	1781-86
GREZIN,-	Die-maker	1797-1800
GROSS, Genrikh Ivanovich (1713-65)	Diplomat	1730s, 1735-65
GROSS, Fedor Ivanovich	Embassy	1764-65
GUR'EV, Semen Emel'ianovich (1764-1813)	Tutor	1792-93
GUR'EV, -	Tourist	1783

H

HARDER, David Johann (GARDER, David Davidovich) (1769-1833)	Doctor	1796
HEDENBERG, Pilers Christoph	Merchant	1790s

I

IAKOVLEV, Lev Alekseevich (1764-1839)	Navy	1795-96 1797-1800
IASTREMBSKII, Ioann	Church	1737-39
ISAKOV, Pavel	Embassy	1733
ITALINSKII, Andrei Iakovlevich (1742-1827)	Doctor	1775
IURASOV, Tikhon	Shipbuilding	1715-
ISUPOV, Fedor	Navy	1762-
IUSUPOV, Prince Nikolai Borisovich (1750-1831)	Tourist	1776
IUZEFOVICH,-	Embassy	1790s
IVANOV, Ivan	Navy	1762
IVANOVSKII, Stepan (d. 1765)	Church	1737-65
IZVOL'SKII, Aleksei	Mechanic	1797

K

KAMENSKII (PARCHIKALOV), Aleksei	Church	1737-
KAKHOVSKII, Count Evgenii Mikhailovich	Tourist	1800
KALMYKOV, Denis Spiridonovich (1687-1746)	Navy	1706-13
KANAEV, -	Shipbuilding	1785-
KANTEMIR, Prince Antiokh Dmitrievich (1708-44)	Diplomat	1732-38
KAPNIST, Petr Vasil'evich (d. 1826)	Tourist	-1781?
KARAMYSHEV, Efrem	Apprentice	1782-88
KARAMYSHEV, Ivan	Navy	1707-
KARAMZIN, Nikolai Mikhailovich (1766-1826)	Tourist	1790
KARTASHEV, Iakov Tikhonovich	Navy	1763-
KARTASHEV, Pavel Petrovich	Navy	1793-98
KARZHAVIN, Erofei Nikitich	Commerce	1753
KARZHAVIN, Fedor Vasil'evich (1745-1812)	Commerce	1753
KASATKIN,-	Student	1777-
KASSANO, Varfolomei (1697-1746)	Church	1716-46
KAZANTSEV, Vasilii Ivanovich	Navy	1706-13

KHANENKO,-	Embassy	late 1790s
KHANYKOV, Petr Ivanovich (1743-1813)	Navy	1762-
KHLEBNIKOV, Grigorii	Navy	1710-
KHOVANSKII, K.	Courier	1792
KHOVANSKII, Prince Vasilii Petrovich	Navy	1716-
KHRIPUNOV, Fedor	Navy	1706-
KIRILOV, Ivan	Navy	1707-
KIRILOV, Vasilii	Navy	1707-
KISELEV, Mikhail	Navy	1706-
KLAVUTSKII, Aleksei Vasil'evich	Agriculture	1776-84
KLINGSHTEDT, Timofei Ivanovich (1710-86)	Official business	1772
KLIUCHAREV, Ivan	Navy	1706
KOBLIAKOV, Aleksei	Shipbuilding	1716-
KOCHUBEI, Apollon Pavlovich	Tourist	1783
KOCHUBEI, Viktor Pavlovich (1768-1834)	Embassy	1789-91, 1792
KOKUSHKIN, Estafii	Mechanic	1794-1800
KOLMAKOV, Aleksei Vasil'evich (d. 1804)	Church	1776-84
KOLYCHEV, Stepan Alekseevich (1746-1805)	Tourist	1770-72
KOMAROV, Ivan	Shipbuilding	1716-
KOMAROVSKII, Count Evgraf Fedotovich (1769-1843)	Courier	1787
KOMOV Ivan Mikhailovich (1750?-92)	Agriculture	1776-84
KONOVNITSYN, Count Petr Petrovich	Courier	1785-86
KORMILITSYN, Ivan	Navy	1706-
KOROLEV, Vasilii	Shipbuilding	1716-
KORONATSKII, Aleksandr	Embassy	1780s
KORONATSKII, Petr Semenovich	Embassy	1784
KORSAKOV, Ivan	Navy	1770
KORSAKOV, Nikolai Ivanovich (1749-88)	Engineer	1774-77
KOSHELEV, Ivan (d. 1732)	Navy	1707-13
KOSHELEV, Ivan Rodionovich (d. 1818)	Embassy	1770-73
KOSTIURIN, Petr	Student	1745-49
KOSTLIVTSOV,	Navy	1797-1802
KOTELEV, Ivan	Navy	1706-
KOZHIN, Aleksandr Ivanovich	Navy	1711-13
KOZHUKHOV, Mikhail	Navy	1762-
KOZLIANINOV, Timofei Gavrilovich (d. 1798)	Navy	1762-66, 1769
KOZLIATEV, Petr	Navy	1762-
KOZLOV, Gerasim	Agriculture	1781-86
KOZLOVSKII, Prince Sergei Petrovich	Tourist	1773

KRETOV,-	Navy	1795-97
KRIVOV, Aleksei Iur'evich	Student	1745-49
KROLL, Adam	Merchant	1786, 1800
KRUZENSHTERN, Ivan (Adam) (1770-1846)	Navy	1793-1800, 1814
KULIKOV, Nikula	Shipbuilding	1716-
KURAKIN, Prince Aleksandr Borisovich (1752-1818)	Tourist	1772
KURAKIN, Prince Boris Ivanovich (1676-1727)	Diplomat	1710, 1714-15
KURDEVSKII, Iakov	Navy	1706-
KUREPANOV,-	Shipbuilding	late 1790s
KUTUZOV, Mikhail Illarionovich (1745-1813)	Tourist	1776
KUTYGIN, Ivan	Shipbuilding	1776
KUZMIN, Andrei	Shipbuilding	1715-

L

LANCHINSKII,-	Embassy	1707-
LANSKOI,-	Courier	1786, 1788
LAPIN, Koz'ma	Navy	1707-11
LEBEDEV, Fedor	Navy	1709-13
LEBEDEV, Gerasim Stepanovich (1749-1817)	In transit	1784, 1799
LEBIADNIKOV, Boris	Navy	1701-09
LEKSEL', Andrei (LEXELL, Andreas) (1740-84)	Academy of Sciences	1781
LEONT'EV, Aleksandr Ivanovich	Navy	1708-16
LEONT'EV, Iakov	Gunsmith	1785-
LEONTOVICH, Konstantin Stepanovich (d. 1811)	Navy	1793-98
LEVASHOV, Aleksei	Student	1779-80
LEVASHOV, Pavel Artem'evich	Tourist	1787
LEVITOV, Mikhailo	Navy	1706-
LEVKEN, Ivan	Medallist	1731
LEVSHIN (LEVSHINOV), Aleksei Georgievich	Student	1765-71
LISIANSKII, Iurii Fedorovich (1773-1839)	Navy	1793-1800, 1802-03, 1812-13
LITH, Albrecht von der	Diplomat	1711-13
LITKEVICH, Leontii (1762?-after 1834)	Church	1780-1830s
LITVINOV,-	Courier	1788

LIVANOV, Mikhail Egorovich (1751-1800)	Agriculture	1776-84
LIZAKEVICH, Vasilii Grigor'evich	Embassy	1765-1800
LEZEL,-	Mechanic	1797-1802
LODYZHENSKII, Aleksei Iur'evich	Navy	1710-
LOMEN, Fedor Iakovlevich (d. 1822)	Navy	1778-81
LOMEN, Iakov Iakovlevich (d. 1781)	Navy	1778-81
LONGINOV, Nikolai Mikhailovich (1779-1853)	Church	1798-1806
LOPUKHIN, Gavriil Fedorovich	Navy	1710-
LOPUKHIN, Stepan Vasil'evich	Navy	1708-17
LUDERS, Fedor	Embassy	1760s
LUKIN, Vasilii Ignat'evich (1737-94)	Freemasonry	1772
LUNIEVSKII, Petr	Shipbuilding	1701-14
LUNIN, Iosif	Navy	1711-13
LUPANDIN, Efim Maksimovich	Navy	1762-64
LUTOKHIN, Egor Ivanovich (d. 1840)	Navy	1793-98
L'VOV, Prince Ivan Borisovich	Navy	1708-16

M

MAIEV, Stepan	Navy	1706-
MAIKOV,-	Tourist	1791
MAKAROV, Petr Ivanovich (d. 1805)	Tourist	1795
MAKSIMILIAN,-	Church	1711
MAKULOV, Prince	Embassy	1787
MALINOVSKII, Vasilii Fedorovich (1765-1814)	Embassy	1789-91
MALIUTIN, Ivan	Shipbuilding	1715-
MAL'TSOV, Petr Semenovich	Embassy	1762
MAL'TSOV, Timofei	Navy	1706-
MARK, -	Embassy	1770s?
MARTINIANOV, Antipa	Church	-1749
MARTOV, Petr	Navy	1706-
MASAL'SKII, -	Shipbuilding	1788
MATVEEV, Andrei Artamonovich (1666-1728)	Diplomat	1707-08
MATVEEVSKII, Semen Ivanovich (b. 1748?)	Student	1765-71
MELEKHOV,-	Shipbuilding	1796-99
MESHCHERSKII, Prince Sergei Vasil'evich	Tourist	1762
MESHCHERSKII, Prince Vasilii	Tourist	1788
MAISNOI, Danilo Ivanovich	Navy	1708-
MICHURIN, Ivan	Shipbuilding	1701-14
MIKHAILOV, Kirill	Church	1879s

MIKHAILOV, Vasilii	Navy	1707-
MILLER, Fedor Ivanovich (1705-83)	Academy of	1730-31
(MÜLLER, Gerard-Friedrich)	Sciences	
MILLER (MÜLLER), Petr	Student	1709
MILLER, Sergei	Embassy	-1784
MOKRINSKII, Petr	Navy	1706-
MONOMAKHOV, Fedor	Navy	1707-11
MORDVINOV, Nikolai Semenovich	Navy	1774-77
(1754-1845)		
MORKOV,-	Courier	1763
MOZOLEVSKII, Aleksandr	Embassy	-1738
MULOVSKII, Grigorii Ivanovich (d. 1789)	Navy	1769-71
MURAV'EV, Nikifor	Shipbuilding	1716-
MURAV'EV, Nikolai Nazar'evich	Navy	1797-1802
(1775-1845)		
MUSIN-PUSHKIN, Aleksei Semenovich	Diplomat	1765-79
(1732-1817)		
MUSINA-PUSHKINA, Ekaterina	Diplomat's wife	1765-79

N

NARTOV, Andrei Konstantinovich	Mechanic	1719
(1680?-1756)		
NARYSHKIN, Aleksandr L'vovich	Navy	1708-21
NARYSHKIN, Aleksei Vasil'evich	Tourist	1773
(1742-1800)		
NARYSHKIN, Ivan L'vovich	Navy	1708-21
NARYSHKIN, Semen Kirillovich	Diplomat ·	1742
(1710-75)		
NASHCHOKIN, Petr Fedorovich	Tourist	1777
NAZAREVSKII, Andrei Vasil'evich	Agriculture, then Embassy	1784-1801
NAZIMOV, Aleksandr	Embezzler fled to England	1778-79
NAZIMOV,-	Navy	17.70
NEELOV, Petr Vasil'evich (1749-1848)	Architect	1771-
NEELOV, Vasilii Ivanovich	Architect	1771
(1722-82)		
NEKRASOV, Nikolai (d. 1783)	Church	1740s-83
NEPEIN, Ivan	Navy	1707-11.
NERONOV, Stepan	Navy	1707-
NESSELRODE, Count Wilhelm	Tourist	1786

NESVITAEV, Ivan	Embassy	1735-
NEVEROV,-	Engineer	1774
NIKITIN, Vasilii Nikitich (1737-1809)	Student	1765-75
NIKOLAI (NICOLAY), Pavel Andreevich (1777-1866)	Embassy	1798-1803, 1804-08,
NOVIKOV Dmitrii	Shipbuilding	1812-18
NOVIKOV, Mikhail	Courier	1787
NOVOSELOV, Artemii Pavlovich	Commerce	1735
NOVOSIL'TSOV, Nikolai Nikolaevich (1761-1836)	Diplomat	1793-1801, 1804-05

O

ODINTSOV, Astafii	Navy	1763-66
ODOEVSKII, Prince Ivan	Navy	1716-
ORLOV, Aleksandr Vladimirovich (d. 1787)	Tourist	1787
ORLOV, Count Grigorii Grigor'evich (1734-83)	Tourist	1775
ORLOV, Stepan	Embassy	1762
ORLOV, Count Vladimir Grigor'evich (1743-1831)	Tourist	1772-73
OSIPOV, Vasilii	Navy	1706
OSTROUMOV, Grigorii	Shipbuilding	1715-
OVTSYN, Dmitrii	Mechanic	1797

P

PERMSKII, Mikhail (1741-70)	Church	1758-60
PESSOROV,-	Student	1776
PETROV Vasilii Petrovich (1736-99)	Student	1772-74
PLESHCHEEV, Mikhail Ivanovich	Embassy	1762-73?
PLESHCHEEV, Sergei Ivanovich (1752-1802)	Navy	1765-70
PLESHCHEEV, Vasilii Ivanovich	Navy	1765-70
PISCHEKOV, Daniil Iakovlevich (1758-1825)	Student	1782-85
PANIN, Ivan	Shipbuilding	1716-
PODKOL'ZIN, Iakov Efremovich	Navy	1797-1802
POGGENPOL' (POGGENPOHL), Vil'gel'm	Embassy	1780s-
POGUTKIN, Afanasii	Navy	1707-
POLIKUTI, Mikhail	Navy	1793-
POLTORATSKII, Fedor Markovich	Student	1783
POLTORATSKII, Dmitrii Markovich (1761-1818)	Student	1783
POLUBOIARINOV, Nikifor	Navy	1762-65

POPOV, Ivan	Navy	1706-
PORTNOV, Mikhail	Shipbuilding	1765-69
POROSHIN, Tikhon	Student?	1756
POSLUSHATELEV, Ivan	Navy	1706-
POSPELOV,-	Shipbuilding	1784-
POSTNIKOV, Petr Vasil'evich (1666-1731?)	Doctor	1698, 1702
POTEMKIN, Count Pavel Sergeevich (1743-96)	Tourist	1775
PROKOPOVICH (PROKOF'EV), Vasilii Prokof'evich (d. 1792)	Agriculture	1776-84
PROTASOV, Pavel Ivanovich	Student	1784-86
PROTOPOPOV, Stepan	Shipbuilding	1715-
PUSHKIN, Aleksei	Navy	1762-

R

RACHINSKII, Stepan Ivanovich (b. 1762)	Student	1774-77
RAEVSKII,-	Church	-1778
RAMEIKOV, Petr	Navy	1707-13
RAZNOTOVSKII, Ivan Vasil'evich	Freemasonry	1774
RAZUMOV,-	Shipbuilding	1796-99, 1802
RAZUMOVSKII, Count Aleksei Kirillovich (1748-1822)	Tourist	1768-69
RAZUMOVSKII, Prince Andrei Kirillovich (1752-1836)	Tourist	1768-69
RAZUMOVSKII, Count Kirill Grigor'evich (1728-1803)	Tourist	1766
RAZUMOVSKII, Count Petr Kirillovich (1751-1823)	Tourist	1768-69
REINHARD,-	Mechanic	1797-
REPNIN, Prince Nikolai Vasil'evich (1734-1801)	Tourist	1773
RIKORD, Petr Ivanovich (1776-1855)	Navy	1796, 1803-05
RIMSKII-KORSAKOV, Aleksandr Mikhailovich (1753-1840)	Official business	1793
ROGOV,-	Embassy	1711
RONTSOV, Aleksandr Romanovich	Tourist	1780
ROSLAVLEV,-	Embassy	1797-98
ROSTOPCHIN, Count Fedor Vasil'evich (1763-1826)	Tourist	1787-88, 1820
ROZHNOV, Ivan	Navy	1793-
RUMIANTSEV, Count Sergei Petrovich (1755-1838)	Tourist	1780-81

RUMIANTSEV, Count Mikhail Petrovich (d. 1806)	Tourist	1782
RZHEVSKII, Petr	Navy	1716-

S

SABAKIN, Ivan L'vovich I (d. 1802)	Mechanic	1797-1802
SABAKIN, Lev Fedorovich (1746-1813)	Mechanic	1784-86, 1797-99
SALDERN, Karl-Heinrich	Tutor	1771-72
SALMANOV, Ivan	Navy	1762-
SALTYKOV, Fedor Stepanovich (d. 1715)	Navy	1711-15
SAMARIN, German Fedorovich	Navy	1797-1802
SAMBORSKAIA, Anna Andreevna (1770-1844)	Priest's family	1770-80
SAMBORSKAIA (later MALINOVSKAIA), Sofiia Andreevna (1772-1812)	Priest's family	1772-80
SAMBORSKII, Aleksandr Andreevich (1776-92)	Student	1776-80, 1784-92
SAMBORSKII, Andrei Afanas'evich (1732-1815)	Church	1765-80, 1784
SAMOILOV, Count Aleksandr Nikolaevich (1744-1814)	Tourist	1770s?
SAMSONOV, Ivan	Navy	1763-65
SARVILOV, Grigorii	Agriculture	-1785
SARYCHEV,-	Shipbuilding	1785-
SELIFONTOV, Ivan Osipovich (1744-1822)	Navy	1762-
SELIVACHEV, Nikifor	Navy	1763-
SEMENNIKOV, Lev	Embassy	1730s
SEMTSOV,-	Embassy	c. 1758
SENIAVIN, Grigorii Alekseevich	Navy	1785?-88
SENIAVIN, Ivan Fedorovich	Navy	1762-
SENIAVIN, P. A.	Navy	1715
SHAK (SCHACK), Baron Bertram von	Diplomat	1713-16
SHAPILOV, Ivan	Navy	1715-20
SHAPKIN, Vasilii (d. 1732)	Navy	1706-19
SHARAPOV, Vasilii	Embassy	1770s
SHCHEPIN, Petr	Navy	1706-
SHCHEPOTEV, Aleksei Ivanovich	Navy	1711-
SHCHEPOTEV, Vasilii Andreevich	Navy	1714-19
SHCHEPOTEV, Vasilii	Navy	1714
SHCHERBATOV, Prince Ivan Andreevich (1696-1761)	Diplomat	1738-42, 1743-46

SHEBONIN, Afanasii Iakovlevich	Commerce	1735
SHEREMETEV, Aleksei Petrovich	Navy	1708-16
SHEREMETEV, Fedor Vladimirovich	Navy	1709-
SHEREMETEV, Ivan Petrovich	Navy	1708-16
SHEREMETEV, Count Nikolai Petrovich (1751-1809)	Tourist	1771
SHEREMETEV, Vasilii Vasil'evich (d. 1729)	Navy	1709-16
SHERLAIMOV, Ivan	Student	1778-80
SHIPILOV, Ivan	Shipbuilding	1715-
SHISHKOV, Aleksandr Semenovich (1754-1841)	Navy	1776
SHISHORIN, Osip Ivanovich	Instrument maker	1780-85
SHISHUKOV, Ivan Nikolaevich	Student	1774-47
SHLATTER (SCHLATTER), Fedor Ivanovich	Medallist	1797
SHLEIKIN, Ivan	Navy	1707-14?
SHTELIN (STAHLIN), Petr Iakovlevich	Embassy	c. 1780
SHUBIN, Fedot Ivanovich (1740-1805)	Tourist	1773
SHUMAKER, Ivan (1690-1761)	Academy of Sciences	1721-22
SHUMLIANSKII, Aleksandr Mikhailovich (1748-1795)	Doctor	1785-86
SHURLOVSKII, Semen	Navy	1706-
SHUVALOV, Count Ivan Ivanovich (1727-97)	Tourist	1765
SHUVALOVA, Countess Ekaterina Petrovna (née SALTYKOVA) (1743-1817)	Tourist	1786
SHVARTS (SHWARTZ), Ivan Ivanovich	Tutor	1787
SIDNEV, Semen	Commerce	1799
SILOV, Galaktion Ivanovich	Student	1772-74
SIMANSKII, Koz'ma	Navy	1707-
SIMOLIN, Aleksandr Matveevich	Embassy	1780s
SIMOLIN, Ivan Matveevich (1720-99)	Diplomat	1779-85
SINIAVICH, Iakov	Embassy	1710s
SIVERS (SEIVERS), David	Embassy	1790s
SIVERS (SIEVERS), Count Jakob Johann (d. 1808)	Embassy	1750s
SKAVRONSKII, Count Pavel Martynovich (1757-93)	Tourist	1776
SKORODUMOV, Gavrila Ivanovich (1755-1792)	Engraver	1773-82
SMIRNOI, Sergei	Navy	1707-
SMIRNOV Iakov Ivanovich (1754-1840)	Church	1776-1840

SMIRNOV, Ivan Ivanovich	Embassy	1788-1808
SOFON'KOV (SAPONKEVICH), Ivan	Agriculture	1781-86
SOKOLOV, Petr	Shipbuilding	1715-
SOLOV'EV, Osip	Navy	1715-
SPESHNEV, Onufrii (d. before 1737)	Embassy	1732-
STAROV,-	Tourist	c. 1796
STEPANOV, Filiter (1745?-97)	Artist	1775-97
STEPANOV, Mikhail Stepanovich	Shipbuilding	1785-
STOROZHEVSKII, Vasilii	Navy	1707-
STREKALOV,-	Tourist?	1788
STROGANOV, Count Pavel Aleksandrovich	Tourist	1790?
SUDAKOV Ivan Ivanovich	Agriculture	1784-85
SUKHANIN, Akim	Navy	1793-
SUKHANOV, Erofei	Navy	1707-13
SURNIN, Aleksei Mikhailovich (1767-1811)	Gunsmith	1785
SUVOROV, Prokhor Ignat'evich (1750-1815)	Student	1765-75
SVESHNIKOV, Vasilii	Commerce	1766-69
SVESHNIKOV, Vasilii Konstantinovich	Instrument maker	1780-85
SYTIN,-	Navy	1733

T

TALYZIN, Ivan Luk'ianovich (1700-77)	Navy	1716-
TARBEEV, Vasilii	Navy	1762-65
TATISHCHEV, Ivan Ivanovich (1743-1802)	Embassy	1769-1775
TATISHCHEV, Mikhail Ivanovich	Embassy	1766-70s
TAUBERT, Ivan Ivanovich (1717-71)	Academy of Sciences	1748
TEL'NOI, Ivan	Navy	1707-11
TEREKHOVSKII, Martyn Matveevich (1740-96)	Doctor	1785-86
TIKHONOV, Andrei	Navy	1707-
TIMOFEEV,-	?	late 1790s
TISHINSKOI, Aleksei	Shipbuilding	1716-
TOMARINSKII, Klim	Church	1758-60
TRAPPE, Georg von	Recruiting agent	1788, 1797-98
TREPOL'SKII, Osip Vasil'evich	Tourist?	1789
TRET'IAKOV, Andrei	Shipbuilding/ Embassy	1715-30s
TRET'IAKOV, Ivan Andreevich (1735-76)	Student	1761-67
TROMPOVSKII, Christian	Commerce	1783

TUFIAKIN, Prince Ivan	Tourist	1771
TUGANOV,-	Mechanic	1797-1801
TULUB'EV, Nikolai (d. 1764)	Navy	1762-64
TURCHANINOV, Grigorii (d. 1717)	Navy	-1714

U

URUSOV, Prince Aleksandr Iakovlevich	Navy	1710-16
URUSOV, Prince Ivan Alekseevich	Navy	1708-
URUSOV, Prince Vasilii Alekseevich	Navy	1708-
USHAKOV, Fedor	Serf settled in England	1780s-
USHAKOV, Semen	Navy	1706
USLEMOV, Ivan	Shipbuilding	1715-
UVAROV,-	Tourist	1780s

V

VALLES, Petr	Navy	1766-
VALUEV,-	Courier	1780s
VASIL'EV,-	Student	1800
VEDENSKII ? (WETENSKY),-	?	1747
VELIKII, Semen Afanas'evich (1772?-94)	Navy	1793-94
VELIKOGAGIN, Prince Nikolai (d. 1722)	Navy	1716-19
VESELOVSKII, Abram Pavlovich (1686?-1783)	Political refugee	1720s
VESELOVSKII, Fedor Pavlovich (d. after 1760)	Diplomat	1715-38
VIAZEMSKII, Andrei Ivanovich (1754-1807)	Tourist	1783
VOLCHKOV, Daniil	Navy	1762-66
VOLKONSKII, Fedor (d. 1742)	Navy	1716-18?
VOLKOV, Ivan	Embassy	early 1780s
VOLYNSKII, Vasilii Ivanovich	Navy	1708-
VOROB'EV,-	Mechanic	1780-81
VORONTSOV, Aleksandr Romanovich (1741-1805)	Diplomat	1762-64
VORONTSOV, Ivan Alekseevich	Embassy	1753-62
VORONTSOV, Mikhail Semenovich (1782-1856)	Diplomat's family	1785-1801
VORONTSOV, Semen Romanovich (1744-1832)	Diplomat	1785-1832
VORONTSOVA, Ekaterina Semenovna (1784-1856)	Diplomat's family	1785-1856

Z

ZHDANOV, Il'ia	Student	1786-
ZHDANOV, Prokhor Ivanovich (d. 1802)	Church	-1766
ZHEREBTSOV, Nikita	Shipbuilding	1715-
ZHEREBTSOV,-	Embassy	1797-1801
ZHUKOV, Petr	Shipbuilding	1715-
ZHUKOV, Vasilii	Embassy	-1784
ZHURAKHOVSKII, Aleksandr	Mechanic	1719
ZINOV'EV, Vasilii Nikolaevich (1755-1827)	Tourist	1775, 1785-86
ZOLOTOI, Vasilii	Navy	1706-
ZOTOV, Konon Nikitich (1690-1742)	Navy	1700s
ZUBRILOV, Nikolai Vasil'evich	Commerce	1780-
ZVERAKA (ZVEREV), Evstafii Fedorovich (1751-1829)	Student	1776-79
ZVEREV, Aleksei (d. 1732)	Navy	1707-17
ZVEREV, Andrei	Shipbuilding	1716-
ZYBIN, Vasilii	Student	1780-81

INDEX OF NAMES